Data Processing in the UNIX Environment

Other McGraw-Hill Books in Mini and Mainframe Computing

ISBN	AUTHOR	TITLE
0-07-062879-3	Tare (hardcover)	*UNIX™ Utilities*
0-07-062884-X	(softcover)	
0-07-056578-3	Sherman	*The CD-ROM Handbook*
0-07-039006-1	Lusardi (hardcover)	*Database Experts' Guide to SQL*
0-07-039002-9	(softcover)	
0-07-016609-6	DeVita (hardcover)	*Database Experts' Guide to FOCUS*
0-07-016604-8	(softcover)	
0-07-036488-5	Larson (hardcover)	*Database Experts' Guide to Database 2*
0-07-023267-9	(softcover)	
0-07-048550-X	Parsons	*Database Experts' Guide to IDEAL*
0-07-008207-3	Brown	*Database Experts' Guide to SAS/DB2*
0-07-065120-5	Tran	*Introduction to DB2 Programming*
0-07-000474-9	Adrian	*The Workstation Data Link*
0-07-057336-0	Simpson, Casey	*Developing Effective User Documentation*
0-07-007248-5	Brathwaite	*Analysis, Design and Implementation of Data Dictionaries*
0-07-035119-8	Knightson	*Standards For Open Systems Interconnection*
0-07-044938-4	McClain (hardcover)	*VM and Departmental Computing*
0-07-044939-2	(softcover)	
0-07-046302-6	Nemzow	*Keeping the Link*
0-07-038006-6	Lipton	*User Guide to FOCUS™*
0-07-057296-8	Simon	*How to Be a Successful Computer Consultant*
0-07-016188-7	Dayton	*Integrating Digital Services*
0-07-002673-4	Azevedo	*ISPF: The Strategic Dialog Manager*
0-07-050054-1	Piggott	*CICS: A Practical Guide to System Fine Tuning*
0-07-043152-3	Morgan, McGilton	*Introducing UNIX™ System V*
0-07-050686-8	Prasad	*IBM Mainframes*
0-07-065087-X	Towner	*IDMS/R Cookbook*
0-07-045001-3	McGilton, Morgan	*Introducing the UNIX System*
0-07-062295-7	Su	*Database Computers*
0-07-041920-5	Milenkovic	*Operating Systems Concepts and Design*
0-07-010829-3	Ceri/Pelagatti	*Distributed Databases*

Data Processing in the UNIX Environment

With INFORMIX-SQL, Embedded-SQL, C-ISAM, and TURBO

Ramkrishna S. Tare

DP-Tech Computer Services
Edison, New Jersey

McGraw-Hill Publishing Company

New York St. Louis San Francisco Auckland Bogotá
Caracas Hamburg Lisbon London Madrid Mexico
Milan Montreal New Delhi Oklahoma City
Paris San Juan São Paulo Singapore
Sydney Tokyo Toronto

Library of Congress Cataloging-in-Publication Data

Tare, Ramkrishna S.
Data processing in the UNIX environment: with INFORMIX-SQL. Embedded-SQL, C-ISAM, and TURBO / Ramkrishna S. Tare.
p. cm.
Includes bibliographical references.
ISBN 0-07-062885-8
1. Data base management. 2. UNIX (Computer operating system)
I. Title.
QA76.9.D3T374 1989
005.4'3 – dc19

89-37276
CIP

234567890 DOC/DOC 9654321

ISBN 0-07-062885-8

The editors for this book were Theron Shreve and Kay Magome. Production supervisor was Richard A. Ausburn. Project supervision was by The Total Book.

Printed and bound by R. R. Donnelley & Sons Company.

For more information about other McGraw-Hill materials, call 1-800-MCGRAW in the United States. In other countries, call your nearest McGraw-Hill office.

TO

Ahilya Bai

Sonu Atya

and

Yeshwant Bhau

Colophon

This book was typeset using the rich document preparation tools of the UNIX system and printed on a POSTSCRIPT printer. The entire manuscript was prepared using *troff*, *pic*, *eqn*, and *tbl*. The power and elegance of these tools in conjunction with file manipulation and project management utilities offered by the UNIX system created a very sophisticated and congenial environment for typesetting and maintaining the various bits and pieces of this project. The POSTSCRIPT language was also used to design the title page. The book uses several font types including Times Roman, Times Italic, Helvetica Bold, ZapfChancery MediumItalic, Courier, and Courier Bold.

Contents

Preface

In the last few years, the UNIX operating system has grown from use in computer laboratories in academic and research institutions to serious commercial usage. UNIX is no longer merely an environment for professors to train their students and for hackers to demonstrate their programming expertise. Nothing signifies the commercial acceptance of an operating system more than its widespread use for data-processing applications. Indeed, UNIX is increasingly becoming the standard operating environment for data-processing applications which were dominated for numerous years by vendor-specific operating systems. This acceptance has fueled a fierce battle among vendors to provide database management systems for a wide variety of applications.

INFORMIX has been among the first vendors to realize the tremendous potential for database management systems in the UNIX world. Combining the advantage of being a first comer with a series of state-of-the-art products, the company has the most versatile and yet the most efficient product line in the UNIX DBMS market.

UNIX itself provides all the necessary ingredients to build a flat file system with its wide range of utilities. The fine blending of its numerous tools with the use of pipes and redirections and the power of the shell makes it the most attractive choice for any applications developer.

This book unfolds the power of UNIX for data-processing needs. It shows how simple commands can be used to build powerful systems with very little development time. The first half of the book concentrates on the use of UNIX tools for development needs. The second half of the book explains different INFORMIX products and how they interact with one another. Indeed, in keeping with the UNIX philosophy, INFORMIX products can be used separately or in conjunction with one another.

This book expects you to have a basic familiarity with the UNIX system. Some chapters also require you to have knowledge of C programming.

Though this book is written for the professional database designer in the UNIX environment, it would serve well as a reference for any course in data management.

Most of the INFORMIX products discussed here are continually updated. This book describes generic features offered by the product and not any version-specific details. The textbook style presented here to describe INFORMIX products differs significantly from the style used in the product manual. This book, however, is not a substitute for either UNIX or INFORMIX manuals. The book provides an excellent supplement to the manuals. The best way to utilize this book is to have access to a UNIX system with the INFORMIX software installed.

The first chapter looks at the internals of the file system. Like UNIX itself, the file system continues to evolve, leaving behind it a trail of versions. Fortunately, most file systems can be categorized under two categories: System V and Berkeley. This chapter briefly discusses the internals of these two file systems. Understanding of the file system provides an insight into the working of the UNIX utilities and the database management software. This chapter goes beyond the display on the screen to the bits and bytes on the disk. Those readers without any exposure to UNIX may skip this chapter entirely.

Chapter 2 discusses UNIX tools available for processing flat files. Chapter 3 demonstrates the use of UNIX tools for developing flat file systems. Chapter 4 introduces database concepts, explains several widely used terms in database jargon, and looks at some of the theoretical foundations on which relational database management systems are built. Chapter 5 is devoted entirely to the popular Structured Query Language (SQL).

Chapter 6 starts a new section of the book. It introduces INFORMIX-SQL with all its paraphernalia. Chapter 7 uses the INFORMIX product ESQL/C to demonstrate the power of the SQL language when it is embedded in the C programming language. Chapter 8 explains how C-ISAM (yet another INFORMIX product) functions can be used in C programs to provide direct access to UNIX files and other powerful features. Chapter 8 explains how INFORMIX satisfies the need for reliable and high performance on-line transaction processing (OLTP) applications in the UNIX environment.

This book was written with the wide variety of tools available in the UNIX world. UNIX utilities, including *awk*, *troff*, *tbl*, *pic*, and *SCCS*, were used frequently.

It is a pleasure to acknowledge the help and guidance of numerous friends and colleagues during the writing of this book. I wish to thank Anthony DeCicco, consulting manager, and David Kosenko, senior consultant at Informix Software, Inc., for providing continuous technical support. David Kosenko also reviewed the entire book and suggested numerous changes. In addition, Simon Tse and Andrew Wild of AT&T Bell Laboratories, Dhiren Kakkad and Tom Roehr of DP-Tech Computer Services, and many other friends and colleagues provided some invaluable suggestions. The inevitable errors, are, however, strictly mine. I would like to thank Todd McAlister for providing support for the AT&T 6386 system on which most of the examples in this book were tested. I also wish to thank Kay Magome, Theron Shreve, and Kate Scheinman of McGraw-Hill Publishing Co. for their help and cooperation throughout this project.

I enjoyed writing this book. I hope you enjoy reading it!

Ramkrishna S. Tare

Introduction

Data processing is a widely used term with different connotations. Very few terms have had such a remarkable usage in the public's vocabulary as the term data processing. It seems to have its origin in the term *electronic data processing*, or EDP. With advances in electronics, the first word, *electronic*, was dropped from the term. Traditionally, data processing was used to refer to the area in computer science which dealt with programming business applications such as inventory control, payroll management, and so on. Today, almost every area of computer science deals with some form of processing of data, and the term data processing is no longer used to refer only to business applications.

The technology of database management systems (DBMS), on the other hand, is relatively new. It is being used to replace traditional methods of data processing. Various database management system packages are available for different hardwares and operating systems. UNIX is one such operating system. The increasing acceptance of UNIX in the commercial computing environment has led to the development of several database management systems. This book discusses the INFORMIX DBMS. It is one of the most popular DBMS in the UNIX environment, and according to the author it is also among the best. The next few paragraphs discuss some of the basic terms and definitions which are used in the area of data processing. These terms are defined and explained with emphasis on their usage in the UNIX world.

Fields, *records*, and *files*: A field is an elemental data item which contains the smallest quantum of information. Fields either are separated by a character which is referred to as the field separator or they are of a fixed length. Fixed-length fields are recognized by their starting and ending position in a record. A record itself is a collection of fields. A file is a collection of records. The following file has fixed-length records. Each record has the same length because the size of corresponding fields in each record is the same.

```
john 34123-345-1212
bob 154112-242-5461
rick   121-889-1901
```

The same information can be stored in a file which has records with fields separated by field separators. The following file shows the use of a colon (:) to separate the fields:

```
john:34:123-345-1212
bob:154:112-242-5461
rick::121-889-1901
```

Note that the last record has the second field value missing. Such fields are called *null-valued fields*. UNIX utilities and DBMS packages handle null-valued fields differently.

In the UNIX environment, a file is actually a collection of bytes. A record is a set of characters terminated by the newline character.

Databases and DBMS: A database is a collection of data organized in a special form. The software which is responsible for managing the database is called a database management system (DBMS). The terms DBMS and database, therefore, connote different meanings and should not be used interchangeably.

Data model: Data in a database can be stored in various formats and structures. This choice determines the data model in use. There are three accepted data models. They are hierarchical, network, and relational. Most UNIX-based DBMS support the relational model. In the relational model, data is stored in the form of tables without any physical links from one table to another.

Query Language: Once the data is stored in the database, the user must be able to access it. The language provided by the software package for the user to manage the data is called the *query language*. Clearly, it would be convenient to have a standard language for the user to interact with the database. The Structured Query Language (SQL) is one such language which is available on most UNIX-based DBMS.

Access methods: The data stored in UNIX files can be read sequentially or can be accessed directly. Sequential access requires that to read the fifteenth record in a file, the first fourteen records must also be read first. Clearly, this slows down the processing. To avoid this problem, UNIX provides direct access to any specified byte position within a file. All DBMS packages make use of this facility to enhance the performance of the software and to provide a wide range of access methods which are superior to sequential access.

Database recovery: Databases have integrity constraints which are enforced by the user through mechanisms provided by the DBMS software. Bugs in the user software, hardware failures, or inadvertent data entry can result in the loss of integrity of the database. Database recovery refers to the procedure which is used to restore the database to a user-specified status. Some DBMS provide this feature as an integral part of the DBMS software. In the absence of recovery features, the user has to resort to UNIX backups to restore the status of the database.

Filter: Any program that can read from the standard input and write to the standard output is called a filter. Normally, the output of a filter depends on its input.

Pipe: The output of one command can be made the input of another command by the connection of the two commands with a pipe (|). For example, *comm1 < inpfile|comm2 > outfile* will have the command *comm1* read from the file inpfile and feed the output to the command *comm2*. The command *comm2* will store its output in the file outfile.

Regular expressions: Regular expressions are used by many UNIX utilities. They provide a way to specify patterns to be matched. The shell also uses these expressions to generate file names. Regular expressions use a group of characters, known as metacharacters, which are interpreted differently from other characters. The interpretation of the metacharacters varies across utilities.

The sample programs in this book are available on disk for a nominal price of $20.00 from DP-Tech Computer Services. DP-Tech Computer Services also provides consulting, training, and technical writing services for UNIX-based database management systems including INFORMIX, SYBASE, and ORACLE. For more information, please call (201) 906-1212 or write to:

DP-Tech Computer Services
Suite 12, 25 S. Main St.
Edison, NJ 08837
U. S. A.

1 The UNIX File System

Data processing, either traditional flat file systems or DBMS supported, involves managing information that is stored in files. These files are stored on secondary devices such as tapes and disks. This chapter deals with data storage on disks. The bytes in a file may not be physically contiguous. The user perceives a file as a stream of logically contiguous characters. The data structures and the associated algorithms used to provide this view to the user are collectively referred to as the UNIX file system. In addition, the file system is responsible for managing and maintaining the physical aspect of data storage. This includes allocation of space to new files and maintaining information on free space.

The UNIX file system has undergone various changes since its inception. The basic theory still remains the same, but variations have been made to improve its performance and flexibility. The most widely used file system which forms the backbone of other UNIX versions is the Seventh Edition implementation still used in System V. The discussion in this chapter will concentrate on the System V and Berkeley file systems and will conclude with a brief note on distributed file systems.

1.1 Types of Files

There are several types of files within the UNIX system. On most versions a file can be categorized as either a regular file, a pipe file, a directory file, or a special file such as a device file.

A regular file is used to store information as an array or a group of bytes. The storage appears to the user to be sequential, though physically that may not be the case.

A pipe file is used to communicate between processes, and unlike reads from a regular file, reads from a pipe file are destructive; the same data can be read only once.

UNIX supports a hierarchical file system. All files in a directory have their names stored in a specific format in a file which is referred to as the directory file. Thus when a user makes a new file within a directory, the contents of the directory file itself are changed. Users are not allowed to change the contents of this file directly. Allowing the users to do so would result in loss of integrity of the directory structure and contents.

Special files, such as device files, serve as an interface between processes and devices. With the UNIX system, devices are considered to be special files. The device driver is the software responsible for interacting with these special files.

In a data processing environment, users store their data in regular files. This may be done directly by the user or by the DBMS that controls the structure and contents of the data. Mass storage devices such as disk packs are used to store these regular files.

1.2 Physical Structure of a Disk Pack

A disk pack is composed of platters, tracks, cylinders, and sectors. Figure 1.1 illustrates the importance of these terms. From a user point of view, a file is a logical grouping of bytes. These bytes are grouped into blocks. Thus a file is made up of blocks. Blocks correspond to sectors in Figure 1.1. However, the correspondence need not be one to one. A block may be made up of more than one sector.

1.3 The System V File System Structure

Each disk pack can be segmented into one or more partitions. Each partition houses a file system. A file system is made up of several blocks. Some of

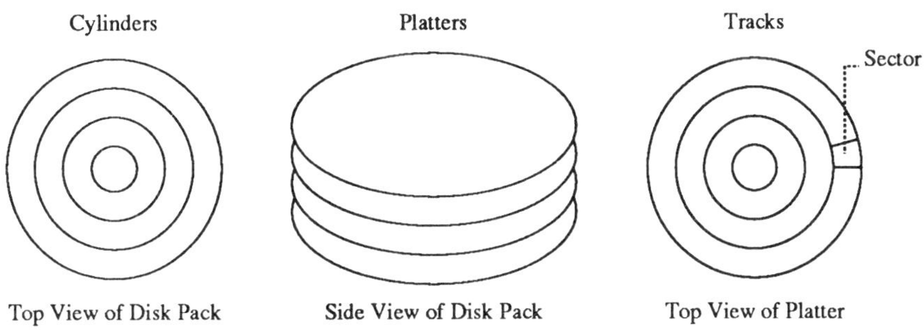

Figure 1.1 Structure of a Disk Pack

these blocks store data while others store control information. It is important to understand the structure and contents of the blocks which store the control information in order to fully understand the file system.

As discussed earlier, the blocks of a file may not be stored sequentially. It is the task of the operating system to determine where the blocks of a file are stored. In order to do so, the file system maintains appropriate tables which store this information. When a file grows, new blocks have to be allocated to it. When a file is removed, the blocks associated with it must be deallocated so that they can be used in the future by new files. The next few sections explain how the blocks of a file are maintained.

1.3.1 Directories and Files

A regular file in the UNIX System must have a name. System V imposes a limit of 14 characters on a file name. Further, a file must be associated with a directory; it must belong to a directory. Subsequently, a directory has one or more files. A directory has a 16-byte entry for each file within it. The first 2 bytes identify the file by an integer number. This number is called the inode number of the file. The *-i* option of the *ls* command displays the inode number of the specified file. The next 14 bytes are used to store the name of the file. In addition, there are two more entries: one for the directory itself and another for the parent directory. The structure of the directory can be examined by using the *od* command. The following example displays the structure of the directory file /tmp.

```
od -c /tmp
0000000  \0   7   .  \0  \0  \0  \0  \0  \0  \0  \0  \0  \0  \0  \0  \0
0000020  \0 002   .   .  \0  \0  \0  \0  \0  \0  \0  \0  \0  \0  \0  \0
0000040 006 235   .   t   m   p  \0  \0  \0  \0  \0  \0  \0  \0  \0  \0
0000060 007   p   e   r   r  \0  \0  \0  \0  \0  \0  \0  \0  \0  \0  \0
0000100 007   X   t   .   t   r  \0  \0  \0  \0  \0  \0  \0  \0  \0  \0
0000120 002   X   .   w   i   n   l   o   a   d  \0  \0  \0  \0  \0  \0
0000140 007 206   n   e   w   t  \0  \0  \0  \0  \0  \0  \0  \0  \0  \0
0000160 007   d   1  \0  \0  \0  \0  \0  \0  \0  \0  \0  \0  \0  \0  \0
0000200 007 217   t   .   s   h  \0  \0  \0  \0  \0  \0  \0  \0  \0  \0
0000220 007 221   t  \0  \0  \0  \0  \0  \0  \0  \0  \0  \0  \0  \0  \0
0000240 003 031   R   x   .   c  \0  \0  \0  \0  \0  \0  \0  \0  \0  \0
```

The octal dump shows the first 2 bytes representing the inode number and the next 14 bytes representing the name of the corresponding file. The directory is the only file/data structure where the name of a file is stored. The operating system identifies the file by its inode number. The inode number specifies an entry in a table called the inode table. The size of the inode table determines the maximum number of files that a file system can accommodate. Each entry in the inode table is called an inode. While the data blocks store information *in* a file, the inode is used to store information *about* a file. In particular, the inode stores the following information:

- Type of the file: This identifies the type of the file: regular, pipe, directory, or special.
- Owner identification (Id): This identifies the owner of the file. The ownership information is stored as an integer. The actual user name can be retrieved from the /etc/passwd file.
- Group Id: This identifies the group ownership of the file. It stores the group ownership information as an integer. The group name can be retrieved from the /etc/group file.
- Number of links: This identifies the number of links to the file. A file can be made to appear in more than one directory. Physically, only one copy of a file can be stored. The number of links is the number of directories in which the same file is present.
- File size: This is the size of the file in bytes.
- File access time: This gives the time when the file was last accessed.
- File modification time: This gives the time when the file was last modified.
- Inode change time: This gives the time when the inode itself was last

modified. Note that reading a file will change its access time but not its inode modification time.

- Array of data-block numbers: This is an array of 13 data-block numbers. These data-block numbers are used to identify the data blocks which are associated with the file.

The commonly used UNIX command *ls* retrieves the file information from its inode.

1.3.2 File Creation

When a new file is created, a new entry is added to the directory in which it is created. The UNIX file system will get a new inode number for this file which can be retrieved by the user by examining the first 2 bytes of the entry in the directory. The inode will also be allocated with the file size field set to zero.

The creation process will fail if there are no more free inodes available. Of course, the user must have the appropriate permissions to create the file in the directory.

1.3.3 Growth of a File

If the inode allocation is successful and the file is created, then the user can add data to the file. The first time a data block is allocated, its block number is entered in the first entry in the array of data block numbers in the inode. If the file grows to more than one block, then another block is allocated and its number is entered in the second entry in the array. This continues up to 10 data blocks. If the file still continues to grow, then the eleventh entry gives the number of the block which has a list of data-block numbers. These numbers are the numbers of the data blocks which will store the data if the file continues to grow. The block which stores the list of data block numbers is called an indirect block.

If a block is identified by a 4-byte integer and if the block size is 1K bytes, then a block can hold 256 block numbers. If all the blocks referred by the indirect block were to be used, then the maximum size of the file would be 1K*10 + 256*1K = 266K bytes. This is a very small limit for most environments. There are still two more entries available in the inode which can be used to allocate more blocks. If the file continues to grow, the twelfth entry points to a block, called the double indirect block, which stores the block numbers of indirect blocks. These indirect blocks store the block

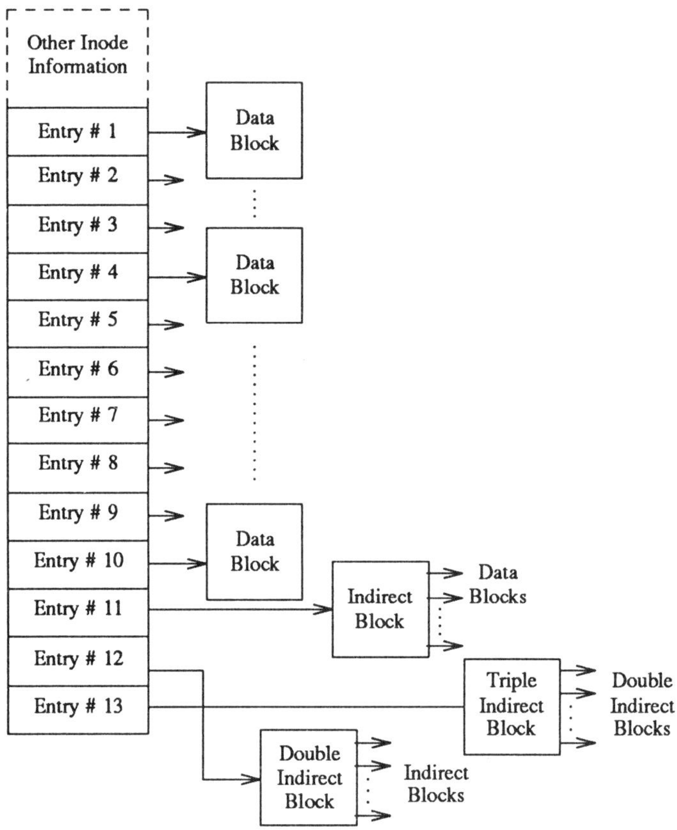

Figure 1.2 Array of Free Data Block Entries in Inode

numbers of actual data blocks which will be allocated as the file grows. The use of the twelfth entry in the array allows the file size to grow to 1K*10 + 256*1K + 256*256*1K = 65802K. The thirteenth entry is still unused. If the file grows further, it is used to store the block number of a block which stores the block numbers of 256 double indirect blocks. As you may have guessed, this new block is called the triple indirect block because it points to double indirect blocks. The new file size limit is now increased to 1K*10 + 256*1K +256*256*1K + 256*256*256*1K = 16843018K. This is the maximum size that a UNIX System V file can have. Another limiting factor is the size of an integer and the number of bytes which can be addressed using that integer.

Figure 1.2 shows the structure of the inode and the array of 13 data block numbers that it stores.

1.3.4 Free Block List

When a fresh file system is created, the list of free blocks available is organized as a linked list. Each free block is a node in the list. Each node of the linked list contains an array of block numbers of blocks which are free. The first block number in this array points to the next node of the linked list. Consider the status in Figure 1.3.

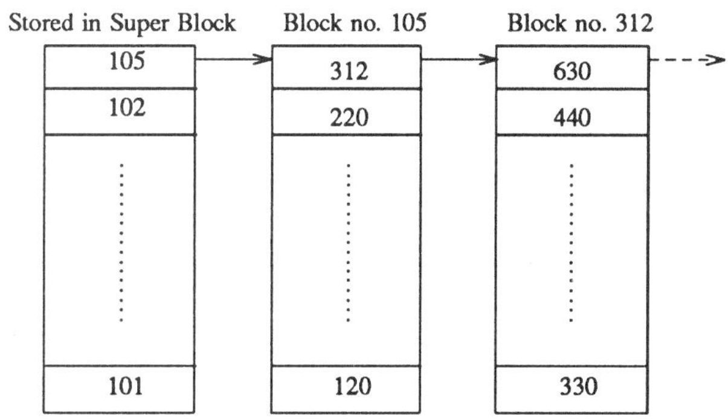

Figure 1.3 Free Block List

The first node of the linked list is stored in the super block, which is discussed later. The array entry 105 in this node refers to block number 105, which is the next node and has its own array of free block numbers. Similarly, block number 312 is the third node of the linked list, and its number is the first entry in the second node.

1.3.5 Free Inode List

As explained earlier, each file has a unique inode associated with it. A list of inodes, often referred to as the ilist, is stored on disk. An inode is considered to be free if its mode field has a zero (NULL) value. The simplest possible mechanism to assign a free inode would be to search the ilist on the disk until a free inode is retrieved. However, such a mechanism would be extremely slow. A subset of the list of free inodes is readily available in the super block. This eliminates the need to do a disk read whenever a new inode is required.

1.3.6 The Super Block

The most critical block of a file system is the super block. This block stores information about the file system, just as the inode stores information about a file. It always starts from a fixed offset from the beginning of a file system's disk partition. The super block contains the following information:

- File system size: This field specifies the size of the file system.
- Number of free blocks: Here the total number of blocks available in the file system is stored.
- Number of free inodes: This field stores the number of free inodes available in the file system.
- Size of the inode list: This field stores the total number of inodes that the file system can allocate.
- Free block list: This field stores the first node of the free blocks linked list. The node itself is an array of block numbers which are free.
- Free inodes list: This refers to the array of inode numbers which are free. As explained earlier, this is not a complete list but one that is maintained to avoid disk searches when a new inode is required.
- Index in the free block list: This stores the index into the first empty slot in the super block list of free data blocks.
- Index in the free inode list: This stores the index into the first empty slot in the super block list of free inodes.
- Super block modification flag: The super block is, of course, read into main memory. This is done when the file system is brought on-line by the use of the *mount* command. Changes to the file system may result in changes to the super block itself. If the super block itself is modified, then it is critical that its disk copy be updated. The modification flag is checked by programs which are reponsible for performing this operation. The *sync()* system call, for example, checks to see if this flag was modified.
- Read only flag: If this flag is set, then the file system can only be read. This option can be set when the file system is brought on-line.
- Lock fields: These fields are used to lock the free block list and the free inode list.

1.3.7 Allocating and Deallocating Inodes

The first step in creating a new file is to assign an inode for the file. The super block maintains an array of free inode numbers and an index into the array which is used to fetch the next available inode in the array. When a new inode is required, the index is decremented and the inode it points to is allocated. If the inode list in the super block is empty, then the disk copy of the list of inodes is read and the super block is populated with a fresh set of free inode numbers. It is important to note that the super block maintains an array of free inode numbers. The inodes themselves are on disk.

Once an inode number is allocated, the count of free inodes in the super block is decremented. The disk copy of this inode is read into memory and the appropriate fields are initialized. In addition, the type field of the inode on the disk is changed from zero (NULL) to indicate that it is no longer free.

If a file is removed, the inode of this file can be reused. Several steps are taken to indicate that an inode has been freed. First, the type field in the disk copy of the inode is updated to indicate that the inode is free. Also, the count field in the super block which indicates the total number of free inodes in the file system is incremented. These steps should suffice to free the inode. However, for efficiency reasons, the newly freed inode is put in the array of inodes maintained by the super block and the index which points to this list is incremented.

If the super block list of inodes does not have an empty slot, then the newly released inode number is compared with the first entry in the super block array of inode numbers. If the new inode number is smaller than the existing inode number in the first entry, then the new inode number is made the first entry in the super block array and the existing inode number there is discarded. Note that discarding it has no side effects on its availability because it can be fetched later from the disk copy of the inodes where it is still marked as a free inode. This approach has the advantage that if all the inode numbers in the super block are used and a new list of free inodes is to be fetched from the disk, then the search for free inodes can start at the inode number in the first entry of the super block inode numbers list. This eliminates the need to search blocks of the disk copy of the inodes with no free inodes.

1.3.8 Allocating and Deallocating Data Blocks

When a file is newly created and requests a data block, it is allocated a block from a list of free data blocks. Once again, like the inode allocation, the super block maintains a list of free data block numbers. There is also an index into this array which is decremented to point to the first empty entry in the list. The array in the super block is actually the first node of a linked list which is used to store the list of free block numbers. This was explained earlier with the help of Figure 1.3. If a new block is needed and the list of free block numbers in the super block has only one entry left, then the block pointed to by that entry is read and its contents are used to populate the array in the super block. After this, the block itself is allocated to satisfy the request.

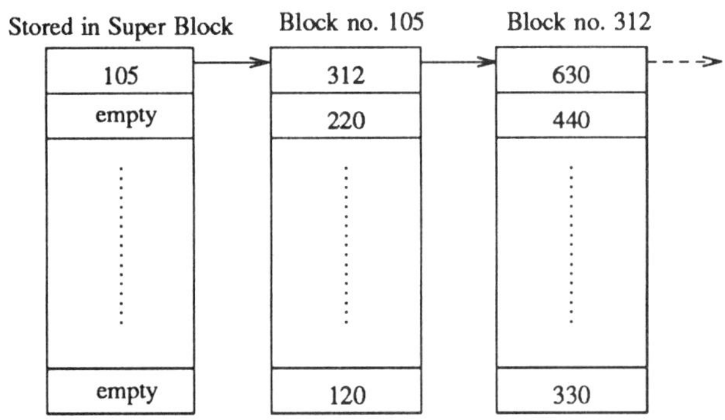

Figure 1.4 Before Allocating Block No. 105

Figure 1.4 shows the status of the list before block number 105 is allocated, and Figure 1.5 shows the same list after block number 105 is allocated.

Deallocating a block requires that the number of the new data block be put in the linked list of free data-block numbers. The index used to point into the array of free block numbers in the super block points to an empty slot in the array. Therefore, the new data-block number is entered in the empty slot and the index itself is incremented.

The process of deallocating a block is slightly complicated when the list of free block numbers in the super block is full. When this occurs, the array in the super block is copied into the newly released block, and its block number is placed in the first slot of the array of free block numbers in the super block. Figure 1.5 shows the status of the list before block number 621 is deallocated, and Figure 1.6 shows the same list after the deallocation process is completed.

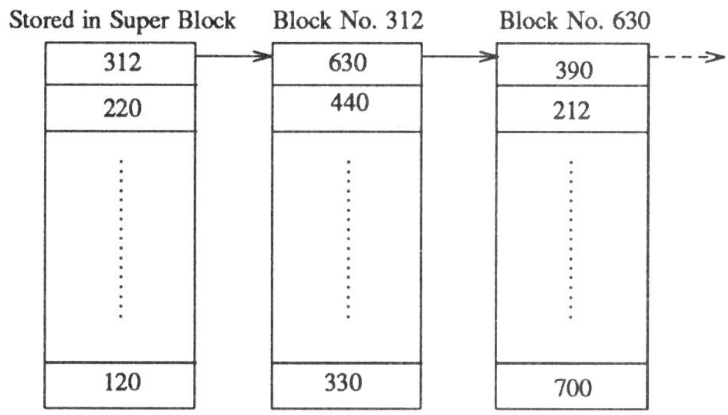

Figure 1.5 After Allocating Block No. 105

1.3.9 Holes in Files

Holes exist in files if the user tries to seek and write bytes into a file at a position which does not currently exist. If a user tries to seek at a position which may result in unused blocks, then the blocks will not be actually allocated and the block number entries in the inode for these unused blocks will be zeroed.

1.3.10 System Buffered I/O

When a process attempts to access a segment of a file, the transfer is made from the file to an intermediate area in main memory called the buffer cache. Buffering the data from the file has several advantages associated with it.

First, data on disk can only be modified in terms of blocks. In the absence of system buffers, a process attempting to access data which is not equal to a block would have to write additional code to handle input/output (I/O) operations.

If a file is processed sequentially, then the next block is brought into the buffer cache before a request for it is actually made. This *read ahead* saves considerable time, as the process does not have to wait for an I/O operation to start processing the next block. A buffer is not written to disk every time a user issues a write call to it. This *delayed write* mechanism saves I/O processing time if the user wishes to access the block again. A similar situation arises when the user wishes to read a block. The block that is read is in the buffer cache, and no I/O operation is required if the user wishes to read it again.

Swapping of processes from core would be difficult if there were no buffering scheme. Processes initiating an I/O would have to wait for the I/O completion before getting swapped out of memory. With the use of buffers, the process requesting an I/O can get swapped out while the I/O request is being serviced. When the process is swapped in again, the I/O may be completed and the process can continue execution.

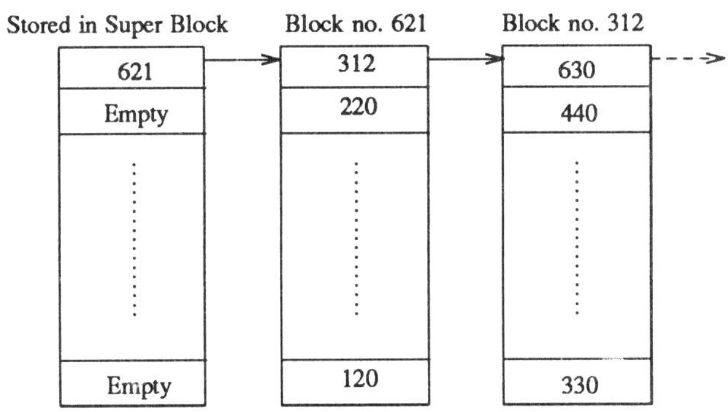

Figure 1.6 After Deallocating Block No. 621

For buffering the data, a certain segment of memory is allocated to store the array of buffers. Each buffer has two parts: the first is the data part, which stores the actual data corresponding to the disk block, and the second part is the buffer header, which has information about the buffer. This information gives the mapping of the buffer into the file system and its current status. The mapping indicates the block in the file system which the buffer represents. The current status of a buffer indicates if it is currently being used, if a process is waiting for another process to free it, if the kernel is reading or writing the contents of the buffer, etc.

When a process requests data from a file, it could either be a sequential read or a direct *seek* followed by a read. In either case, the process needs to read a segment of the file starting at a specific byte number. This byte number is first translated into a block number. A search is then made among the list of buffers. If a buffer is found corresponding to the file and block number that the user has requested and if it is not currently used by another process, then the buffer search is completed. If it is found but is in use, then the process will go to sleep and will be awakened later when the buffer is free. If a corresponding buffer is not found, then a new one is allocated from a list of buffers which are not currently in use. More complicated situations can also arise, but they will not be discussed here.

1.3.11 Locking Mechanism

New releases of UNIX System V have a locking mechanism. A locking mechanism is used not to provide additional security but to maintain integrity of updates and reads by providing a synchronization mechanism. This mechanism provides a facility to user processes to lock records and files so that other processes will not be able to access the file or record and will be able to detect that a lock has been set. C programmers can use the system call *fcntl()* or the library function *lockf* to use this feature.

Record locking refers to the feature which allows the user to lock any segment of the file. File locking is therefore only a special case of record locking where the record starts at the beginning of the file and is as long as the file itself. Locks can either be read locks or write locks. If a file is "read-locked," then other processes can read it but cannot write it. If a file is "write-locked," then other processes can neither read nor write that file. A lock can be promoted by a process from read to write. Once a read lock is set on a record, that record can also be read-locked by other processes. The same record will have to be unlocked before a write lock can be applied by another process. Once a write lock is set on a record, no other process can lock that record.

A process may unlock only a part of a record that it had locked previously. In that case, the remaining part or parts will continue to be locked. The locking mechanism discussed thus far is called advisory locking, and it is not enforced by the I/O subsystem. Several "commands" were added to the *fcntl* system call to implement the advisory locking capabilities. Another form of record locking which is enforced by the I/O subsystem is called mandatory locking. It offers an extra synchronization check in addition to that implemented by the user processes, but it has additional system overheads. The *chmod* command with the *+l* option can be used to set mandatory locks on a file. For example,

```
chmod +l file1
```

will set a mandatory lock on file1. Once set, the advisory record locks applied by a process will be enforced on the locked records. Other records of the file can be accessed as if no mandatory locks were applied. There is a major overhead associated with mandatory locks. Every I/O operation will have to check if the record is locked.

1.3.12 Relevant UNIX Commands

In order to interact with a UNIX file system, you have at your availability several UNIX commands. Some of these commands are discussed here.

The *mkfs* command is used to create a UNIX file system. File system creation requires that a disk be formatted. Formatting commands and procedures vary among UNIX systems and hardware. A file system cannot be created on an unformatted disk. Formatting a disk or making a new file system removes existing data from the disk. The following command creates a file system on the device named "/dev/fp002" with 2000 blocks and 400 inodes:

```
mkfs /dev/fp002 2000:400
```

If the number of inodes is not specified, it defaults to a number which is usually the number of blocks divided by 4.

Counts on free inodes and blocks available on a file system can be printed with the use of the *df* command. In addition, the *-t* option can be used to get counts on total blocks and inodes. Here is an example:

```
df
/          (/dev/fp002):     85144 blocks    13073 i-nodes
df -t
/          (/dev/fp002):     85144 blocks    13073 i-nodes
                  total:    120944 blocks    15104 i-nodes
```

A report of inode numbers and corresponding file names can be generated by the use of the *ncheck* command. The *-a* option can be used to print entries for "." and "..", which are suppressed by default. A file system can also be specified optionally. Here is an example in which only the first 20 lines of the output are reported:

```
ncheck -a|head -20
/dev/fp002:
2       /./.
2       /../.
3       /bin/.
```

```
15      /mnt/.
16      /etc/.
30      /dev/.
55      /tmp/.
56      /lib/.
272     /lost+found/.
273     /mnta/.
274     /mntb/.
275     /u/.
300     /.profile
301     /UNIX3.51
301     /unix
302     /usr/.
3       /bin/./.
2       /bin/../.
4       /bin/sh
```

A file system can be brought on-line by the use of the *mount* command, and a mounted file system can be unmounted, or taken off-line, by the use of the command *umount*. *Umount* will complain if the file system is currently in use. A file system is considered to be in use if it has an open file or if it has a directory which is a user's current directory as reported by *pwd*.

1.3.13 File System Corruption and Recovery

The structure of a UNIX file system, as explained in the previous sections, leaves ample room for inconsistencies to slip into it. These inconsistencies may be a result of bad system administration such as shutting the system off without taking appropriate measures, or it may be a result of a system crash. Several file system inconsistencies are possible. An inode may be indicated as allocated, but it may not have an entry in any directory. The super block itself may be corrupted. The block numbers may be invalid. A directory may be corrupted; the size of a directory may not be an integral multiple of 16. A block may be allocated more than once. The number of free inodes as given by the super block entry may not match the number of free inodes detected by examining the free inodes list on disk. The list of possible inconsistencies is very long.

Some inconsistencies can be rectified, while others are fatal. The UNIX program *fsck* can be used to check and repair a UNIX file system. It can be run in interactive as well as noninteractive mode on an unmounted file system. The file system should be unmounted because *fsck* is a multipass program and the status of the file system must not be changed between passes. In interactive mode the user/operator can direct the action of *fsck* in response to a prompt. In a noninteractive mode a default action is taken. If invoked with a *-p* option, *fsck* will limit the consistency checks to the following:

- Unreferenced inodes
- Link counts in inodes too large
- Missing blocks in the free list
- Blocks indicated as missing and also allocated to files
- Invalid counts in the super block (e.g., number of free inodes).

If any other error is detected, *fsck* will exit with an abnormal return status. It can then be invoked in interactive mode to fix the problem. If invoked with a *-y* option, it will assume a *yes* response to all questions prompted by it. If *fsck* detects a directory/file which is not linked to the file system, it will link it to the lost+found directory.

At startup time, *fsck* should be invoked in the system initialization script *.rc*. If a corrupted file system is used without being repaired, the inconsistencies will multiply and will ultimately result in an irreparable file system.

The *clri* command can be used to clear an inode. The syntax of the command is:

`clri` *file-system i-number*

Execution of this command results in the writing of zeros in the inode fields of the specified inode. Clearly, inadvertent use of this command can be disastrous. This command is used to remove an inode which does not have a directory entry. Such a file would not have a name and therefore cannot be removed by the *rm* command. It should not be used to remove an inode for which a directory entry exists.

1.3.14 File System Debuggers

File system debuggers such as *fsdb* are used to repair a damaged file system. *Fsdb* is particularly useful to fix the file system when *fsck* is unable to do so. *Fsdb* has several interesting features. It can change the contents of any segment of the file system, including an inode or the super block. The file system can be severely damaged if this tool is used carelessly. The following session shows the use of *fsdb* to display the contents of an inode and to change the number of links to inode number 4 from 3 to 2.

```
fsdb /dev/fp020
/dev/fp021(): 1K byte Block File System
FSIZE = 316, ISIZE = 96
4i
i#:  4  md: f---rwxr--r--    ln:  3  uid: 0  gid:  0  sz: 3638
a0: 89  a1:  92  a2:    95  a3:  98  a4: 0   a5:  0  a6:  0
a7:  0  a8:  0   a9:    0  a10:  0  a11: 0  a12:  0
at: Mon Sep 19 13:51:38 1988
mt: Mon Sep 19 13:51:38 1988
ct: Mon Sep 19 13:51:38 1988
ln=2
4i
i#:  4  md: f---rwxr--r--  ln:  2   uid:  0   gid:  0  sz: 3638
a0: 89  a1:    92  a2: 95  a3: 98   a4:  0    a5:  0  a6:  0
a7:  0  a8:     0  a9:  0 a10:  0   a11:  0   a12:  0
at: Mon Sep 19 13:51:38 1988
mt: Mon Sep 19 13:51:38 1988
ct: Mon Sep 19 13:51:38 1988
```

The inode fields are displayed with the following labels:

i#	Inode number
ln	Count of links
uid	User Id number
gid	Group Id number
sz	Size of the file
a0-a12	Refer to the 13 data block numbers entry in the inode
at	Last access time
mt	Last filc modification time
ct	Last inode modification time

The *fsdb* instruction *4i* is used to select inode number 4, and the instruction *ln=2* is used subsequently to change the number of links to the inode to 2. Similarly, other instructions exist to move around in the file system and to change various fields in the super block, inodes, directories, and files.

1.3.15 Overheads and Limitations

The UNIX System V file system has few overheads if the file is not bigger than 10 blocks. However, a file size of more than 10 blocks has different levels of overheads associated with it. To access a file, the system has to read the inode itself; if an indirect block is involved, it must also be read to get to the data block. This operation is still slower if the data block has to be accessed via the triple indirect block. In terms of space inefficiency, the indirect blocks, double indirect blocks, and triple indirect block are not used to store any data.

It is not possible to allocate less than a block of data to a file. If the block size is 1024 bytes and if the file size is 1025 bytes, then the file will need two blocks and the remaining 1023 bytes in the second block will be wasted. In addition, two logically sequential data blocks may not be physically contiguous. They may not be on the same cylinder, which will force additional seeks for applications requiring sequential processing of data.

Users can consume any amount of disk space on file systems on which they have permissions to create files. There is no mechanism provided by the file system maintenance software to restrict the amount of disk space that users can consume. This can result in unfair use of disk space, which is a critical resource in some environments. Unsocial users can create dummy files to reserve space and then remove them as space is required by their processes, thus depriving other users of available disk space. Further, a process performing a file write inside an infinite loop can fill up the entire file system affecting the performance and result of other processes accessing the same file system. Disk quotas cannot be allocated to individual users.

The structure of the directory restricts the maximum length of a file name to 14 characters. This is not enough for some environments where suffixes, such as .idx, take 4 characters leaving the user with only 10 characters.

1.4 Berkeley File System Internals

The Berkeley file system was designed to reduce some of the deficiencies in the traditional UNIX file system. It also incorporated features to eliminate several limitations and improve reliability. The internals of the new file system as implemented in BSD 4.3 is described briefly in the next few paragraphs.

Berkeley implementation of the UNIX file system has a super block which is duplicated. The super block itself has some redundant information, and the fields in it that are irrecoverable do not change with new activities on the file system. This eliminates the need to update the duplicated copy of the super block which is accessed only if the main copy is destroyed. This mechanism protects the file system against catastrophic loss of information resulting from a super block corruption due to hard-disk errors such as a head crash. The super block in the Berkeley system, as in System V, is located at the beginning of the file system and describes the file system.

Perhaps the most significant feature of the Berkeley Software Distribution (BSD) file system design is that data blocks allocated to a file need not have a fixed size. Smaller data blocks allocated to a file are referred to as fragments. With a big block size, the throughput of the system can be increased. Fragments can be allocated to small files to eliminate wasted space. The ability to allocate fragments of a block saves space not only for small files but also for big files where the last block can now be a fragment. For example, for a file which is 4097 bytes long on a file system with 4096-byte blocks, the wasted space is no longer 4095 bytes. Instead, if the fragment size is 512 bytes, then the wasted space is only 511 bytes.

The size of the data blocks or the fragments need not be the same for all file systems on any given UNIX system. The super block stores the block size and the fragment size, and these parameters can be specified when the file system is made using the *mkfs* command. The fragment size is constrained by the sector size. The minimum size of a block is 4096 bytes. Both the fragment size as well as the block size must be powers of 2. In addition, the block size to fragment size ratio cannot be more than 8.

1.4.1 Cylinder Groups

The new file system divides the disk partition allocated to the file system into areas called cylinder groups. The super block maintains a description of the cylinder groups. A cylinder group is made up of a set of consecutive cylinders. A cylinder itself is explained in Figure 1.1. Each cylinder group has a copy of the super block and other information relevant to the group. This information includes the following:

- The time the cylinder group was last written
- The number of the cylinder group
- The number of cylinders in this group
- The number of inode blocks in the group
- The number of data blocks in the group
- The number of directories in the group
- The number of free blocks in the group
- The number of free inodes in the group
- The number of free fragments in the group
- The position of the last-used block
- The position of the last-used fragment
- The position of the last-used cylinder
- The position of the last-used inode
- The count of available fragments
- The map of used inodes

- The map of total blocks available for each cylinder in the group
- The map of the position of free blocks within each cylinder

The cylinder group information is not located at the beginning of each cylinder group. This would make the top platter extremely critical, as all cylinder group information, including the duplicate copies of the super block, would be placed on the top platter and any damage to this platter would render the file system useless and any data on it irrecoverable. To avoid this situation, the cylinder group information is placed at varying offset from the beginning of the cylinder group. The space between the beginning of the cylinder group and the position where the information is stored is not lost, but it is used to store data blocks.

The map of the position of free blocks within each cylinder refers to the rotational position. The number of distinct rotational positions is 8.

1.4.2 Fragment Allocation

As a file grows, fragments and blocks are allocated to it. On a system with 4096 bytes as the block size and 1024 bytes as the fragment size, a file of size 7200 bytes will occupy one full block and three small fragments. The performance factor is actually user dependent. If the user creates the file by writing out one fragment or less of an unit at a time, then only one fragment will be allocated at a time if space does not already exist in the current fragment. When the file grows to a block size, these fragments will be copied into one contiguous block if they are not already so. There will be a performance degradation due to the additional step involved in copying the fragments. On the other hand, if the user programs write one block at a time, this overhead can be eliminated. Of course, this need not be the case for writing the last segment of the file, as it may be less than a block.

1.4.3 Hardware Parameters

The physical parameters of the hard disk can drastically change the performance of the file system. In System V, when a file grows, the "next" block is allocated from the list of free blocks. The block allocation algorithm does not take into consideration the time it would take to access this block if the file were to be read sequentially. For improving the performance, the task of allocating the "next" block to a file is nontrivial. First, it depends on several factors, including the type of processor and the time it takes a processor to service an interrupt. In processors which use an interrupt driven

I/O mechanism, once a block is read, a certain amount of time must elapse before the next block can be read. The optimal position of the next block is where the disk head is expected to be at this time. This block position is dependent on several factors, including the processor speed, the drive revolutions per minute (rpm), and the number of blocks per track. If I/O channels are available, then the physical consecutiveness of the two blocks would enable them to be read sequentially in a minimum amount of time.

The cylinder group information stores the count of available blocks at different rotational positions. The super block stores configuration parameters such as disk revolutions per second and number of milliseconds for optimal next block allocation. These parameters are used by the BSD file system to locate the optimum "next" block from the list of available blocks. The file system parameters in the super block describing the hardware characteristics of the environment and the disk pack can be changed while the file system is mounted and in use. This feature is required to avoid performance degradation when the disk pack is moved to a processor having a different speed.

The BSD file system requires many administrator-supplied parameters to create a file system. Supplying wrong parameters or letting them default to incorrect ones can degrade the performance. The file /etc/disktab has information on these parameters for different disk drives. For each drive it specifies parameters such as the number of sectors per track, the number of tracks per cylinder, the number of cylinders per disk, the rpm, the sector size, partition sizes, etc.

1.4.4 Allocation of Data Blocks and Inodes

Data blocks are selected, as discussed above, from "optimal" positions so that the access time is reduced. Ideally, they would be placed on the same cylinder or at least in the same cylinder group. However, such a policy would cause big files to be forced to one cylinder group. If a small file is located in the same cylinder group and needs to grow, the blocks for the new file can be allocated only from other cylinder groups. Having a cylinder group full can result in performance degradation, as a new block to be allocated may not find a free block in the most optimum cylinder/cylinder group. The policy adopted is to force blocks to different cylinder groups after a specified file size is reached and to change the new cylinder group again at intervals of 1 megabyte.

Each cylinder group maintains a list of free inodes. When a new directory is to be created, it is stored in the cylinder group with the maximum number of free inodes and the least number of directories. This allows the inode entries for a directory to grow in the same cylinder group as more files are added to the directory. The clustering of inodes of a directory to one cylinder group improves performance for user commands such as *ls* which require access to information on all files in the same directory. This allocation strategy of a cylinder group to a directory ensures uniform distribution of files.

Unlike the System V file system, BSD maintains another parameter called the free-space reserve, which is the minimum number of free blocks which must be available for a block to be allocated to a user file. The purpose of this parameter is to localize the allocation of blocks to a file. If the file system is nearly full, localization attempts will be delayed, or fail, resulting in the degradation of system performance. The access rate of blocks in a file will therefore be better if the file is created on an empty file system as opposed to an 80% full file system. If a file is created on a near full file system and other files are removed from it at a later date, then the access times of the blocks of the old file will not improve unless the file is recreated by copying it as another file and then renaming it.

1.4.5 The Super Block Structure

The super block structure of the BSD file system is considerably different from the super block structure of the old System V file system. The super block has to store many more fields because of the increased complexity of the file system structure. There are several configuration parameters, such as disk speed, which are also stored here. The following are some of the important fields stored in the super block:

- The time the super block was last written
- The number of data blocks in the file system
- The number of cylinder groups
- The block size of the file system
- The size of a fragment
- The minimum percentage of free blocks
- The number of cylinders in a cylinder group
- The number of tracks per cylinder
- The number of sectors per track
- The number of sectors per cylinder
- The number of cylinders in a file system
- The number of inodes per cylinder group
- The number of fragments in a group
- The block address of cylinder-group information area
- The size of cylinder-group information area
- A flag for optimization preference

Some of these fields are redundant and can be calculated from others. The flag for optimization preference can be set when the file system is created. It can be set to optimize the file system for either space efficiency or time efficiency. Other fields, such as block size and fragment size, are required because their values need not be the same for different file systems used on the same UNIX system.

1.4.6 Relevant UNIX Commands

Like in the System V environment, in BSD several UNIX commands are available for use by the system adminstrator to maintain file systems. Some of these commands need root privileges in order to be run.

The *mkfs* command is used to make new file systems. The BSD command diiffers from its System V counterpart in that it takes many optional parameters to tune the file system. These parameters include the block size, the number of sectors, the number of tracks, the fragment size, the minimum percentage of free disk space, the revolutions per second of the drive, and the optimization preference. The optimization preference can be specified as *s* for space optimization and *t* for time optimization.

The *newfs* command is a front-end to the *mkfs* command, as it forks a *mkfs*. It is used primarily to let *mkfs* pick up appropriate parameters from the file /etc/disktab. It, therefore, needs the disk type as one of its parameters. *Mkfs* options can also be specified to override parameters specified in the /etc/disktab file.

The *mount* and *umount* commands are used to mount and unmount file systems.

The *tunefs* command can be used to tune existing file system parameters. Parameters such as optimization preference, minimum free space, and the time to service an I/O interrupt can be changed using this command. The file system itself may be mounted and in use.

1.4.7 User Perspective

From a user's perspective, differences between the UNIX System V file system and the Berkeley file system discussed so far only affect the performance of their read/write operations on the disk. There are several other enhancements which directly affect the end user. These are discussed here.

In the System V implementation, there was no mechanism to restrict disk space usage to users. The only restriction was the physical availability of disk space and the access to the file system mounted on it. The BSD file system has a mechanism called quotas which can be used by the administrator to enforce a limit on disk usage. Two types of limits can be set: soft and hard. When a soft limit is set, a warning message is generated. A hard limit is equivalent to running out of physical disk space; all write operations will fail if this limit is reached. Administrators can turn the quota mechanism on and off by using the *quotaon/quotaoff* command.

In the System V file system, file names could only be 14 characters long. This limit was eliminated in the BSD implementation. A directory in the BSD file system grows in "chunks" of 512 bytes. Each file entry consists of four fields: the inode number of the file, the size of the entry, the length of the file name contained in the entry, and the file name terminated by a null character and padded to a 4-byte boundary, using more null characters if required. The inode number occupies 4 bytes; the entry length and the file name length occupy 2 bytes each; and the current limit on the file name itself is 255 characters. The following sessions demonstrate the structure of a directory and its entries:

```
mkdir dir1
ls -ld dir1
drwxr-xr-x  2 rst      grp           512 Sep 21 12:54 dir2
od -cd dir1
0000000   o 240   \0  \0   \f  \0 001  \0    .  \0   \0  \0   \f 310   \0  \0
          41071    00000    00012    00001    00046    00000    51212    00000
0000020 364 001 002  \0    .   .  \0  \0   \0  \0   \0  \0   \0  \0   \0  \0
          00500    00002    11822    00000    00000    00000    00000    00000
0000040  \0  \0   \0  \0   \0  \0   \0  \0   \0  \0   \0  \0   \0  \0   \0  \0
          00000    00000    00000    00000    00000    00000    00000    00000
*
0001000
```

Here a new directory, dir1, is created. The size of the empty directory is 512, as opposed to 32 in System V. The first 4 bytes represent the inode number for the "." entry in the directory. The inode number for the "." directory in this example is 41071. The next 2 bytes represent the size of the entry, which is 12; the third field stores the length of the file/directory name, which is 1. The second entry of the directory starts at byte 13 because the first entry is 12 bytes long. The second entry, as in the System V directory, is for the parent directory ".." and in this example has an inode number of 51212, an entry length of 500, a file-name length of 2, and a file name ".." padded with null characters. The entry length is 500 bytes because the first entry occupied 12 bytes and the chunk is 512 bytes long.

If a new file is added to the directory, the entry changes as follows:

```
cp f1 dir1/filename1.data.final
od -c dir1
0000000   o 240  \0  \0  \f  \0 001  \0   .  \0  \0  \0  \f 310  \0  \0
          41071      00000     00012     00001     00046     00000     51212     00000
0000020  \f  \0 002  \0   .   .  \0  \0   w 240  \0  \0 350 001 024  \0
          00012      00002     11822     00000     41079     00000     00488     00020
0000040   f   i   l   e   n   a   m   e   1   .   d   a   t   a   .   f
          26982      25964     24942     25965     11825     24932     24948     26158
0000060   i   n   a   l  \0  \0  \0  \0  \0  \0  \0  \0  \0  \0  \0  \0
          28265      27745     00000     00000     00000     00000     00000     00000
0000100  \0  \0  \0  \0  \0  \0  \0  \0  \0  \0  \0  \0  \0  \0  \0  \0
          00000      00000     00000     00000     00000     00000     00000     00000
*
0001000
```

The size of the second entry for ".." is now changed to 12. The size of the third entry must therefore be 488 to make the total of all entries equal to 512. The inode allocated to the new file is 41079, and the length of the file name is 20.

If a second file, filename2.data.final, is added to the directory, the directory structure changes as follows:

```
od -cd dir1
0000000   o 240  \0  \0  \f  \0 001  \0   .  \0  \0  \0  \f 310  \0  \0
          41071      00000     00012     00001     00046     00000     51212     00000
0000020  \f  \0 002  \0   .   .  \0  \0   w 240  \0  \0      \0 024  \0
          00012      00002     11822     00000     41079     00000     00032     00020
0000040   f   i   l   e   n   a   m   e   1   .   d   a   t   a   .   f
          26982      25964     24942     25965     11825     24932     24948     26158
0000060   i   n   a   l  \0  \0  \0  \0   y 240  \0  \0 310 001 024  \0
          28265      27745     00000     00000     41081     00000     00456     00020
0000100   f   i   l   e   n   a   m   e   2   .   d   a   t   a   .   f
          26982      25964     24942     25965     11826     24932     24948     26158
0000120   i   n   a   l  \0  \0  \0  \0  \0  \0  \0  \0  \0  \0  \0  \0
          28265      27745     00000     00000     00000     00000     00000     00000
0000140  \0  \0  \0  \0  \0  \0  \0  \0  \0  \0  \0  \0  \0  \0  \0  \0
          00000      00000     00000     00000     00000     00000     00000     00000
*
0001000
```

The size of the third entry is changed to 32, and the size for the last entry is now 456 bytes to give a total of 12+12+32+456 = 512 bytes. Now if the file filename1.data is removed, the directory structure appears as follows:

```
rm filename1.data.final
od -c dir1
0000000   o 240  \0  \0  \f  \0 001  \0   .  \0  \0  \0  \f 310  \0  \0
          41071   00000   00012   00001   00046   00000   51212   00000
0000020   ,  \0 002  \0   .   .  \0  \0   w 240  \0  \0      \0 024  \0
          00044   00002   11822   00000   41079   00000   00032   00020
0000040   f   i   l   e   n   a   m   e   1   .   d   a   t   a   .   f
          26982   25964   24942   25965   11825   24932   24948   26158
0000060   i   n   a   l  \0  \0  \0  \0   y 240  \0  \0 310 001 024  \0
          28265   27745   00000   00000   41081   00000   00456   00020
0000100   f   i   l   e   n   a   m   e   2   .   d   a   t   a   .   f
          26982   25964   24942   25965   11826   24932   24948   26158
0000120   i   n   a   l  \0  \0  \0  \0  \0  \0  \0  \0  \0  \0  \0  \0
          28265   27745   00000   00000   00000   00000   00000   00000
0000140  \0  \0  \0  \0  \0  \0  \0  \0  \0  \0  \0  \0  \0  \0  \0  \0
          00000   00000   00000   00000   00000   00000   00000   00000
*
0001000
```

Removing file filename1.data.final from the directory increases the size of the previous entry by the size of the entry of the file to be removed. The file to be removed has an entry size of 32 bytes. The previous entry, for "..", had an entry of 12 bytes. Thus removal of the file has changed the entry size for ".." to 44.

The addition of a new file to the directory attempts to make use of previously released space as follows:

```
cp /etc/rc dir/newname.data.final
od -cd dir1
0000000   o 240  \0  \0  \f  \0 001  \0   .  \0  \0  \0  \f 310  \0  \0
          41071   00000   00012   00001   00046   00000   51212   00000
0000020  \f  \0 002  \0   .   .  \0  \0   w 240  \0  \0      \0 022  \0
          00012   00002   11822   00000   41079   00000   00032   00018
0000040   n   e   w   n   a   m   e   .   d   a   t   a   .   f   i   n
          25966   28279   28001   11877   24932   24948   26158   28265
0000060   a   l  \0   l  \0  \0  \0  \0   y 240  \0  \0 310 001 024  \0
          27745   27648   00000   00000   41081   00000   00456   00020
0000100   f   i   l   e   n   a   m   e   2   .   d   a   t   a   .   f
          26982   25964   24942   25965   11826   24932   24948   26158
0000120   i   n   a   l  \0  \0  \0  \0  \0  \0  \0  \0  \0  \0  \0  \0
```

```
          28265   27745   00000   00000   00000   00000   00000   00000
0000140   \0  \0  \0  \0  \0  \0  \0  \0  \0  \0  \0  \0  \0  \0  \0  \0
          00000   00000   00000   00000   00000   00000   00000   00000
*
0001000
```

The entry for ".." had enough space to accommodate the new entry and is accordingly split into two entries of 12 and 32 bytes. The 32-byte entry is assigned to the newly added file.

1.4.7.1 Locking Mechanism

Berkeley UNIX has an elementary locking mechanism which can be used by user programs but cannot be enforced. This implies that if a process locks a file, other processes can check if a lock exists on the file but can go ahead and access the file even if one exists. Locks, therefore, do not guarantee consistency. Locks can only be applied to open files. If a process applies a lock and then terminates abnormally or if there is a system crash, the lock will be terminated automatically; no manual intervention is required. This is done by maintaining lock fields in only the in-core copy of the inode, not in the disk copy of the inode.

The system call *flock(2)* can be used to apply locks on files. There are two types of locks which can be applied to a BSD opened file. The first, called shared lock, can be applied to a file many times. The other, called exclusive lock, can be applied only once. The user has the choice to make an attempt to lock a file and block the process if the lock cannot be applied immediately. For example, an attempt to apply an exclusive lock on a "locked" file will block the process. Such blocked processes may be awakened by signals. The user may only check for the existence of a lock without blocking the process by just examining the return status of a system call to lock the file.

1.4.8 Links

Links are used to have a file "appear" in more than one directory without having the data physically duplicated. If a file is created and a new link is added to it at a later time, this new link is indistinguishable from the original one. Such links are called hard links. They cannot span across file systems and are equivalent to links available on System V. In BSD, soft links can be used to link files across file systems if you use the -s option on the *ln* command line. With the use of hard links, if the original directory entry of a file is removed but the newly created link is not removed, the file is still guaranteed to exist. Symbolic links, on the other hand, are implemented bv file name substitution. They can span across file systems, and therefore it is possible to remove the original file while the file system with the link is not mounted.

1.5 Raw I/O

If the user does not like the UNIX file system there is an alternative process to access the data on the disk. This process, which bypasses the file system, is called raw I/O. At least one process, called the swapper which manages swap space when processes are swapped from and to main memory uses raw I/O.

Many DBMS use raw I/O to manage their own disk space. This is done to reduce some of the overheads of using the UNIX file system. Of course, the DBMS must keep track of all used and unused space on the device as well as control access to it. The advantages of using the buffer cache may be lost if raw I/O is used without some buffering scheme.

1.6 Distributed File Systems

A distributed file system provides the user with a view of file systems residing on multiple machines as if they were all mounted on a single machine. A heterogeneous distributed file system is one which provides a single view of files which may reside on multiple computers running different operating systems. Several distributed file systems are currently available from different vendors. Perhaps the most popular of these is the Network File System from Sun Microsystems. Several systems on a network can share a file as a common resource. There are several benefits of using a distributed file system.

First, sharing a file as a common resource on multiple machines eliminates the need to make the file physically available on different machines. In addition to saving substantial disk space, it increases the integrity of the file, as the file need not be updated on multiple machines. This is true for both software and data. Updating a version of a software package need be done only once. Associated with this benefit is the low cost of maintaining a single copy. A distributed file system must be able to provide the benefits without subjecting users to make any changes in their commands or programs. In addition, users must be able to get a consistent view of the data and be assured of reliability and security of the data.

Sun Microsystem's Network File System implements a distributed file system by incorporating several changes in the file system internals. The implementation uses the Remote Procedure Call (RPC) mechanism. RPCs are functions that can be executed on remote machines. A system that makes files available to other systems is called a server, and systems which use files residing on remote computers are called clients. If the data representation such as byte ordering and alignment of basic data types on different computers is different, then there must be an additional layer to do appropriate conversions to a standard format. The External Data Representation (XDR) protocol is used by RPC to resolve such problems.

A client can access remote file systems by *mount*ing them. Servers can make file systems accessible to clients by *export*ing them. The *mount* and *export* commands can be used for this purpose. The server has a file called /etc/exports which lists the available directories. When an NFS server is booted, the startup script /etc/rc.local starts up a program called exportfs. This program is responsible for enforcing permissions on the exported file system. File systems can also be exported and unexported after the booting process is complete.

AT&T's Remote File Sharing (RFS) provides file systems on one machine to be shared by users on other machines as if the file systems were mounted on the machine they are logged into. The system administrator can make any directory and the files in it sharable by making it known to other machines using the *adv* command. Remote machines can mount the advertised directory on a local directory, and the advertised directory will then appear to users as if it is a local directory. Remote mounting of an advertised directory can be stopped by using the *unadv* command. This command does not affect the machines on which the directory is already mounted.

1.6.1 Closing Thoughts

The UNIX file system continues to evolve, incorporating new techniques and methodologies for managing data. A detailed discussion on the algorithms and data structures used in the different versions of UNIX is beyond the scope of this book. Though there are different file systems in use, newer versions of UNIX would provide access to different file systems mounted on the same UNIX system. And perhaps, one day, there will be only one UNIX version!

2 File Processing

UNIX offers a wide range of tools for examining the contents of a file. These tools have some common features and many incongruous options. They can read a standard input file and write to the standard output. Such utilities, often called filters, are powerful enough to serve the data processing needs of small databases and files; however, they provide only sequential access and can be slow for search operations. They do not modify the contents of the input file, but will simply write the result to the standard output. The following sections show how these utilities can become a powerful arsenal for both casual and serious UNIX users.

2.1 Head and Tail

Head is used to display the specified number of records from the top of a selected file. The most commonly used option is the one that specifies the number of records to be displayed. If you do not have *head* on your system, then you probably have a *more* or a *pg* command which will let you do a *head* and something more! *Tail* does the same as *head*, but in the reverse direction: it displays the specified number of lines from the end of the file. In most UNIX versions, *tail* allows only a limited number of lines to be displayed. This limit depends primarily on the record size of the file to be displayed. Here is an example of *head* usage:

```
head -5 file1
John     23      123-38-9073
Michael 23      321-12-8921
James    25      142-32-4564
Paul     26      231-34-1212
Tom      23      123-12-1245
```

In the above example we have used an option to display the first five lines. By default, *head* displays the first 10 lines of selected files.

2.2 More and Pg

More and *pg* are used to examine the contents of a file. These utilities can be used to display a file one screen at a time or a specified number of lines at a time. Thus

```
more bigfile
```

can be used to display the file bigfile one screen at a time, while

```
more -10 bigfile
```

can be used to display the file 10 lines at a time. They also provide a mechanism to search for regular expressions. Most options are common to both *pg* and *more*. *More* is more popular and commonly used on the Berkeley Software Distribution (BSD) version, while *pg* is normally available on the System V version of UNIX. They provide numerous command line options and search features. We will look at the most commonly used features of these utilities.

2.2.1 Examining a File

To examine a file, use the command along with the name of the file to be examined, as follows:

```
more somefile
or
pg somefile
```

Either of these commands will display the first screenful of the file. *More* and *pg* will then wait for the user response. If you are using *pg*, a carriage return in response to the prompt will display the next screenful. If you are using *more*, entering a space character in response to the prompt will display the next screenful. A control D (^D) will display the next 11 lines, or half a screenful. To skip some lines while using *more*, specify the number of lines to be skipped followed by the letter *i*, and *more* will position itself after the specified number of lines. *Pg* allows you to scroll backward and forward with the *l* command. A negative number preceding this command can be used to specify the number of lines to be scrolled backward. A positive number with the + sign will scroll the file forward, and an unsigned number will display a screenful beginning at the specified line. In addition, the *$* command in *pg* can be used to display the last screen of the file.

2.2.2 Searching for Regular Expressions

Pg and *more* also enable us to search for regular expressions in the file. In *pg*, the command *i/regular expression/* is used to search forward for the *i*th occurrence of the regular expression. The command *i?regular expression?* is used to search backward for the *i*th occurrence of the regular expression. In *more*, the command *i/regular expression* is used to search forward for the *i*th occurrence of the regular expression. In *more*, there is no command to search backward.

2.2.3 Escaping to the Shell

More and *pg* allow us to escape to the shell and execute a UNIX command by the use of *!command*, where *command* is any UNIX command.

2.2.4 Examples of More and Pg Usage

Here are some examples of *more* and *pg* usage:

```
man cat|more -200 > catman
```

will store the first 200 lines of the manual page of the *cat* command in the file catman.

```
pg -l file1
John    23      123-38-9073
l/^J/
James   25      142-32-4564
```

In the above session we invoke *pg* to peruse file1 one line at a time and then display the next line which starts with the letter *J*.

On-line help for using these commands is available by using the *h* command.

2.3 Cut

Each record of a file can be considered as a collection of characters or fields. The fields may be separated by any field separation character. Data processing requirements often make an extraction of only certain character positions or fields from a file. *Cut* is the UNIX utility that provides these capabilities. The syntax of *cut* is as follows:

```
cut -f list [-d char] file1 file2...
        or
cut -c list file1 file2...
```

List is a comma-separated list of integers or range of integers. For example, 1,3−5,7 would project the first, third, fourth, fifth, and seventh positions. The first form is used to cut specified fields from a file with the field separator *char*. The second form is used to cut columns based on character positions. The only option required for a *cut* by character positions is the −*c* option which specifies a list of character positions to be projected. Here is an example of a *cut* by character positions:

```
cat file1
John,P  23      123-38-9073     75
Phil,R  23      321-12-8921     59
Mike,T  25      142-32-4564     32
Rick,L  26      231-34-1212     65
Jack,T  23      123-12-1245     90
```

```
cut -c1-4,10-15 file1
John    123-3
Phil    321-1
Mike    142-3
Rick    231-3
Jack    123-1
```

The file named file1 has four fields separated by a tab character which has been expanded in the display. A cut by field positions is more commonly used. Let us look at another example in which we will cut a list of fields from the same file:

```
cut -f1,3-4 file1
John,P  123-38-9073     75
Phil,R  321-12-8921     59
Mike,T  142-32-4564     32
Rick,L  231-34-1212     65
Jack,T  123-12-1245     90
```

The default field separator is a tab, but it can be changed by using the *−d* option on the command line. In the following example the fields are separated by a blank character:

```
cat file1
John,P 23 123-38-9073 75
Phil,R 23 321-12-8921 59
Mike,T 25 142-32-4564 32
Rick,L 26 231-34-1212 65
Jack,T 23 123-12-1245 90
```

```
cut -f2,1,3 -d" " file1
John,P 23 123-38-9073
Phil,R 23 321-12-8921
Mike,T 25 142-32-4564
```

```
Rick,L 26 231-34-1212
Jack,T 23 123-12-1245
```

When specifying the field delimiter, only characters which have a special meaning to the shell have to be enclosed in quotes; otherwise quoting is not required. *Cut* will give an error diagnostic if the line length is greater than 1023 characters.

2.4 Paste

Paste is used to paste several files together. It is similar to the UNIX utility *cat* except that while *cat* concatenates files vertically, *paste* concatenates files horizontally. The number of records in the output file is equal to the number of records in the longest input file. The syntax of the *paste* command is as follows:

paste *[-s] [-d char] file1 file2 ...*

The output file contains a record for each record in the longest input file. These records are concatenated together, and their newline characters replaced by tab characters, except for the records of the last file which retain their newline characters. The tab character can be replaced by another character by using the *−d* option. The file names can be substituted by the minus (−) characters. This indicates that the records of the file must be read from the standard input. A *−s* option is useful for reading lines from the same file and pasting them together. Here are some examples of the use of *paste*:

```
cat f1
a
b
c
d
cat f2
1
2
3
4
5
6
```

Example 1

```
paste f1 f2
a       1
b       2
c       3
d       4
        5
        6
```

Example 2

```
paste -d" " f1 f2
a 1
b 2
c 3
d 4
 5
 6
```

Example 3

```
paste -s f1
a       b       c       d
```

Example 4

```
cat f1 | paste - -
a       b
c       d
```

In example 1, *paste* was used to simply paste horizontally the records of the two files f1 and f2. The newline character of file f1 was replaced by the tab character. In example 2, we pasted f1 and f2, but this time the newline character of file f1 was replaced by a blank character. This was specified by the $-d$ option. In example 3, we used the records in the same file f1 to be pasted together into one record. In the last example, the input consisted of two files. Records for both files were taken from the standard input. This option is used to convert a file of n records into a file containing n/x records, where x is the number of minus signs on the command line. The first record contains the first x records pasted together as described earlier, the second record contains the next x records from the input file, and so on.

2.4.1 Using Cut and Paste Together

Cut and *paste* can be used together to restructure the columns of a file. Let us move the first column of file1 to the end of the record. This can be done as follows:

```
cat file1
John,P 23 123-38-9073 75
Phil,R 23 321-12-8921 59
Mike,T 25 142-32-4564 32
Rick,L 26 231-34-1212 65
Jack,T 23 123-12-1245 90

cut -f1   -d" " file1 > file2
cut -f2-4 -d" " file1 > file3
paste -d" " file3 file2 > file1

cat file1
23 123-38-9073 75 John,P
23 321-12-8921 59 Phil,R
25 142-32-4564 32 Mike,T
26 231-34-1212 65 Rick,L
23 123-12-1245 90 Jack,T
```

In this example, we first cut the first field of file1 and stored it in file2. Next, we cut the remaining fields of file1 and stored this segment in file3. We then pasted file3 and file2 and redirected the output into file1. The new file1 is now restructured as desired.

2.5 Od: Unraveling the Hidden

One of the frustrating things in programming is to display nongraphic characters in a file. Attempts to display a file which has these characters can create problems, as these characters may alter some of the terminal settings. *Od* helps us to display these characters in various formats. The syntax of *od* is as follows:

```
od [-bcdosx] [file] [[+]offset[.][b]]
```

Let us try to dump the contents of a directory file using *od*. The directory file in the UNIX System V consists of a 16-byte entry for each file. The first 2 bytes store the i-number of the file. The i-number is used to locate an inode for the file being accessed. The remaining 14 bytes store the name of the file. If you try to *cat* the directory file, you will see strange characters because the first 2 bytes of a file entry may not represent graphic ASCII characters. Let us use *od* to dump one such directory file:

```
ls dirfile
s.t.c
dummy.c
a.out
core
test.c
od -c dirfile
0000000   \0    b    .   \0   \0   \0   \0   \0   \0   \0   \0   \0   \0   \0   \0   \0
0000020    6    a    .    .   \0   \0   \0   \0   \0   \0   \0   \0   \0   \0   \0   \0
0000040   \0  211    s    .    t    .    c   \0   \0   \0   \0   \0   \0   \0   \0   \0
0000060  003  340    d    u    m    m    y    .    c   \0   \0   \0   \0   \0   \0   \0
0000100  036    @    a    .    o    u    t   \0   \0   \0   \0   \0   \0   \0   \0   \0
0000120   \0  206    c    o    r    e   \0   \0   \0   \0   \0   \0   \0   \0   \0   \0
0000140  001    f    t    e    s    t    .    c   \0   \0   \0   \0   \0   \0   \0   \0
0000160
```

The $-c$ option instructs *od* to interpret the bytes in ASCII. The first column indicates the character position in octal; thus the first row starts with 0000000, indicating that the first character is at position 1. The second row starts with the octal number 0000020, or decimal 16, indicating that the first character in the second row is at position 17. The ASCII graphic characters are printed appropriately. If the character does not have a graphic representation, then it is printed as a C escape character or a three-digit octal number. The first two bytes of each file entry have some characters which are nongraphic, as may be expected. The \0 represents the NULL character in C escape format.

When *od* is invoked with the $-d$ option, 2 adjacent bytes are clubbed together and their decimal equivalent is printed as an integer value. Here is the output of *od* with the $-c$ and the $-d$ options on the same directory file:

```
od -cd dirfile
0000000   00098   11776   00000   00000   00000   00000   00000   00000
         \0   b   .  \0  \0  \0  \0  \0  \0  \0  \0  \0  \0  \0  \0  \0
0000020   13921   11822   00000   00000   00000   00000   00000   00000
          6   a   .   .  \0  \0  \0  \0  \0  \0  \0  \0  \0  \0  \0  \0
0000040   00137   29486   29742   25344   00000   00000   00000   00000
         \0 211   s   .   t   .   c  \0  \0  \0  \0  \0  \0  \0  \0  \0
0000060   00992   25717   28013   31022   25344   00000   00000   00000
        003 340   d   u   m   m   y   .   c  \0  \0  \0  \0  \0  \0  \0
0000100   07744   24878   28533   29696   00000   00000   00000   00000
        036   @   a   .   o   u   t  \0  \0  \0  \0  \0  \0  \0  \0  \0
0000120   00134   25455   29285   00000   00000   00000   00000   00000
         \0 206   c   o   r   e  \0  \0  \0  \0  \0  \0  \0  \0  \0  \0
0000140   00358   29797   29556   11875   00000   00000   00000   00000
        001   f   t   e   s   t   .   c  \0  \0  \0  \0  \0  \0  \0  \0
0000160
```

The second row shows the ASCII character representation, and the first row displays the same characters with their decimal equivalent. For example, ASCII characters \0 and b represent binary values 00000000 and 01100010. If we club them together, we get 0000000001100010. This number, with the most significant bit at the left side, represents the decimal number 98. This number is shown above the two characters it represents. If the bit order on the machine is different, the decimal number displayed will be different. There are certain software packages which create files with integer data stored in their binary representation. Data in these files can be examined by using *od* *−d*. The *−b* option dumps the characters in their octal representation. The *−o* option dumps two characters clubbed together as a word in their octal representation. The *−x* option gives the hexadecimal representation, and the *−s* option is identical to the *−d* option except that it interprets the most significant bit as a sign bit.

Od also offers a feature to look at only a certain segment of the file. This feature can be used by specifying the byte offset from where *od* is to start reading the file. This offset is interpreted as an octal number. If this offset is followed by a dot (.), then it is interpreted as a decimal number. If a *b* is specified along with the offset, then the offset is multiplied by 512. Finally, if data is piped into *od* and an offset is desired, then a plus (+) must be specified. Here are some examples of using *od* with an offset. Try to compare the results with earlier outputs from the same file.

```
od -c dirfile 10
0000010  \0  \0  \0  \0  \0  \0  \0  \0   6   a   .   .  \0  \0  \0  \0
0000030  \0  \0  \0  \0  \0  \0  \0  \0  \0 211   s   .   t   .   c  \0
0000050  \0  \0  \0  \0  \0  \0  \0  \0 003 340   d   u   m   m   y   .
0000070   c  \0  \0  \0  \0  \0  \0  \0 036   @   a   .   o   u   t  \0
0000110  \0  \0  \0  \0  \0  \0  \0  \0  \0 206   c   o   r   e  \0  \0
0000130  \0  \0  \0  \0  \0  \0  \0  \0 001   f   t   e   s   t   .   c
0000150  \0  \0  \0  \0  \0  \0  \0  \0
0000160
od -c dirfile 10.
0000010  \0  \0  \0  \0  \0  \0   6   a   .   .  \0  \0  \0  \0  \0  \0
0000026  \0  \0  \0  \0  \0  \0  \0 211   s   .   t   .   c  \0  \0  \0
0000042  \0  \0  \0  \0  \0  \0 003 340   d   u   m   m   y   .   c  \0
0000058  \0  \0  \0  \0  \0  \0 036   @   a   .   o   u   t  \0  \0  \0
0000074  \0  \0  \0  \0  \0  \0  \0 206   c   o   r   e  \0  \0  \0  \0
0000090  \0  \0  \0  \0  \0  \0 001   f   t   e   s   t   .   c  \0  \0
0000106  \0  \0  \0  \0  \0  \0
0000112
```

In the first example, *od* started reading the file from offset 8, which is the decimal equivalent of octal 10. In the second example we have specified the offset as a decimal number by the use of a dot (.); therefore *od* started reading the file from offset 10. *Od* continues dumping the data until it reaches the end of the file.

2.6 Sort

Most applications involving data processing with flat files require that the input files be sorted. UNIX offers the *sort* utility for sorting files. The syntax of the command with its many options is:

sort *[*-**bdfnr***] [sort-field] [*-**cmu***]*
[-**o** *output-file] [*-**T** *directory] [*-**y kmem***] [*-**y** *kmem] [*-**z** *recz] filename*

If file1 is the input file, it can be sorted by using the *sort* command in its simplest possible form as follows:

```
cat file1
John:44:Engineer
Tom:32:Programmer
Mary:0019:Dancer
Shalan:0022:Biologist
sort file1
John:44:Engineer
Mary:0019:Dancer
Shalan:0022:Biologist
Tom:32:Programmer
```

The input file was sorted in ascending order using the ASCII collating sequence, character-by-character from left to right. By default, the output is directed to the terminal (stdout). It can be redirected to another file by using the *−o* option. In the following example, the sorted output is directed into the file file.out.

```
sort -o file.out file1
```

Redirecting the output to the original file will destroy it.

Records in a file are made up of fields. Each field may be separated by a character known as the field separator. File file1 has three fields separated by a colon(:). *Sort* can be used to sort a file based on a field position. Here is an example:

```
sort -t: +1 -2 file1
Mary:0019:Dancer
Shalan:0022:Biologist
Jacob:039:Actor
Tom:32:Programmer
John:44:Engineer
```

Here the *−t* option is used to specify the field separator. The sort field is determined by using the arguments beginning with a + or a − sign.*+1* specifies that the first field is to be skipped for sorting purpose, and a *−2* specifies that the sorting should stop at the second field. The output is, therefore, sorted on the second field. It is possible to sort on a character position within a field by suffixing a field position with a *.number*, where *number* refers to the number of additional characters to skip before determining the sort position. To sort on two characters starting from the third character in the third field and ending at the fourth character in the same field, use:

```
sort -t: +2.2 -2.5 file1
John:44:Engineer
Mary:0019:Dancer
Tom:32:Programmer
Shalan:0022:Biologist
```

The *−r* option can be used to reverse the order of the sort. The file in the example can be made to sort in reverse descending order on the second field by using the command:

```
sort -t: -r +1 -2 file1
John:44:Engineer
Tom:32:Programmer
Shalan:0022:Biologist
Mary:0019:Dancer
```

A file can be sorted in numeric order by using the *−n* option. To sort the file on the second field in numeric order on the second field use the command:

```
sort -t: -n +1 -2 file1
Mary:0019:Dancer
Shalan:0022:Biologist
Tom:32:Programmer
John:44:Engineer
```

The *−f* option can be used to fold uppercase letters to lowercase only for comparison during the sort. The *−b* option can be used to ignore leading space characters when determining the starting and ending positions of a field. The *−d* option can be used to enforce dictionary order. Only letters, digits, and the white-space characters are considered significant in comparisons.

2.6.1 Merging Files

The *sort* utility can be used not only to sort files but also to merge them. The *−m* option can be used for this purpose. Here is an example:

```
cat f1          cat f2
Mike:12                Lilian:22
Judy:24                Joseph:24
Lilian:40              Naomi:50
Nutan:70               Kim:99
sort -t: -m +1 -2 f1 f2
Mike:12
Lilian:22
Joseph:24
Judy:24
Lilian:40
Naomi:50
Nutan:70
Kim:99
```

To use the *−m* option, the input files must be sorted on the merge field. The *−u* option can be used to output only the records with unique sort field values. In the above example, there are two records with the sort field value of 24. The *−u* option can be used to enforce uniqueness in the output as follows:

```
sort -t: -m -u +1 -2 f1 f2
Mike:12
Lilian:22
Joseph:24
Lilian:40
Naomi:50
Nutan:70
Kim:99
```

The *−u* option can also be used without the *−m* option.

Finally, *sort* will print a warning message if the last record does not have a newline character. It will also append one to the output.

2.6.2 Limitations and Precautions

The *sort* command consumes both space and CPU time. Numerous temporary files are created during the sort phase. By default, these files are created in the /tmp directory. To sort large files, there must be approximately 1.5 times the input file size available in this directory. The user may not find the required space in this directory. If an attempt is made to sort the file in the absence of disk space for intermediate files, the sort will terminate abnormally. The alternative to this problem is to find another writable directory on a file system with enough space and let *sort* use it to create temporary files. The *−T* option is provided for this purpose.

Records in the input file are expected to have a maximum length of 1024 characters. If the length of an input record is found to exceed this number, *sort* will terminate the sort abnormally or truncate the record silently. A limit on the maximum length is required because it is neccessary to allocate buffer space during the sorting process. The *−z* option can be used to specify the maximum length of an input record.

Sort starts with a default main memory size and then continues to request more space as the need arises. The performance can be enhanced by specifying a memory size that *sort* can start with. The *−y* option can be used for this purpose.

The following *sort* command sorts the input file file1, using a starting memory of 512K bytes and the directory /u/t as the temporary directory:

```
sort file1 -T /u/t -y 1
```

It is a waste of system resources to sort an already sorted file. The *−c* option can be used to check if the input is sorted. An output will be produced only if the input is not sorted.

2.7 Join: Joining Data in Two Files

Join is a utility that supports the relational database operator *natural join*. It enables extraction of data from two files having a field that is defined over some common domain. While this definition may sound theoretical, understanding what it means is worthwhile. Let us consider two files: suppliers and parts. The suppliers file has three fields, representing supplier number, supplier name, and part number of the part supplied. The parts file also has three fields, representing part number, part name, and part description. If you needed to create a file having supplier name and part name, it would be necessary to make a comparison of the two files based on information in the part number column of each file. Since the part numbers in both files have the same type and represent the same object, we can say that the part number fields in the two files are defined over the same domain. The comparison of the two files based on the field defined over the same domain can therefore be made by using the *join* utility. The syntax of *join* is:

```
join [options] file1 file2
```

File1 and file2 are the two input files. These files have to be sorted by the field on which a comparison is to be made. Each output line is made up of the common field followed by a line of file1 followed by a line of file2. This output can be modified by using the various options that *join* is equipped with. Here is an example to create a file having supplier name and part name.

```
cat suppliers
S0101:PRS, Inc:p123
S0230:Tare, Inc:p123
S1213:Unicomp Corp.:p223
S0202:Strakers, Inc:p23
S3030:Ritecore, Inc:p234

cat parts
p123:Resistors:multi
p223:Boards:brown
p234:Gloves:blue

join -j1 3 -j2 1 -o 1.2 2.2 -t: suppliers parts
PRS, Inc:Resistors
Tare, Inc:Resistors
Unicomp Corp.:Boards
Ritecore, Inc:Gloves
```

The output shows how the records are joined over the common fields. There is no output record corresponding to the supplier record *S0202:Strakers, Inc:p23* because there is no parts record for part number *p23*. If there are records with duplicate keys in the same file, the join is performed on all the duplicate key records. Since we have two records in the suppliers file with the same part number *p123*, we also have two records with part name *Resistors* in the output.

This example employs the most commonly used options of *join*. The *−j* option is used to specify the common fields on which the join is to be made: *−j1 3* means join on the third field of the first file, *−j2 1* means join on the first field of the second file. The *−o* option is used to specify a list of fields to be output. The list contains blank-separated field specifiers in the form *m.n*, where *m* is the file number and *n* is the position of the field in the file. Thus, *−o 1.2* means output the second field in the first file. The *−t* option is used to specify the field separator character, a colon in this example. By default, the field separators are blank, tab, or newline characters. Multiple blanks and tabs count as one field separator.

It is possible to create output records for unpairable lines in the input files. This is particularly helpful when the purpose of the *join* is to append some data from one file to another without losing any records. *Join* provides the *−a n* and *−e str* options to output records for unpairable lines. The *−a n* option produces a line for each unpairable record in file *n*, where *n*=1 or 2. The *−e str* option replaces the empty fields for the unpairable file by the string specified by *str*. If we require a suppliers parts file with the part name attached if known and the string *NA* attached if it is not known, here is how we would request it:

```
join -a1 -e NA -j1 3 -j2 1 -o 1.1 1.2 1.3 2.2 -t: suppliers parts
S0101:PRS, Inc:p123:Resistors
S0230:Tare, Inc:p123:Resistors
S1213:Unicomp Corp.:p223:Boards
S0202:Strakers, Inc:p23:NA
S3030:Ritecore, Inc:p234:Gloves
```

Join is very helpful when we need to attach information from one file to another file when the two files are of different lengths and/or are sorted by different fields. A *cut* and *paste* works as long as the two files have exactly the same number of records sequenced exactly the same on the common field.

2.8 Sed: A Stream Editor

Sed is a noninteractive editor that can be used to edit files which are too large for *ed*. This is possible because *sed* does not read the entire file into a buffer, rather it reads only a few required lines at a time. *Sed* is a filter because it does not change the original file: it reads the input file and creates a new file which is sent to standard output by default. *Sed* can be invoked as follows:

```
sed [-n] [[-e command]...] [-f] [file]
```

The *−e* option is used to specify that there are multiple commands in the *sed* command string. This is not required if we have only one *sed* command. Let us get started with some simple *sed* scripts.

2.8.1 Getting Started

The minimum requirements to run *sed* are an input file and a command to let *sed* know about the transformations that should be applied on this file to create an output file. Let us run *sed* to change all occurrences of *"and,"* to *"and"* in the input file file1 and then output only the changed lines.

```
cat file1
It follows,then,that the divine, being good,
is not, as most people say,
responsible for everything that happens to mankind,
but only for a small part;
for the good things in human life are far fewer than
the evil, and, whereas the good must be ascribed to heaven only,
we must look elsewhere for the cause of evils.*

sed  -n s/and,/and/p file1
the evil, and whereas the good must be ascribed to heaven only,
```

We used the $-n$ option to specify that only those lines selected for printing (p) should be output. By default, *sed* will print all lines in the input file. Edited lines will replace the original lines in the input file. The *s/and,/and/p* string is the *sed* command string. The *s* instructs *sed* to do a pattern substitution. This is followed by the string to be searched for, which is enclosed in slashes, and then by a string that should replace the searched pattern. The final *p* instructs *sed* to print the edited lines. If the $-n$ option was not given, we would get both the edited line as well as the entire input file, as follows:

```
sed s/and,/and/p file1
It follows,then,that the divine, being good,
is not, as most people say,
responsible for everything that happens to mankind,
but only for a small part;
for the good things in human life are far fewer than
the evil, and whereas the good must be ascribed to heaven only,
the evil, and whereas the good must be ascribed to heaven only,
we must look elsewhere for the cause of evils.
```

If the *sed* editing command was not terminated by the *p* option, we would get only the edited file as the output:

**The Republic of Plato*, translated by Francis Comford, 1945.

```
sed s/and,/and/ file1
It follows,then,that the divine, being good,
is not, as most people say,
responsible for everything that happens to mankind,
but only for a small part;
for the good things in human life are far fewer than
the evil, and whereas the good must be ascribed to heaven only,
we must look elsewhere for the cause of evils.
```

2.8.2 Sed Commands

Sed commands have the general syntax

line1,line2 [edit commands] [opt commands]

This instructs *sed* to apply the edit commands and the optional (opt) commands on the input file but only on the segment of the file from line number *line1* to line number *line2*. *Line1,line2* can be substituted by just one line number, in which case the following command operates only on that particular line of the input file. It is also possible to use pattern matching to select the lines. This is done by enclosing the pattern in slashes for selecting the lines. For example, the command */John/s/tare/Tare/* substitutes the string *Tare* for *tare* only in those lines which have the string *John* in them. If the line specification is missing, the edit commands are applied to all the lines in the file. The most commonly used edit commands are shown in Table 2.1.

TABLE 2.1 Commonly Used Edit Commands

Command	Explanation
s	Substitute one string with another string.
a	Append newlines in the file.
i	Insert newlines in the file.
d	Delete lines from a file.
c	Change lines from a file to user-specified lines.
p	Print the specified/edited lines.
w	Write selected lines into a specified file.

2.8.3 Examples of Sed Usage

All of the following examples assume the same input file, file1, which was used in the previous examples. Let us use *sed* to display lines 3 to 4 of file1:

```
sed -n 3,4p file1
responsible for everything that happens to mankind,
but only for a small part;
```

Let us create a file with the third and fourth lines deleted:

```
sed  3,4d file1
It follows,then,that the divine, being good,
is not, as most people say,
for the good things in human life are far fewer than
the evil, and, whereas the good must be ascribed to heaven only,
we must look elsewhere for the cause of evils.
```

Here is an example that deletes lines containing the string *the*:

```
sed /the/d file
is not, as most people say,
responsible for everything that happens to mankind,
but only for a small part;
```

The program presented below handles more than one *sed* command on the command line. It substitutes the occurrence of the string *the* with the null string. It also deletes lines with occurrences of the word *for*.

```
sed -e s/the// -e /for/d file1
It follows,n,that the divine, being good,
is not, as most people say,
 evil, and, whereas the good must be ascribed to heaven only,
```

In the above example we had to use the $-e$ option because we have more than one command. In this example we see that the string *the* is still present in the output, though our command was to substitute this string by a null string. Here is what happened: Unless we specify a global substitution, the substitution takes place on only the first occurrence of the string *the* in a line.

The second and any subsequent occurrences of the string will not be changed. In order to do a global substitution, we have to use the optional command *g*. Here is how we can do it:

```
sed -e s/the//g -e /for/d file1
It follows,n,that  divine, being good,
is not, as most people say,
 evil, and, whereas  good must be ascribed to heaven only,
```

2.8.4 Sed Commands from a File

We have so far used only the *−e* and the *−n* command line options. The *−f* option is used to store the edit commands in a file and then inform *sed* to take the edit commands from this file. This option is particularly helpful if the edit commands are long; it is also useful for appending or inserting new lines. The *sed* command below performs the same task as the previous *sed* command; however, this time the *sed* edit commands are stored in a file.

```
cat editfile
s/the//g
/for/d
sed -f editfile file1
It follows,n,that  divine, being good,
is not, as most people say,
 evil, and, whereas  good must be ascribed to heaven only,
```

Multiple options can also be used, as shown in the following example:

```
sed -n -f optfile file1
It follows,n,that the divine, being good,
for  good things in human life are far fewer than
 evil, and, whereas the good must be ascribed to heaven only,
we must look elsewhere for  cause of evils.
```

2.8.5 Appending and Inserting New Lines

In *sed*, appending of new lines is done with the *a* command. This command appends lines after the specified line number. Like all other *sed* commands, if a line number is not specified, the append command operates on all lines. The *a* command has to be followed by a backslash (\). The lines to be appended are then specified after the command line. Each line except the last line must be terminated by a backslash character. Let us add a line containing underscores after each line in the input file.

```
cat addfile
a \
-----------------------------------------------------
sed -f addfile file1
It follows,then,that the divine, being good,
-----------------------------------------------------
is not, as most people say,
-----------------------------------------------------
responsible for everything that happens to mankind,
-----------------------------------------------------
but only for a small part;
-----------------------------------------------------
for the good things in human life are far fewer than
-----------------------------------------------------
the evil, and, whereas the good must be ascribed to heaven only,
-----------------------------------------------------
we must look elsewhere for the cause of evils.
-----------------------------------------------------
```

The new lines added are not affected by subsequent deletes, as shown here:

```
cat add_del
a\
-----------
1,3d
head -4 file1 | sed -f add-del
-----------
-----------
-----------
but only for a small part;
-----------
```

The addition of new lines does not affect the line number counter in the same *sed* command file. In the above *sed* command we have not specified a line number; therefore the lines were appended after every record in the input file. Note how the command to delete the first three lines does not affect the newly added lines. The insert (*i*) command is identical to the append command except that the lines are inserted before the specified line number.

2.8.6 Writing Output to Files

It is possible to write the output of selected or edited lines to a file by using the *w* command. Let us output the first two lines of the input into a file called firsttwo, lines having the string *the* into a file called thefile, and finally, substitute the string *good* with the string *nice* and output the result into a file called nicefile. The *sed* command below performs these tasks:

```
cat writefile
1,2w firsttwo
/the/w thefile
s/good/nice/w nicefile

sed -n -f writefile file1

cat firsttwo
It follows,then,that the divine, being good,
is not, as most people say,

cat thefile
It follows,then,that the divine, being good,
for the good things in human life are far fewer than
the evil, and, whereas the good must be ascribed to heaven only,
we must look elsewhere for the cause of evils.

cat nicefile
It follows,then,that the divine, being nice,
for the nice things in human life are far fewer than
the evil, and, whereas the nice must be ascribed to heaven only,
```

2.8.7 Use of Regular Expressions in Sed

UNIX filters thrive on the use of regular expressions, and *sed* is no exception to this rule. Until now we have selected lines for operations to be performed by *sed* commands by explicitly specifying the line numbers or by specifying a string so that the *sed* commands could operate on lines having this string. We can extend this line selection capability by specifying a regular expression. The *sed* commands would then operate on lines which have a string that matches the regular expression. *Sed* regular expressions are either text characters, which match verbatim, or operator characters, which have special interpretations. Operator characters are

```
"\[]^-?.*+()$/
```

Table 2.2 explains the special meaning associated with eight of the available operator characters. These characters will suffice for most purposes and are more than enough to get started. Meanings for the remaining operator characters can be found in the UNIX system documentation.

TABLE 2.2 Sed Operator Characters in Regular Expressions

Character	Meaning	Examples
.	Matches any character except a new-line character.	#.* matches a string starting with a # character until the end of a line. Typically used for removing comment lines.
$	Used at the end of an expression to indicate that a string should match the regular expression preceding this operator only if it occurs at the end of a line.	p$ matches any lowercase letter *p* occurring at the end of a line.
"	Used to match a string containing operator characters. The special meaning of the operator characters is turned off.	"Tip*Top" matches the string *Tip*Top*.
\	Also used to turn off the special meaning of an operator character. This character can be followed by a number to give an octal representation.	Tip*Top matches the string *Tip*Top*. \40 matches a single blank.

TABLE 2.2 Sed Operator Characters in Regular Expressions (contd.)

Character	Meaning	Examples
//	Matches the last regular expression compiled.	
*	Matches zero or more occurrences of the preceding element of an expression.	*bc*d* matches strings like *bd*, *bcd*, and *bccd*.
[ ]	Used to specify character classes. Within a character class, three characters have special meanings. The minus (–) character is used to indicate a range of characters. It loses its special meaning if it occurs at the beginning of a character class. The ^ character is used to indicate the complement set of characters, i.e., all characters specified except those in the character class. The \ character is used as explained above.	[A–Za–z_][A–Za–z0–9]* matches any C variable name. [^0–9] matches all characters except the digits 0 to 9. [0\–9] matches the three characters 0, 9, and –.
^	If this character occurs outside a character class and at the beginning of an expression, it matches the expression only if it starts after a newline character.	^"New line" matches the string *New line* only if it starts on a new line.

Here are some examples of the use of regular expressions for specifying lines:

Example 1

```
sed -n /^It/p file1
It follows,then,that the divine, being good,
```

In this example, only lines which began with the word *It* were selected. The next example uses the [ ] operator characters to match lowercase letters. The –*n* option is used once again to output only lines selected for printing.

Example 2

```
sed -n /p[a-z]/p file1
is not, as most people say,
responsible for everything that happens to mankind,
but only for a small part;
```

Here a line was selected if it had a word with the letter *p* followed by any other lowercase letter.

Example 3

```
sed -n /" "p[a-z]/p file1
is not, as most people say,
but only for a small part;
```

In this example, a line was printed only if it had a word that was preceded by a blank character and that began with the letter *p*. In both example 2 and example 3, the selected word had to be at least a two-letter word and the second letter had to be a lowercase letter.

Example 4

```
sed -n s/,$//p file1
It follows,then,that the divine, being good
is not, as most people say
responsible for everything that happens to mankind
the evil, and, whereas the good must be ascribed to heaven only
```

In example 4, we deleted all line-terminating commas and printed the edited lines. With these examples we conclude the discussion of *sed*.

2.9 Egrep

Egrep is a utility which can search for patterns or regular expressions in a file. It is simple to use and comes in three flavors: grep, egrep, and fgrep. The predecessor of *egrep* is *grep*. *Egrep* is an extension of *grep* and can handle more powerful regular expressions. *Fgrep* is a subset of *egrep* that can handle only strings of fixed size, and it is faster to use to search for such strings. In this book we will discuss the use of *egrep*.

2.9.1 Getting Started with Egrep

Egrep can be invoked as follows:

```
egrep [options] [regular expression] files
```

It is always safe to enclose the regular expression in single quotes to protect it from the shell. For the purpose of illustrating the use of *egrep*, we will use the same input file, inpfile, in all the examples. Here is a very simple *egrep* command:

```
cat inpfile
And if a man is temperate and free from the love of money,
meanness, pretentiousness, and cowardice, he will not be hard to
deal with or dishonest. So, as another indication of the
philosophic temper, you will observe, from youth up, he is fair-
minded, gentle, and sociable.

egrep 'So,' inpfile
deal with or dishonest. So, as another indication of the
```

In this example we displayed only those lines in which the string *So,* appeared. *So,* is a very simple regular expression that we were looking for. Like *sed*, *egrep* also has some special characters that allow *egrep* to form regular expressions. The interpretation of these characters is identical to the operator characters in *sed* and is explained in Table 2.2. The following examples show how *egrep* can be used to search for regular expressions in a file:

Example 1

```
egrep '-$' inpfile
philosophic temper, you will observe, from youth up, he is fair-
```

Example 2

```
egrep ',.*,.*,' inpfile
meanness, pretentiousness, and cowardice, he will not be hard to
philosophic temper, you will observe, from youth up, he is fair-
```

Example 3

```
egrep '(^[A-Z])|([a-z]$)' inpfile
And if a man is temperate  and  free  from  the  love  of  money,
meanness,  pretentiousness, and cowardice, he will not be hard to
deal  with  or  dishonest.  So,  as  another  indication  of  the
```

Example 1 printed lines which end with a hyphen. Example 2 printed lines which have more than two commas in them. Finally, example 3 displayed lines which either start with an uppercase letter or end in a lowercase letter. Note the use of the ( ) operator characters to group regular expressions.

2.9.2 Command Line Options with Egrep

Egrep provides several command line options. The most useful ones are listed in Table 2.3.

TABLE 2.3 Egrep Command Line Options

Options	Description
−v	Print lines which do not match the regular expression.
−c	Do not print any lines but give the count of the number of lines that matched the regular expression.
−i	Do not distinguish between lowercase and uppercase letters.
−n	Print the line numbers along with the lines.
−e	Print lines which begin with a − (minus).
−f	Get regular expression from a file which is specified after this option.

Here are some examples which use command line options:

Example 1

```
egrep -e '-$' -v inpfile
And if a man is temperate  and  free  from  the  love  of  money,
meanness,  pretentiousness, and cowardice, he will not be hard to
deal  with  or  dishonest.  So,  as  another  indication  of  the
minded, gentle, and sociable.
```

Example 2:

```
egrep -c '.' inpfile
2
```

Example 3:

```
egrep -n ',.*,.*,' inpfile
2:meanness,  pretentiousness, and cowardice, he will not be hard to
4:philosophic  temper, you will observe, from youth up, he is fair-
```

Example 4:

```
cat exprfile
,.*,.*,

egrep -n -f exprfile inpfile
2:meanness,  pretentiousness, and cowardice, he will not be hard to
4:philosophic  temper, you will observe, from youth up, he is fair-
```

In example 1, *egrep* printed lines which do not end in a minus (−). Example 2 gave a count of periods (.) in the input file. Example 3 displayed lines which have at least three commas. In example 4, *egrep* performed the same function as in example 3 but the regular expression was taken from the file exprfile.

Though we have showed the use of *egrep*, the usage of *grep* and *fgrep* are identical except that the regular expressions are restricted. In particular, *fgrep* should be used if the size of the string to be searched is fixed. For this purpose it is documented to be more efficient than *egrep*.

2.10 Awk

Awk is a pattern scanning and processing language. It is undoubtedly the most popular and the most powerful filter available in the UNIX environment. It is particularly helpful because it supports field-oriented processing. It also has capabilities for matching on regular expressions. *Awk* has many built-in functions and supports many conventional arithmetic expressions. *Awk* statements and expressions are C-like. *Awk* supports scalar variables and arrays, has many built-in variables, and has a wide range of operators. *Awk* does not need any declarations of variables. The data type of the variable is inferred from its context. *Awk* has been updated recently to extend its capabilities as a high-level language. If some of the features of *awk* discussed here do not work on your system, you probably have an old version of *awk*.

2.10.1 Invoking Awk

Awk can be invoked as follows:

```
awk [-Fsep] ' pattern {action}
              pattern {action}
              .
              .
              ' filenames
              or
awk [-Fsep] -f pattern-action-file filenames
```

Awk checks to see if the input records in the specified files satisfy the *pattern*, and, if there is a match, then execute the action associated with it. If the pattern and action sequences are long, it is convenient to store them in a file, referred to in the syntax as *pattern-action-file*, and then invoke *awk* with a *-f* option as shown in the second form. The field separator can be specified by the *-F* option as shown above where *sep* is the field separator string. By default, *awk* fields are separated by white space.

Patterns are defined as follows:

```
BEGIN
END
/regular expression/
relational expression
pattern && pattern
pattern || pattern
(pattern)
!pattern
pattern, pattern
```

Actions consist of a list of zero or more statements separated by semicolons or newline characters. Braces can be used to group statements. *Awk* supports the following statements:

```
if (expression) statement [else statement]
while (expression) statement
for (expression;expression;expression) statement
break;
continue;
next;
```

exit
variable = expression
print [expression] > [expression]
print [expression] | [expression]
for (var in array) statement

2.10.2 Getting Started with Awk

A common use of *awk* is to select some records based on a value in some field. Fields can be referred to in *awk* by prefixing the field number with a dollar sign ($). Thus $1 refers to the first field, $2 refers to the second field, etc. $0 refers to the entire record. Let us look at a small file containing student name, major, and age and then run a sample *awk* program on it:

```
cat students
John,P  Physics  20
Rick,L  Mechanical  21
Jack,T  electrical  23
Larry,M  Chemical   22
Phil,R  Electrical  21
Mike,T  mechanical  22
Paul,R  Chemical    23
John,T  Chemical    23
Tony,N  Chemical    22
James,R Electrical  21

awk '$3 > 22 { print $1 }' students
Jack,T
Paul,R
John,T
```

In this example, we printed the first field of all records where the third field was greater than 22. The pattern is *$3 > 22* and the action consists of one statement: *print $1*. The pattern can be categorized as a relational expression.

Now let us print out the names of all students whose major is electrical. Since we know that when the data was entered, *Electrical* was also entered as *electrical*, we have to make use of regular expressions to do the searching. Here is the *awk* command:

```
awk '$2 ~ /[Ee]lectrical/ { print $1} ' students
Jack,T
Phil,R
James,R
```

The relational operator ~ is used for matching regular expressions. The !~ means that the condition is satisfied if the regular expression is not matched. The complete set of regular expressions supported by *awk* is shown in Table 2.4.

TABLE 2.4 Regular Expressions in Awk

Element	Meaning
c	Matches any nonspecial character c.
\c	Matches c even if c is a special character.
.	Matches any character but newline.
^	Matches beginning of line or string.
[xyz..]	Matches any of the specified characters. A minus (−) may be used to specify a range, e.g., [a−z] matches any lowercase letter. A ~ may be used to negate the character class.
ex1|ex2	Matches either the regular expression ex1 or the regular expression ex2.
ex+	Matches one or more occurrences of the regular expression element ex.
ex*	Matches zero or more occurrences of the regular expression element ex.
ex?	Matches zero or one occurrence of the regular expression element ex.
(ex)	Matches the regular expression element ex. It can be used for grouping in order to resolve ambiguities in regular expressions.

Here are some examples of regular expression usage in *awk*:

Example 1

```
awk '$0 ~ /^J.*/ {print $0} ' students
John,P  Physics  20
Jack,T  electrical  23
John,T  Chemical    23
James,R Electrical  21
```

Example 2

```
awk '$1 !~ /[A-Zb-z]*a[A-Zb-z]*/ {print $0}' students
John,P  Physics  20
Rick,L  Mechanical  21
Phil,R  Electrical  21
Mike,T  mechanical  22
John,T  Chemical    23
Tony,N  Chemical    22
```

In the first example, we displayed all fields of all records where the record began with the letter *J*. In the second example, we displayed all fields of all records where the first field did not have a single lowercase letter *a* in it.

2.10.3 Awk Operators

Apart from the two relational operators, ~ and !~, that *awk* uses for matching regular expressions, it also has six other relational operators. They are <, <=, >, >=, !=, and ==. These relational operators have the same meaning as the C relational operators. *Awk* also supports the logical operators ||, &&, and ! to signify a logical OR, a logical AND, and a logical negation, respectively. The operators +, −, /, *, %, ^=, +=, -=, /=, %=, *=, ++, and -- have the same meanings as in C. Exponentiation can be done by the use of the operator ** or ^ in the proper context. Finally, the operator $ is used to refer to a field, as indicated earlier.

2.10.4 Using Awk Statements

So far we have been using the capabilities of the *pattern* section of *awk* for selecting records. *Awk* also provides statements that can be used for selecting records and performing operations on the contents of these records. The statements that *awk* supports are listed in Section 2.10.1. Let us look at an example of *awk* that uses some of these statements:

```
cat awkprog1
{sum += $3
 ++no
}
END {printf "The average of the ages is %.2f\n", sum/no}
```

```
awk -f awkprog1 students
The average of the ages is 21.80
```

The *awk* program listed above calculates the average of the third field of the file, student age. We have used the variable *no* to keep count of the number of input records. The variable *sum* is used to keep track of the sum of the third fields from all the records input. The pattern END is a special pattern. Statements associated with this pattern are executed after the end of the input file is reached. Similarly, the pattern BEGIN can be used to execute statements before reading any records from the file. We used the *printf* statement to print the result. This statement is almost identical to the *printf* statement in C. It provides a way to print output in a format specified by the first double-quoted argument.

2.10.5 Awk Defined Variables

Awk defines a number of variables that have special meaning. These variables provide access to values that are very commonly used. *NR* is one such variable. It keeps track of the number of the record that is currently being processed. It will have a value of zero if it is accessed in statements associated with the BEGIN pattern. If it is accessed in the action associated with the pattern END, then it will have a value corresponding to the number of records in the input file. Let us rewrite the earlier examples to calculate the average age of the students, using the variable *NR*:

```
cat awkprog2
 {sum += $3
 }
END {printf "The average of the ages is %.2f\n",sum/NR}
awk -f awkprog2 students
The average of the ages is 21.80
```

Other variables defined by *awk* are listed in Table 2.5.

2.10.6 More on Awk Statements

Awk statements provide us with many features. In the next few examples we will see how these statements can be used. We have seen two versions of the

TABLE 2.5 Awk Variables

Variable	Description
FILENAME	Name of the current file being read
NR	Number of records read so far
NF	Number of fields in current record
RS	Input record separator
ORS	Output record separator
OFS	Output field separator
FS	Input field separator
OFMT	Output format for numbers (default: %.6g)
FNR	Record number in current file (Same as NR unless more than 1 input file)

awk print statements. One provides unformatted output and the other provides formatted output. In the previous examples, this output was written to the standard output. It is possible to write the output of the print statements to files other than the standard output. The *awk* program listed below would create two files. The first file, Jfile, would contain the data of all students whose name starts with the letter *J*. The second file, Pfile, would contain data of all students whose name starts with the letter *P*:

```
awk '{ if ($1 ~ /^J/) printf "%s\n", $0 > "Jfile"
       if ($1 ~ /^P/) printf "%s\n", $0 > "Pfile"}' students

cat Jfile
John,P  Physics  20
Jack,T  electrical  23
John,T  Chemical    23
James,R Electrical  21

cat Pfile
Phil,R  Electrical  21
Paul,R  Chemical    23
```

Notice that the *if* statement has been used to select records where the first field starts with the required letter. It is also possible to do this selection by specifying the appropriate regular expression in the pattern section of the *awk* program.

Awk also provides some functions that can be invoked in the same way that functions are used in programming languages. The most commonly used functions are shown in Table 2.6.

TABLE 2.6 Commonly Used Awk Functions

Function	Description
length(string)	Returns the length of *string*
substr(string,st,l)	Returns substring of *string* starting at position *st* and of length *l*
index(str1,str2)	Returns position of string *str2* in *str1*; if not found, returns 0
sprintf(frmt,expr-list)	Returns a string formatted according to format *frmt* using the values in the expression list
int(num)	Returns the truncated integer value of *num*
cos(x)	Returns the cos of *x*; *x* is in radians
exp(x)	Returns the exponential of *x*
sin(x)	Returns the sine of *x*; *x* is in radians
sqrt(x)	Returns the square root of *x*

It is also possible to define and use your own functions. In the next example, we will make use of *awk* functions to create a file having the initials of each student, followed by a three-character abbreviation of the student's major, followed by the student's age. We will sort this file before outputting it and do all this using *awk*.

```
awk '{ pos = index($1,",");
        lname = substr($1,pos+1,1);
        fname = substr($1,1,1);
        major = substr($2,1,3);
        name  = fname lname;
        printf "%s\t%s\t%s\n", name,major,$3 | "sort";
        }' students
JP      Phy     20
JR      Ele     21
JT      Che     23
JT      ele     23
LM      Che     22
MT      mec     22
PR      Che     23
PR      Ele     21
RL      Mec     21
TN      Che     22
```

The first *awk* statement located the position of the comma in the first field.

The second *awk* statement used this position to get the initial letter of the last name and stored it in the variable *lname*. The third statement got the first letter of the first field, student first name, and stored it in *fname*. Similarly the next statement fetched the three-character abbreviation of the student major from the second field. Then *fname* and *lname* were concatenated using the next statement to give us the two-character abbreviated name. The final statement output the result into a pipe. The *sort* command read from this pipe, sorted the input, and provided the final sorted result.

2.10.7 Arrays in Awk

Awk supports one-dimensional arrays. Array elements may be numeric or nonnumeric. The latter facility is particularly helpful for string processing. Since the size of the array is not fixed but can grow indefinitely, the statement *for (var in array) stat* executes the statement *stat* for each defined element of the array.

Here is an example of array usage in *awk*. Let us try to get the distribution of students in each major:

```
cat awkprog
{ if ($2 == "electrical") $2 = "Electrical";
  else if ($2 == "mechanical") $2 = "Mechanical";
  else if ($2 == "chemical")   $2 = "Chemical";
  else if ($2 == "physics")    $2 = "Physics";
  major[$2]++
}
END {
  for (i in major)
  printf "There are %d student(s) majoring in %s\n",
                                               major[i],i
}

awk -f awkprog students
There are 4 student(s) majoring in Chemical
There are 3 student(s) majoring in Electrical
There are 1 student(s) majoring in Physics
There are 2 student(s) majoring in Mechanical
```

Notice that we changed the second field so that it uniformly starts with an uppercase letter. Thus it will suppress the distinction between majors like *Electrical* and *electrical*. The statement *major[$2]++* increments the count of the major referred by $2. Finally, at the end of the file, we print each element of the defined array *major* along with its subscript. The element itself has the count and the subscript is the string representing the major.

2.10.8 Command Line Arguments and Parameters

Usage of arguments and parameters make *awk* programs flexible and powerful. Parameters are variable values that can be set during the invocation of *awk*. Command line arguments are arguments that can be specified while invoking *awk* and can be accessed in the *awk* program as the shell positional argument. Let us write an *awk* program to calculate the area of a circle, a square, or a rectangle given the required parameters. For example, if we store the *awk* program in a file named area, we can invoke the program as *area circle 12* to calculate the area of a circle with radius 12 units, as *area square 12* to calculate the area of a square with side 12 units, or as *area triangle 5* to calculate the area of a triangle with side 5 units. The program is listed below:

```
cat area
awk ' BEGIN {pi = 3.14
if ("'$1'"=="circle")
    printf "Area of the circle is %d\n", pi * '$2' ** 2;
else if ("'$1'"=="square")
    printf "Area of the square is %d\n", '$2' ** 2;
else if ("'$1'"=="triangle")
    printf "Area of the triangle is %d\n", '$2' ** 2 * 0.5
    }'

area triangle 12
Area of the triangle is 72
```

The single quotes in the above example were required to protect the *awk* program from the shell. The positional parameters were excluded from the quotes because it was desired that the shell interpret them.

Let us now rewrite the *awk* program to perform the same task. This time we will use parameters instead of positional command line arguments. Here is the *awk* program:

```
cat awkprog
BEGIN {
  pi = 3.14;
  if  (figure=="circle")
    printf "Area of the circle is %d\n", pi* param **2
  if  (figure=="square")
    printf "Area of the square is %d\n", param**2
  if  (figure=="triangle")
    printf "Area of the triangle is %d\n", param**2*0.5
}
awk -f awkprog figure=circle param=3
Area of the circle is 28
```

As you can see from this program, *awk* variables can be initialized on the command line. In older versions of *awk*, these values are not assigned to the respective *awk* variables in the statements associated with the BEGIN pattern.

2.10.9 Awk: Closing Thoughts

In the preceding sections we have shown selected features of *awk*. A language as powerful as *awk* cannot be covered in its entirety in a few pages. Awk has been used for a variety of purposes ranging from database management systems (DBMS) to language processors and data processing tasks. If you are not a C programmer, do not wish to learn C, and yet you need to do some processing that cannot be done by the other utilities, *awk* may just be the tool you are looking for. Give it a try; you will love it!

2.11 Uniq

The *-u* option of the *sort* command will produce unique records for duplicates on sort field values. The *uniq* utility can be used to output only unique records from an already sorted file. The following example outputs only unique records from file file4.

```
cat file4
12:aabede
12:aabede
777:xybdca
777:xybdca
```

```
uniq file4
12:aabede
777:xybdca
```

2.12 Find

The *find* command is used to search files in a list of directories based on a specified search criterion. Once the required files are found, specified commands can be executed on these files. This command can be used for several data-processing needs such as locating a lost file, removing old files, etc.

If a directory is inaccessible, a message will be displayed indicating that it is. Several options can be used as a search criterion. These options evaluate to true or false, depending on the condition. The files which satisfy the given search criterion can be used as arguments to the specified UNIX commands. Two commonly used commands are *print*, which list the names of the files, and *exec* which executes a specified command with the matched file name as the argument. One of the most commonly used option is *−name* which is used to specify the name of the file to be searched. Here is an example of a *find* command to locate the full path of a file:

```
find / -name passwd -print
find: cannot chdir to /etc/fixes
find: cannot chdir to /u/class/students.dbs
/bin/passwd
/etc/passwd
```

The first two lines of the display lists directories which could not be searched because of permission problems. The *−atime* option can be used to find files which have been accessed in a specified number of days. The following *find* command can be used to list the names of files in directory /u/class which have not been accessed for over 15 days.

```
find /u/class -atime +15 -exec ls {} ;
```

Similarly, to list the names of files in the same directory which were accessed in the last 15 days, you must specify the number of days with a negative sign. For example, the command

```
find /u/class -atime -15 -exec ls {} ;
```

can be used to display a list of files which were accessed in the last 15 days. If the sign is not specified, the command will list the names of files which were accessed exactly 15 days back.

Several other options for searching a file can be specified. The *-size* option can be used to search files bigger than, smaller than, or equal to the specified size. The size specified defaults to the number of blocks unless it is followed by a *c* in which case it is taken as the number of bytes. The following *find* command gives a long listing of files in directory /usr/bin which are less than three blocks big:

```
find /usr/bin -type f -size -3 -exec ls -l {} ;
-rwxr-xr-x  1 bin     bin           740 Jan  1  1970 /usr/bin/arconvert
-rwxr-xr-x  1 bin     bin           109 Jan  1  1970 /usr/bin/fdfmt.nl
-rwxr-xr-x  1 bin     bin           109 Jan  1  1970 /usr/bin/fdfmt.sl
-rwxr-xr-x  1 bin     bin           109 Jan  1  1970 /usr/bin/fdfmt.vl
-rwxr-xr-x  1 bin     bin           113 Jan  1  1970 /usr/bin/fdfmt10.nl
-rwxr-xr-x  1 bin     bin           113 Jan  1  1970 /usr/bin/fdfmt10.sl
-rwxr-xr-x  1 bin     bin           113 Jan  1  1970 /usr/bin/fdfmt10.vl
-rwxr-xr-x  1 bin     bin           652 Jan  1  1970 /usr/bin/tutor
-rwxr-xr-x  1 bin     bin           410 Aug 12 04:16 /usr/bin/greek
-rwxr-xr-x  1 bin     bin           307 Aug 12 04:27 /usr/bin/diff3
-rwxrwxrwx  1 bin     bin           842 Aug 17 11:31 /usr/bin/troff
```

The *-type* option is used to specify the type of the files to be searched. Among the file types recognized are *f* and *d* which are used to specify regular files and directories, respectively. In the absence of the *-type* option in the above example, the command *ls -l* would have been executed on regular files as well as directory files which have a size less than three blocks.

Additional options include *-mtime*, which can be used to search for files based on modification times, and *-ctime*, which can be used to search files based on inode modification times. Also, the *-user* and *-group* options can be used to search files on user and group ownership IDs, the *-perm* option can be used to search for files which have the specified permission flags, and the *-link* option can be used to search for files which have a certain number of links.

The options discussed here can be combined together to form an expression using parentheses which must be escaped using backslash characters. The *-o* option can be used to provide a logical *or* operation among the search conditions. For example, the following example is used to search for all C program files as well as files which start with the letter *A*.

```
find /u/bk \( -name '*.c' -o -name 'A*' \) -print
/u/bk/index/hyphen.c
/u/bk/chapters/t.c
/u/bk/chapters/Ax
/u/bk/chapters/A
/u/bk/chapters/Axxxx.c
/u/bk/Ax.c
```

The expression used in specifying the name of the file has to be quoted to protect the metacharacters from the shell. If multiple options are provided without the use of the *-o* option, then a logical *and* operation is implied. If a list of all C program files which start with the letter *A* is required, the following *find* command can be used:

```
find /u/bk -name '*.c' -name 'A*' -print
/u/bk/chapters/Axxxx.c
/u/bk/Ax.c
```

The *find* command is very often used in conjunction with the *cpio* command for backing up files. This will be discussed in the next chapter.

2.13 Encrypting and Decrypting Files

UNIX provides security to files by letting the user change the permission modes of the file. This level of security is sufficient for most systems. Of course, files with permission modes set off can still be read by users with "root" privileges. The *crypt* command is available to encrypt and decrypt the contents of a file. Once encrypted, the original file can be removed. The encryption process requires an encryption key which serves the purpose of a password. The key must be known in order for the encrypted file to be decrypted. If file.inp is an input file to be encrypted, the *crypt* command can be used as follows:

```
crypt mykey < file.inp > file.crpt
```

Once the file file.inp is encrypted, it can be removed. At a later time, you can retrieve the original file by using the same key, as follows:

```
crypt mykey < file.crpt > file.inp
```

The algorithm used by *crypt* to encrypt the file is not foolproof. However, the amount of attempt required would be large enough to deter any attempts to break the encryption.

2.14 Compressing and Expanding Files

Big files can be compressed temporarily to save space. When they are required again they have to be expanded because the contents of the file are, of course, changed after the compression process. The *pack* command can be used to compress files, and the *unpack* command can be used to expand previously compressed files. Typically, *pack* results in reducing the file to 60 to 75% of its original size. The actual reduction depends on two main factors, the number of bytes in the input file and the distribution of the characters. When used on a file, *pack* removes the original file and creates a new file with the suffix *.z* appended to the original file name. Here is an example:

```
ls -l original
-rw-r--r--  1 bk      108       80491 Oct 20 19:16 original
pack original
pack: original: 38.8% Compression
ls -l original*
-rw-r--r--  1 bk      108       49263 Oct 20 19:16 original.z
```

Pack will not proceed with the compression if at least a block of file space cannot be saved. *Pack* also does not work on files with links or on directory files.

2.15 Other Commonly Used Filters

UNIX offers a multitude of filters; it would take a whole book to discuss all of them. Some of the other widely used file processing utilities are discussed briefly in this section. The *bdiff* utility shows us the differences between two files. It displays the result of its comparison in the form of *ed* commands. It is possible to get the second file from the first file by applying these *ed* commands to the first file. *Diff* also displays the lines in the two files which create the differences in them.

```
cat file1
file1a
file1fr
file1b
file1c
file1d
file1e
file1f
file1g
file1h
```

```
cat file2
file1a
file1b
file1d
file1e
file1f
file1fn
file1g
file1h
```

```
diff file1 file2
2d1
< file1fr
4d2
< file1c
7a6
> file1fn
```

In this example the differences between file1 and file2 are displayed. The < refers to the affected lines which are in the first file. The > refers to the affected lines which are in the second file. *Ed* commands used are *c, a*, and *d*, which refer to changes, additions, and deletions to be made to the first file. The number after the command refers to the second file; thus, the first line of the display informs us that the second line of the first file has to be deleted. The next line, < *file1fr*, is the line to be deleted. Similarly, the next two lines inform us that line number 4 from file1 is also to be deleted. Finally, the last two lines tell us that a new line, *file1fn*, has to be added to file1 after line number 7.

Two files can also be compared using the *cmp* command. This command compares two files and prints the character position from the beginning of the file of the first difference encountered, as shown in the following example:

```
cat cmpf1
pqrs
abcd
cat cmpf2
lmno
abed
cmp cmpf1 cmpf2
cmpf1 cmpf2 differ: char 1, line 1
```

```
cmp -l cmpf1 cmpf2
      1 160 154
      2 161 155
      3 162 156
      4 163 157
      8 143 145
```

The $-l$ option can be used to get a long listing of all differing characters. The output specifies the byte number in decimal and the differing bytes in octal. Clearly the differing bytes in files cmpf1 and cmpf2 are at positions 1, 2, 3, 4, and 8. Do not forget to count the newline byte!

Another file comparison utility is *comm*. This utility requires that the input file be sorted. The output is in the form of three columns. The first column contains lines that exist only in the first file listed on the command line, the second column lists lines that are found only in the second file listed on the command line, and the third column lists lines that are common to both files. If file comm1 is:

```
cat comm1
1
2
3
4
5
```

and file comm2 is

```
cat comm2
1
2
4
7
```

then a *comm* on these two files will display:

```
comm comm1 comm2
                  1
                  2
3
                  4
5
         7
```

Yet another utility for comparing two files is *sdiff*. It uses the output of *diff* to produce a more readable report of the differences between the two files. Let us use *sdiff* to report the differences between the two files comm1 and comm2. Here is the output:

```
sdiff -w 20 comm1 com2
1           1
2           2
3         <
4           4
5         | 7
```

The files are listed side by side. Records which differ are marked with a vertical bar (|). A record which exists in the first file but not in the second file is marked with the < character, and a record which exists in the second file but not in the first file is marked with the > character. The $-w$ option is used to control the width of the output record. The default width is 130 characters. Only records from the first file of identical records can be made to output by the use of the $-l$ option. Outputting of identical records can be suppressed by the use of the $-s$ option. This option results in an output similar to the output of the *diff* command.

Tr is a utility that is available for translating occurrences of a set of characters in a file to another set of characters. It also allows for deletion of characters and squeezing of adjacent occurrences of the same character into a single character. Here are some examples of *tr* usage:

```
cat inpfile
asdfasdf      asdfasdf        asdfsdaf
adsf asdfasdf aaadsf asdf
```

Example 1:

```
tr  -ds  "df" " " <inpfile
asas asas assa
as asas aaas as
```

Example 2:

```
tr "as" "pq" < inpfile
pqdfpqdf      pqdfpqdf        pqdfqdpf
pdqf pqdfpqdf pppdqf pqdf
```

In example 1, we used the $-d$ and $-s$ options. The $-d$ option is used to delete all occurrences of the characters in the first string. In the example, the first string is made up of two characters, *d* and *f*. The $-s$ option allows us to squeeze multiple, adjacent occurrences of the characters in the second string to a single character. Since our second string consists of a single character which is a blank, all adjacent blanks are squeezed into a single blank character.

In example 2, the character *p* is substituted for the character *a* and the character *q* for the character *s*.

Split is a utility that is used to break big files into smaller files. The size of the small files can be specified explicitly or a default value of 1000 bytes is used. The files created are named xaa, xab, xac, ..., xzz. Although *x* is the default prefix, it can be changed by specifying the desired prefix on the command line. Let us split the file splfile into small files of four records each, specifiying the prefix *new*:

```
cat splfile
1
2
3
4
5
6
7
8
9
0

split -4 splfile new

cat newaa        cat newab        cat newac
1                5                9
2                6                0
3                7
4                8
```

Split can be used for various purposes. It is especially useful when a file is too large to be edited and most of the editing is to be done in one segment of the file. *Split* can be used to separate the segment, which can then be edited. The new updated file can be created by simply *cat*ing the old segments and the updated segment in the correct sequence.

2.16 Summary

In this chapter, the various tools for manipulating the contents of a file were discussed. Some tools can operate only on the whole record, while others like *awk* can manipulate individual fields within a record. Most of these tools also support a search on regular expressions. It is important to recognize that these tools can be used by users without any knowledge of programming. Further, UNIX provides a congenial environment for using these tools in conjunction with one another. Indeed, with some knowledge of shell programming and with the use of the pipeline mechanism, users can design their own tools using the utilities discussed in this chapter as building blocks.

The next chapter shows how these tools can be used for a wide variety of data processing applications.

3 Flat Files Systems

In Chapter 2 several UNIX utilities for file manipulation were examined. This chapter will demonstrate the power behind these tools for building systems of moderate sizes. None of the tools provided by UNIX for file handling have direct access or capabilities to update files. This forces the user to create temporary files and then move (*mv*) these files to give the final updated version. The major advantage of the UNIX environment for data processing for the casual user is that he or she is not expected to have any knowledge of programming techniques.

All examples in this chapter are based on a sample system consisting of three files. The first section of the chapter describes the system. Next, UNIX tools explained in the previous chapter are used to query and update the flat file system. The use of document preparation tools to generate fancy reports is also illustrated here. Subsequent sections deal with miscellaneous issues concerning data management using flat files. The emphasis here will be on the use of the tools and not on shell programming or database design. Some basic knowledge of shell programming is assumed.

3.1 System Description

The system discussed in this chapter is used to maintain information on programmers, projects, and software packages. Programmers, projects, and software packages are assigned a unique number so that they can be identified. Associated with each programmer is her or his name, salary, and the number of a software package with which she or he is familiar. Associated with each project are two fields. One field identifies the status of the project and the other field is used to identify the programmer working on it. Finally, associated with each software package number is the name of the package and the machine on which it is installed. Fields in the three files have variable lengths. A field separator is therefore required to separate the fields. The colon (:) character is selected as the field separator.

3.1.1 File Formats

As stated earlier, there are three files in the system. The first file, referred henceforth as the programmer file, has the following format:

Field position	Data
1	Programmer number
2	Programmer name
3	Software package number
4	Programmer salary

The software package number stores information about the package with which the programmer is familiar.

The second file, referred to as the project file, has the format:

Field position	Data
1	Project number
2	Project status
3	Associated programmer

This file thus provides information about the status of each project and the programmers who are working on it. The status of a project is identified by an integer. A status code of 1 indicates that the project was just started, a 2 indicates that it is nearly half done, a 3 indicates that it is more than half complete, and a 4 indicates that it is nearing completion.

The third file, referred to as the software file, has the following information:

Field position	Data
1	Software package number
2	Software package name
3	Machine on which installed

This file provides information about the software packages and the machines on which they are installed.

3.1.2 File Contents

For the purpose of explaining the tools, the files used here have a very small number of records. Specifically, the current contents of the programmer file are:

```
cat prog.d
11:John Doe:212:34000
11:John Doe:11:34000
11:John Doe:214:34000
13:Nutan Vaghmare:313:33000
19:Eileen Bush:12:30000
101:Michael Gatting:214:42000
141:Alan Lamb:213:52000
141:Alan Lamb:212:52000
15:David Rose:114:42000
29:Joan Jackson:320:39000
29:Joan Jackson:315:39000
29:Joan Jackson:114:39000
412:Shama Parab:113:42000
412:Shama Parab:11:42000
```

The contents of the project file are:

```
cat proj.d
P1:2:11
P1:2:412
P1:2:29
P2:1:11
P2:1:412
P2:1:29
P2:1:101
```

```
P3:3:141
P3:3:15
P4:3:101
P5:4:141
P5:4:19
```

The contents of the software file are:

```
cat soft.d
11:Rsys:M1
11:Rsys:M2
12:C--:M2
113:DieBase:M1
114:Engres:M1
212:NKS:M1
212:NKS:M2
212:NKS:M3
212:NKS:M4
213:NeVS:M3
214:TCP/NP:M3
313:Divify:M4
315:WolfBASE:M3
315:WolfBASE:M1
315:WolfBASE:M2
320:Y-Windows:M4
```

The examples in the rest of the chapter will use these files as input.

3.2 Processing Retrievals

The three files in the system have related information. A query may require one or more files as input. The examples in this section deal only with retrieval of data.

Query 1
Retrieve the total annual salary paid to programmers.

```
cut -d: -f1,4 prog.d|sort|uniq|
awk -F: '{ tot += $2};
 END { print  "Total salary of all programmers is: ", tot
     }'
Total salary of all programmers is:  314000
```

The *cut* command is used to cut the first and the fourth fields of the file. These fields are the programmer code and the programmer salary, respectively. The output is then sorted and *uniq*ued to give the list of programmer codes and their salaries. Finally, *awk* is used to sum the salary field.

Query 2

Retrieve names of programmers who are not currently working on any project

```
cut -d: -f3 proj.d|sort|uniq > /tmp/t1
cut -d: -f1 prog.d|sort|uniq > /tmp/t2
comm -13 /tmp/t1 /tmp/t2 > /tmp/t3
sort -t: +0 -1 -o /tmp/t4 prog.d
join  -t: -j1 1 -j2 1  -o 1.2 /tmp/t4 /tmp/t3
Nutan Vaghmare
```

The programmer code field is cut from both the programmers and the projects files using the *cut* command. *Comm* is used to get the number of programmers who are in the programmer file but not in the project file. The programmer numbers of the required programmers are retrieved in the file /tmp/t3. Finally, the prog.d file has to be sorted on the programmer code field and joined to the /tmp/t3 file to get the name(s) of the required programmers.

Query 3

Generate a report with programmer number, programmer name, and a list of projects the programmer is associated with.

```
cat query3.sh
sort -t: +2 -3 proj.d |
awk -F: ' {
        # Set "prev" to the programmer number in the
        # first record.
        if (NR == 1) prev=$3;

        # If there is a change in programmer number
        # print the array of projects.
        if (prev != $3)
              {
                      printf "%s", prev;
                      for (j=1;j<i+1;++j)
                            printf ":%s", projects[j];
                      printf "\n";
```

```
            i=0;
                    prev = $3;
            }

        # If the programmer number has not changed,
        # add the project number to the list
        projects[++i] = $1;
       };
        # Print the record for the last programmer
       END {
                    printf "%s", prev;
                    for (j=1;j<i+1;++j)
                            printf ":%s", projects[j];
                    printf "\n";
                    i=0;
                    prev = $3;

       }' > /tmp/t1
cut -d: -f1,2 prog.d|sort -t: +0 -1|uniq > /tmp/t2
join -t: -a1 -j1 1 -j2 1  /tmp/t2 /tmp/t1
rm /tmp/t1 /tmp/t2
```

query3.sh

```
101:Michael Gatting:P2:P4
11:John Doe:P1:P2
13:Nutan Vaghmare
141:Alan Lamb:P3:P5
15:David Rose:P3
19:Eileen Bush:P5
29:Joan Jackson:P1:P2
412:Shama Parab:P1:P2
```

The *sort* command is required to sort the project file on the programmer field. The sorted output is piped to the *awk* script to generate an output consisting of programmer number and a list of projects the programmer is associated with. The next step is to get the names of these programmers. The programmer number and the programmer name fields are cut from the programmer file. This output has to be sorted and then uniqued. The two files /tmp/t1 and /tmp/t2 are joined on the programmer number field to give the required output. The *-a1* option in the *join* command is used to output records for programmers who do not have any project assigned to them. Programmer number 13, for example, does not have any project assigned to her. Her record would have been lost in the absence of the *-a* option. Finally, all the temporary files are removed.

Query 4
List programmer numbers of programmers who are working together on at least one project.

```
cat query4.sh
sort -t: +0 -1 -o proj.d proj.d
join -t: -j1 1 -j2 1 -o 1.3 2.3  proj.d proj.d|
awk  -F: '{
        if ($1 > $2)
                print $1,$2;
        else
                if ($1 < $2)
                        print $2, $1;
        }' |sort|uniq
query4.sh
101 11
101 29
141 15
141 19
29 11
412 101
412 11
412 29
```

The first problem is to sort the project file on the project number field, which is accomplished very easily by the use of the *sort* command. Once the file is sorted, it is joined with itself on the project number field. The purpose of doing this is to get the list of programmers who are working on the same project. The problem, however, is that joining will also result in output records such as 11:11, 11:412, and 412:11. The first record indicates that programmer number 11 is working with himself on at least one project! The second and the third records clearly indicate a duplicate occurrence of the same pair. The output of the *self* join is therefore filtered through the *awk* script to eliminate records where both the first and the second fields are the same. In addition, the *awk* script also outputs records of the type 11:412 as 412:11. Only after this transformation is done can the output be sorted and uniqued to display the final result.

Query 5
For each programmer, output the count of the number of projects that he or she is currently working on and the count of software packages that he or she knows.

```
cat query5.sh
cut -d: -f3 proj.d|sort|uniq -c > /tmp/t1
cut -d: -f1 prog.d|uniq -c > /tmp/t2
join -a2 -e 0 -j1 2 -j2 2 /tmp/t1 /tmp/t2|
awk '{
        if (NF==2)
                print $1,"0",$2;
        else
                print $1,$2,$3;
     }'
query5.sh
101 2 1
11 2 3
13 0 1
141 2 2
15 1 1
19 1 1
29 2 3
412 2 2
```

In the first line, the *sort* and the *cut* commands are used to get a sorted output of programmer numbers from the project and programmer files. The *-c* option of the *uniq* command is used to retrieve the count of the occurrences of a programmer number in the input. The file /tmp/t1 will have the count of the number of projects the programmer is working on. The file /tmp/t2 will have the count of the number of software packages that the programmer knows. The programmer file is the master file. All programmers are guaranteed to have an entry in this file. The count of the number of software packages that a programmer knows is derived from this file and is therefore also guaranteed to be complete. However, all programmers may not have an entry in the project file. The *join* on the /tmp/t1 and /tmp/t2 file has a *-a* option to retain records for programmers who may not be currently associated with any project. Finally, an *awk* script is used to output a zero as a project count for these programmers. Without this *awk* script the third record in the ouput would appear as *13 1* instead of *13 0 1*.

Query 6
Display the average programmer salary associated with each project.

```
cat query6.sh
cut -d: -f1,3 proj.d|sort -t: +1 -2        > /tmp/t1
cut -d: -f1,4 prog.d|sort -t: +0 -1 |uniq > /tmp/t2
join -t: -j1 2 -j2 1 -o 1.1 2.2 /tmp/t1 /tmp/t2|sort -t: +0 -1|
awk -F: '{
        # Initialize prev to the project number
        # in the first record
                if (NR==1)
                        prev=$1;

        # If there is a change in the project number, then
        # output the computed averages
                if ($1 != prev)
                        {
                        print prev, tot/no;
                        prev = $1;
                        no = tot = 0;
                        }

        # Increment the number of records and add salary to
        # the tot variable
                ++no;
                tot += $2;
        };
        END{
                print prev, tot/no;
        }'
rm /tmp/t1 /tmp/t2
query6.sh
P1 38333.3
P2 39250
P3 47000
P4 42000
P5 41000
```

To calculate the average, you need to put together a file with project numbers and programmer salaries. The first *cut* projects out the project number and the programmer number fields from the project file. The second *cut* projects out the programmer number and programmer salary fields from the programmer file. This file has to be sorted and uniqued to remove duplicates. The *join* operation joins the two temporary files to give the following output:

```
P2:42000
P4:42000
P1:34000
P2:34000
P3:52000
P5:52000
P3:42000
P5:30000
P1:39000
P2:39000
P1:42000
P2:42000
```

This output has the project number as the first field and the programmer salary as the second field. Only the average salary associated with a project is required; therefore, this output is sufficient. It is sorted and piped to the *awk* script to calculate the average salary. The *awk* script keeps track of the project number. When the number changes, the *awk* script outputs the average; otherwise, it adds the salary to the tot variable and increments the no variable which is the count of the input records for the project. The print statement associated with the *END* is used to output the average for the last record.

Query 7

Create a new master file for programmers with the following information:

Field Position	***Data***
1	*Programmer number*
2	*Programmer name*
3	*Programmer salary*
4-8	*List of 5 software packages the programmer is knowledgeable about*
9-13	*List of 5 projects the programmer is associated with*
14-18	*The corresponding status of the projects*

Use NULL-valued fields where appropriate.

cat -n query7.sh

```
# Program to generate a master file with all relevant
# information for each programmer
sort -t: +0 -1 prog.d|
awk -F: '{
        if (NR==1)
                  {
                        prev   = $1;
                        name   = $2;
                        salary = $4;
                   }
        if (prev != $1)
                {
                printf "%s:%s:%s", prev,name,salary
                for (j=1;j<6;++j)
                        if (j<=i)
                                printf ":%s", packages[j];
                        else
                                printf ":";
                printf "\n"
                prev   = $1;
                name   = $2;
                salary = $4;
                i = 0;
                }
        packages[++i] = $3;
        };
        END {
                printf "%s:%s:%s", prev,name,salary
                for (j=1;j<6;++j)
                        if (j<=i)
                                printf ":%s", packages[j];
                        else
                                printf ":";
                printf "\n"
        }' > /tmp/t1
# Output programmer number, a list of projects that he
# is currently working on and their status.
sort -t: +2 -3 proj.d|
awk -F: '{
        if (NR==1)
                        prev   = $3;
        if (prev != $3)
```

```
                {
                printf "%s", prev
                for (j=1;j<6;++j)
                        if (j<=i)
                                printf ":%s", projects[j];
                        else
                                printf ":";
                for (j=1;j<6;++j)
                        if (j<=i)
                                printf ":%s", status[j];
                        else
                                printf ":";
                printf "\n"
                prev   = $3;
                i = 0;
                }
        projects[++i] = $1;
        status[i]    = $2;
        };
        END {
                printf "%s", prev
                for (j=1;j<6;++j)
                        if (j<=i)
                                printf ":%s", projects[j];
                        else
                                printf ":";
                for (j=1;j<6;++j)
                        if (j<=i)
                                printf ":%s", status[j];
                        else
                                printf ":";
                printf "\n"
        }' > /tmp/t2
# join the two lists in /tmp/t1 and /tmp/t2
join -t: -a1 -j1 1 -j2 1 /tmp/t1 /tmp/t2|
# For programmers who are not involved in any projects
# append NULL-valued fields.
awk -F: '{
                if (NF == 18)
                        print $0;
                else
                        printf "%s::::::::::\n", $0
        }'
```

```
query7.sh
101:Michael Gatting:42000:214::::P2:P4::::1:3:::
11:John Doe:34000:11:212:214:::P1:P2::::2:1:::
13:Nutan Vaghmare:33000:313:::::::::::::
141:Alan Lamb:52000:212:213:::P3:P5::::3:4:::
15:David Rose:42000:114::::P3:::::3::::
19:Eileen Bush:30000:12::::P5:::::4::::
29:Joan Jackson:39000:114:315:320:::P1:P2::::2:1:::
412:Shama Parab:42000:113:11::::P1:P2::::2:1:::
```

The process of generating the required file is completed in three steps. First, a temporary file, /tmp/t1, is generated with programmer numbers and a list of software packages about which the programmer is knowledgeable. This is done in the first 35 lines of the shell script. Next, from line numbers 36 to 75, another file, /tmp/t2, is generated with programmer numbers, a list of projects that the programmer is currently working on, and the status of the projects. Finally, the two files are joined. The output of the *join* is piped to an *awk* script which appends null-valued fields for programmers who are not involved in any project. The string *::::::::::* is appended to these records to ensure that each record has the same number of fields.

The *awk* scripts to generate the list are simple. The aim here is to read each record and accumulate the information for each programmer. When a record for a new programmer is encountered, print the accumulated information, initialize the variables, and continue the processing. The action associated with the END pattern is executed for the last programmer in the input. Without this segment of the program, there will be no output record for the last programmer in the input. The *-a* option in the *join* command is used to retain a programmer record in the output file even if the programmer is not associated with any project.

3.3 Generating Troff Reports

With the wide availability of laser printers, *troff*, the UNIX typesetting tool has increased tremendously in popularity. It comes equipped with several preprocessors such as *pic*, *tbl*, etc. UNIX file manipulating tools can be used very effectively in conjunction with *troff* and its preprocessors to produce high quality reports. The following example illustrates how *troff* can be used with *awk* and *tbl* to generate a laser-quality report.

Query:

Generate a report with the following information:

a. Programmer number

b. Programmer number

b. Number of projects he or she is currently assigned to

cat report.sh

```
# Get count of projects a programmer is associated with
# in file /tmp/t1
cut -d: -f3 proj.d|sort|uniq -c|
        awk '{ printf "%s:%s\n",$2,$1}' > /tmp/t1

# Get programmer number and programmer name in file /tmp/t2
cut -d: -f1,2 prog.d|sort -t: +0 -1|uniq > /tmp/t2

# Join the two files but don't lose idle programmers!
join -t: -a1 -j1 1 -j2 1 /tmp/t2 /tmp/t1 > /tmp/t3

awk -F: 'BEGIN {
# Print Page header for the first time
        printf ".ll 4.5i\n.lt 4.5i\n";
        printf ".sp 2\n";
        printf ".ft HB\n"
        printf ".ps 9\n"
        printf ".tl %c%cPROGRAMMER ACTIVITY REPORT%cPage No: %% %c\n",
                39,39,39,39;
        printf ".ps 8\n";
        printf ".sp 2\n";
        printf ".TS\n";
        printf "center;\nc c c\nn a n.\n";
        printf "NUMBER\tNAME\tPROJECTS\n=\n";
        printf ".ft H\n"
        }
            { if (line_no > 50)
# If more than 51 lines per page, generate new page
                {
        line_no=0;
        printf ".TE\n";
        printf ".bp\n";
        printf ".sp 2\n";
        printf ".ft HB\n";
        printf ".ps 9\n";
        printf ".tl %c%cPROGRAMMER ACTIVITY REPORT%cPage No: %% %c0,\
                39,39,39,39;
```

```
        printf ".ps 8\n";
        printf ".sp 2\n";
        printf ".TS\n";
        printf "center;\nc c c\nn a n.\n"
               printf "NUMBER\tNAME\tPROJECTS\n=\n";
               printf ".ft H\n";
               }
          ++line_no;
        # This statement prints the input record
          printf "%s\t%s\t%d\n",$1,$2,$3;
         };

# At End of file
        END {
        printf ".TE\n";
        }' /tmp/t3 > /tmp/t4
tbl /tmp/t4|troff -Tps|lp
rm /tmp/t1 /tmp/t2 /tmp/t3
report.sh
```

When executed, the following report will be printed:

PROGRAMMER ACTIVITY REPORT **Page No: 1**

NUMBER	NAME	PROJECTS
101	Michael Gatting	2
11	John Doe	2
13	Nutan Vaghmare	0
141	Alan Lamb	2
15	David Rose	1
19	Eileen Bush	1
29	Joan Jackson	2
412	Shama Parab	2

The program here has made use of very elementary *troff* and *tbl* commands. With the use of these commands, the readability of the program has improved significantly. The advantages and disadvantages of creating intermediate files as opposed to using pipes is discussed later in this chapter. However, in this example, it is important to redirect the output of the main *awk* program which generates *tbl* and *troff* commands into a temporary file, /tmp/t4 in this example. This redirection is necessary because one or more pages of the report can be missing or damaged because of printer problems such as a paper jam. The presence of a temporary file is useful in these circumstances, as only the required pages can be printed using the *-o* option of *troff* without rerunning the entire job. The temporary file /tmp/t4 can then be removed after the printing is completed successfully. *Troff* commands can also be used to highlight an "exception" record. For example, the names of programmers who do not have a project assigned to them can be printed in bold fonts. This can be achieved by changing the line

```
printf "%s\t%s\t%d\n",$1,$2,$3;
```

which prints each record in the input in the *awk* script to

```
if (NF==2)
  {
   printf ".ft HB\n";
  printf "%s\t%s\t%d\n",$1,$2,$3;
  printf ".ft H\n";
  }
else
  printf "%s\t%s\t%d\n",$1,$2,$3;
```

which will generate the following output:

PROGRAMMER ACTIVITY REPORT **Page No: 1**

NUMBER	NAME	PROJECTS
101	Michael Gatting	2
11	John Doe	2
13	**Nutan Vaghmare**	**0**
141	Alan Lamb	2
15	David Rose	1
19	Eileen Bush	1
29	Joan Jackson	2
412	Shama Parab	2

With the use of appropriate *tbl* and *troff* commands, fancier ouputs can be generated. Some programmers/users insert *tbl/troff* commands manually in the ouput. For long reports this method is impractical and prone to errors. While using *troff* for generating reports, users must take necessary measures to guarantee that none of the data lines begin with a period. *Troff* will, of course, look at these lines as commands, resulting in the loss of these records.

3.4 Processing Updates

As discussed earlier, there are no tools available in the UNIX environment to directly update files. Of course, one can write a C program to do so. However, in this chapter we will restrict our processing capabilities to standard UNIX tools.

Updates can be made to a file by creating a new version of the file and then renaming the new version to the old one. Though inefficient, it suffices for small applications. In this section, the update capabilities of UNIX tools will be explained with the use of examples. The three files used in the earlier section will be used again as the input.

Update 1

Add a new set of programmers to the programmer file. The new set is stored in the file new.pr.d.

```
cat new.pr.d
111:J. Owens:315:32000
112:Mike Powers:110:42000
11:John Doe:11:34000
cat new.pr.d prog.d > /tmp/tl
mv /tmp/tl prog.d
```

This appears to be a fairly trivial job. Several validation checks must be performed before any updates are made to maintain the integrity of the database. For example, a check could be made to see that the programmer name isn't already there in the prog.d file with a different programmer number. Another check could be made to see that a programmer number in use is not reassigned to a new programmer. Further, the software package number must have an entry in the soft.d file. The following shell script checks if the programmer already exists in the prog.d file. It should be executed before the update commands are run.

```
cat check1.sh
cut -d: -f1-3 prog.d   |sort > /tmp/t1
cut -d: -f1-3 new.pr.d|sort > /tmp/t2
join -t% /tmp/t1 /tmp/t2 > /tmp/t3
if test -s /tmp/t3
then
        echo Error, duplicate programmer entries:
        cat /tmp/t3
        rm /tmp/t1 /tmp/t2 /tmp/t3
fi
check1.sh
Error, duplicate programmer entries:
11:John Doe:11
```

Cut is used to project the first three fields from the existing and new programmer files. The output is then sorted and put in temporary files. *Join* is used to detect any common records in the two files. The *-t%* option is used to force a join on the entire record. Of course, it is assumed that there is no possibility of a % character occurring in any record. Ideally, there should be no output from the *join* command. If there is any output, then it is stored in the file /tmp/t3. Finally, the size of this file is checked using the *test* command. If it is greater than zero, an error message is displayed along with the duplicate errors.

As was pointed out before, it is also necessary to check that the software package numbers in the new programmers file have an entry in the soft.d file. The following shell script is used to check the same:

```
cat check2.sh
cut -d: -f3 new.pr.d|sort|uniq > /tmp/t1
cut -d: -f1 soft.d   |sort|uniq > /tmp/t2
comm -23 /tmp/t1 /tmp/t2        > /tmp/t3
if test -s /tmp/t3
then
        echo Invalid software package number in records:
        sort -t: +2 -3 -o new.pr.d new.pr.d
        join -t: -j1 1 -j2 3 -o 2.1 2.2 2.3 2.4 /tmp/t3 new.pr.d
        rm /tmp/t3
fi
rm /tmp/t1 /tmp/t2
check2.sh
Invalid software package number in records:
112:Mike Powers:110:42000
```

In this shell script, we first cut the software package numbers from the soft.d file and the new.pr.d file. The *comm* command is used to locate software package numbers in the new.pr.d file which are not in the soft.d file. These numbers are stored in a temporary file /tmp/t3. Finally, the size of this temporary file is checked and an error message along with the set of error records is displayed. Note that the join requires the use of the *-o* option to force the fields in the output to appear in the same order as the fields in the input.

Validation checks in any updates can be extremely involved. In addition to the two validation checks that were performed earlier, another possible validation check would be to check if there are common programmer names in the new file and the old programmer master file. If there are any common names, then the programmer numbers for these names must also be the same. Here is a shell script to detect such inconsistencies:

```
cat new.pr2.d
11:Jim Date:11:34000
112:Mike Powers:110:42000
111:J. Owens:315:32000
cat check3.sh
cut -d: -f1,2 new.pr2.d|sort -t: +0 -1|uniq > /tmp/t1
cut -d: -f1,2 prog.d|sort -t: +0 -1|uniq > /tmp/t2
join -t: -j1 1 -j2 1 /tmp/t1 /tmp/t2|
awk -F: '{
  if ($2 != $3)
    printf "Programmer no %s has multiple names: %s, %s\n", $1,$2,$3
        }'
rm /tmp/t1 /tmp/t2
check3.sh
Programmer no 11 has multiple names: Jim Date, John Doe
```

Once again, *join* is used to retrieve the names from the two programmer files on the programmer number field. The output of join has three fields. The first field is the programmer number, the second and the third fields are programmer names from the two programmer files. *Awk* is used to compare the names in the output records. If these names are not the same, then an error message is displayed.

Here is another example of the use of UNIX tools for updating files:

Update 2
Change the status of a project

```
cat update2.sh
# Check if program is invoked correctly
if test $# -ne 2
then
        echo "Usage: update2.sh <project-no> <new-status>" 1>&2
        exit 1
fi

# If project number is equal to the first argument
# Output a record with the new status code
awk -F: '{
        if ($1 == "'$1'")
                {
                printf "%s:%s:%s\n",$1,"'$2'",$3 > "/tmp/t1";
                ++entries;
                }
        else
                printf "%s:%s:%s\n",$1,$2,$3 > "/tmp/t1";
        };
# print statistics on records updated
        END{
        if (entries >0)
                printf "%d entries were updated\n", entries
        else
                print "Project ","'$1'"" not found\n" | "cat 1>&2";
        }' proj.d
mv /tmp/t1 proj.d
update2.sh P1 3
3 entries were updated
update2.sh P9 2
Project P9 not found
```

In this example, the status of a project can be changed by invoking the shell script update2.sh with two arguments. The first argument specifies the project number, and the second argument specifies the new status code. If the program is not invoked with two arguments, an error message is displayed. An error message is also displayed if the specified project is not found.

In the *awk* program, as records are read, the project number is checked against the first argument specified on the command line. If it matches, then the status code is changed to the second argument on the command line. The variable *entries* is used to keep a count of the number of matched records. After all the records are read, if no record is encountered in the input with the specified project number, then an error message is displayed, otherwise a count of matched records is displayed. The error message is redirected to *stderr* by using a pipe and redirecting *cat* to *stdout*. If the specified project is found, then the project status entry is changed. All changes are incorporated in the /tmp/t1 file which is finally renamed to the proj.d file.

The next example shows how to delete records from a file. Clearly, it is not possible to delete records from the original file, as it would leave holes in the blocks of the file! The only way is to create a new version of the file and rename it. The following shell script can be used to delete names of programmers who are not assigned to any project. First, the programmers who are not assigned to any project must be identified by perusing the projects file. Once identified, these programmers must be deleted from the programmer file. Here is the required shell script:

Update 3

Delete programmers who are not assigned to any project

```
cat update3.sh
cut -d: -f3 proj.d|sort|uniq > /tmp/t1
sort -t: +0 -1 -o prog.d prog.d
join -t: -j1 1 -j2 1 prog.d /tmp/t1 > /tmp/t2
cut -d: -f1 prog.d|sort|uniq|wc -l > /tmp/count
echo "Number of programmers before deletion:" `cat /tmp/count`
echo "Number of programmers after  deletion:" `cat /tmp/t1|wc -l`
mv /tmp/t2 prog.d
rm /tmp/t1 /tmp/count
update3.sh
Number of programmers before deletion: 8
Number of programmers after  deletion: 7
```

The programmers who have at least one project assigned to them are first identified by cutting out the third field from the project file and then redirecting the output to the /tmp/t1 file. The *sort* and *uniq* are required to eliminate duplicate programmer numbers. The programmer file is then sorted on the programmer number field and joined to the /tmp/t1 file. This join eliminates all programmers who are not in the project file. The output of this join is redirected to the /tmp/t2 file. Before the /tmp/t2 file is renamed, it is used to display a count of the number of programmers in the file before the deletion. A count of the number of programmers after deletion is also displayed. The count will be correct only if all programmers identified in the project file also have an entry in the programmer file. This is an integrity requirement and will be checked in the next example.

All queries and updates are guaranteed to be correct only if the integrity of the files across the system is maintained. Inadvertent updates to a file can result in a loss of integrity, and therefore systems using flat files or a DBMS must be constantly subjected to integrity checks. The simple system used in the preceding examples is subjected to a set of elementary integrity checks in the following shell script.

```
cat check.sh
#cut all key fields
cut -d: -f1 prog.d|sort|uniq > /tmp/progs
cut -d: -f3 proj.d|sort|uniq > /tmp/proj.progs
cut -d: -f3 prog.d|sort|uniq > /tmp/prog.softs
cut -d: -f1 soft.d|sort|uniq > /tmp/softs

#check if programmers in project file have an entry in
#the programmer master file: prog.d
comm -23 /tmp/proj.progs /tmp/progs > /tmp/err.1

#check if software packages in programmer file
#have an entry in the software file: soft.d
comm -23 /tmp/prog.softs /tmp/softs  > /tmp/err.2

### Check if the same programmer has multiple salaries!
sort -t: +0 -1 +3 -4 -o prog.d prog.d
awk -F: '{
        if (NR==1) {
                prev = $1;
                salary = $4;
        }
        if ($1==prev) {
                if (salary != $4)
                        {
                        print prev, "", salary > "/tmp/err.3"
                        print $1, "", $4  > "/tmp/err.3"
                        }
                }
        else {
                prev = $1;
                salary = $4;
        }
        }' prog.d
```

```
### Display results
if test -s /tmp/err.1
then
        echo Invalid programmer numbers in project file:
        cat /tmp/err.1
        rm /tmp/err.1
else
        echo Validation check for programmer numbers successful
fi

if test -s /tmp/err.2
then
        echo Invalid software package numbers in programmer file:
        cat /tmp/err.2
        rm /tmp/err.2
else
        echo Validation check for software package numbers successful
fi

if test -s /tmp/err.3
then
        echo Multiple salaries for same programmer:
        echo "Prog_no Salary"
        echo "======= ======"
        cat /tmp/err.3
        rm /tmp/err.3
else
        echo "Validation check for programmer salaries successful"
fi
```

The first part of the shell script checks for interfile consistency. Specifically, it checks to see if programmers in the project file proj.d have an entry in the programmer file prog.d and if a software package number in the programmer file is present in the file soft.d. Integrity checks, such as the ones performed in this example, which require that values of a field in a certain file also exist in another file are referred to as referential integrity checks.

This shell script also checks to see if there are multiple entries for the same programmer with different salaries in the prog.d file. The same segment of the *awk* program with minor modifications can be used to check for multiple names for the same programmer number in the prog.d file. Finally, appropriate messages are displayed indicating the outcome of the validation check.

3.5 Records with Fixed-Length Fields

Though records with fields separated by a field separator are more popular in the UNIX environment than records with fixed length fields, UNIX tools can also be used to handle these records. Consider the following file:

```
cat suppliers.d
01121DP-Tech Computer Services25 South Main St.   Edison    NJ07104
01131Innovative Technologies  318 W. Wilkes St.   Easton    PA18042
01231Creative Technologies    212 Shalan St.      N. Nutley PR19042
```

The fields is this file have a fixed length. Positions 1 to 5 are used to store the supplier number. The supplier name is stored from positions 6 to 30. The next 20 characters are used to store the street address. The town where the supplier is located is stored in the next 10 characters, and finally the last 2 and 5 characters are used to store the state and zip codes, respectively.

Files with such formats can be handled by *awk* very easily. Here is an *awk* script which can be used to print mailing labels from this file:

```
cat labels.sh
awk '{
        name    = substr($0,6,25);
        address= substr($0,31,20);
        town    = substr($0,51,10);
        num     = split(town,t," ");
        state   = substr($0,61,2);
        zip     = substr($0,63,5);
        printf "%s\n%s102s\n%s", \
                number, name, address, t[1];

        for (i=2; i <= num; ++i)
                printf " %s",t[i];

        printf ", %s %s\n\n\n", state, zip

        }' suppliers.d
labels.sh

DP-Tech Computer Services
25 South Main St.
Edison, NJ 07104
```

```
Innovative Technologies
318 W. Wilkes St.
Easton, PA 18042



Creative Technologies
212 Shalan St.
N. Nutley, PR 19042
```

The *substr* function was explained in the previous chapter. It is used here to extract fields from the input records. The *split* function is used here to break the town field into an array of words. The first argument is the string to be split. The second argument is the name of the array in which the target strings are to be stored. Finally the third argument is the word separator. If the town field was printed directly as:

```
printf "%s,", town
```

it would print the variable *town* with several blanks between the town and the comma character. *Split* is used here to suppress the trailing blanks. This method also compresses multiple blanks within the name of a town to a single blank. Once the required fields are extracted, additional processing can be done as if the file had records with fields separated by a field separator.

3.6 A Picture Is Worth a Thousand Records

A picture is worth a thousand words. In the data processing world it is worth a thousand lines of output records! UNIX tools can be used to generate graphics commands which can generate pictures such as pie charts and histograms. *Pic* is a *preprocessor* to *troff* and can be used to generate elementary geometric figures such as squares and circles. UNIX file-manipulating tools can be used to output *pic* files to give a pictorial representation of the data. The following example outputs a *pic* file to draw a pie chart of the project status field from the project file. The size of each slice of the pie indicates the number of projects which have that status.

```
awk '{
        # If invalid code, change it to 5
        if ($2 < 0 || $2 > 4) $2=5;

        # increment count of corresponding status
        ++stat[$2];

        # increment count of total number of projects
        ++tot;
    };
    END {

        # Calculate the value of pi
        pi = atan2(0,-1);

        # Calculate the angular span for each slice
        # and add it to the angle for the previous slice
        stat[1] = 2*pi*stat[1]/tot;
        for (i=2;i<6;++i)
                stat[i] = 2*pi*stat[i]/tot + stat[i-1];;

        # Get the x,y coordinates of lines to be drawn
        # to get slices
        for (i=1;i<6;++i)
                {
                x[i] = cos(stat[i])*2.0 + 1.5;
                y[i] = sin(stat[i])*2.0 + 1.5;
                }

        # Get the angular span for the text associated with
        # each slice
        label_angle[1] = stat[1]/2;
        for (i=2;i<16;++i)
                label_angle[i] = (stat[i-1] + stat[i])/2;

        # Get the x and y coordinates for the text label
        # associated with each slice
        for (i=1;i<6;++i)
                {
                labels_x[i] = cos(label_angle[i]) + 1.5;
                labels_y[i] = sin(label_angle[i]) + 1.5;
```

```
                }

        # Start generating the pic specification file
        printf ".PS\n";

        # draw the pie
        printf "circle radius 2i at 1.5i,1.5i\n";

        # draw the horizontal line for the first slice
        printf "move to 1.5i,1.5i; line to 3.5i,1.5i \n";

        # draw the other lines from center to the calculated
        # positions to get the different slices
        for (i=1;i<6;++i)
        {
        printf "move to 1.5i,1.5i \n";
        printf "line to  %.2fi,%.2fi\n", x[i],y[i];
        }

        # start labeling the slices
        printf "\"Err\" at %.2fi,%.2fi\n", labels_x[5],labels_y[5];
        for (i=1;i<5;++i)
                printf "\"%d\" at %.2fi,%.2fi\n",i, labels_x[i],labels_y[i
        printf ".PE\n";
}'  >  pie.pic
pic pie.pic|troff -Tps|lp
```

If the project file proj.d is:

```
cat proj.d
P2:1:101
P4:3:101
P1:3:11
P2:1:11
P3:3:141
P5:3:141
P3:3:15
P5:4:19
P1:2:29
P2:1:29
P1:2:412
P2:7:412
```

```
P2:1:101
P4:3:101
P1:2:11
P2:2:11
P3:3:141
P5:4:141
P3:3:15
P5:4:19
P1:2:29
P2:1:29
P1:2:412
P2:7:412
```

then the *awk* script will generate the following *pic* specification file:

```
.PS
circle radius 2i at 1.5i,1.5i
move to 1.5i,1.5i; line to 3.5i,1.5i
move to 1.5i,1.5i
line to  2.02i,3.43i
move to 1.5i,1.5i
line to  -0.43i,2.02i
move to 1.5i,1.5i
line to  2.02i,-0.43i
move to 1.5i,1.5i
line to  3.23i,0.50i
move to 1.5i,1.5i
line to  3.50i,1.50i
"Err" at 2.47i,1.24i
"1" at 2.29i,2.11i
"2" at 1.00i,2.37i
"3" at 0.79i,0.79i
"4" at 2.11i,0.71i
.PE
```

This *pic* specification file will generate the pie chart shown in Figure 3.1.

This simple shell script, which is written using only *awk*, can be modified easily and adapted to any application. In fact, given that associative arrays in *awk* can have strings as subscripts, pie charts can be drawn for string data types also.

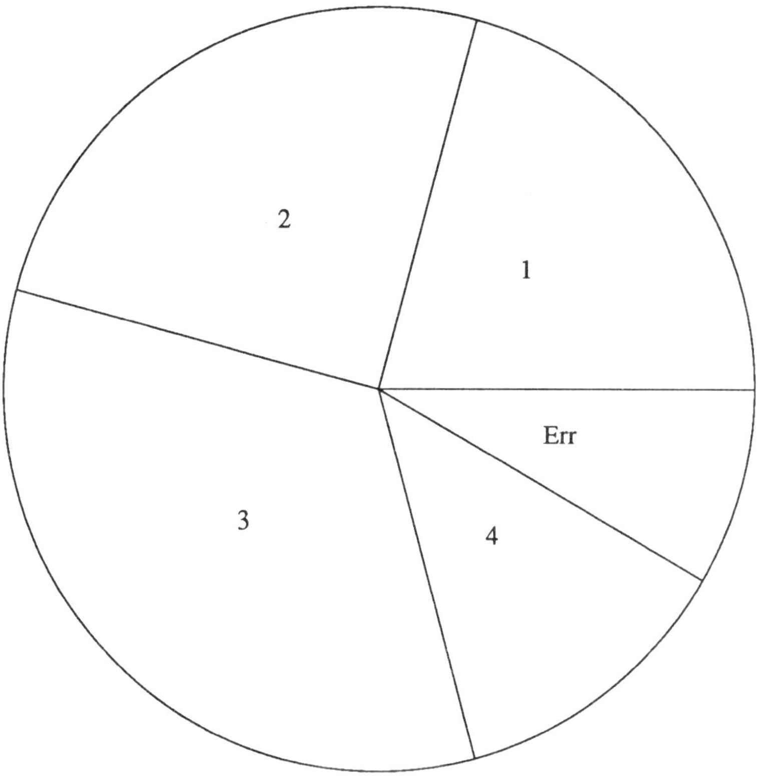

Figure 3.1 Pie Chart for Project Status

3.7 The Performance Factor

The files involved in the system used in this chapter were very small by any standard. When the file size is big, it becomes necessary to consider time and space efficiency involved in using the UNIX tools. The wide range of UNIX tools actually adds to the problem by offering the users several permutations involving different utilities. To write the best possible set of commands, users must be familiar with the overheads associated with the different tools. Some common sense also comes in handy! Here is a list of guidelines to follow:

- If a field is to be cut, use the *cut* command as opposed to using *awk*.

- Perform a selection or a projection (cut) operation on a file before performing a *sort* or a *join.*
- Postpone a *join* operation as much as possible.

In *query 5*, for example, the first two commands

```
cut -d: -f3 proj.d|sort|uniq -c > /tmp/t1
cut -d: -f1 prog.d|uniq -c > /tmp/t2
```

can be rewritten inefficiently as follows:

```
sort -t: +2 -3 proj.d|cut -d: -f3|uniq -c > /tmp/t1
sort -t: +0 -1 prog.d|cut -d: -f1|uniq -c > /tmp/t2
```

Clearly, the sort in the second case is performed on longer records. This is avoided in the first case by cutting the required fields first, thus reducing the size of the file for subsequent processing. Consider the following query:

Query
Retrieve names of programmers
who are working on project P1.

One solution is

```
cat answer1.sh
sort -t: +0 -1 -o prog.d prog.d
sort -t: +2 -3 -o proj.d proj.d
join -t: -j1 1 -j2 3 prog.d proj.d|
awk -F: '{
        if ($5=="P1")
                print $2;
        }'|sort|uniq
answer1.sh
Joan Jackson
John Doe
Shama Parab
```

Another solution to the same problem is

```
cat answer2.sh
awk -F: '{
        if ($1=="P1") print $3;
        }' proj.d|sort > /tmp/t1
cut -d: -f1,2 prog.d|sort -t:|uniq > /tmp/t2
join -t: -j1 1 -j2 1 -o 1.2 /tmp/t2 /tmp/t1
rm /tmp/t1 /tmp/t2
answer2.sh
John Doe
Joan Jackson
Shama Parab
```

In the second solution, records involved in the *join* operation were reduced. In the first solution, the *join* operation was performed on the entire project file. In the first solution, the entire files were sorted. In the second solution, only a segment of the proj.d file was sorted. This example illustrates the need to select and sequence the tools appropriately to avoid degradation in the performance of query execution.

3.8 Pipes vs. Temporary Files

In all the previous examples, pipes and temporary files were used extensively. The number of temporary files can be eliminated by using pipes. There are several advantages and disadvantages associated with the use of pipes and temporary files. Pipes allow several stages of processing to proceed simultaneously. In addition, they eliminate the use of temporary files resulting in space efficiency. However, there are several overheads associated with the use of a pipe. Perhaps, the biggest advantage of the use of temporary files over pipes comes into play after a system crash or after a bug is detected in one of the processes involved in the job. Consider the following scenario:

```
comm1 < inpfile | comm2 | comm3 | comm4 > outfile
```

If there is a system crash during the execution of the above job, all the commands involved in the job will have to be restarted. This is also true if while the job is under execution, the user realizes that command/program comm2 has a bug in it and she or he decides to terminate the job. The same job can be rewritten using temporary files as

```
comm1 < inpfile   > /tmp/t1
comm2 < /tmp1/t1 > /tmp/t2
comm3 < /tmp1/t2 > /tmp/t3
comm4 < /tmp/t3   > outfile
rm /tmp/t1 /tmp/t2 /tmp/t3
```

This job is easy to monitor, as intermediate results can be checked. If the system crashes after the third command, the job can be restarted by commenting the first two lines, thus saving a lot of processing. Of course, it will take more time than the previous solution, though the difference in execution times depends on the nature of the commands involved. Also, temporary files will occupy additional disk space.

In an environment where more than one user is using the same shell script or the same user is running a shell script multiple times, possibly on different input files, the creation of intermediate temporary files with the same name will most certainly lead to disastrous results. The solution, then, is to have temporary files created with names derived from input files. Though this approach alleviates the problem, it does not eliminate it completely.

3.9 Processing EBCDIC Data

In the data-processing world, IBM has traditionally ruled with an iron hand. In the last few years, thanks to improvements in the file system internals and the availability of several DBMS packages, UNIX is increasingly becoming popular in the data-processing world. Some applications are undergoing conversions from IBM systems, which use Extended Binary Coded Decimal Information Code (EBCDIC), to UNIX, which uses American Standard Code for Information Interchange (ASCII). Data from IBM environment becomes difficult to handle because conversion has to be done on both numeric and character data. Character data can be handled easily by using the *dd* command. Customized C programs have to be written to handle the many numeric data formats available in the IBM world.

3.9.1 Using Dd for Data Conversion

Dd is the UNIX utility for converting characters from EBCDIC to ASCII, and vice versa. It can be used with data residing on different device types. Data from the IBM world is normally shipped via tapes or cartridges. An IBM tape may be labeled or unlabeled. If it is labeled, then it has a header record at its beginning before the start of the actual data file. The header record has information about the data on the tape. It is used to name the data set on the tape, the time it was created, the block size of the files on it, and the volume number of the tape, if it is a part of a multivolume set. A multivolume set is one which has a file or a group of files spanning across multiple tapes. It is also possible to get a tape without the header record. Such tapes are referred to as unlabeled tapes. Block size of the data on unlabeled tapes can also be fetched by using *dd*.

Consider the following example:

```
dd if=/dev/rmt0 of=output ibs=12480 cbs=80 conv=ascii
```

In this example, *dd* takes input from the file /dev/rmt0 which is expected to have EBCDIC data and outputs the result to a file called output. The input consists of data blocks which are 12,480 bytes large. The character buffer used for conversion is 80 characters big. The characters are converted to ASCII. Trailing blanks are dropped, and a newline character is added. If *conv=ebcdic* is used, then the ASCII data is converted to EBCDIC. Other conversion specifications include *lcase* and *ucase* which are used to map alphabetic data to lowercase and uppercase alphabets, respectively.

3.9.2 Other Uses of Dd

Dd is far from limited to reading tapes. It can also be used to perform a raw copy from one disk to another. The *dd* command line

```
dd if=/dev/rdsk/2s0 of=/dev/rdsk/3s0 bs=40k conv=noerror,sync
```

performs a raw copy from one disk to another using 40K blocks. This is much faster than single 512 byte filesystem access. The file system should be unmounted to execute this. The use of the *conv=noerror,sync* means that bad spots on the disk will not terminate the program and that output will be resynchronized to input when errors occur. The next example reads and writes just one sector of a file system:

```
dd if=/dev/rdsk/2s0 of=/dev/rdsk2s0 iseek=12456 \
     oseek=12456 bs=512 count=1 conv=noerror
```

This is useful if you have soft ECC errors occuring on that sector. The soft

ECC means that the disk media has lost some information, but it could be reconstructed from error correction techniques. If the same data is forced back out to the same sector, the second write is likely to "stick," and error messages for that sector should cease.

3.10 Taking Backups

In data processing it is extremely important to perform regular backups on both data and program files. It is almost impossible to recover an *rm*ed file in the absence of a backup. There is nothing more frustrating than to inadvertently *rm* a file and then try to restore it from a backup only to realize that no backup was taken. There are several utilities available in the UNIX environment which are used by system administrators to back up file systems. Among them, the most commonly used are *dump* and *volcopy.* In addition, *tar* and *cpio* can be used by other users on the system to backup their own files.

3.10.1 Backups by System Administrators

Both *volcopy* and *dump* can be used by administrators to copy files from a disk to a backup device such as a tape. *Dump* is popular on Berkeley UNIX and its derivatives such as SunOS. *Volcopy* on the other hand is available primarily on System V-based UNIX systems.

Dump and *volcopy* provide incremental backup facilities. Incremental backups refer to partial backups with a selection criterion which is based on two factors. One factor is the time when the file was created or last modified, and the other factor is the time when the last backup was taken. For example, if two files, f1 and f2 were created on Monday, if a backup was taken on Monday night, and subsequently if file f1 was modified on Tuesday morning, then the Tuesday night backup will have the latest copy of file f1 but not f2. The Monday night backup will have copies of the old f1 and f2. If f1 is removed accidentally, it can be restored from the Tuesday night backup or from the Monday night backup, if the old version is required. If f2 is to be restored, it can only be restored from the Monday night backup but not from the Tuesday night backup. Incremental backups save time and backup device space. Unfortunately, they are not enough, because users often forget the time when a lost file was last modified. Also, restoring directories with multiple files having different modification times can be a very long exercise. Therefore, full backups must be taken at regular intervals, in addition to incremental backups. Most sites have incremental backups taken daily, and full backups taken weekly.

3.10.1.1 Dump: File System Backup Facility

Dump takes several options. Some of these options require an argument. Though it is primarily used for backing data to magnetic tapes, *dump* on some systems, such as the Sun386i, can be used to back up data to floppy disks. To back up an entire file system, *dump* can be used as follows:

```
dump 0uf /dev/rmt2 /data1
```

/data1 is the file system to be backed up. *0* is an option to specify that the entire file system is to be backed up. An incremental backup can be done by specifying an option other than *0*. Any single digit can be used to specify the backup level. All files that have been modified since the last backup was performed at a lower dump level are copied to the tape. *f /dev/rmt2* specifies that the file system is to be copied to a tape mounted on device */dev/rmt2*. The *u* option is used to write the date the dump was completed to the file /etc/dumpdates. Consider the following sequence of activities:

Monday:	Files f1 and f2 are created
Monday night:	Level 2 backup is performed
Tuesday morning:	File f1 is modified
Tuesday night:	Level 4 backup is performed
Wednesday:	File f2 is modified
Thursday:	Level 3 backup is performed

Both the original copies of files f1 and f2 will be on the level 2 backups performed on Monday. The modified version of f1 will be on the level 4 Tuesday night backup. The level 3 backup performed on Thursday has the modified copy of file f2 but it also has a copy of the new f1 file, though it was not modified on Wednesday. It is copied again because the backup level of Wednesday was not lower than the backup level of Thursday.

How does *dump* know when the last backup was taken? The use of the *u* option updates a file called /etc/dumpdates. An entry is added to this file to indicate the time and level of the update. Several other options are also available with the *dump* utility. The *c* option is available on some versions to specify a cartridge instead of a tape. The *d* option is used to specify the tape density. In the absence of this option, the default tape density used is 1600. The *b* option is used to specify the blocking factor. The default is 20 blocks per write. Each block has a size of 512 bytes. The list of file systems which require backing up can be listed by using the *w* option. Of course, it can also be retrieved by examining the contents of the file /etc/dumpdates. *Dump* displays numerous verbose messages while executing. Here is an example of *dump* as executed on a Sun 3/60 running SunOS 3.4:

```
dump 3uf /dev/rmt3  /datal
DUMP: Date of this level 3 dump: Wed Oct 26 21:29:06 1988
DUMP: Date of last level 0 dump: Sun Oct 23 20:12:07 1988
DUMP: Dumping /dev/rsdld(/datal) to /dev/rmt3
DUMP: mapping (Pass I)[regular files]
DUMP: mapping (Pass II)[directories]
DUMP: estimated 11587 tape blocks on 0.30 tapes
DUMP: dumping (Pass III)[directories]
DUMP: dumping (Pass IV)[regular files]
DUMP: DUMP: 1589 tape blocks on 1 tape(S)
DUMP: DUMP IS DONE
DUMP: level 3 dump on Wed Oct 26 21:29:06 1988
DUMP: Tape rewinding
```

The number of tapes which will be required is estimated based on the length of each tape, the block size, BPI, etc. The default tape length of 2300 feet is assumed. It can be changed by using the *s* option.

Once backed up, any file can be restored using the *restore* command. The general form of the command is

restore *options* [*file name*]

The *file name* is optional. Several options are available. The *x* option is used to extract the specified file from the backup. The *f* option can be used to indicate the drive on which the tape is mounted. The *b* option can be used to specify the blocking factor. The *t* option can be used to list the names of the files on the tape. Here is a simple *restore* command to check if file f3 is present on the tape:

```
restore tf /dev/rmt2 f3
```

If found, it can be restored by using the following command:

```
restore x /dev/rmt2 f3
```

If a directory name is specified instead of a file name, then the files in the directory are extracted recursively. All files or directories are restored into the current directory. Once restored, the ownerships of these files have to be changed by using the *chown* command.

It is also possible to use *restore* in interactive mode when invoked with the *i* option. *Restore* displays several messages about the tape and then displays the prompt *restore* >. UNIX commands such as *cd* and *ls* can be used to locate the file/directory on the backup tape. Files to be extracted can be marked by using the *add* command in response to the "restore >" prompt. Finally, all such marked files can be extracted by using the *restore* command *extract*.

3.10.1.2 Volcopy: Another File System Backup Facility

Volcopy is another file system backup facility which is popular on System V environments. It is used to back up entire file systems. It is not possible to back up only selected files or directories using this tool because it copies a block-by-block image. Therefore, to restore only selected files from a *volcopy*, first the entire backup must be restored to a temporary disk partition and then the required files copied to the appropriate destination. *Volcopy* has several other disadvantages associated with it. It is not possible to back up multiple file systems on the same tape. Also, *volcopy* does not understand incremental backups, it does not keep track of the date and time the last backup was made. For most data-processing needs, it is necessary to have the capability to restore only selected files. Because of its inability to do so and also because of the numerous disadvantages associated with it, *volcopy* will not be discussed in detail here.

3.10.2 Backups by Individual Users

The backup utilities *dump*, *restore*, and *volcopy* are designed for use by system administrators. Two other utilities, *tar* and *cpio*, are more suitable for users to take their own backups.

3.10.2.1 Tar: A Tape File Archiver

Tar is the programmer's tool to store files on tapes and restore them when required. If you wish to store all the files in your current directory and its subdirectories on a tape mounted on a drive designated as /dev/mt/1h, here is how you would do it:

```
tar cf /dev/mt/1h
```

Simple! This can save you a lot of trouble if you inadvertently remove a file and don't wish to interact with the administrator. The syntax of *tar* is

```
tar function-selector [options] [files]
```

The *function-selector* controls the primary action of *tar*. The optional parameters can be used to provide additional information to *tar*. Finally, the files to be extracted from the archive or the files to be archived are specified. In the example, *c* is the primary function selector and *f* is the additional parameter specified. The *c* function selector is used to create a new tape file. The optional parameter *f* is used to specify that the next argument, /dev/mt/1h, be used as the name of the archive. A dot (.) in the example indicates that all files in the current directory are to be archived.

A minus (−) as the name of the archive causes *tar* to write to the standard output or read from the standard input. Commonly used archive or device names have the form /dev/mt/*nd*, where *n* is the tape drive number, and *d* is the tape density, which can be *l*, *m*, or *h* for low (800 bpi), medium (1600 bpi), or high (6250 bpi) density, respectively.

Having stored the files on a tape, how do you extract these files from the tapes? The following command extracts all the files from the tape mounted on the tape drive designated as /dev/mt/2h and copies these files to the current directory:

```
tar xf /dev/mt/2h
```

If it is not necessary to extract all the files on the tape, then the names of the required files should be specified, as in

```
tar xf /dev/mt/2h file1 file2
```

which will extract only file1 and file2.

The following additional primary options are used by *tar*:

- *r* The specified files are written at the end of the tape.
- *t* The names of all the files on the tape are listed.
- *u* Normally the specified files are written on the tape

even if they are already on the tape. This option specifies that a file is to be added only if it is not already present or if it was modified after it was copied to the tape.

Tar also provides a set of additional options that can be used to control its action. They are:

v This option provides output consisting of the name of each file preceded by the primary option. This lets you see the file names as the files are written to or read from tape.

w This option provides an interactive session with *tar*. Before taking any action, *tar* prints the name of the file and the action to be taken, then waits for the user input. If the user response starts with a *y*, the action is executed, otherwise the action on the file is neglected and *tar* continues with the next file.

b This option is used to specify the blocking factor. The default blocking factor is one. When writing lots of data to tape, it is common to use a blocking factor of 20.

m By default, *tar* restores the modification times as files are copied onto tape. Using this option causes *tar* to restore files as if they were modified during the execution of *tar*.

o Files extracted from a tape retain the user and group ids as they appear on the tape. This option overrides this default action and causes the group and user id to be that of the user running *tar*.

To display verbose information about the files on the archived tape mounted on device /dev/mt/1h, you would use the following command (sample output follows the command):

```
tar tvf /dev/mt/1h
rw-rw-r--2407/1011   5730 Sep  2 10:00 1986 c0.c
rw-rw-r--2407/1011  56488 Sep  2 10:00 1986 c2.c
```

The *v* optional parameter is used above to display the information about the tapes on the file in verbose mode. This information is displayed in the same format as the output of the *ls −l* command. In addition, the numerical user id and group id of the file owner is displayed. This option is used to check that the appropriate version of the files has been retrieved. It is also handy for monitoring the writing or reading of *tar* tapes.

Here is an example of using *tar* in interactive mode:

```
tar wxf /dev/mt/1h c?.c
x c0.c :y
x c1.c :n
```

Here *tar* displays the action to be taken on the file. The *x* displayed indicates that the file is to be extracted. *Tar* then waits for the user response. A response starting with a *y* means that the file is to be extracted. Any other response means that the file is to be omitted from the *tar* command. In the above session, only the c0.c file is to be extracted.

3.10.2.2 Cpio: Copy Archives In and Out

Cpio is used to read a list of file or path names and to copy these files to the standard output in a special format. *Cpio* can also be used to extract these files from the formatted file. It is very useful when many small files (perhaps in several directories) need to be moved as a group from one machine to another. *Cpio*, in effect, bundles all of the files into one package. The package can be moved as a single unit and then unbundled in its new location.

There are three main options accepted by *cpio* and they are *−o*, *−i*, and *−p*. In addition, many key words are provided to control the action of *cpio*. *Cpio* can also be used to archive files on a tape. The *−o* option is used to read the names of files from the standard input and redirect these files into a single file. The default output file is the standard output. The output file also stores status information about the input files. The *−i* option is used to extract specified files from a *cpio* formatted file. The *−p* option is used to read a list of file or path names from the standard input and to copy these files into the output directory.

Cpio files can be created using the *−o* option. *Cpio* expects a list of file or path names from the standard input. It organizes these files into a single file. The status of the files is also copied. The output file size is an integer which is a multiple of 512. It has trailer records with the string *TRAILER!!!* in them. The following example copies the files /ds5/us1/rprt/c4 and /ds5/us1/rprt/*.c into the tape file /dev/mt/1m:

```
ls /ds5/usl/rprt/c4 /ds5/usl/rprt/*.c | cpio -o > /dev/mt/1m
392 blocks
```

Cpio displays the number of blocks in the output file. The *v* option can be used to display a verbose output of *cpio* action. It displays the names of the files as they are written to tape. It is good practice to also use the *c* option to write the *cpio* header information in ASCII characters. This permits portability, so that a *cpio* file created on one machine can be read on another machine. The *B* option can be used to control block size when the output is directed to a tape file. The *a* option is used to reset the access times of the files after they have been copied. Here is another example:

```
ls /ds5/usl/rprt/*.c | cpio -ova /dev/mt/1m
/ds5/usl/rprt/ nice.c
/ds5/usl/rprt/bkp.c
/ds5/usl/rprt/debug.c
/ds5/usl/rprt/filters.c
/ds5/usl/rprt/getpwent.c
/ds5/usl/rprt/m1.c
/ds5/usl/rprt/m2.c
/ds5/usl/rprt/match.c
/ds5/usl/rprt/passwd.c
o/ds5/usl/rprt/try.c
/ds5/usl/rprt/yacc.c
/ds5/usl/rprt/ymdhms.c
392 blocks
```

The names of the files were generated by the use of the *v* option.

The *−i* option can be used to extract files from a *cpio* archive. Let us extract files m1.c and m2.c from the *cpio* archive file created in the previous example:

```
cat /dev/mt/1m | cpio -i m*.c
112 blocks
```

Several options are available to control the files to be extracted. Depending on the current directory, it may be necessary to create new directories during the extract process. By default, *cpio* will not create new directories. The *d* option can be used to create new directories, if required. The *t* option can be used to print a table of contents of the input archive file. The following *cpio* command prints a verbose output describing the contents of the archive file arout:

```
cat arout | cpio -itv
153 blocks
100664 rst       5978  May 29 17:42:26 1986  ../ml.c
100664 rst       6034  May 29 17:44:35 1986  ../m2.c
100664 rst      65969  Sep  6 13:40:18 1986  c4
153 blocks
```

Normally, files are not replaced if a file with the same name exists and has a more recent modification time. The *u* option is used to unconditionally replace files. To unconditionally extract files m1.c and m2.c from the archive file arout, use the following command:

```
cat arout | cpio -iu ../m?.c
153 blocks
```

Note that the pattern defines the full path name as it appears in the archive. Multiple patterns can also be specified, as in

```
cat arout | cpio -iu ../ml.c c4
153 blocks
```

which will extract files ../m1.c and c4.

Cpio can be used with the *f* option to copy all files except those that match the specified patterns. The command

```
cat arout | cpio -if c4
153 blocks
```

will copy all files from the *cpio* archive except file c4. The *m* option can be used to retain the previous modification time. The *r* option can be used to rename the extracted files interactively. The file can be skipped by responding with a null line. Here is an example:

```
cat arout | cpio -iru
Rename <../ml.c>
mnl.c
Rename <../m2.c>
<null line>
Skipped
Rename <c4>
cx
153 blocks
```

Only files ../m1.c and c4 were extracted from the archive. It is important to note that not only were the file names changed in the above example, but in the case of ../m1.c the target directory was also changed. *Cpio* did not extract the file ../m2.c, because a null line was specified as the new name of the file.

When used with the $-p$ option, *cpio* reads a list of path names of files from the standard input and copies these files into the specified directory. Some of the options discussed earlier can be used to control the copying of files. Here is an example:

```
pwd
/usr1/dst1

ls -l dir2
total 0

ls  /usr1/dst/m1 /usr1/dst/m2 | cpio -pdu dir2
36 blocks

find dir2 -print
dir2
dir2/usr1/dst
dir2/usr1/dst/m1
dir2/usr1/dst/m2
```

The *d* option was used to create directories as necessary. The *u* option was used to copy the files unconditionally. Note how the files were copied into the new directory. The *find* command was used to display the entire hierarchy of the dir2 directory.

Unlike the $-i$ and the $-o$ options, the $-p$ option copies the files relative to the specified directory and not to the standard output. The following example shows how the files are copied relative to the destination directory if the full path names are not specified for the input files:

```
pwd
/usr1/dst1/dir1

ls
file1 file2 file3 dir3

ls ../f*.c
file4.c
```

```
ls ../f*.c file1 /usr/dst1/dir1/file2 | cpio -pud dir3
247 blocks

find dir3 -print
dir3
dir3/usr/dst1/dir1/file2
dir3/file1

ls f*.c
file4.c
```

Note that the input file ../f*.c is copied in the current directory because all path names originate from the destination directory.

3.11 Concluding Remarks

This chapter discussed how UNIX provides a productive set of tools for programmers and nonprogrammers to do basic data processing. As files grow, the tools used here become unacceptable as the performance deteriorates significantly. In addition, users need a friendlier interface than running UNIX commands with arguments. None of the standard UNIX tools can be used to develop forms or menus. Also, shell scripts have to be written to generate reports. As report formats become complicated, the shell programming involved may require programming skills beyond the reach of the casual user. The solution to this dilemma is to provide an interface which the user can customize without extensive programming. That is the purpose of Database Management Systems which are available commercially in the UNIX world. The next chapter discusses the theoretical concepts and terms associated with DBMS.

4 Database Management Systems

The last two chapters discussed data processing using commands provided by UNIX. Systems built using these commands have limited power and become slow as the file size increases. The need to create an intermediate file to update an existing file introduces another element of inefficiency. The user can write programs in a language like C to update a file without creating an intermediate file. The problem is that every user in the UNIX environment may not know C. It is also difficult for casual users to generate formatted reports with the use of UNIX tools. Generation of forms is almost impossible without any C programming.

Given all the limitations, the only other alternative is for users to write their own programs using a language such as C. Clearly, this is inefficient but gives the users complete freedom to implement any system, as they will be dealing at a much lower level by using a third generation programming language. Database Management Systems are software packages which allow users to implement systems without the need to do much programming. They provide tools to eliminate the need to write programs in a language such as C. Unfortunately, they take away some flexibility from the user and impose additional limitations on the system. They provide tools to query a database for users who are not knowledgeable about UNIX commands and shell programming. They also provide tools for the design of data-entry screens. They come equipped with report writers which allow users to generate customized reports. They also provide facilities such as transaction management and crash recovery. This chapter provides the theoretical background required for a user to understand DBMS. The aim is to demystify the jargons which are often used in the DBMS world and to prepare the user to use a DBMS package such as INFORMIX.

4.1 Database vs. DBMS

A database is a repository for stored data. DBMS on the other hand are the tools provided to manage the database. In a flat-file mangement system the set of data files can be referred to as a database and the shell scripts written to generate reports, update the data files, and perform other data management tasks can be perceived as a DBMS. In addition to providing the necessary tools to manipulate the database, commercially available DBMS also offer the following advantages:

- Data can be stored with minimal redundancy.
- Data integrity can be maintained
- Data can be shared efficiently by multiple users.
- Applications can become independent of the way in which the data is stored.
- Security and standards can be enforced more easily.

Though DBMS offer these advantages, it is the user's responsibility to exploit them to the fullest. The tools provided by a DBMS makes it easy for the user to implement a system, but he or she still has to design the system. Expert systems exist to help in the design of databases, but the experienced database designer will always remain irreplaceable.

4.2 The Relational Model

There has been a considerable amount of research into deciding the best possible way of storing data for any application. This research has given birth to a term that is widely used in database jargon, data model. There are three important and commonly accepted data models: hierarchical, network, and relational. The relational model is considered state-of-the-art, and most of the DBMS available today on the UNIX system support this model. For this reason, only the relational model will be discussed in this book.

4.3 Commonly Used Terms

A relational database is a collection of tables. Tables are physically represented by files. There need not be a one-to-one relationship between tables and their physical representation in terms of files. In fact, more than one file may exist for a table, and several tables may be physically stored in one file as done by the UNIFY DBMS. Tables are also referred to as relations. Files are made up of records. Similarly, tables or relations are made up of rows. These rows are also referred to as tuples. Each tuple, like a record, is made up of fields. Fields are called attributes in relational jargon. They are like columns of a table. Here is an example of a relational database with two relations:

> *Relation:* Parts
>
> *Attributes:* Part no, part name, color, quantity in stock, and cost
>
> Relation: Suppliers
>
> *Attributes:* Supplier no, supplier name, and part no

The number of attributes in a relation is called the degree of the relation and the number of tuples in a relation is called its cardinality. Relation "parts" in the example is 5-ary because it is a relation of degree 5. Relation "suppliers" is ternary because it is a relation with 3 degrees. Relations with 1 degree are referred to as unary relations and relations with 2 degrees are called binary relations. The cardinality of the two relations will depend on the number of tuples in them.

From a strictly theoretical definition of a relation, tuples in a relation cannot be duplicates. In practice, DBMS allow duplicates to exist in a table. A set of attributes which can uniquely identify a record form a candidate key. Clearly, several combinations of attributes can exist to satisfy the uniqueness criterion. Any one of these can be selected and designated as a primary key. The other keys in the relation are then called alternate keys. If an attribute has a restriction that values assigned to it must exist as values of a primary key in another relation, then that attribute is called a foreign key. In the example, if a restriction is placed on the value of attribute "part no" in the supplier table that it must also exist in the "part no" attribute in the parts table, then the "part no" attribute in the supplier table becomes a foreign key. Of course, this is based on the assumption that the "part no" attribute is a primary key in the parts table.

The concept of null-valued attributes is important in relational databases. If an attribute in a record has a value missing, then that attribute is said to be null-valued. A null-valued field is distinctly different from a field with a value of zero or spaces.

4.4 Designing a Database System

One of the major advantages of a relational database is the simplicity it offers. The only data structure used to represent a relational database is a record! Therefore, designing a relational database involves the grouping of fields to be put together to form a record. In the other two data models, links are used to establish relationships between two record types. In a relational model, links are themselves represented by records. While some designers design databases solely on intuition, such ad hoc designs often suffer from inefficiencies and redundancies in data storage. To start the database design, you can start with a single big relation which has all the attributes in the database. Such a relation is called a universal relation. A universal relation is unrealistic and has been a subject of much debate; however, it serves as a good starting point to begin the design process. The design process decomposes the universal relation into a set of smaller relations. Another approach to database design is to start from relationships or dependencies among attributes and then create relations progressively as a synthesis approach in the design phase. Either way, the final relations must be subjected to some design criterion by checking the relations against a set of rules which are commonly referred to as normal forms. There are five such normal forms. Normal forms have undergone some criticism, because they tend to degrade the performance of retrieval operations; however, performance is enhanced if there are frequent updates on nonkey fields. It is not always necessary to subject database designs to all the normal forms. The five normal forms are explained briefly in the next section.

4.4.1 Normal Forms

The explanation of the five normal forms given below is simplified and may deviate slightly from theoretically pure definitions.

The first normal form defines a given relation in a database as having a fixed number of fields. This means that all record occurrences for the same record type must have the same number of fields.

The second normal form states that a nonkey field must describe the whole key and not just a subset of the key. Consider the following relation:

supplier no.	city code	part supplied	city name

In the above relation, if "supplier no." and "city code" form a composite key, and "city name" relates only to "city code" and not to "supplier no.," then this relation has to be decomposed to form the following two relations:

supplier no.	city code	part supplied

and

city code	city name

The third normal form states that a nonkey field must not describe another nonkey field. The following relation violates third normal form:

part no.	description	storage loc. no.	storage location

The third normal form is violated here because "storage location" describes "storage loc. no.". The relation has to be decomposed into two separate relations to satisfy the third normal form. These new relations are shown below:

part no.	description	storage loc. no.

and

storage loc. no.	storage location

The fourth normal form is violated when a relation contains two or more independent multivalued facts about an entity. The following example should help to make this form clear. Consider a relation consisting of the following three fields:

student no.	course	friend

This relation violates the fourth normal form because we have a many-to-many relationship between students and courses and another many-to-many relationship between students and friends. In addition, these two relationships are independent of each other. The above relation must therefore be decomposed into two relations in order to satisfy the fourth normal form:

student no.	course

and

student no.	friend

The fifth normal form states that a record type must not be structured in such a way that its contents can be reconstructed from smaller record types. Of course, it is always possible to restructure a record into smaller records with the same key field. This case is excluded from the above restriction.

Normal forms are applied sequentially. A database design must first be subjected to the first normal form, followed by the second, followed by the third, and so on.

4.4.2 Practical Approach

Normalized relations tend to have a few number of attributes. In fact, if all the normalization rules are followed carefully, the designer will probably end up with many binary relations. The theoreticians have overemphasized the process of normalization as a tool for a good database design. The fact is that "overnormalizing" a design can degrade its performance. Normalization should be used only as one of the tools for database design. The designer must be familiar with the system and the needs of the end users. Decisions of grouping fields must take user needs into account. Static databases which are not subjected to many updates suffer in performance if overnormalized. The fact that a database is static is known only by interacting with end users. A good designer will design the relations only after repeated discussions with users and only after all the fields and record types involved are clearly understood.

Normalization, if applied blindly, achieves the elimination of data redundancy. Strangely enough, data redundancy is sometimes desirable to minimize data retrieval times. Consider the following relation:

supplier no.	area code	phone number	city	state

If "supplier no." is the primary key, this relation is not normalized completely because there is a relationship between the two fields "area code" and "state." To normalize it would require the decomposition of this relation into the following two relations:

supplier no.	area code	phone number	city

and

area code	state

This process of normalization has clearly reduced the amount of space that will be required to store the data, because the state and area code mapping is a small static table and therefore the state code need not be stored as a part of the supplier record. Also, updates to the supplier file will not need the state code, as it can be derived from the area code field. This will eliminate the possibility of violating data integrity by having multiple states for the same area code. Associated with this advantage is a major disadvantage for retrieval operations. If all the information for a supplier is needed, it will have to be accessed from two tables. A *join* operation will have to be performed on the two tables. As indicated in the previous chapter *join* is a fairly expensive operation. The first solution would be good for a static database, the second for a database involving frequent updates. The information about the stability of a database can be learned only by repeated interaction with end users. A good approach to database design is first to fully normalize the relations and then after sufficient interaction with the users to denormalize them based on practical issues. The denormalization process will introduce redundancy. Sufficient control must be retained on the redundancies to ensure that the integrity of the database is not jeopardized.

4.4.3 Additional Factors

A good database design must be based not only on the overall structure of the data but also on the volume of the various attributes involved in the database. For example, the design of a database involving suppliers and parts must take into consideration the number of suppliers and parts. In particular, the relative size of each relation must be taken into consideration. In addition, the frequency of access of a relation must also be taken into consideration. Also, the attribute on which the relation will be searched should be known. This information is not only useful in the database design process in terms of grouping the attributes into a relation but is also helpful at a later stage when access methods (to be discussed later) are to be selected. Normalization algorithms do not take these factors into consideration.

4.4.4 Data Independence

A widely used term in relational database design theory is data independence. It refers to the independence provided by the DBMS to application programs from changes to both the logical and physical structure of the database. Application programs, once written, do not require rewriting or even recompilation if changes are made to the database definition. Data independence also ensures that applications are resilient to changes in the physical representation of the relations. The relational model does not specify any physical representation of the relations. That aspect is left to the particular implementation. Users must be aware of the DBMS implementation to find the level of data independence that it supports.

Data independence is an extremely desirable feature because it facilitates the modification of the database design. New tables can be added to the database, new attributes can be added to existing tables, existing tables and attributes can be dropped, and all this can be done without significantly affecting the application that uses the database. It also allows the designer to change the access methods used as usage pattern of the database changes. If a DBMS does not support data independence, then tuning the database design to optimize its performance will require recompilation and even rewriting of application programs. A database designer must take the level of data independence offered by the DBMS into account during the design phase.

4.4.5 Database Integrity and Security

Designing a database for optimized run-time performance should not be the only goal of the database designer. Integrity and security of the database must also be taken into consideration. The relational model as defined by E. F. Codd provides two integrity rules. They are

- A primary key or any of its components cannot accept null values.
- Let "prim" be an attribute of relation "rel1" and let it also be the primary key of that relation. Let "forn" be an attribute and a foreign key of relation "rel2" matching the primary key "prim" of relation "rel1." Then, every value of "forn" appearing in relation "rel2" must also appear as the value of the attribute "prim" in relation "rel1" or it must be null.

It is important to emphasize here that these rules may not be supported by all DBMS implementations. In addition to these rules, database designers may add their own integrity constraints based on the application.

Security in relational models can be provided by letting the user access only a "view" of the database. The view is actually only a subset of the physical database; thus, the remaining segment of the database remains protected. Views are discussed in detail later in this chapter. Data manipulation languages also support statements to restrict access to specified users. This access restriction can be enforced at various levels. As access is restricted to lower levels, the overhead increases. For example, putting access restrictions at the database level is much easier than doing the same at field level. Operating systems also provide another level of security. For example, a directory containing a database and/or its files can be made inaccessible to other users by changing the permissions using the *chmod* command. Some DBMS make use of the operating system security mechanism to implement their security features. Sometimes, this is not possible. For example, UNIX does not provide any security mechanism at the record level. DBMS running in the UNIX environment have to implement this feature without any explicit support of the operating system.

4.5 Entity-Relationship Diagrams

Entity-Relationship (E-R) diagrams give a pictorial representation of all the attributes and their relationships in a database. They can be used by database designers to represent the dependencies of attributes in the database. In its simplest form, an E-R diagram is made up of entity sets. Entities, like tuples, are described by attributes. A set of entities, like a relation, is made up of tuples. A relationship depicts interaction between entity sets. An E-R diagram uses entity sets, relationships, and attributes as building blocks. Relationships are represented by diamonds, entity sets by rectangles, and attributes by circles. A relationship can be one-to-one, one-to-many, many to one, or many-to-many. Attributes, represented by circles, are attached by an undirected edge to the entity set which they describe. Undirected edges are also used to connect entity sets to the relationships in which they participate. These edges are labeled "1" or "N", depending on the type of relationship between the entity sets. An edge is labeled "1" if it contributes a single entity in a one to many relationship between entity sets. The label "N" is used if the entity set contributes more than one entity in a one-to-many, many-to-one, or many-to-many relationship.

Consider a simple database consisting of three entity sets: suppliers, parts, and projects. The entities in the entity set parts are identified by three attributes: part no., part name, and supplier no. Entities in the entity set suppliers are identified by three attributes: supplier no., part no., and supplier name. Finally, projects are identified by the attributes project no., project status, and part no. The suppliers entity set is "related" to the parts entity set via the relationship "supplier supplying the part." The projects entity set is related to the parts entity set via the relationship "parts used in the project." The supplier entity set is related to the project entity set via the relationship "supplier supplies to a project." An E-R diagram representing this system is shown in Figure 4.1.

One of the major advantages of the E-R diagram is that it can give a complete representation of the entire database at the conceptual level without going into the intricacies of the physical representation of the database. It must be used during the "fact collecting" phase when the database designer is interacting with the users who would be using the database. The representation is independent of the DBMS which would be ultimately used to implement the database. Further, like the design of a database, an E-R diagram representation may not yield a unique representation for the same system. This is primarily due to variations in perception about attributes, entity sets, and relationships among different designers.

The E-R diagram represents only the conceptual view of the database. It represents neither the logical relations nor the physical representation of the entity sets or relationships. It is possible to translate an E-R diagram into a set of tables by representing entity sets by tables consisting of the given attributes and by representing relationships also by tables consisting of attributes which contribute to the relationship. However, such a design may not yield a normalized set of relations. The E-R diagram must, therefore, be used as a system modeling tool. The relationships in the database can then be designed from the E-R diagram representation.

4.6 Testing a Database Design

The database design process is nondeterministic. For a given database there is no algorithm to determine if a design is optimum. Conversely, there is no algorithm to design an optimum database. There are, however, several tests which should be applied to a database design to test for potential flaws. In particular, the following tests should be applied:

- Can the contents in one relation be derived from the other relations in the database? If it can be, then that relation is redundant.
- Are all the relationships among all the attributes represented in the database? If not, the design is either incomplete or incorrect. If incomplete it may need the use of another relation to represent the missing relationship.
- Is a relationship represented in two different relations? If so, it will create update anomalies.

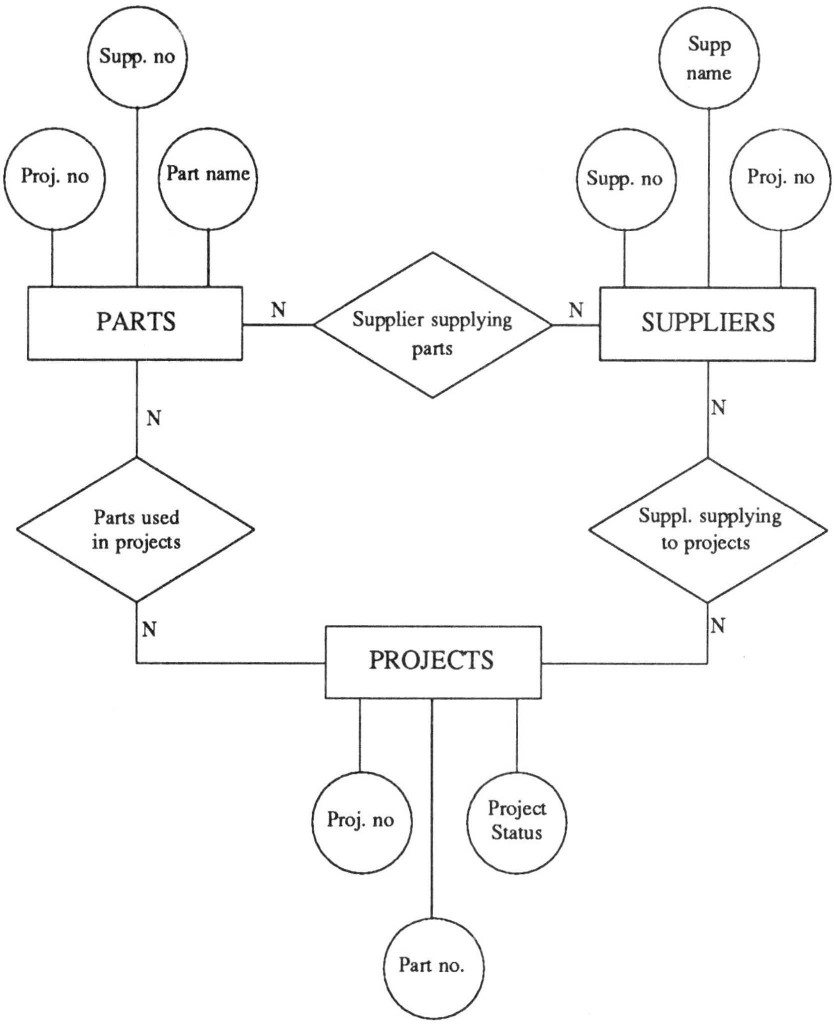

Figure 4.1 E-R diagram for Suppliers-Parts-Projects System

These tests check for correctness in the normalization procedure. In addition, performance factors must also be taken into consideration. If the response time is too slow for retrieval, then the relations are overnormalized and must be denormalized meticulously by redefining the database relations. Database design is almost always an iterative process. The designer must run performance tests on the design to fine tune it to reach the optimal design. Performance tests must be run on a regular basis because usage patterns on the database may change, resulting in the user resorting to different access paths to the database. Changes to the database design, to improve its performance, must be transparent to application programs. Changes to the database design are also required because of additions of new relations and relationships to the database. Thus, data independence plays a major role in the never-ending database design process.

4.7 Views

Tables in relational databases have a physical representation in terms of one or more files. Views, on the other hand, do not have files directly representing them, but to the user they appear to exist just like tables. They provide the user a window into the database. The DBMS stores the definition of the view rather than the data in the view.

One use of views is to provide security. Database administrators can restrict access to a segment of a database by providing the user with a view of the database which is a subset of the whole database. Another use of views is to simplify queries. The output of most queries in relational systems appear in tabular forms. As queries become more complicated, they can be divided into smaller modules which are easier to understand. The format of the output of each subquery can then be looked at as a definition of a table. This definition is called a view. Users can use views in writing queries. The DBMS will distinguish a view from a table and do the appropriate computation or translation of the view by referring to its stored definition. This process is transparent to the user.

Though views are popular for writing complex queries for retrieving data, they can also be used for updating the database. Updates using views depend on DBMS implementations. Some DBMS do not allow updates on views. Others allow only restricted updates on views. The logical data independence provided by a DBMS is significantly enhanced if it provides complete but controlled updates to views. Updates to views involving joins on multiple tables are more difficult. Updates to views involving multiple tables involve several atomic update operations on each table. The DBMS must guarantee that either all tables used in the view definition are updated or none at all.

4.8 Query Languages

Though the word query connotes a question to be asked, in DBMS terminology it covers operations such as updates and deletes to the information in the database. Query languages supported by most relational DBMS are based on three mathematical concepts. They are the relational algebra, tuple relational calculus, and domain relational calculus. Commercially supported languages provide the capabilities of these mathematical languages and have several additional features which are not covered by them.

4.8.1 Relational Algebra

Relational algebra is defined in terms of several basic operations. These are discussed here by using the following relations:

Relation: parts

part number	part_name
p1	name_p1
p2	name_p2
p4	name_p4

Relation: local_suppliers

supplier no.	supplier name	part no.
s1	name_s1	p1
s2	name_s2	p2
s2	name_s2	p1

Relation: foreign_suppliers

supplier no.	supplier name	part no.
s5	name_s5	p4
s6	name_s6	p1

The *union* operation on two relations is a relation consisting of tuples from both the relations. The union of relations local_suppliers and foreign_suppliers consists of the following tuples:

```
s1   name_s1  p1
s2   name_s2  p2
s2   name_s2  p1
s5   name_s5  p4
s6   name_s6  p1
```

This operation can be applied only if the two relations have the same degree, i.e., if they have the same number of attributes. The *difference* operation on two relations gives the set of tuples in one which are not in the other. The difference of relations local_suppliers and foreign_suppliers is the set of tuples in the relation local suppliers because there is no tuple common to both the relations. The *intersection* of two relations with the same number of attributes is the set of tuples which are common to the two relations. The intersection of the two supplier relations will give zero number of tuples because there are no tuples which are common to the two relations. The cartesian product of two relations gives a relation with the number of attributes equal to the sum of the number of attributes in each input relation. The number of tuples in the output is equal to the product of the number of tuples in each input relation. In addition, if there are *n1* attributes in the first relation and *n2* attributes in the second relation, then the first *n1* attributes of the output tuples when uniqued form the first input relation, and the next *n2* attributes when uniqued form the second input relation. The cartesian product of the parts and foreign_suppliers relations gives the following set of tuples:

```
p1   name_p1  s5   name_s5 p4
p2   name_p2  s5   name_s5 p4
p4   name_p4  s5   name_s5 p4
p1   name_p1  s6   name_s6 p4
p2   name_p2  s6   name_s6 p4
p4   name_p4  s6   name_s6 p4
```

The *project* operation on a relation gives a set of tuples with only the specified attributes from the input relation. After a projection is applied, all duplicate tuples are removed from the output. While the projection operation yields a vertical subset of the input relation, another operation called the *select* outputs a horizontal subset based on a selection criterion. The selection criterion can be constructed from constants, logical operators, and attributes. The *selection* operation when applied to the parts relation with the selection criterion that the part number be equal to p1 outputs the following tuple:

```
p1         name_p1
```

The *division* operation divides a relation with *n1* number of attributes by a relation with *n2* number of attributes, where *n1* > *n2* and outputs a set of tuples with *n1*−*n2* attributes. The tuples in the dividend relation can be conceived as having two composite attributes. The first attribute, *a1*, is composed of the first *n1*−*n2* attributes, and the second attribute, *a2*, is composed of the next *n2* attributes. Similarly, the tuples in the divisor relation can be conceived to be composed of one single composite attribute, *a2*, made up of *n2* attributes. The result of dividing A by B is the set of values of *a1* such that the pair of values for *a1* and *a2* in the dividend relation appear for all values of *a2* in the divisor relation. Consider the following relations:

Relation: rel1

```
a1        b1        x
a2        b2        x
a3        b3        x
a1        b1        y
a2        b2        y
a1        b1        z
a2        b2        z
a3        b3        z
```

Relation: rel2

```
x
y
z
```

The division operation on the two relations will yield the following set of tuples:

```
a1 b1
a2 b2
```

The relational algebra operation *join* was explained in Section 2.7. It is actually derived from the cartesian product operation by specifying a condition that the cartesian product operation be applied only if the value of a specified attribute of the tuple in the first relation match the value of a specified attribute of the tuple in the second relation. If the *join* operation is applied to the parts and local_suppliers relations on the attribute part_no, then the output is the following set of tuples:

```
p1  name_p1  s1  name_s1
p1  name_p1  s2  name_s2
p2  name_p2  s2  name_s2
```

4.8.2 Relational Calculus

Like relational algebra, relational calculus offers a base for a relational query language. It does not have any links to mathematical calculus. It offers a set of rules to define an expression. If this expression is applied to one or more relations, then the output itself is a relation. The output can be used to define a new relation, to query a subset of an existing relation, or to update an existing relation. Expressions using relational calculus are constructed using the following elements:

- Tuple variables which represent relations. If T is a tuple representing relation R, then T[i] is the ith attribute of that tuple.
- Conditions of the type A *op* B, where *op* is a relational operator (=,!=,<,>,<=, or >=) and at least A or B is an element of the form T[i] as defined above. A or B can also be a constant.
- Logical operators such as AND, OR, and NOT and quantifiers such as "exists" and "for all."

With these elements, relational calculus expressions can be written. Commercial implementations use the dot (.) operator to refer to a named attribute. For example, the supplier_no field of the supplier relation can be written as "supplier.supplier_no." Here are two examples of a relational calculus expression:

```
THERE EXISTS supplier(qty_supplied > 20)

NOT (supplier_no = 10)
```

With such expressions, a query using relational calculus takes the form

retrieve *a list of attributes*
        where *relational calculus expression*

The explanation about relational calculus here is simplified to avoid theoretical details which are not required to use the languages which are based on it.

4.8.3 Popular Query Languages

The UNIX DBMS market is largely dominated by products which support the Structured Query Language (SQL) language. It is now informally accepted as the standard relational query language. Another popular relational query language is QUEL, which is supported by INGRES and a few other products. INGRES as marketed by Relational Technology, Inc., also has support for the SQL language, but the standard INGRES version that comes with Berkeley UNIX 4.3 does not have support for SQL. It is for this reason that QUEL is more popular in academic circles. There are differences in syntax between QUEL and SQL. Also, QUEL is based on the theory of relational calculus, while SQL is based on both relational algebra and relational calculus. A third language called Query-By-Example (QBE), developed by IBM, has several additional features not supported by either QUEL or SQL. Unlike QUEL and SQL, it is screen-driven and is not, strictly speaking, a language. Most DBMS in the UNIX environment provide features reminiscent of Query-By-Example through their forms management package. The user can enter a known value or an expression in some fields of a displayed screen, and the system retrieves the rows which satisfy the search criteria and populates the remaining fields on the screen.

4.9 Components of a DBMS

A DBMS has several components. The most important component of a DBMS is the query processor. The query processor interacts with the user via statements specified in a language called the query language. The query processor analyzes the input query to check for any errors in syntax. If none are found, the query processor tries to execute it. The query execution may fail because the user may be violating security restrictions. It may also fail if the specified relation or tuple does not exist in the database.

Query languages are powerful and flexible enough to offer multiple solutions to a problem. Thus it is possible to write a query in several forms to perform the same task. These forms may not be equally efficient. It is the task of the query processor to transform a query written by the user to a form that can be executed most efficiently. The component of the query processor that does this is called the query optimizer. Most DBMS claim to have some form of query optimizers. Unfortunately, most implementations do not provide good query optimizers. Users must be aware of these deficiencies and must make attempts to write efficient queries themselves rather than depending on the query optimizer.

Query execution algorithms try to decompose complex queries into simpler and more manageable queries. This process is called query decomposition. The process of decomposing a query is closely linked to the process of query optimization. Users can have more control over a query by breaking a complex one into smaller queries and creating intermediate relations. This process is analogous to the creation of temporary files in flat file systems as discussed in the previous chapter. Normally, this is not required unless the user wishes to monitor intermediate results.

4.9.1 Access Methods

In order to execute a query efficiently, the query processor must be able to access the required data in the least amount of time. Several access methods are provided by DBMS to improve the performance of query processors. It is the responsibility of the database designer to specify the access methods to be used on tables, leaving the query processor the task of utilizing them in the most optimum form. Several forms of access methods are supported by currently available DBMS in the UNIX environment. These can be categorized under two major classes:

a. Indexed Sequential Access Method (ISAM).
b. Hashing.

Though the underlying principles are the same, each of these access methods have implementation differences which vary across DBMS. In its simplest form, a relation which is stored with an ISAM structure has a data file and an index file. The index itself has two elements. The first element is the key value and the second is the offset in the data file where a record corresponding to this key value is stored. As the number of key values increases, so does the index file. At some point it becomes necessary to provide an index to the main index to expedite the search in the index. As the index to the main index grows, still another level of index is added. As more levels are added, the index file appears to a have a treelike structure. The internal structure of the index file is implementation-dependent. The chapter on C-ISAM discusses the implementation strategy used by INFORMIX.

Hashing is another access method used by some DBMS. In its simplest form, it consists of a function, called the hash function, which takes a key value as its input. The output of this function is an integer value which is in a prespecified range. This output value is used as an index into an array called the hash table where the data corresponding to the key value is stored or will be stored. A good hashing function ensures that the integer values which it outputs are uniformly distributed throughout the range. When the hashing function yields the same index value for two different inputs, the condition is called a collision. There are several schemes to resolve collisions. The most widely used is called chaining and it involves the linking of records which hash to the same index into the hash table. If a key hashes to a chain, all records in the chain have to be searched to get data for the specified key.

Most DBMS provide more than one access method. Almost all UNIX-based relational DBMS provide ISAM. ISAM is particularly good for search on a range of values. Hashing is good for search on exact values. Hashing does not require any extra storage. ISAM requires extra storage to store the index. The selection between the two is a design issue which must take the pattern of end-user requests into consideration. In the absence of any of the above access methods, tuples may be stored in a heap without any order. A search on a file with such organization is extremely inefficient because the entire file has to be perused sequentially to locate the desired record.

4.9.2 Report Writers

The successful execution of a query yields results in a default format over which the user has little or no control. Clearly, end users, to be appeased, need something fancier than a dump of a table with column names as headings. Report writers are tools which provide this mechanism. The query processor retrieves the required data, and the report writer takes this data and a format specification as input and outputs a formatted report. The process of generating the report is depicted in Figure 4.2. Some DBMS provide a report writer which combines report writer format specification and the query into one single specification file. Most report writers do a lot more than simply formatting the output of the query. They may have additional features to output summaries, calculate additional information based on the query output, and even provide an interface to a programming language like C.

Most report writers provided by DBMS in the UNIX environment provide the same features with differences in syntax and implementation. They take as input data in a tabular form. The data may be derived from one or more tables from the database as an output of a user specified query. Some report writers (for example, the one provided by the UNIFY DBMS) are more flexible and can generate a report from data taken from a flat file. The tabular input is read by the report writer, and some additional values are computed and printed in accordance with the user specification.

Typically, a report writer specification file consists of several sections. Some of these sections are optional. There is almost always a section which indicates to the report writer the source of input data. Normally, this section is in the form of a query. Another section is used to declare variables to be used in the specification file. These variables are in addition to the names of the columns in the database. Formatting sections have statements associated with them which are executed at different stages in the report generation process. For example, statements associated with a *page header* section are executed when a new page is generated. These statements are used to print page titles with information such as date, page number, report title, etc. Similarly, the

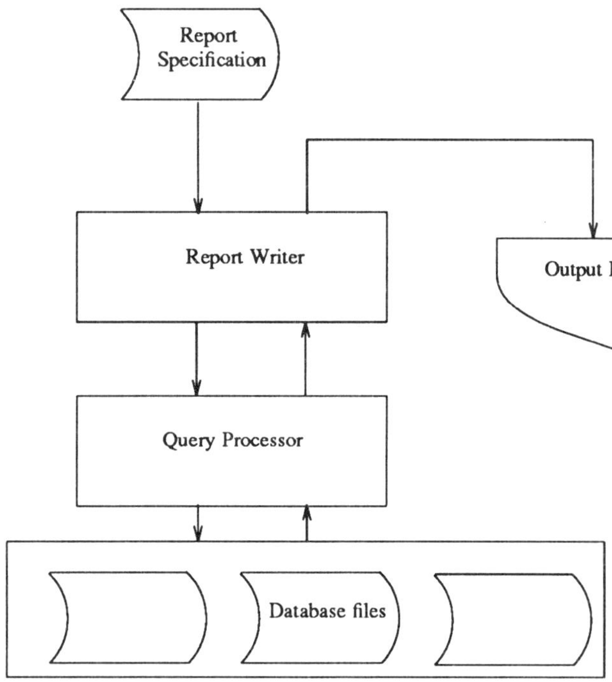

Figure 4.2 How a Report Writer Works

page footer section has statements which are used to print information at the bottom of every page. Statements associated with *report headers* are printed at the start of the report, and those associated with *report footers* are executed at the end of the entire report. In addition, a section is provided to execute statements after every input record is read. The term "detail record" is sometimes used to refer to individual records which are read by the report writer.

If the input is sorted on one or more columns and if there are multiple records with the same value for the sorted column, then statements can be executed to print a heading before the start of a set of records with a new sort column value or to print a summary about the set of records immediately after all records with the same sort column value are read. The *control* here is on the sort column value.

4.9.3 Form Generators

Users can update and query the database by learning the query language which the DBMS supports. End users cannot be expected to learn query languages. Forms provide a user-friendly interface to the end user to add, delete, update, and retrieve information in the database. These forms can be generated using programming languages such as C and packages such as *curses*. To minimize the programming involved, the DBMS software comes equipped with a form generator. Form generators take as input a specification file which describes the layout of the form, the database tables and columns with which the form interacts, a set of validation rules for data entry, error messages to be displayed, etc. Once the form specification file is compiled, the form is ready to be used by an end user who may not have any knowledge of the underlying software or hardware.

4.9.4 Menu Generators

Report writers and form generators provide a user-friendly interface to a database. The user must still know enough about UNIX to run the commands to generate the reports and forms. Menu generator is a tool to design menus. Menus provide options to end users who may not have any knowledge of UNIX to generate reports, display forms, execute UNIX shell scripts, etc.

4.9.5 Host Language Interface

The purpose of a DBMS, among other things, is to eliminate programming efforts. Though a substantial amount of programming is eliminated by the use of DBMS tools, the ultimate goal of eliminating the need to program in a language such as C is not always met. Complicated systems require that the DBMS tools interface with programs written in C. Programming interfaces to these tools come in various flavors. Some DBMS offer the use of library functions which can be called from C programs. Others also offer a preprocessor to the C language which allows the use of a query language within a C program. In addition, programming interfaces are also available with other DBMS tools such as report writers and form generators.

4.9.6 Transaction Processor

Though this module of a DBMS may not be as distinct as the other modules discussed here, the transaction processor which is built within the query processor of the DBMS must deal with the issues of database integrity, recovery, and concurrency control. A transaction is an atomic unit of a database operation which must be executed either completely or not at all. The transaction processor must therefore deal with recovery, because the atomicity must be preserved in case of hardware or software failures and in case of concurrent execution. In a relational database environment, application programs may be written to update several tables as a single transaction. The transaction processor must then guarantee that either all the tables are updated or none at all. In the case of a failure during an update, it must undo the transaction that was partially completed.

4.9.7 Data Dictionary

The data dictionary keeps track of the databases existing on the system which are currently being managed by the DBMS. In addition, it stores information about the tables and columns in the database, the access methods used, the access privileges on them, etc. Clearly, it is one of the most critical parts of the DBMS. Unlike the other components of the DBMS, the data dictionary changes with usage. Some DBMS, such as INFORMIX do not have a global data dictionary for the entire system but maintain a separate dictionary for each database. For such DBMS, the data dictionary can be perceived as a segment of the database rather than that of a DBMS.

4.10 Selecting a DBMS

One of the major problems that a database designer can encounter during the project is to select the right DBMS. What constitutes the best DBMS in the UNIX environment really depends on the application. Benchmarks have indicated that some DBMS are ideal for applications involving extensive inquiries, while others are more suitable for applications involving frequent updates. Many DBMS are continually being enhanced, with improved versions frequently available. For an application in need of a DBMS, the selection of a DBMS, based on existing DBMS studies, comments from users of any particular DBMS, and vendor literature, can be a confusing issue. A database package that lacked desired features a year ago may now have those features. The selection of a DBMS must be based on several factors, with each factor weighed to determine its importance based on the application under consideration. The list of factors to be considered while evaluating a DBMS package is endless. The following are some features to be considered:

- It should be possible to reconfigure the database elegantly. For example, UNIFY stores the entire database in one file, and therefore changes to the structure of a single table often requires that the whole database be restructured.
- If security features are important for the application, the DBMS should support field-level security. Password features are also desirable.
- The DBMS must be able to support various data types, such as date, money, time, boolean, and serial, in addition to the standard data types integer, float, and character strings.
- The DBMS must be able to support a search on UNIX regular expressions.
- The DBMS must have a rich set of functions at the query level.
- The DBMS must have a menu generator.
- In an environment where disk storage is important, it is important to have a DBMS that requires minimal disk storage.
- The DBMS must have a good recovery feature to ensure data integrity after a system crash.
- A good DBMS will allow for easy loading of data into the database from flat files. It will also provide a feature to dump tables from the database into flat files.
- The DBMS should allow multiple users to use the same database without it losing integrity or tying itself into a deadlock. This could be important for databases which have multiple users.
- The DBMS must also be supported on various hardware configurations. This is necessary if there is a likelihood of the hardware being upgraded or changed. It would be disastrous if the DBMS was not supported on the new hardware.
- The DBMS should offer good error messages. Informative messages are helpful for any software system, and DBMS are no exception to this rule. Unfortunately, some DBMS which are available commercially provide very cryptic error messages, and some provide error numbers rather than error messages!
- Some DBMS packages can handle a limited number of fields per record, records per file, or files per database. These limitations are normally not a barrier for most applications; however, it is always advisable to check into these restrictions.
- Technical support is a very important feature that is very often neglected during the evaluation phase. Technical support from some vendors is

so poor that sometimes problems in using the software are interpreted by evaluators as bugs! Regular training programs can be helpful to both vendors and users.

- Most vendors provide trial copies. This trial copy should be tried by the potential user before any decision is made, especially one based on vendor-supplied literature.

Access to user groups, magazines, reviews of DBMS, and current users of the DBMS being considered can be very helpful in the evaluation process. Commercially available DBMS packages discussed in this chapter are continuously enhanced; new features are added and old drawbacks eliminated. The drawbacks of some of the DBMS packages discussed here may no longer be true.

4.11 Distributed DBMS

A distributed database is one that is not physically stored on one computer system. A distributed DBMS is one that can handle such a database. With the advent of distributed file systems, distributed databases are becoming increasingly popular. Though some distributed DBMS may make use of the distributed file system architecture to manage scattered data, others provide their own software to manage UNIX files belonging to the database but resident on remote computers. In a distributed database environment, the term data independence takes on a new notion. Application programs must also be independent of the site where the data is actually stored. This feature is called distribution transparency.

Several terms associated with centralized databases have to be redefined in a distributed database environment. The query processor transforms global queries into fragment queries, executes the fragment queries at remote sites, synchronizes the execution process, and finally accumulates the result of the different fragment queries to generate the end result of the global query.

Query optimization must be done at the global and local level. At the global level, the optimizer must look for the most efficient method to access the database. At the local level, the optimizer functions as if the database is centralized at the physical site. The function of the data dictionary is also enhanced; it must now also keep track of the location of each fragment of the database. Security of a distributed database is no longer in the hands of a single database administrator. With the database physically residing on several sites, control of the database, or a segment of it, lies with the local administrator. With the degree of distribution increasing, the number of administrators having control of the database increase providing a security problem. In addition, security problems are intrinsic to distributed systems in general, because communication networks can represent a weak point with respect to security.

Maintaining database integrity is also complex, as multiple users may be accessing the same record across the network. Updating a single transaction involving multiple records residing on different machines is complex both from a concurrency and failure point of view. It is complex from the concurrency point of view because the records involved must be locked for access from all machines. It is complex from a failure point of view because the atomicity of the transaction must now be observed across machines. A transaction involving updates to multiple relations residing on different machines must either be completed successfully or not at all. The DBMS must be able to handle the case where a machine may crash while completing a transaction involving updates to multiple records on different machines.

4.11.1 Types of Distributed DBMS

Distributed DBMS can be classified into two main categories: heterogeneous and homogeneous. Heterogeneous distributed DBMS are those which can handle databases stored using different operating systems, different hardware and even different DBMS on local sites. There is no implementation of such a distributed DBMS; however, distributed DBMS do exist which can handle databases using the same DBMS on different hardware. This is probably due to the features of UNIX rather than those of the distributed DBMS. A homogeneous DBMS can handle only databases which are stored at remote locations using the same DBMS, the same hardware, and the same operating system.

4.11.2 Types of Distributed Databases

Distributed databases are often categorized on the type of database distribution or fragmentation. There are primarily two types of fragmentation: horizontal and vertical. Horizontal fragmentation refers to the fragmentation of a database in which tuples of a relation are scattered at different sites. Vertical fragmentation refers to the fragmentation of a database in which attributes of a relation are distributed across different sites. The choice as to which of the two types of fragmentation to use depends on the nature of the application. For applications in which different sites perform the same function but on different segments of the database, horizontal fragmentation is more appropriate. Vertical fragmentation is suitable for applications in which different sites are performing variegated functions on the same logical database. Mixed fragmentation is also possible, but it is difficult to manage. As indicated earlier, the function of the data dictionary is augmented to keep track of the location of each fragment.

4.11.3 Advantages of a Distributed DBMS

There are several advantages associated with a distributed DBMS. Some corporations are geographically located at different sites, with each site performing a different function. Though all the sites involved have access to information in a common database, a site may be accessing data related to its function more often than other data in the database. A centralized database would require that all locations access a common location for all their needs. Clearly, with communication costs on the rise, this is not a cost effective solution. By keeping the segment of the database which is used frequently at the local site, communication costs can be reduced. If a site has to access a less frequently used segment of the database stored at a remote site, it can still do so. The application program does not have to be aware that the access is made to a remote segment because of the distribution transparency feature.

In a distributed database environment, the availability of the database is significantly improved. If one site is down, the other sites can still continue to operate.

If a database is fragmented efficiently, access times can be reduced significantly. Consider, for example, a suppliers database with several thousand local and a few foreign suppliers. In a centralized database, the entire supplier file will have to be scanned to locate a foreign supplier. In a distributed database, the suppliers relation may be fragmented into two fragments, local suppliers and foreign suppliers. The table of foreign suppliers can then be stored at a site which deals mostly with foreign suppliers (e.g., the overseas department). The access time to locate a foreign supplier will be significantly reduced. Note that there are two levels of searches required in a distributed database. First, the data dictionary must be searched to retrieve the location of the required data fragment. Next, the actual record must be located at the identified site. However, if the distributed database is designed efficiently, the overhead of two levels of searches is easily offset by the need to search only a smaller relation.

5 Structured Query Language

Structured Query Language (SQL) is the most popular query language in the UNIX DBMS market. It was introduced by IBM around 1974 as SEQUEL. It had to undergo several changes before it assumed the name SQL. The first commercial implementation of SQL was offered by IBM under System R. After the initial success of System R, several vendors started offering SQL-based relational DBMS. Today there are more than a hundred SQL-based DBMS packages in both the UNIX and the non-UNIX environment. The popularity of SQL among commercial vendors has made it the standard query language for relational databases. The "standard" normally refers to the ANSI accepted standard. All the commercial SQL-based DBMS products attempt to support this standard, but minor differences still exist across the different implementations currently available. In this chapter, all examples will be discussed using the INFORMIX-SQL package. All implementation details discussed here are relevant only to this package.

SQL is both a Data Manipulation Language (DML) and a Data Definition Language (DDL). The DDL part of it allows the creation and modification of the basic structure of the database both at the physical and at the logical level. The DML part of it is used to manipulate the contents of the database.

5.1 Getting Started

Before we invoke any INFORMIX-SQL commands, the environment must be appropriately set. In particular, two shell environmental variables must be set correctly. The *INFORMIXDIR* variable must be set to the name of the directory where INFORMIX is installed. Also, the *PATH* variable must be augmented to have the directory with all the INFORMIX binaries. If INFORMIX is installed in the directory /usr/informix, then these variables can be set and exported as follows:

```
PATH=$PATH:/usr/informix/bin
INFORMIXDIR=/usr/informix
export INFORMIXDIR
```

The informix command which interprets SQL statements is *isql.*

5.2 Using SQL as a DDL

SQL can be used as a DDL. This feature of the SQL language allows it to be used for the creation and modification of a database and its schema. A database schema consists of the database itself, a definition of the tables and views in it, and a definition of the indexes used to facilitate faster access. The next few sections discuss these features with an example of a simple database to be used by a florist.

5.2.1 Creating a Database

The first step in the use of SQL is to create a database. Let us create a database for storing information about customers and orders for a florist. This database consists of two tables: customers and orders. The customer table stores the following information:

```
Customer number
Customer last name
Customer first name
Customer address line1
Customer address line2
Customer town
Customer state code
Customer zip
```

and the order table stores the following information:

```
Customer number
Order number
Amount
Order date
Order description
Delivery charge
Amount Paid
```

Before we create the required tables, the database to store the tables must also be created. The SQL statement *create database* can be used to create a new database. Though there are several ways of executing an SQL statement, the most convenient method is to store all the SQL statements in a .sql-suffixed file. This file can be run subsequently using the *isql* command with two arguments. The first argument is the name of the database on which the SQL script is to be run; the second argument specifies the file name without the .sql extension from which the SQL commands are to be fetched. When a database is to be created, the first argument can be a -. The florist database can be created as shown here:

```
cat cr.sql
create database florist
isql - cr
Database created.
```

An interactive session can be initiated by using a - as the first and the second argument. The florist database can also be created by invoking *isql* as:

```
isql - -
> create database florist
^D
Database created
```

5.2.2 Creating Tables in a Database

Once the database is created, there are no user tables in it and therefore the database is not functional. SQL statements must be executed to create these tables. The definition of these tables must be determined after going through the design process. For the florist database, there are two tables to be created. The database design process defines the columns to be grouped within a table. Once the design is completed, the field names and their data types must also be fixed. Certain data types also require the maximum length of the data in that field. The florist database tables can be redefined now in terms of the column names, data types, and length of each field.

Table: *customers*

column name	data type	length
c_no	character	10
c_lname	character	20
c_fname	character	20
c_addr1	character	20
c_addr2	character	20
c_state	character	2
c_town	character	20
c_zip	character	5

Table: *orders*

column name	data type	length
c_no	character	10
o_no	integer	
o_amt	money	
o_date	date	
o_desc	character	30
o_del_chg	money	
o_paid	money	

The SQL statements to create the actual tables corresponding to the above definitions are:

```
create table customers
(
c_no    char(10),
c_lname char(20),
c_fname char(20),
c_addr1 char(20),
c_addr2 char(20),
c_town  char(20),
c_state char(2),
c_zip   char(5)
);
```

```
create table orders
(
c_no    char(10),
o_no    integer
o_amt   money,
o_date  date,
o_desc  char(30),
o_del_chg       money,
o_paid  money
)
```

If these statements are stored in a file called create.sql, then the *isql* command to run these statements can be executed as follows:

```
isql florist cr

Table created.


  201: A syntax error has occurred.
Error in line 16
Near character position 0
```

The cr.sql file has two SQL statements. Multiple SQL statements must be separated by a semicolon (;). The first statement did not have any errors and was therefore executed successfully. The second SQL statement has an error in syntax in line 16. The comma after the definition of the column in line 15 is missing. The line

```
o_no   integer
```

should be

```
o_no   integer,
```

After making the required changes, let us run the same command again:

```
isql florist cr
```

```
   310: Table (customers) already exists in database.
Error in line 11
Near character position 1
```

Trying to run the same set of SQL statements now poses a new problem. The first SQL statement tries to create the customers table again; however, the table is already there and therefore *isql* aborts. The solution to this problem is to either delete the first statement from the file or comment it out. Any portion of an SQL file can be commented by being enclosed in a set of braces. The modified lines of the cr.sql files are shown below:

```
{create table customers
);}
o_no    integer,
```

The *isql* command can now be executed with the required changes incorporated in the cr.sql file to create the second table.

A table can also be referred to by another name with execution of the *create synonym* statement. The synonym is effective only for the user who creates it, and it can be deleted subsequently by the *drop synonym* statement. The following SQL statement creates a synonym called *custs* for the customers table.

```
create synonym custs for customers
```

This can be eliminated at a later time by the following SQL statement being executed:

```
drop synonym custs
```

5.2.2.1 SQL Data Types

Though only a few data types were used in the example, INFORMIX-SQL supports a wide range of them. These are shown below:

Type	Description
Smallint	An integer with values from -32,767 to 32,767
Integer	An integer with values from -2,147,483,647 to 2,147,483,647
Decimal	A decimal floating point number
Smallfloat	A binary floating point number
Float	A binary double precision floating-point number
Money	A data type stored as a decimal but displayed with a leading dollar sign ($)
Serial	If a new record, with a field of this data type, is added, then a unique sequential integer is assigned automatically by the SQL processor to this field. Only one field in a table can have this data type
Date	This data type is associated with fields which are used to maintain dates. Internally, the date field is stored as an integer representing the number of days since Dec. 31, 1899.

Other SQL implementations may not support all these data types. In particular, the serial data type is not available on most implementations.

5.2.2.2 Handling Null Values

Null-valued fields were discussed in the preceeding chapters. INFORMIX-SQL accepts null values for fields unless a *not null* clause is specified along with the data type at table creation time. For example, to force the customer number field to have only non-null values, use the following line in the SQL *create* statement:

```
c_no   char(10) not null,
```

Some SQL implementations have a *unique* clause which forces uniqueness on that field. If specified, no two records in the table can have the same value for the specified field.

5.2.3 Creating Indexes

Once the tables in the database are created, the database is ready for use. Data can now be added to the various tables in the database. As the database grows in size, its performance deteriorates. For example, to retrieve the address of customer no. 2019061212, it will be necessary to scan all the records in the table until the required customer is located. Such sequential searches are inefficient for most applications. To speed up the searching process, an index can be provided. Database indexes work like the index of a book. At first, only one level of an index is created. At some point, the index itself becomes big, so an index to the index is built. As the database continues to grow, the second index also becomes big so a third-level index is provided. The different levels are collectively referred to as an "index" in database jargon and are stored as a tree structure in a single file. The presence of an index on a table reduces the time it takes to retrieve a record. Indexes can be built on an empty or a loaded database.

An index can be built on one or more fields. If the index is on multiple fields, it is called a composite index. The order of the individual fields in a composite index is important. For example, a composite index on two fields *c_fname* and *c_lname* in that order is different from a composite index on the same fields in the order of *c_lname* and *c_fname*. The first index is useful for searches given values for both the *c_fname* and *c_lname* fields. It can also be used for searches on the field *c_fname* alone. However, it is useless for searches involving only the values of field *c_lname*. Let us create two indexes for the customer table: a composite index on the name fields and a simple index on the customer number. Let us also create a simple index on the *customer no.* field for the orders table. Here are the SQL statements to create these indexes:

```
cat ind.sql
create distinct index c_index1 on customers(c_fname, c_lname);
create index c_index2 on customers(c_no);
create index o_index1 on orders(c_no)
```

The first statement creates an index which forces uniqueness on the name fields combination. The *distinct* option is used to force this. Each index has a name. This name can be used later either to delete the index or to alter its structure. The next two statements create indexes on a single field. The *isql* command can be used to execute these SQL statements, as was indicated earlier. A message is displayed for every index created, as shown below:

```
isql florist ind

Index created.

Index created.

Index created.
```

Once the index is created, it is automatically updated as records are added, deleted, and modified from the table for which the index is built. The physical order of the records in the table can be forced to be the same as the order in the created index with use of the *cluster* option. For a table there can, of course, be only one index with the *cluster* option.

5.2.4 Creating a View

Views were explained in Section 4.7. In SQL, views can be created with use of the *create view* statement. Let us create a view consisting of only *c_no* and *c_town* as the two fields in it. Here is the SQL statement to create this view:

```
create view no_town as
        select c_no, c_town
        from customers
```

The view is called *no_town*. It is like a table but does not have a separate physical existence. It is made up of two fields selected from the customers table: *c_no* and *c_town*.

It is also possible to create a view by drawing fields from different tables. Such views can be used to simplify complex queries. Here is an example of a view which has two fields, a customer number (*c_no*) and an order description (*orders*), for those customers who have at least one record in the orders table:

```
create view ord_info as
        select customers.c_no, o_desc
        from customers, orders
        where customers.c_no = orders.c_no
```

The *select* statement is used to specify the fields in the view and the segment of the data which should appear in the view.

5.3 Loading the Database

Once the database and the tables in it are created, it has to be loaded with data. The statements to create tables only create the required structures to accept the data. Data can be loaded into the database in a wide variety of ways. Forms can be designed specifically for data entry. SQL can be used to load data into the database in one of two ways: either one record can be loaded at a time or a whole flat file can be dumped into the specified table. The *insert* statement can be used to load one record at a time. It can also be used to take data from other tables in the database and dump it in the specified table, for example, to load the following customer record:

c_no	: 2019061212
c_lname	: DP-Tech Computer Services
c_fname	:
c_addr1	: Suite 12
c_addr2	: 25 South Main St.
c_state	: NJ
c_town	: Edison
zip	: 08837

The SQL *insert* statement can be used as shown here:

```
cat ins.sql
insert into customers
values ( "2019061212","DP-Tech Computer Services",
        "","Suite 12", "25 South Main St.",
        "NJ", "Edison", "08837"
        )
isql florist ins

1 row(s) inserted.
```

If the length of a string is greater than the field length, it is silently truncated. The value for the *c_lname* field in the example is greater than the field length and will therefore be truncated. The values are in the same order as the definition of the columns in the table. If the order of values is different from the column order in the original definition of the table, then the order must be specified. Also, if a value is missing, it must still be indicated as a null value. Otherwise, the SQL processor will be confused about the mapping of the fields and their values. Let us add another customer record with the zip value specified first:

```
cat ins2.sql
insert into customers
       (
       c_zip, c_no, c_fname, c_lname,
       c_addr1, c_addr2, c_state, c_town
       )
values ( "08837", "2012428055","John",
       "Doe","Suite 12", "25 South Main St.",
       "NJ", "Edison"
       )
isql florist ins2

1 row(s) inserted.
```

Data from other tables in the database can be extracted with use of the SQL *select* statement and loaded into the specified table with use of *insert*. In the following example, a temporary table, *S_custs* is created, and the customer number of those customers whose last name starts with the letter *S* is inserted:

```
create table S_cust
(
c_no    char(10)
);
insert into S_cust
       select c_no from customers
              where c_lname matches "S*"
```

The *select* statement is used to retrieve the required customer numbers. This statement will be discussed later.

5.3.1 The Load Statement

The SQL *load* statement can be used to dump data from a flat file into a database table. Let us dump three records from the file cust.d into the customers table:

```
cat file.d
2014852216|Umesh|Parab|32 Marcela St.||Newark|NJ|07104
2014852216|Todd|McAlister|12 Jones Drive||Plainfield|NJ|07060
2152500254|Rick|Sanders|13 Jonathan Terrace||Belleville|NJ|07103

cat ld.sql
load from "file.d"
insert into customers
isql florist ld

3 row(s) loaded.
```

The file file.d must have records with the same number of fields and in the same order as the columns in the table. If the order is different, then it must be specified, in parentheses, after the table. A list of column names may also be used if the number of fields in the input file does not match the number of fields in the database table. By default, the field separator used is the "|" character. However, other characters can also be used by setting the environment variable *DBDELIMITER*. For example, to use the ":" character as a field separator, the environment variable *DBDELIMITER* can be set as follows:

```
DBDELIMITER=:
export DBDELIMITER
```

Character data fields exceeding the length of a column are silently truncated. A field with a length of zero is interpreted as a null-valued field. Fields with the date data type must appear in the format *mm/dd/yyyy* or *mm/dd/yy*. If it appears in the later form, it is interpreted as *mm/dd/19yy*. If a different format for date is to be used, the *DBDATE* environment variable can be used to specify it. For example, if *DBDATE* is set to *DMY4/*, then the date is accepted in the format *dd/mm/yy* or *dd/mm/yyyy*. At load time the date field is validated for possible inconsistencies such as invalid month or day of the month.

5.4 Retrieving Schema Information

Once the database is created and perhaps loaded with data, INFORMIX SQL offers the *info* statement to retrieve information about the schema. This statement can be used to display information about tables, columns, and indexes. To display the list of tables in the florist database, use the *info* statement as follows:

```
cat info1.sql
info tables
isql florist info1

Table name

customers orders
```

The *info* statement can also be used to retrieve information for the columns in a given table. Here is an example in which information about the columns is displayed in the customers table:

```
cat info2.sql
info columns for customers
isql florist info2

Column name          Type                Nulls

c_no                 char(10)            yes
c_lname              char(20)            yes
c_fname              char(20)            yes
c_addr1              char(20)            yes
c_addr2              char(20)            yes
c_town               char(20)            yes
c_state              char(2)             yes
c_zip                char(5)             yes
```

Information about indexes on any table can also be fetched with the *info* statement, as in:

```
cat info3.sql
info indexes for customers
isql florist info3

Index name          Owner     Type     Cluster  Columns

c_index1             rst       dupls    No        c_fname
                                                  c_lname
```

```
c_index2            rst       dupls   No        c_no
```

The *Type* column indicates if duplicates are allowed. The *Cluster* column indicates if the records in the table are in the same order as the index. The last column indicates the fields in the index.

The current status of a table can also be displayed with use of the *info* statement as follows:

```
cat info4.sql
info status for customers
isql florist info4

Table Name          customers
Owner               rst
Row Size            117
Number of Rows      5
Number of Columns   8
Date Created        10/27/1988
Audit Trail File
```

Here the status of the customers table is displayed. The *Audit Trail File* status will be explained later. The access privileges for a table can be displayed with use of the *access for* or the *privileges for* options of the *info* statement. The access status for the customers table can be displayed with use of the *info* statement, as in:

```
cat info5.sql
info access for customers
isql florist info5

User      Select   Update   Insert    Delete  Index  Alter

public    All      All      Yes       Yes     Yes    No
```

Public here refers to all users of the system. These privileges can be changed, as is explained later.

5.5 Altering the Schema

Due to modifications in the application, the database schema may require some change. Sometimes, changes are required to fine tune the performance of the system. The *alter* statement can be used to change the database schema. This involves changing the structure of a table or its indexes. The definition of a table can be changed to delete an existing column, to add a new column, or to modify the data type of an existing column. The field length of the *c_lname* field in the customers table can be changed to 30 with use of the *alter* statement:

```
alter table customers
        modify (c_lname char(30))
```

When the execution is successful, the following message will be displayed:

```
Table altered.
```

Similarly, an existing column may be deleted from a table with use of the *alter* statement with the *drop* option, as in:

```
alter table customers
        drop (c_addr2)
```

which deletes the *c_addr2* column from the customers table. A new field can be added to a table with use of the *add* option of the *alter* statement. By default, the new field is added after the last column of the table. The *before* option can be used to position the new column before any existing field. For example, the *c_addr2* field can be added again to the definition of the table with use of the following *alter* statement:

```
alter table customers
        add (c_addr2 char(20) before c_town)
```

The *alter* statement can also be used to change the physical order of the records in a table either by the dropping of the *cluster* option currently associated with an index or by the addition of one to an existing index. Dropping the *cluster* option of an index will not actually reorder the records, but if new records are added, they will no longer follow the earlier cluster order. All records in the customers table can be ordered according to the order of the *c_index2* index with use of the *alter* statement:

```
alter index c_index2 to cluster
```

The database schema can also be altered by the deletion of tables, indexes, and views. The *drop* statement can be used for this purpose. To delete the customers table from the database, use the following statement:

```
drop table customers
```

The *drop* statement can also be used to delete an index. For example, the *c_index2* index can be dropped by using the SQL statement:

```
drop index c_index2
```

Similarly, views can be dropped by using the *drop view* statement. It is also possible to eliminate the entire database by using the *drop database* statement. The entire florist database can be eliminated by using the following *drop database* statement:

```
drop database florist
```

Changes to the schema can also be made by merely renaming tables and columns. The *rename* statement can be used for this purpose. To change the name of the column *c_state* to *c_state_cd* in the customers table, the following *rename* statement can be used:

```
rename column customers.c_state to c_state_cd
```

The table name has to be specified as a qualifier to the old column name because several tables may have a column with the same name. The name of the table itself can be changed as in:

```
rename table customers to clients
```

which changes the name of the customers table to *clients*.

The user must have appropriate permissions to make changes to the database schema. Permissions can be granted by using the *grant* statement which is explained in the following section.

5.6 Granting Access Privileges

In addition to the UNIX *chmod* command, which restricts access to files in a multiuser environment, INFORMIX imposes its own security restriction to limit access to the tables in the database. The *grant* statement can be used to specify different levels of access to the tables and columns in the database. The syntax of this statement to grant table-level access is:

```
grant privileges on table-name to
        user-list
```

This statement grants the desired *privileges* to the specified *user* on the indicated *table*. Different levels of privileges can be specified. They are

Privilege	**Description**
alter	Allows the user to modify the definition of the table
delete	Allows the user to delete any number of rows from the table
index	Allows the user to create indexes on the table
insert	Allows the user to insert rows in the table
select	Allows the user to retrieve data from the table
update	Allows the user to update existing rows in the table
all	Grants the user all the above privileges

User-list is a list of comma-separated login names. *Public* can be used to specify all users on the system. A list of columns can be optionally specified along with the *select* and *update* privileges which grant those permissions only on the specified columns. The following statement can be used to allow all users the privilege to access data from the customers table:

```
grant select on customers to public
```

Database-level access can also be specified with use of the *grant* statement. For example, to grant the Data Base Administrator (DBA) status to user *tpm*, use the following statement:

```
grant dba to tpm
```

Two other privileges can also be specified. They are *connect* and *resource*. The *connect* privilege allows access to the database but does not allow the user to create new permanent tables and indexes. This additional control is available if the *resource* privilege is also granted to the user.

The *revoke* statement can be used to remove access privileges given by the *grant* statement. It has almost the same syntax as the *grant* statement. The only difference is that it is not possible to revoke column-level privileges. Only table-level or database-level privileges can be revoked. If column-level privileges are to be changed, then they can be revoked in entirety on the whole table and then regranted on the desired columns. Only the DBA can revoke database-level privileges.

5.7 Retrieving Data

SQL offers the *select* statement to retrieve data from the database. Data may be retrieved from one or more tables in a single *select* statement. This statement is probably the most powerful statement offered by SQL. The general syntax of an SQL statement is:

```
select unique-option
          list-of-columns
from list of tables
where condition for retrieval
additional clauses
```

The *from* clause is mandatory. Other clauses are optional. The *select* statement provides all the relational algebra operators, including *project*, *select*, and *join*. In addition, it has several features which are defined neither by relational algebra nor by relational calculus expressions. It is one of the most widely used statements for benchmarking DBMS systems. The user does not have to specify the names of the indexes to be used; the SQL processor is expected to make that decision. The implementation of an SQL processor therefore becomes a nontrivial task.

5.7.1 Getting Started

All the examples discussed in this section will use the schema for the florist database as defined in section 5.2.2. The customers table is loaded from the following UNIX flat file:

```
2012428055|Doe|John|Apt. 2|782 Clifton Ave.|Shalantown|NJ|07104
8000011212|Smith|Mike|32 Palisade Ave.||Ringwood|NJ|07456
2011212451|McAlister|Todd|44 Park Ave.||Plainfield|NJ|07060
2013211234|Parab|Umesh|55 Slick St.||Midland Park|NJ|07432
2014561412|Dev|Kapil|55 Cricket Drive||Ocean|NJ|07712
2013211341|Botham|Ian|72 Fast Avenue||Nutley|NJ|07110
2014311211|Lillee|Dennis|92 Australia St.||Orange|NJ|07051
2018911211|Roberts|Maria|72 Cinconni Dr.||Lakewood|NJ|08701
2016667777|Marshal|Jennifer|11 Indies Lane||Paramus|NJ|07652
6091212121|Hadlee|Richard|112 Allround St.||Princeton|NJ|08540
```

and the orders table is loaded from this file:

```
2012428055|1|45.70|12/12/1987|A dozen roses|5.00|15
2012428055|2|50|2/12/1988|Centerpiece|15.00|20
2013211234|1|872.00|1/24/1988|Wedding Arrang.|7.00|400.00
2013211234|2|70.00|1/24/1988|Birthday Arrang.|7.00|00.00
2013211341|1|25.00|2/12/1988|Basket Willis|6.00|55.00
2018911211|2|55.00|2/12/1988|Casket Spray|3.00|75.00
2016667777|4|75.00|3/27/1988|Birthday Arr.|4.00|85.00
6091212121|1|12.00|6/19/1988|Baby Girl Arr.|5.00|100.00
6091212121|2|50.00|2/2/1988|A dozen roses|2.00|10.00
6091212121|3|70.00|3/2/1988|Funeral Wreath|2.00|10.00
2123211411|1|100.00|3/12/1988|2 Dozen roses|5.00|90.00
```

5.7.2 Elementary Select Statements

The *select* statement can be used to project only the required columns from a table, as in:

```
select c_no,c_lname from customers
```

which gives the following output:

```
c_no       c_lname

2013211234 Parab
2011212451 McAlister
8000011212 Smith
2012428055 Doe
2014561412 Dev
2013211341 Botham
2014311211 Lillee
2018911211 Roberts
2016667777 Marshal
6091212121 Hadlee

10 row(s) retrieved.
```

The output consists of column headings and the actual data. In addition, the total number of rows retrieved is also displayed.

To display all the columns of the table, use an asterisk (*) instead of the complete list of columns. Columns of only selected records can be displayed with use of the *where* clause. For example, to display all the columns for those customers whose first name is "John," use the following *select* statement:

```
select * from customers
where c_fname="John"
```

which will display the following information:

```
c_no     2012428055
c_lname  Doe
c_fname  John
c_addr1  Apt. 2
c_addr2  782 Clifton Ave.
c_town   Shalantown
c_state  NJ
c_zip    07104
```

```
1 row(s) retrieved.
```

The INFORMIX-SQL processor will not display the output in a table format if it cannot fit a row in one line. The *where* clause can have a set of selection conditions connected by the logical operators *and*, *or*, and *not*. For matching strings with regular expressions, the operator *matches* can be used. Relational operators such as =, <, !=, etc., are supported. The next query retrieves the customer number of customers whose last name starts with an *M* and whose state code is *NJ*.

```
select c_no from customers
        where c_lname matches "M*" and
              c_state matches "NJ"
```

which displays the following output:

```
c_no

2011212451
2016667777

2 row(s) retrieved.
```

The wildcard character * matches zero or more characters. All the wildcard characters are reminiscent of the shell metacharacters. The *?* character matches any single character. A class of characters can be specified by being enclosed in square brackets. For example, *[a-dk]* matches the letters *a,b,c,d,* and *k*. The special meaning of wildcard characters is lost if they are preceded by a backslash character. Null-valued fields can be detected with use of the *is null* comparison criterion. The *not* operator can be used to negate the search criterion. For example, the query

```
select c_lname from customers
where c_addr2 is not null
```

displays the last names of customers whose address exceeds one line. The output displayed is:

```
c_lname

Doe

1 row(s) retrieved.
```

A field can also be checked for a range of values. Here is an example which displays a list of order descriptions with an order amount ranging from $70.00 to $100.

```
select o_desc, o_amt from orders
where o_amt between 70 and 100
```

which displays:

```
o_desc                                       o_amt

Birthday Arrang.                            $70.00
Birthday Arr.                               $75.00
Funeral Wreath                              $70.00
2 Dozen roses                              $100.00

4 row(s) retrieved.
```

5.7.3 Retrieval from Multiple Tables

The *select* statement can be used to retrieve information from multiple tables. It can be used to join two or more tables on one or more fields. For example, the following query retrieves the customer numbers and customer names of customers who have an outstanding amount of more than $200.00 to be paid. Outstanding amount is calculated as:
order amount + delivery charge − amount paid.

```
select orders.c_no,c_fname,c_lname
       from customers, orders
       where customers.c_no   = orders.c_no
       and    (o_amt + o_del_chg - o_paid) > 200.00
```

When executed, the *select* statement displays

```
c_no       c_fname          c_lname

2013211234 Umesh            Parab

1 row(s) retrieved.
```

The customers and orders table are joined here on the *c_no* fields. Column names which appear in more than one table must be qualified; the table name must be specified so that any ambiguity is avoided. Here is another query which joins the two tables to retrieve the last names of customers who have at least one record in the order table.

```
select c_lname
       from customers, orders
       where customers.c_no = orders.c_no
```

It outputs:

```
c_lname

Parab
Parab
Doe
Doe
Botham
Roberts
Marshal
Hadlee
Hadlee
Hadlee

10 row(s) retrieved.
```

Clearly there are several duplicates in the output. These duplicates can be eliminated with use of the *distinct* clause. In addition, the output can be sorted with use of the *order by* clause. Here is the modified *select* statement:

```
select distinct c_lname
        from customers, orders
        where customers.c_no = orders.c_no
        order by c_lname
```

which outputs:

```
c_lname

Botham
Doe
Hadlee
Marshal
Parab
Roberts

6 row(s) retrieved.
```

The output does not have an entry for customer no. 2123211411. This customer has an order, but there is no record in the customers table! This is a data integrity problem. In a *select* statement, retaining such records is possible with use of an outer join. If tables *t1* and *t2* are involved in a join and if all records in table *t2* are to be retained in the output, then the table *t1* must be described as an outer table in the *from* clause of the *select* statement. For example, the query to retain the record for customer no. 2123211411 in the join operation on the customers and orders table is

```
select distinct orders.c_no,c_lname
        from outer customers, orders
        where customers.c_no = orders.c_no
        order by c_lname
```

which displays:

```
c_no       c_lname

2123211411
2013211341 Botham
2012428055 Doe
6091212121 Hadlee
2016667777 Marshal
```

```
2013211234 Parab
2018911211 Roberts

7 row(s) retrieved.
```

5.7.4 Using the Group By Clause

The *group by* clause is used to arrange the incoming rows such that all rows with the same values in the *group by* fields are clustered together. Once the rows are grouped, only values which are associated with each input group can be selected. Each group appears as a single row. For simplification, only two types of values can be extracted. First, columns specified in the *group by* clause can be extracted because they are guaranteed to be the same among the clustered rows. Second, aggregate functions can be applied to columns in the clustered rows of a group, and the result of the applied function can be extracted. The following query extracts the total order amount for each customer:

```
select c_no, sum(o_amt)
from orders
group by c_no
```

which displays

```
c_no                (sum)

2012428055          $95.70
2013211234         $942.00
2013211341          $25.00
2018911211          $55.00
2016667777          $75.00
6091212121         $132.00
2123211411         $100.00

7 row(s) retrieved.
```

The aggregate function *sum* is used here to add the order amount for all rows in the same group. Several other aggregate functions are also supported by SQL. They are listed below:

Count	Retrieves the number of rows in the group
Sum	Retrieves the sum of all the values in the specified column for all rows in the group
Avg	Retrieves the average of all values for the specified column in the group
Max	Retrieves the maximum value of the specified column within the group
Min	Retrieves the minimum value of the specified column within the group

When the functions *count*, *sum*, or *avg*, are used, the word *distinct* may precede the column name. This word is used to eliminate duplicate values before the function is applied. It is possible to eliminate records before any grouping is done by using the *where* clause. For example, to get the average order amount for the year 1988, you can use the following query:

```
select avg(o_amt)
from orders
where o_date >= "1/1/1988"
  and o_date <  "1/1/1989"
```

which displays

```
          (avg)

        $137.90

1 row(s) retrieved.
```

The *having* clause can be used to do a selection on groups. For example, the query to display the total order amount for each customer can be modified to display the same information only for those customers who have an order amount greater than $100.00. The modified query is

```
select c_no, sum(o_amt)
from orders
group by c_no
having sum(o_amt) > 100.00
```

and it displays the following results:

```
c_no                     (sum)

2013211234            $942.00
6091212121            $132.00

2 row(s) retrieved.
```

To get the number of customers who have at least one order, use the following query:

```
select count(distinct c_no)
       from orders
```

which displays

```
    (count)
        7

1 row(s) retrieved.
```

The total number of records in a table can be counted by using the special form of *count*: *count(*)*. For example, you can retrieve total number of orders by using the following query:

```
select count(*)
       from orders
```

which displays

```
  (count(*))
         11

1 row(s) retrieved.
```

Count(*) can also be used to count the number of records in a group. For example, here is a query which displays the customer number and the number of orders for that customer:

```
select c_no, count(*)
from orders
group by c_no
```

which displays

```
c_no          (count(*))

2012428055             2
2013211234             2
2013211341             1
2018911211             1
2016667777             1
6091212121             3
2123211411             1

7 row(s) retrieved.
```

Note that the output is not sorted. The *order by* clause can be used to sort the output on any specified field.

5.7.5 Date Functions

There are several functions which are designed specifically for the date data type.

The *date* function returns the date data type from numeric or character arguments. For example, *date(1000)* returns the thousandth day after Dec. 31, 1899. String arguments can also be used. For example, date("1/1/1988") returns a date data type from the specified string type. The *day* function returns the day of the month. The argument must be of type date. The *mdy* function takes three arguments which can be expressions but must evaluate to integers. These arguments represent the month, day, and year, in that order. The function returns a type date value. Three other functions, *month*, *weekday*, and *year*, return an integer which represents the month, weekday, and year for the specified argument of type date. Weekday is returned as an integer in the range from 0 to 6. A 0 represents Sunday and a 6 represents Saturday. Finally, the *today* function returns today's date.

Here is an example which displays only the year of each order:

```
select year(o_date) which_year
  from orders
```

The output of this query is:

```
which_year

      1987
      1988
      1988
      1988
      1988
      1988
      1988
      1988
      1988
      1988
      1988

11 row(s) retrieved.
```

The word *which_year* is called a display label. It is used to provide a readable heading to an output column. It is particularly useful for columns which are evaluated as an expression. In the absence of an explicit display label, they are labeled as "(expression)"!

5.7.6 The User Function

The *user* function returns the login id. of the user running the query. For example, the query

```
select distinct user who_am_i,today today_is from customers
```

displays

```
who_am_i today_is

rst      10/30/1988
```

```
1 row(s) retrieved.
```

In the absence of the *distinct* option, there will be as many rows in the output as the number of rows in the customers table. Strictly speaking, the output has nothing to do with the customers table, but syntactical requirements force the use of at least one table in a *select* statement.

5.7.7 Nested Subqueries

The *select* statement can be nested. The value of an expression in an outer *select* can be checked against values fetched from an inner *select* statement. The inner statement is called a subquery. It is normally associated with the outer query by the use of the *all*, *any*, and *in* predicate. If these predicates are used, several forms of nested subqueries are possible. These are explained with examples in the following sections.

5.7.7.1 The All and Any Predicate

Queries involving *all* or *any* associated with a subquery have the following format:

```
select ...
where  expression relational-operator
all/any
( select ...
)
```

For every *expression* in the outer query a comparison is made, using the specified relational operator, with the set of values returned by the inner query. If the comparison is true for all the values returned by the inner query, then the result is true if *all* was used. If the comparison is true for at least one value in the set, then the result is true if *any* was used. The following query displays customer numbers of customers who placed at least one order after customer no. 2012428055 placed *any* order.

```
select distinct c_no from
        orders where
        o_date > any
        (select o_date from orders
```

```
        where c_no = "2012428055"
        )
```

The output of this query is

```
c_no

2012428055
2013211234
2013211341
2018911211
2016667777
6091212121
2123211411

7 row(s) retrieved.
```

If *all* is used instead of *any*, the query will display the list of customer numbers who placed at least one order after customer no. 2012428055 placed his last order. Here is the modified query:

```
select distinct c_no from
        orders where
        o_date > all
        (select o_date from orders
        where c_no = "2012428055"
        )
```

which will output the following result:

```
c_no

2016667777
6091212121
2123211411

3 row(s) retrieved.
```

If the relational operator = is to be used with *any*, then = *any* can be replaced by *in*.

5.7.7.2 Using the Existential Quantifier

Nested *select* statements which use the existential quantifier *exists* take the following form:

```
select ...
where exists (
select ...    )
```

The inner statement is executed, and if it does not retrieve any row, then the result of the evaluation is false; otherwise, the result is true. Most queries using *exists* require that a column from the outer query be used by the inner query in its *where* clause. Here is a query which retrieves the customer number, first name, and last name from the customers table for the customer with the highest order amount:

```
select c_no, c_fname, c_lname from
        customers where
        exists (
        select * from orders
         where customers.c_no = orders.c_no
         and o_amt in (
                select max(o_amt)
                       from orders
                )
        )
```

There are two subqueries in the statement. The innermost subquery retrieves the highest order amount. The outermost query reads each record from the customers record. It passes customer number to the middle-level subquery which checks to see if the order amount for this customer is equal to the highest order amount. When the SQL statement is executed, the output is

```
c_no       c_fname             c_lname

2013211234 Umesh               Parab

1 row(s) retrieved.
```

Users are tempted to write the following query to solve the above problem:

```
select customers.c_no, c_fname, c_lname
from customers, orders
where customers.c_no = orders.c_no
and             o_amt = max(o_amt)
```

If an attempt is made to run this query, it will give the following error message:

```
  303: Expression mixes columns with aggregates.
Error in line 5
Near character position 0
```

Clearly, SQL does not allow the use of aggregate functions in a *where* clause. The *max* function must be evaluated by a separate subquery.

5.7.8 Using Temporary Tables

INFORMIX-SQL provides a mechanism for storing the output of a *select* statement into a temporary table. This temporary table can be used in subsequent queries in the same SQL script. After the entire script is executed, the table is removed. Here is an example:

```
select c_no, c_lname
       from customers
       into temp temp1;
select c_no
       from orders
  where o_amt > 70
  into temp temp2;
select temp1.c_no from temp1, temp2
where
       temp1.c_no = temp2.c_no
```

which when executed outputs

```
10 row(s) retrieved into temp table.

3 row(s) retrieved into temp table.
```

```
c_no

2013211234
2016667777

2 row(s) retrieved.
```

Temporary tables are used if the result of a subquery is used in multiple queries. Also, complicated queries can be simplified if they are decomposed into smaller subqueries. Temporary tables cannot have indexes on them and therefore can degrade the query execution performance.

5.8 Unloading Data

The *select* statement retrieves data with column headings. Also, if the rows are long, *select* does not format the output in a table format. Sometimes, it is desirable to have the data from a table unloaded to a flat file. There are several reasons why this could be required. First, users on another system may be using a different DBMS and may need to have access to the data in the database. It then becomes necessary to unload this data into a flat UNIX file which can then be reloaded into a database which uses another noncompatible DBMS. Also, several packages exist which store data in their own internal form. These packages cannot interface with the data stored in the DBMS-specific format. Data must then be unloaded from the database and reconverted to a structure that the package understands. Utilities associated with the package can do the reconversion once a flat file is available. The SQL statement *unload* can be used to extract data from the database and to create a UNIX flat file. Each record has fields separated by a field separator. The output of any *select* statement can be unloaded to a file. Here is an example:

```
unload to "/u/bk/unp.orders.d"
        select * from orders
                where o_amt+o_del_chg < o_paid
```

When executed, the statement displays the following message:

```
4 row(s) unloaded.
```

The specified file is created. It can now be used with any other UNIX filters or a file management utility. Here is the contents of that file:

```
cat /u/bk/unp.orders.d
2013211341|1|25.0|02/12/1988|Basket Willis|6.0|55.0|
2018911211|2|55.0|02/12/1988|Casket Spray|3.0|75.0|
2016667777|4|75.0|03/27/1988|Birthday Arr.|4.0|85.0|
6091212121|1|12.0|06/19/1988|Baby Girl Arr.|5.0|100.0|
```

5.9 Updating the Database

The *insert* and the *load* statements can be used to load data into the database. Once the data is loaded into the database, existing records can be changed with use of the *update* statement and removed with use of the *delete* statement.

The following *update* statement changes the amount paid field for order no. 2 of customer number 2013211234 to $879.00:

```
update orders
       set o_paid = 879.00
       where c_no = "2013211234"
       and   o_no = 1
```

If the update is successful, the statement displays

```
1 row(s) updated.
```

Several columns can also be updated simultaneously, as in

```
update orders
       set o_no = 7, o_amt=170.00
       where c_no = "2013211234"
       and   o_no = 1
```

This statement can also be rewritten with use of a different syntax, as shown below:

```
update orders
        set (o_no, o_amt) =
             (7,    170.00)
        where c_no = "2013211234"
        and    o_no = 1
```

The new values to be used in the *update* statement can be specified as the output of a *select* statement. The table to be updated cannot be used in the *select* statement. It is an error if the *select* statement retrieves more than one row. The following query changes the order description of order no. 2 of customer no. 2018911211 to her last name!

```
update orders
        set (o_desc) =
        (( select c_lname
        from customers where c_no = "2018911211"
        ))
        where c_no = "2018911211" and
               o_no = 2
```

The extra pair of parentheses are required for the *select* statement. If more than one column is to be updated, then some of the columns may get the input data from a *select* while the remaining columns may have a constant value specified in the statement. Here is a modified version of the previous *update* statement which also changes the order amount:

```
update orders
        set (o_desc,o_amt) =
        (( select c_lname
        from customers where c_no = "2018911211"
        ),65)
        where c_no = "2018911211" and
               o_no = 2
```

In the absence of the *where* clause, all records in the table are updated.

The *delete* statement can be used to remove specified records from the table. Records to be removed can be specified through use of the *where* clause. In the absence of the *where* clause all records in the table are deleted.

To delete all records in the orders table for customer no. 2012428055, use the following statement:

```
delete from orders
       where c_no="2012428055"
```

Deleting all records from a table does not remove the table itself.

5.10 Transaction Processing

Transaction processing refers to a sequence of operations to be performed on a database which are guaranteed to be atomic; they are either all executed successfully or none at all. There are two reasons why a transaction may not be completed. First, the user may request that it be aborted midway during its completion. Second, the system may crash while executing the transaction. In both cases, a good DBMS must be able to recover the partially completed processing.

The transaction must remain under the control of the user and must be completed when the user explicitly issues a statement to do so. Once completed, the transaction must not be lost because of any system failures. In addition, the DBMS must guarantee serializability of transactions. This means that if two transactions are to be executed concurrently, the end result must be the same as if they were executed serially in some order. Transactions must be executed in isolation. This means that the result of a transaction must not be visible unless the user issues a statement to commit the transaction.

The above-discussed features of a good transaction processor are required so that the integrity of the database is maintained. To achieve this feature, the DBMS implementation becomes nontrivial. Also, there are additional overheads associated with each transaction which slow updates to the database. A DBMS should, therefore, give the option to the database designer to decide if such a feature is desirable. Clearly, some applications may not need the additional level of reliability. Periodic backups can be taken and restored in the event of a system failure. The database can then be rolled forward through the application of the same set of transactions again. The isolation of a transaction results in other processes waiting for it to be completed. This reduces the availability factor of the database.

5.10.1 Transaction Processing Using INFORMIX-SQL

This section discusses the mechanism of managing transactions using INFORMIX-SQL statements. The transactions applied to a database are actually stored in another file called the transaction log. A database must be created with a transaction log; otherwise, transaction management statements cannot be used on the database. A database with a transaction log can be created by the following SQL statement:

```
create database mydb with log in "/u/rst/mydb/dblog"
```

which will create the database and an empty transaction log file:

```
ls -l /u/rst/mydb/dblog
-rw-rw----  1 rst       informix      0 Nov  1 20:25 dblog
```

A transaction log file can also be created after the database is created through use of the following SQL statement:

```
start database mydb with log in "/u/rst/mydb/dblog"
```

The *start database* statement can also be used to restart a new transaction log and is normally done prior to a database backup operation. Once the database is created, the tables and indexes can also be created. Let the database have only one simple table which is created by the following SQL statement:

```
cat cr.sql
create table mytable
(
col1   integer,
col2   integer
)
isql mydb cr

Table created.
```

Let mytable.d be a flat file with the following data:

```
cat mytable.d
12|24
32|42
111|12
```

If an attempt is made to load this file in the only table in the database by using the SQL *load* statement, the statement will report an error as in:

```
cat ld.sql
load from "mytable.d"
insert into mytable
isql mydb ld

  255: Not in transaction.
Error in line 2
Near character position 32
```

The *load* statement must be explicitly specified to be a transaction, and this is done by using the *begin work* statement before the *load* statement. If the load statement is to be committed to the database, the *commit work* statement must be executed afterwards, as in

```
cat ld.sql
begin work;
load from "mytable.d"
insert into mytable;
commit work
isql mydb ld

Started transaction.

3 row(s) loaded.

Data committed.
```

The following query displays a count of the number of rows in the table:

```
cat count.sql
select count(*) how_many from mytable
{Count the number of rows in the table}
```

```
isql mydb count

   how_many

          3

1 row(s) retrieved.
```

If the SQL script with the *load* statement is modified to

```
begin work;
load from "mytable.d"
insert into mytable;
rollback work
```

and executed on the mydb database, the following messages are displayed:

```
Started transaction.

3 row(s) loaded.

Transaction rolled back.
```

The query to count the number of rows in the database reports the following:

```
   how_many

          3
1 row(s) retrieved.
```

Indeed, after the *rollback work* statement is executed, the effect of the *load* statement is reversed. The *rollback work* statement gives the user the control to abort the transaction.

5.10.1.1 Rolling a Database

The status of a corrupted database can be restored from a backup. If the database has been updated since the backup was taken, then all the transactions will ordinarily be lost. The transaction log can be used to bring the database up-to-date. A new transaction log file must be started before a backup of the database is taken, as done here:

```
cat start.sql
start database florist with log in "/u/bk/chaps/newlog.d"
isql - start
Database started.
find florist.dbs -print|cpio -oBc > /dev/rfp021
100 blocks
```

If the *load* statement is executed again, then the database is updated to have three more records to give a total of six records. If the database is corrupted at this point, then the new transactions can be saved by first restoring the old copy of the database and then by running the *rollforward database* SQL statement. The following session indicates the sequence of commands executed:

```
isql mydb ld

Started transaction.

3 row(s) loaded.

Data committed.
isql mydb count
   how_many

          6

1 row(s) retrieved.
Database is corrupted at this point!!
cpio -iBcdu < /dev/rfp021
100 blocks
isql mydb count

   how_many

          3
1 row(s) retrieved.
cat roll.sql
rollforward database florist
```

```
isql - roll

Database rolled forward.

isql mydb count
   how_many

          6

1 row(s) retrieved.
```

Clearly, the database is now up to date. The backup copy and the transaction log file are both required so that the database restore process is guaranteed. After the database is restored, it must be closed using the *close database* statement which brings it out of exclusive mode. Exclusive mode is discussed later.

5.11 Audit Trail Management

Databases can be restored from backups and transaction log files. Any changes to the database contents are recorded in the transaction log, which results in additional overheads incurred. If only a selected group of tables is critical, then maintaining a transaction log of updates only to these tables should be possible. The audit trail mechanism is provided for this purpose. An audit trail, sometimes referred to as a journal file, is a log of changes made to a table. It has a preupdate and a postupdate image of each transaction that was applied to the table since the audit trail was initiated. There may, therefore, be several audit trails associated with a database, but there can be only one current transaction log file.

To initiate an audit trail on a table, the *create audit* statement can be used. The following SQL statement can be used to create an audit trail file on table mytable in the database mydb.

```
create audit trail for mytable in "/u/bk/chaps/myaudit.d"
```

After the audit trail file is initiated, a backup of the table must be taken. The table should not be updated before the backup is completed. If the table is corrupted at a later time, the backup must be restored and a *recover table* statement must be run. The statement will restore the table up to the last transaction logged in the audit trail file for the table. For example, the following SQL statement can be executed to recover the table mytable:

```
recover table mytable
```

An audit trail can be removed by use of the *drop audit* statement. Here is an example:

```
drop audit for mytable
```

Audit files should be stored on a different physical device than the one on which the database itself is stored. This is required so that any damage to a disk on which the table is stored will not also destroy the audit trail file.

5.12 Using the Locking Mechanism

To ensure the integrity of a database in a multiuser environment, it is necessary to ensure that the final state of the database will be the same irrespective of whether the two transactions are executed concurrently or sequentially.

Locking exists at different levels. At the highest level, the entire database can be locked. At the next level, tables in the database can be locked. Finally, at the lowest level some rows in the database can also be locked. Field level locking is not supported by INFORMIX SQL. The entire database can be locked by opening the database in the exclusive mode. For example, the following SQL statement opens the database florist in exclusive mode:

```
database florist exclusive
```

The opened database remains inaccessible to other users unless a *close database* statement is issued. An entire table can be locked and made totally inaccessible by using the *lock table* statement, as in

```
begin work;
lock table mytable in exclusive mode;
SQL update statements
commit work
```

A table can be made accessible only for reading by use of the *share* mode as in

```
lock table mytable in share mode;
```

In the absence of the *lock table* statement, only those rows which are affected by the SQL statements are locked. If multiple rows are affected by the SQL statement, then a lock is required for each row to be locked. There may be a limitation on the number of locks available. To avoid this problem, the user should lock the entire table if the number of rows to be locked is large. The locked table can be unlocked by use of the *unlock table* statement. If the database has a transaction log, then the *commit work* statement also unlocks all locked records.

The *set lock mode to wait* SQL statement can be used to determine if subsequent SQL statements should wait for a locked record or return an error condition. The default is to return with an error condition. The *to not wait* option can be used to toggle back to the default action.

5.13 Writing Efficient SQL Queries

The process of writing SQL statements to satisfy a user request is nondeterministic. Several equivalent SQL statements can be written to have the same end result. Query optimization can be done by query transformation and by selection of the best access method available for the execution of the transformed query. Query transformation involves the syntactical transformation of queries to produce the same end result. A query, in its transformed or original form, requires that it be decomposed into smaller subqueries. Once decomposed, it can be optimized further by selection of the best method available to access the data to execute it.

Ideally, a DBMS must have a built-in query optimizer which does the required optimization irrespective of the syntax of the query. Unfortunately, all DBMS currently available fall short of this desired feature, leaving the user with the task of writing not only correct queries but also efficient queries. Consider the following query:

```
select table1.col1, table1.col2, table2.col1, table2.col2
       from table1, table2
where
       table1.col1 = table2.col1
    and table1.col2 = table2.col2
    and table1.col1 > 12
```

This query can be executed in several ways. It requires two operations: select and join. The sequence in which these two operations are executed is important. Join is a very expensive operation, as discussed earlier. The input to this operation should therefore be minimized. The select operation can be performed prior to the join to minimize the number of tuples in table1. The query optimizer must select the sequence appropriately. Unfortunately, most DBMS depend on the sequence in which the query is written. For example, if the query under consideration is rewritten as

```
select table1.col1, table1.col2, table2.col1, table2.col2
       from table1, table2
where
        table1.col1 > 12
    and table1.col1 = table2.col1
    and table1.col2 = table2.col2
```

then the query execution time should not change.

Another problem associated with query optimization is the use of an index. Query processors must be able to use indexes even if all the components of the index are not used in the query. Also, the performance of the query must not change by the interchanging of the variable operands of a relational operator. For example, the query under consideration must take the same time, even if it is rewritten as

```
select table1.col1, table1.col2, table2.col1, table2.col2
       from table1, table2
where
        table1.col1 > 12
    and table2.col1 = table1.col1
    and table2.col2 = table1.col2
```

This argument is based on the assumption that the query optimizer can judiciously decide the index to be used in executing the join operation. If an index is not present, the query optimizer must select the appropriate columns on which a temporary index can be built to reduce the query execution time, as is done in INFORMIX. This feature is called auto-indexing. Unfortunately, knowledge of SQL alone is not enough for the user to be able to write efficient queries. Users should also be aware of the idiosyncrasies associated with the query processor so that they can write efficient queries. Fortunately, INFORMIX provides a fairly reliable query optimizer.

5.14 Interaction with the UNIX File System

When a database is created, INFORMIX creates a directory for that database. The directory name is derived from the database name by being suffixed with a *.dbs*. This directory is used to store all the tables and the indexes of the database. In addition, this directory is used to store tables which maintain information about the database definition, permissions, etc. This set of tables is called the system catalog and consists of the following tables:

Table	**Contents**
systables	Describes the tables in the database
syscolumns	Describes the columns in each table
sysindexes	Describes the indexes on each table
systabauth	Describes the table-level privileges
syscolauth	Describes the column-level privileges
sysdepend	Describes the dependency between tables and views
syssynonyms	Maintains the information about different synonyms for tables
sysusers	Maintains information about database-level privileges
sysviews	Maintains information about how views are defined

It is possible to store part of the database outside the *.dbs* directory by use of the *create table* statement with the *in "pathname"* clause, as in

```
create table mytable2
(
mycol   integer
) in "/u/bk/mytable2"
```

which creates the required table in the directory /u/bk. The file name is used as a prefix by INFORMIX to create the required files.

Storing data for different tables in separate files improves the availability of the database. If a file representing a table is corrupted, the remaining tables in the database may still be accessible. Some DBMS store the entire database in one single file, resulting in a complicated data structure which is difficult to "repair" in the event of a system crash.

5.15 INFORMIX Utilities

There are several INFORMIX-SQL commands which can be executed as UNIX commands. The *isql* command was used to execute SQL statements. Two other commands are explained in this section. The *dbload* command is used to load data stored in UNIX flat files into INFORMIX tables. It is much more flexible than the SQL statement *load.* The *dbschema* utility generates a SQL script which can be executed to recreate the database schema.

5.15.1 Dbload

The *dbload* utility is far superior to the SQL *load* statement for bulk loading of data into the database. Its power lies in its ability to load data from different files into multiple tables. It also provides better control over records which cannot be loaded. It provides good transaction management capabilities, the ability to handle records with fixed length fields, a mechanism to handle NULL values, and a feature to load constant values in one or more fields. The basic syntax of *dbload* is

dbload -d *database-name* **-c** *command-file* **-l** *errlog*

Additional options are also available. *Database-name* refers to the name of the database in which the data is to be loaded. *Command-file* is the name of the file in which instructions to *dbload* are stored. *Errlog* refers to the name of the file in which all error messages are to be stored.

The *command-file* is made up of two types of statements. First, statements are used to specify the format of the data in the various files and to label fields in the data file. Second, the SQL statement *insert into* is used to load the data into the specified fields of a table. Consider a simple flat file called custf.d:

```
cat custf.d
012345678901234567890123456789012345678901234567890123456789012345678901234
2012428055Doe       John Apt. 2          782 Clifton Ave.Shalantown    NJ07104
8000011212Smith     Mike 32 Palisade Ave.NA                Ringwood    NJ07456
2011212451McAlisterTodd 44 Park Ave.     NA                Plainfield  NJ07060
2013211234Parab     Umesh55 Slick St.    NA                Midland ParkNJ07432
2014561412Dev       Kapil55 Cricket DriveNA                Ocean       NJ07712
```

Clearly, it is made up of rows with fixed length fields. Here is a *dbload* description of the file followed by an *insert into* statement to load the data in the customers table defined in Section 5.2.2:

```
cat mydb.com
file custf.d (
        field1      1  - 10,
        field2      11 - 19,
        field3      20 - 24,
        field4      25 - 40,
        field5      41 - 56,
        field6      57 - 68,
        field7      69 - 70,
        field8      71 - 75
        );
insert into customers
```

The field names *field1*, *field2*, etc., are user selected. The *dbload* command to do the required loading is

```
dbload -d florist -c mydb.com -l /tmp/err.log
```

which when executed will display the number of rows loaded. The first row in the datafile is actually a header record. The *-i* option can be used to specify the number of records in the input data file to be skipped before loading can start. The first record in the file custf.d can be prevented from being loaded by modification of the *dbload* command line as follows:

```
dbload -d florist -c mydb.com -l /tmp/errlog -i 1
```

Field5 has several rows with the value *NA*. If the user has used this string constant to be interpreted as a "not available" value then it can be loaded as a NULL-valued field in the table by modification of the entry for the field labeled *field* as

```
        field5      41 - 56 null="NA              ",
```

Thus far, the field labels were not used in the *insert into* statements. If the state code was to be uniformly loaded as *NJ* irrespective of the data in the file and if the address lines to be loaded were to be interchanged, then the command file would have to be modified to make use of the field labels, as shown here:

```
file custf.d (
        field1      1  - 10,
        field2      11 - 19,
        field3      20 - 24,
        field4      25 - 40,
        field5      41 - 56 null="NA               ",
        field6      57 - 68,
        field7      69 - 70,
        field8      71 - 75
        );
insert into customers
        values(field1,field2,field3,field5,field4,field6,"NJ",field8);
```

The *values* clause is used here because the sequence of the columns as defined in the system catalog definition for the customers table is not the same as the corresponding data in the custf.d file. Also, a constant string of *NJ* was used to load all the rows with the same value for the state code field. The actual value of the data in *field7* in the input data file becomes irrelevant.

Fields defined in the *dbload* statement can be overlapping. For example, the following command file is valid:

```
file custf.d (
        field1      1  - 5: 3-7,
        field2      11 - 13:1-5,
        field3      71 - 75
        );
insert into customers
        (c_no,c_lname,c_addr1);
```

The first field is made up of 9 characters, the second field has 8 characters, and the third field has 5 characters. Character positions 3 to 5 are used twice in *field1* and once in *field2*. In addition, characters from position 1 to 5 are used in *field1* and *field2*. If the *dbload* command is executed with this command file on the mydb database, the values of the three fields loaded from the flat file are as shown below:

```
c_no       c_lname            c_addr1

0123423456 01201234           01234
3012412428 Doe30124           07104
3000000011 Smi30000           07456
3011211212 McA30112           07060
3013213211 Par30132           07432
3014514561 Dev30145           07712
```

Dbload can also be used to load data from a flat file with variable length fields delimited by a field separator. The command file which describes the format of the input data has to be changed accordingly. The format specification statement

```
file "var.d" delimiter ":" 3
```

can be used to describe a flat file named var.d with fields delimited by a colon (:) character and with each record having 3 fields.

5.15.1.1 Other Options

Dbload comes equipped with a host of options. The *-c*, *-d*, *-l*, and *-i* options were used earlier. Several other options are also available. The *-n* option is used to display a message after the specified number of rows are loaded or committed (for database with transactions) to the database. The default is 100 rows. This option is very useful for monitoring the status of the load process. *Dbload* aborts after 10 bad rows are encountered in the input. This number can be changed by use of the *-e* options. If this number is reached, the uncommitted records are committed automatically before *dbload* aborts the loading process. This action can be changed by use of the *-p* option which prompts the user for confirmation to commit the records read. Finally, the *-s* option can be used to check the command file for errors in syntax. Consider a table created by the following SQL script:

```
create table ex_table
(
first_col      integer,
second_col     integer
)
```

Let mydata.d be a UNIX flat file with the following information:

```
cat mydata.d
12|33
14|55
12313|1212
a12|121
17|109
```

This data can be loaded into the table ex_table by use of the following command file:

```
cat mycom
file "mydata.d" delimiter "|" 2;
insert into ex_table;
```

The following *dbload* command line can be used to initiate the loading process:

```
dbload -p -e 0 -n 2 -d florist -c t.com -l /tmp/err.log
Copyright messages...
2 Row(s) loaded so far to table ex_table.

In insert statement number 1 of raw data file mydata.d.
Row number 4 is bad.

a12|121

Character to numeric conversion error


More than 0 bad rows have been encountered.

Do you wish to rollback to last commit (Y or N): N
```

The *-e 0* option is used here to abort the loading process when a bad record is encountered in the input. The *-n* option is used to specify that records be committed in sets of 2. The *-p* option generates the prompt

```
Do you wish to rollback to last commit (Y or N): N
```

The **N** response terminates the loading process without committing the last uncommitted good record:

```
12313|1212
```

A **Y** response would have forced this record to be committed to the database.

5.15.2 Dbschema

The *dbschema* utility is used to generate an SQL script to create INFORMIX tables, indexes, and views which can duplicate the specified database schema. The *-d* option is used to specify the database name. Several other options are also available. The *-t* option can be used to generate an SQL script to create only a specified table and associated indexes. It can also be used to generate SQL statements to create a view. Here is a *dbschema* command line to generate the SQL *create* statement for the customers table in the florist database.

```
dbschema -t customers -d florist
Copyright message
{bk is owner of table customers}
create table customers
    (
     c_no char(10),
     c_lname char(20),
     c_fname char(20),
     c_addr1 char(20),
     c_addr2 char(20),
     c_town char(20),
     c_state char(2),
     c_zip char(5)
    );
{bk is owner of index c_index2}
create distinct index c_index1 on customers(c_fname, c_lname);
create index c_index2 on customers (c_no);
revoke all on customers from public;
```

The *-p* option can be used to generate SQL statements to grant permissions to the specified user. For example, the command

```
dbschema -p bk -t customers -d florist
```

will also generate the following SQL statement which indicates the permission to the specified user on the table:

```
grant dba to bk;
```

The *-s* option can be used to generate SQL *create synonym* statements for the specified user. *Dbschema* outputs the SQL statements to *stdout*. This output can be saved in a file either by redirection of the output or by use of the *-o* option with a file name in which the output is to be saved.

6 System Development with ISQL

In Chapter 5, the SQL language was used to create a database and to manipulate its contents. Though SQL is a very powerful language it does not have capabilities to develop a complete user-friendly system. INFORMIX offers the *isql* package, often referred to as INFORMIX-SQL, which has several components which interact with one another to provide a powerful environment for developing user-friendly systems. One of its components, the query processor, was used in the last chapter for processing SQL queries. This chapter discusses the other components of the INFORMIX-SQL package. They are the report writer, the forms manager, and the menu interface. These components are first discussed separately. The latter part of the chapter shows how these components can be made to interact with one another.

6.1 Components of Isql

Isql has the following components:

- Query processor

- Report writer
- Forms manager
- User menus interface
- Miscellaneous utilities

In addition to interacting with one another, these tools also use tables in the system catalog for their processing. The query processor was discussed in the previous chapter, the other components are discussed below.

6.2 The Report Writer

The SQL query processor, which was discussed in the previous chapter, is able to manipulate the contents of a database, including complex retrieval operations. The user has little or no control over the format of the data retrieved from the database with SQL statements. For most applications, control on the output format is a desirable feature. Of course, it is possible to write C programs to format the retrieved data, but that defies the very purpose of using a DBMS. The report writer tool is provided for this purpose. Actually, it goes a step further. It provides a set of additional statements and a programming environment not available in SQL that can be used to compute additional information to be reported. It needs two types of specifications. One is used to specify the data to be extracted and the other is used to indicate the format in which this retrieved data, possibly after some computation, is to be reported.

In INFORMIX the report writer is called *ace* and the two types of specifications have to be given in one single file called the report specification file. The report specification file has to be compiled using a compiler provided by the *isql* package. If the compilation is successful, then the compiled code can be executed with the use of another tool to generate the required report.

There are two methods of performing the compilation and the execution. The first method is through the INFORMIX menu interface. The second method is via UNIX-level commands. The INFORMIX menu interface will be discussed later. The rest of this section uses UNIX-level commands used to compile and run report specifications.

6.2.1 Compiling and Running Reports

A report specification file can be created using an editor such as *vi*. This file must be suffixed with the extension *.ace*. Once created, this file can be compiled using the *saceprep* command. If the compiled file has an error, a file suffixed with the extension *.err* is created; otherwise a compiled report file suffixed with the extension *.arc* is created. If errors are detected, the original report source file will have to be edited to eliminate these errors. Several iterations may be necessary to get successful compilation. Once the report specification file is compiled successfully, it can be executed using the *sacego* command. Figure 6.1 shows the process of compiling and generating reports.

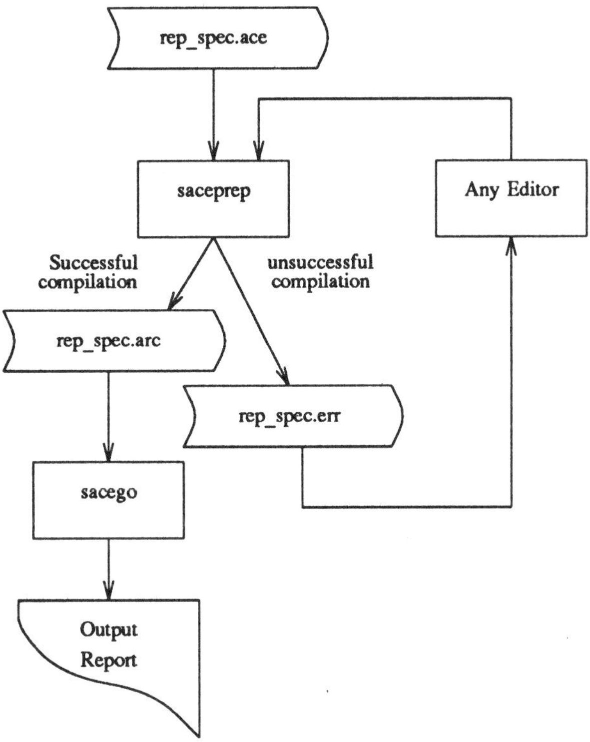

Figure 6.1 Report Generation Process

6.2.2 Getting Started

In this chapter, once again, the sample florist database will be used in all the examples. Report generation does not involve any updates to the database. The customers database is assumed to be loaded with 10 records and the orders database with 11 records. The contents of these records is shown in Section 5.7.1.

A report specification file may contain up to six sections. Some of these sections are mandatory, while others are optional. The mandatory sections are:

- Database section: This section is used to specify the name of the database from which data has to be extracted and reported.
- Select section: This section is used to specify an SQL *select* statement to be used to extract the required data from the database.
- Format section: This is the last section of a report writer and is made of several subsections. Each subsection specifies how the data extracted by use of the *select* statement is to be reported. Subsections in the format section are also called control blocks.

The following is a simple report specification file which generates a report of customer names in a default format:

```
cat repl.ace
database
        florist
end
select c_no, c_fname, c_lname
        from customers
end
format
        every row
end
```

This report specification file can be compiled as shown below:

```
saceprep repl.ace
Copyright & Version No. messages
The file "repl.ace" will now be compiled.

The compilation was successful.  The file that holds
the ACE Report Control tables, "repl.arc", has been created.
```

Once compiled, the *.arc* file can be executed using *sacego* as shown below:

```
sacego rep1
Copyright & Version No. messages
The reading of the database will now begin.

Select statement number 1 will now be processed.

The reading of the database has finished.

     c_no       c_fname             c_lname

     2012428055 John                Doe
     8000011212 Mike                Smith
     2011212451 Todd                McAlister
     2013211234 Umesh               Parab
     2014561412 Kapil               Dev
     2013211341 Ian                 Botham
     2014311211 Dennis              Lillee
     2018911211 Maria               Roberts
     2016667777 Jennifer            Marshal
     6091212121 Richard             Hadlee
```

The *-s* option can be used with *saceprep* and *sacego* to suppress unimportant messages. The formatting statement *every row* is used to print the retrieved columns in a default format. The user can specify the format explicitly using formatting statements as shown below:

```
database
        florist
end
select * from customers
end
format
 on every row
        print c_lname clipped, ", ", c_fname
        print c_addr1
        print c_addr2
        print c_town clipped,", ", c_state, " ", c_zip
        print "===================================="
        skip 2 lines
end
```

When compiled and run, the report generated is

```
Doe, John
Apt. 2
782 Clifton Ave.
Shalantown, NJ 07104
=====================================



Smith, Mike
32 Palisade Ave.

Ringwood, NJ 07456
=====================================



McAlister, Todd
44 Park Ave.

Plainfield, NJ 07060
=====================================



Parab, Umesh
55 Slick St.

Midland Park, NJ 07432
=====================================
    .
    .
    .
```

The formatting statements are self-explanatory. *On every row* is a subsection within the *format* section. Statements associated with this subsection are executed after every selected row is read. A *print* statement prints the specified column, constant, or the value of an expression and generates a new line. The new line can be suppressed by termination of the *print* statement by a semicolon (;). Character fields are printed in a width equal to that of the corresponding column definition. The *clipped* clause can be used with character strings to suppress the printing of trailing blanks. In the generated report there is a blank line after the first address line. This blank line is printed as a result of a NULL value in the *c_addr2* field. It can be suppressed by insertion of the following *if* statement before the statement to print the *c_addr2* field:

```
if c_addr2 is not null then
```

The *if* statement also has an optional *else* segment. Multiple statements can be associated with an *if* or an *else* when the statements are put in a block starting with a *begin* and terminating by an *end*.

6.2.3 The Define Section

If variables are required to compute intermediate results, then these variables can be declared in the *define* section. The SQL data type of the variable to be declared must also be specified. Here is a sample *define* section:

```
define
        variable prev_c_no       char(10)
        variable start          integer
        variable t_o_amt         money
end
```

In the *format* section, values can be assigned to these variables with the *let* statement. For example, a value of 5 can be assigned to the *start* variable as follows:

```
let start = 5
```

The value assigned to the variable can be an expression. The expression is evaluated and the result assigned to the variable.

6.2.4 Report/Page Headers and Footers

A report header is the segment of the report which is printed at the very beginning of the report, and a report footer is one which is printed at the very end. There are two subsections in the format section which can be used to print these segments. The statements associated with the *first page header* subsection in the format section can be used to print report headings. This subsection can also be used to initialize variables defined in the *define* section. Similarly, the *on last row* subsection can be used to print report summary information or a banner indicating end of report.

The *page header* and the *page trailer* subsections can be used to print header lines, report title, page number, date, etc., at the top or bottom of any page.

The *print* statement can be made to start printing from any column by use of the form:

```
print column expr, data_item
```

which will evaluate the value of the expression or constant *expr* and print the *data_item* starting from a column specified by the expression.

Numeric and *date* fields, or variables, can be printed using a format string. Several formatting characters are available. Some of the important formatting characters for numeric fields are

*	Substitute blank characters by this character.
&	Substitute blank character by a zero (0) character.
#	This character can be used to specify the maximum width of the field.
<	This character can be used to print a number left justified.
,	This character is used to print commas in numeric strings. It is printed as a literal only if there is a digit to its left.
$	This character is used to print a floating dollar ($) sign. If several "$" characters are used in the string then only a single "$" will be printed just before the number.

Date fields can be formatted by use of the following formatting characters:

dd	Print day of the month as a 2-digit integer
ddd	Print day of the week as a 3-letter abbreviation; e.g., *Sun* for Sunday
mm	Print month as a 2-digit integer
mmm	Print month as a 3-letter abbreviation; e.g., *Jan* for January
yy	Print year as a 2-digit number
yyyy	Print year as a 4-digit number

Lines can be skipped in a report by use of the statement:

```
skip no lines
```

where *no* is an integer constant. A new page can be forced by use of the statement:

```
skip to top of page
```

Here is a report specification file which prints information about each order and a summary line for each customer:

```
database
  florist
end
define
  variable prev_c_no      char(10)
  variable start          integer
  variable st_o_amt       money
  variable st_o_del_chg   money
  variable st_o_paid      money
end
select * from orders
        order by c_no
end
format
 page header
  skip 2 lines
  print column 11, "CUST. NO",
        column 25, "ORD. AMT",
        column 40, "DEL. CHG.",
        column 55, "AMT. PAID"
  print column 11, "========",
        column 25, "========",
        column 40, "=========",
        column 55, "========="
  skip 2 lines
 on every row
  if start = 0 then
  begin
```

```
      let start = 1
      let prev_c_no = c_no
    end
    if prev_c_no != c_no then
      begin
        print "===================="
        print "Total for ", column 11, prev_c_no,
                                   column 25, st_o_amt   using "$$$$.$$",
              column 40, st_o_del_chg using "$$$$.$$",
              column 55, st_o_paid  using "$$$$.$$"
        print "===================="
        let st_o_amt = 0
        let st_o_del_chg = 0
        let st_o_paid = 0
        let prev_c_no = c_no
      end
    print   column 11 , c_no clipped,
      column 25, o_amt using "$$$$.$$",
            column 40, o_del_chg using "$$$$.$$",
      column 55, o_paid using "$$$$.$$"
    let st_o_amt       = st_o_amt + o_amt
    let st_o_del_chg   = st_o_del_chg + o_del_chg
    let st_o_paid      = st_o_paid + o_paid
  on last row
    print "===================="
     print "Total for ", column 11, prev_c_no,
        column 25, st_o_amt   using "$$$$.$$",
        column 40, st_o_del_chg using "$$$$.$$",
        column 55, st_o_paid  using "$$$$.$$"
    print "===================="
    skip 5 lines
    print "END OF REPORT"
  end
```

When compiled and run, the report generated is

```
              CUST. NO       ORD. AMT        DEL. CHG.       AMT. PAID
              ========       ========        =========       =========


              2012428055      $45.70           $5.00          $15.00
              2012428055      $50.00          $15.00          $20.00
```

```
====================
Total for 2012428055      $95.70          $20.00          $35.00
====================
          2013211234     $872.00           $7.00         $400.00
          2013211234      $70.00           $7.00            $.00
====================
Total for 2013211234     $942.00          $14.00         $400.00
====================
          2013211341      $25.00           $6.00          $55.00
====================
Total for 2013211341      $25.00           $6.00          $55.00
====================
          2016667777      $75.00           $4.00          $85.00
====================
Total for 2016667777      $75.00           $4.00          $85.00
====================
          2018911211      $55.00           $3.00          $75.00
====================
Total for 2018911211      $55.00           $3.00          $75.00
====================
          2123211411     $100.00           $5.00          $90.00
====================
Total for 2123211411     $100.00           $5.00          $90.00
====================
          6091212121      $12.00           $5.00         $100.00
          6091212121      $50.00           $2.00          $10.00
          6091212121      $70.00           $2.00          $10.00
====================
Total for 6091212121     $132.00           $9.00         $120.00
====================



END OF REPORT
```

In this report, each selected record is printed. The control variable here is *c_no*, on which the incoming data is sorted. If the value of this field changes, a summary line is printed. A running total of the three numeric fields is maintained in the variables *st_o_amt*, *st_o_del_chg*, and *st_o_paid*. There is no way to detect end of input in the *for every row* subsection; therefore, the summary line for the last set of records is printed in the *on last row* subsection. The *print* statements use column nos. to align the columns.

6.2.5 Processing Sorted Records

When the incoming records from the *select* statement are sorted on one or more fields, then each set of records with the same value for the sort field can be looked at as a group. The report writer provides subsections which can be used to process groups of records. These subsections are

`after group of` *list-of-fields*
and
`before group of` *list-of-fields*

List-of-fields refers to a comma separated list of fields used in the *order by* clause of the *select* statement. Fields used in the statements associated with the *after group of* subsection have the old values of the group fields. Similarly, fields used in the statements associated with the *before group of* subsection have the new values of the group fields. Several aggregates can be used in statements associated with an *after group of* subsection. These include *count*, *total*, *average*, *min*, and *max*. The previous report specification file can be simplified by use of these subsections and aggregates. Here is a rewrite of the same specification file:

```
database
  florist
end
select * from orders
        order by c_no
end
format
 page header
  skip 2 lines
  print column 11, "CUST. NO",
        column 25, "ORD. AMT",
        column 40, "DEL. CHG.",
        column 55, "AMT. PAID"
  print column 11, "========",
        column 25, "========",
        column 40, "=========",
        column 55, "========="
  skip 2 lines
```

```
after group of c_no
   print "===================="
   print "Total for ",
            column 11, c_no,
            column 25, group total of o_amt    using "$$$$.$$",
            column 40, group total of o_del_chg using "$$$$.$$",
            column 55, group total of o_paid   using "$$$$.$$"
      print "===================="
on every row
   print   column 11 , c_no clipped,
     column 25, o_amt using "$$$$.$$",
     column 40, o_del_chg using "$$$$.$$",
     column 55, o_paid using "$$$$.$$"
on last row
   skip 5 lines
   print "END OF REPORT"
end
```

The *group total of* aggregate prints only the total of the specified fields for the records in the group. This eliminates the need to declare intermediate variables to keep track of this total. Also, the last group is not lost. When end of input is detected, statements associated with the *after group of* subsection are executed. While an aggregate is printed, if *group* is omitted, then a total for all the values in that field for all the selected rows is printed. This is useful for printing the grand total in the *on last row* section. Only summary information can be printed by eliminating the *on every row* subsection. The following report specification file generates a report of customer no., customer name, total number of orders, date of last order, and total order amount:

```
database
  florist
end
select customers.c_no, c_fname, c_lname, o_amt, o_date
  from orders, customers
  where customers.c_no = orders.c_no
  order by c_no
end
format
 page header
  skip 2 lines
  print column 1, "CUST. NO",
        column 13, "NAME",
```

```
            column 34, "ORDERS",
            column 42, "LAST DATE",
            column 54, "AVG. AMT"
      print column 1, "========",
            column 13, "====",
            column 34, "======",
            column 42, "=========",
            column 54, "========"
      skip 2 lines
    after group of c_no
      print column 1, c_no,
            column 13, c_fname clipped, " ", c_lname clipped,
            column 34, group count using "###",
            column 42, group max   of o_date using "mm/dd/yy",
            column 54, group total of o_amt  using "$$$$.$$"
end
```

It is necessary to specify the maximum field width to print the count field. In the absence of a specified maximum field width, the default field width will be assumed. To get the date of the last order, use the *max* aggregate on the *o_date* field. It is possible to do this because the date is stored as a long integer. When compiled and run, the output is

```
CUST. NO    NAME                    ORDERS  LAST DATE   AVG. AMT
========    ====                    ======  =========   ========


2012428055  John Doe                  2     02/12/88      $95.70
2013211234  Umesh Parab               2     01/24/88     $942.00
2013211341  Ian Botham                1     02/12/88      $25.00
2016667777  Jennifer Marshal          1     03/27/88      $75.00
2018911211  Maria Roberts             1     02/12/88      $55.00
6091212121  Richard Hadlee            3     06/19/88     $132.00
```

If a column name appears in two tables, a table name may be required to qualify the column name and make it unique. A reference to a column name along with a table name cannot be used in the *after group of* clause. Display labels can be used to resolve this problem. Here is another example of a report specification file which retrieves customer name and address from the customers table and the order information from the orders table and prints the report in a nontabular format:

```
database
  florist
end
select *, customers.c_no cno
  from orders, customers
  where customers.c_no = orders.c_no
  order by cno
end
format
   before group of cno
     print column 1, c_fname clipped, " ", c_lname
     print column 1, c_addr1
     if c_addr2 is not null then
       print column 1, c_addr2
     print column 1, c_town clipped, " ", c_state," ", c_zip
     print column 1, "==========="
     print column 1, "ORDER INFO:"
     print column 1, "==========="
  on every row
     print column 1, "Order Amt: ", o_amt using "$$$$.$$",
           column 21, "Order Date: ", o_date using "mm/dd/yy",
           column 43, "Description: ", o_desc clipped
  after group of cno
     skip 1 line
     print column 30, "***** # *****"
     skip 1 line
end
```

Note the use of the display label "cno" in the *select* statement and later in the *group by* clauses. The output report generated by this specification file is

```
John Doe
Apt. 2
782 Clifton Ave.
Shalantown NJ 07104
===========
ORDER INFO:
===========
Order Amt:  $45.70  Order Date: 12/12/87  Description: A dozen roses
Order Amt:  $50.00  Order Date: 02/12/88  Description: Centerpiece

                             ***** # *****
```

```
Umesh Parab
55 Slick St.
Midland Park NJ 07432
===========
ORDER INFO:
===========
Order Amt: $872.00  Order Date: 01/24/88  Description: Wedding Arrang.
Order Amt:  $70.00  Order Date: 01/24/88  Description: Birthday Arrang

                              ***** # *****
          .
          .
          .
```

6.2.6 Looping Statements

The report writer provides several other statements for additional computation and flexibility. The *for* and *while* statements provide a looping mechanism. The syntax of the *while* statement is

```
while expr do
  statement
```

The *expr* expression is evaluated; if it is true, then the loop continues and executes the associated statement. This statement can be a compound statement starting with a *BEGIN* and ending with an *END*. The loop exits when the expression is evaluated as false.

The syntax of the *for* statement is

```
for var = expr1 to expr2 step expr3
        do statement
```

In each iteration the statement is executed and the value of the loop control variable incremented. When this value is equal to the value evaluated from expression *expr2*, the loop terminates. By default the loop control variable is incremented by 1 in each iteration. The *step expr3* clause can be optionally used to specify any other increment value.

A line can be drawn in a report, by use of the *for* statement, as in

```
for var1=1 to 25  do
       print "*";
print
```

which will generate a line with 25 asterisks. The second *print* statement is used here to force a new line character. The semicolon terminating the *print* statement in the *for* loop suppresses the printing of the newline character. The equivalent *while* statement would be

```
let var1 = 0
while var1 != 25 do
   begin
       print "*";
       let var1 = var1 + 1
   end
print
```

6.2.7 Other Miscellaneous Statements

The report writer also provides several other statements. The *need* statement is used to skip to a new page if a specified number of lines cannot fit into the remaining lines of the page. This statement is used to prevent the breaking of grouped information, such as address lines, across a page. It is similar to the *.ne* command of *troff*. The *pause* statement suspends the display of the report until the user enters the "Return" key. If the report is directed to a printer or a file, then this statement has no effect. An external file can be included in a report at any stage by use of the statement

```
print file "filename"
```

where *filename* is the name of any UNIX file to be included in the report. This statement can be used to generate reports where a part of the report, which is not dependent on the database contents, may change. This part can be kept in an external text file and included dynamically at run time. This eliminates the need to recompile the report specification file. It also reduces its size.

6.2.8 The Output Section

The optional *output* section is used to direct the output of a report file to a program, printer, or file. In addition, the page length, margins, and width can also be specified here.

The *left margin* statement sets the left margin for the report. For example, the statement

```
left margin 10
```

sets the left margin to 10. The default left margin is 5. The *right margin* statement sets the right margin for the report. The default right margin is 132 characters. Similarly, the top margin and the bottom margin can be set by using the *top margin* and the *bottom margin* commands, respectively. The default for both is 3 lines. The *page length* command sets the number of lines on each page. The default page length is 66 lines. The *report to* statement is used to direct the output of the report to a file, printer, or program. This is particularly useful if the output has to be passed through some preprocessor before it is sent to the printer. For example, a report specification file can be written to generate a *troff* file. This file will have to be piped through *troff* and a postprocessor before it is given to the line spooler. This can be easily handled by use of the *report to* statement, as in

```
report to "troff.sh"
```

where *troff.sh* is a shell script which pipes the input file to *troff*, to its post-processors, and finally to the spooler. All these stages are transparent to the user running the report, who gets a high quality report from a typesetter/laser printer.

6.2.9 Passing Arguments

The flexibility of a program increases if arguments can be passed to it or if it can prompt for values to be assigned to different variables. The INFORMIX-SQL report writer has both these capabilities. Values can be passed to it on the command line at run time. It also has the capability to prompt for values to be assigned to variables. This feature enables the report writer to change the format and the contents of the report dynamically at run time.

Command-line arguments can be passed to the report writer at run time on the *acego* command line. The arguments specified on the command line are passed to the variable declared by use of a *param* statement in the *define* section. The declaration must also specify the mapping of the arguments and the variables. An integer is used in the declaration statements which specifies the position of the argument on the command line. For example, the declaration

```
define
        param [1] fname_arg char(21)
        param [2] num_arg   integer
end
```

can be used to specify that if *acego* is run with two arguments, then *fname_arg* will be assigned the first argument and *num_arg* will be assigned the second argument. The following report specification file generates the name and address of any customer whose number is specified on the *acego* command line:

```
cat rep8.ace
database
        florist
end
define
        param [1] arg_no char(21)
end
output
        left margin 15
end
select *
        from customers
        where c_no = $arg_no
end
format
        on every row
        print c_fname clipped, " ", c_lname clipped
        print c_addr1 clipped
        if c_addr2 is not null then
                print c_addr2 clipped
        print c_town clipped, ", ", c_state," ", c_zip
end
```

Once compiled, the *sacego* command can be invoked on this file as follows:

```
sacego -s rep8 2012428055
               John Doe
               Apt. 2
               782 Clifton Ave.
               Shalantown, NJ 07104
sacego -s rep8 2019061212
```

no output

```
sacego -s rep8

    The number of defined parameters in the ACE program does
not equal the number of actual parameters passed to ACEGO
on the command line.
See error number -9051.
```

Note that in the last invocation of *sacego* where an argument is not given, an error message is displayed to indicate the same. The mechanism of providing an argument on the command line was used here to assign a value to the variable *arg_no*. Note that this variable must be prefixed by a dollar sign ($) to distinguish it from a column name.

Another mechanism to pass a value to the report program is to prompt for a value to be entered at run time and then assign it to the specified variable. This mechanism needs another section, called the *input* section. This section can have one or more *prompt for* statements. The syntax of the *prompt for* statement is:

```
prompt for var-name using "prompt string"
```

where *var-name* is the name of any variable which must be declared in the define section. When the program executes this statement, the *prompt string* is displayed on the screen and the value entered is assigned to the specified variable. The report specification file shown above can be rewritten by use of the mechanism to prompt for the value for the same variable. Here is the rewritten report specification file:

```
database
   florist
end
define
   variable arg_no char(21)
end
```

```
input
   prompt for arg_no using "Please enter customer no.: "
end
output
   left margin 15
end
select *
   from customers
   where c_no = $arg_no
end
format
   on every row
     print c_fname clipped, " ", c_lname clipped
     print c_addr1 clipped
     if c_addr2 is not null then
        print c_addr2 clipped
     print c_town clipped, ", ", c_state," ", c_zip
end
```

When compiled and executed, this program will run as shown below:

```
sacego -s rep9
Please enter customer no.: 2012428055

               John Doe
               Apt. 2
               782 Clifton Ave.
               Shalantown, NJ 07104
```

6.2.10 Miscellaneous Functions

INFORMIX-SQL also offers several miscellaneous functions and expressions (key words) which can be used to report items which are frequently associated with reports. The *lineno* expression gives access to the line number that is currently being displayed. The *pageno* expression returns the value of the page number that is currently being printed. The *day* function returns the day of the month for the specified date. Similarly, the *month* function returns an integer corresponding to the month (1-12) for the specified date. The *date* expression returns today's date. Here is a sample *page header* section:

```
page header
  for i = 1 to 60 do
    print "=";
  print
  print column 1, "Page no.:", pageno using "###",
        column 40, "Date: ", date
  for i = 1 to 60 do
    print "=";
  skip 2 lines
```

When executed, the top of every page of the report would be printed as shown below:

```
============================================================
Page no.:  1                            Date: Mon Dec 19 1988
============================================================
```

6.2.11 Comments

Comments can be included in a report specification file by being enclosed within braces. For example, the line

```
{ This report prints the customer name and address }
```

is a valid comment line in the report specification file and will be ignored by *saceprep*.

6.2.12 Interfacing C Functions

Though ACE is a powerful report writer, there are several requirements which cannot be handled by it. In particular, it does not have a wide selection of functions. When ACE cannot handle the report requirements, interfacing modules written in the C language to the report file becomes necessary. The process of interfacing requires that the C function to be interfaced be written in a specified format. This program file must then be compiled and linked with the necessary library functions in order for a customized version of *sacego* to be created. A shell script, called *cace*, is provided to the programmer to do the compilation and linking. The object file thus created is the customized version of *sacego* and must be used instead of *sacego* whenever the user-defined function is used in the specification file. *Saceprep* can still be used for the compilation of the report specification file.

The functions to be defined in the C program must be declared in the report specification file in the *define* section. For example, the function *sqroot* can be defined as follows:

```
define
        function sqroot
end
```

Once declared, this function can be invoked in the report by use of the statement:

```
call sqroot(some_var)
```

which will ignore the return value of the function or a statement such as

```
let x = sqroot(some_var)
```

where the returned value is assigned to the variable *x*. The C function must use the typedef *valueptr* to declare all arguments passed and returned to and from the function. In addition, the function itself returns a value of type *valueptr*.

Several functions are available to convert a pointer to data of type *valueptr* to a specified C data type. Also, the return value must be of type *valueptr*. Several macros are available to perform the appropriate conversions from regular C data types, such as integers and floats, to a *valueptr* data type.

An array of structures, called *userfuncs*, must be initialized with an entry for each function declared in the program file. An entry for a function consists of two values. The first value is a string indicating the name of the function as used in the report specification file. The other value indicates the name that has been used to declare the function. These two entries provide a mechanism to declare a function with one name and invoke it in the report specification file by another name. Finally, an entry of *0,0* indicates the end of the function array. Consider the initialization shown below:

```
valueptr sqrt, cname;
struct ufunc userfuncs[] =
{
"sqroot", sqrt,
"repname", cname,
0,0
};
```

In this example, the functions are declared in the C file as *sqrt* and *cname*. However, they must be invoked as *sqroot* and *repname*, respectively, in the report specification file.

The ability to interact with C functions adds a new set of capabilities to the report writer. Consider the situation in which the generation of the report is to be restricted to a group of users. If this group is independent of any UNIX groups, then clearly the *chmod* mechanism cannot be used to restrict execution mode. The problem can be solved by entering in a file the login names of all users, who should be allowed to run the report. At run time, the customized version of *sacego* can get the login name of the user and compare it against the set of login names stored in the file. If the user's login name is not found, then the program can be forced to exit without generating the report. The file in which the login names of all valid users is stored can be under the control of the database administrator who can add and delete users without recompiling the report specification file.

The function to validate the user should be invoked in the *first page header* subsection. Here is a skeleton report specification file:

```
database
  florist
end
define
  function validate
  function abort
  variable whoami  char(15)
  variable i integer
end
select * from customers
end
format
first page header

  { Check if user is allowed to run this report }
  if validate(whoami) = 1 then
```

```
    begin
        print "No authorization to run this report "
        call abort()
    end
  else
       skip 1 line

       { Generate Report Banner }
  for i=1 to 50 do
    print "=";
  print
  print column 4, "Report Initiated by ",
        whoami clipped, " on ", date
  for i=1 to 50 do
    print "=";
  print
    .
    .
    .
on every row
  { process each row here }
    .
    .
    .
end
```

The following is the C program with the function *valid* which is used in the report specification file:

```
#include "ctools.h"
#include <stdio.h>

valueptr valid(),abort();

struct ufunc userfuncs[] =
{
  "validate", valid,
  "abort", abort,
  0, 0
};
valueptr abort()
{
```

```
    exit(1);
    }
    valueptr valid(user)
    valueptr user;
    {
      char fuser[9], *cuserid();
      int eof=2;

      FILE *fp;
      /* Open the file with valid login names */
      fp = fopen("repfile", "r");
      cuserid(user->v_charp);
      while (1)
      {
        eof=fscanf(fp,"%s",fuser);

        /* If EOF then not found, return 1 */
        if (eof == EOF)
            intreturn(1);

        /* If found return 0 */
        if (strcmp(fuser,user->v_charp)==0)
            intreturn(0);

      }
    }
```

The file *ctools.h* must be included, as it has all the definitions of the macros and the various typedefs. The macro ***intreturn*** returns a value of type ***valueptr*** for any specified integer value. Similar functions are available for returning values of other data types as indicated in the last column of Table 6.1.

The argument *user* is of type *valueptr*, the construct *user->v_charp* returns a pointer to string. Other constructs are available to return other data types from a *valueptr* data type. Functions are also available to perform the same task. Table 6.1 gives a map of the different constructs and functions which can be used for converting a *valueptr* type variable named *vptr* to the indicated numeric C data type. A more detailed list is available in the reference manual.

TABLE 6.1 Handling a Valueptr Data Type

C data type	Function	Alternative construct	Return function
int	toint	vptr->int	intreturn
long	tolong	vptr->v_long	lngreturn
double	todouble	vptr->v_double	dubreturn
float	tofloat	vptr->v_float	floreturn
struct decimal	todecimal	vptr->v_decimal	decreturn

6.3 Form Management

Forms provide a very user-friendly interface to any system. They can be used to retrieve and update a database without the user having to know a query language such as SQL. Clearly, end users cannot be expected to know SQL, and forms provide a more natural interface to the users by hiding the implementation intricacies and the idiosyncracies of the operating environment. The process of creating a form is identical to that of creating a report. First, a form specification file must be created and compiled by use of the *sformbld* utility. After this file is compiled, the form can be displayed by use of the *sperform* command. If the form is compiled successfully, a file suffixed with *.frm* is created; otherwise, a file suffixed with a *.err* is created with error messages and can be perused to locate the error. The file suffixed *.frm* is used by *sperform* to display the form and perform data entry and retrieval.

6.3.1 Creating a Form Specification File

A form specification file can be created with any editor and must have the following sections:

- *Database* section: This section is used to specify the name of the database to be used in the form.
- *Screen* section: This section is used to describe the layout of the screens as they should appear to the end user.
- *Tables* section: This section is used to specify the tables and columns which will be used in the form.
- *Attributes* section: This section describes the correspondence between the fields specified in the screen section and the database columns. Additionally, it is used to describe the appearance of the field on the screen and identify the acceptable values, default values, instructions to be displayed at the bottom of the screen, and other attributes to be

associated with the screen fields.

- *Instructions* section: This section is optional and offers additional features which are not available otherwise. These features include the capability to control cursor movements between fields, perform action after data is entered in a field, execute user specified statements after a record is added to the database, and specifying the default field delimiter characters.

6.3.2 Getting Started

In the last chapter, SQL statements were used for data entry. This section shows how the data entry process can be made user-friendly with the design of forms. In fact, the form can be used for retrieval, updates, and deletion operation also. The following form specification file can be used to interact with the customers table in the database:

```
cat customer.per
database florist
screen
{

        ==============================
            CUSTOMER MAINTENANCE
        ==============================

Customer No. : [c1         ]

First Name   : [c2                  ]
Last  Name   : [c3                  ]

Address:
[c4                   ]
[c5                   ]
Town :  [c6                   ]
State: [c7]
Zip  : [c8    ]

}
tables
        customers
attributes
```

```
c1 = customers.c_no;
c2 = customers.c_fname;
c3 = customers.c_lname;
c4 = customers.c_addr1;
c5 = customers.c_addr2;
c6 = customers.c_town;
c7 = customers.c_state;
c8 = customers.c_zip;
end
```

The database section is used to specify *florist* as the name of the database to be used. The screen section has several fields in which data can be displayed or entered. Each field has an optional field title, a field tag, and delimiters to indicate the area into which data is to be entered by the user or by the system. The default delimiters are the *[,]* characters. For example, in the line:

```
Customer No. : [c1          ]
```

Customer No. is a field title and *c1* is a field tag within the delimiters *[* and *]*. A field tag inside the delimiters is used to identify the field. This field tag subsequently can be used in the attributes section to associate the field with database columns. All fields need not be directly associated with a database column. Such fields are called display-only fields. Text appearing in the screen section is like a comment in a program. It is displayed on the screen verbatim.

All field tags must have an entry in the attributes section which associates them with database columns or specifies that they are display-only fields. For example, the line

```
c1 = customers.c_no;
```

indicates that the field identified by the tag *c1* will be used to display and enter the *c_no* field in the customers table. The form specification file can be compiled by use of the utility *sformbld*. Once compiled, the form can be displayed by using the *sperform* command. The displayed form is shown in Figure 6.2.

The box in the figure is used to indicate the highlighted option, usually a reverse video display or an underline. Any option can be selected by moving the highlight to the desired option and then pressing the "Return" key or by entering the first letter of the option. Once the desired option is selected, it may be executed immediately or it may wait for another user response. For

```
PERFORM [Query] Next  Previous  Add  Update  Remove  Table  Screen ...
Searches the active database table          ** 1: customers table**

                    ============================
                        CUSTOMER MAINTENANCE
                    ============================


Customer No. : [           ]

First Name   : [                     ]
Last  Name   : [                     ]
Address
[                     ]
[                     ]
Town : [                     ]
State: [  ]
Zip  : [     ]
```

Figure 6.2 Form Displayed by Sperform

example, if a new row is to be inserted, then an escape (Esc) key must be entered to signal that all the fields in the form are filled and that the record is ready to be added. Among the options available are

- *Query*: This option is used to query the database based on values entered in one or more screen fields.
- *Next*: If more than one row is retrieved in a query operation, then it is possible to scroll through these rows. The *Next* option allows forward scrolling.
- *Previous*: This option can be used to scroll backward.
- *Update*: Once a record is retrieved, the fields on the screen can be updated by use of this option. An "Esc" key must be pressed to reflect the updated image of the screen to the database row.
- *Remove*: Once a record is retrieved, it can be deleted by use of this option.
- *Output*: This option is used to store the screen image of the current row or the current set of rows into a UNIX flat file.

- *Screen*: If multiple screens are defined in a single form file, then this option can be used to scroll through each screen.

Other available options will be discussed in later sections.

6.3.3 More Attributes

The *attributes* section was used in the previous section to associate a field tag with a database column. Several other attributes can also be associated with a field tag in this section. The order in which the fields are described determines the cursor movement between fields. For example, if the lines describing field tags *c2* and *c3* were interchanged, then the cursor would move to the last name field after the Customer no. is entered. During data entry, when a field is full, the cursor will not automatically advance to the next field unless the *autonext* attribute is used.

During addition of a row, a default value can be made to appear in any field by use of the *default* attribute. For example, a default value of *NJ* can be made to appear in the *state* field by use of the default attribute, as shown below:

```
c7 = customers.c_state,default="NJ";
```

The word *today* can be used to specify today's date as the default value of a date field. Users often need instructions to fill out a form. A comment line can be displayed at the bottom of the screen to provide instruction to the user on data entry about each field. The *comments* attribute can be used to display this message. For example, the description

```
c7 = customers.c_state, default="NJ",
    comments = "Please enter state code";
```

will display the message "Please enter state code" whenever the cursor is on the c7 field. Uppercase letters can be converted to lowercase, and lowercase letters to uppercase by using the attributes *downshift* and *upshift*, respectively. During data entry, some fields must not have any missing data. The attribute *required* can be used to force the user to enter data in the specified field. Only a set or range of values can be made acceptable by use of the *include* attribute. For example, if *NY*, *NJ*, and *PA* are to be made the only acceptable values for the *state* field, then the attribute specification for *c7* must be augmented as follows:

```
c7 = customers.c_state, default="NJ", include=("NY","NJ","PA")
    comments = "Please enter state code";
```

The *picture* attribute can be used to make a *char* type field more readable and to enforce a basic type-checking capability. For example, the user can be forced to enter only numeric characters in the *Zip* field by describing the *c8* field as:

```
c8 = customers.c_zip,picture="#####";
```

The # character is used to force a numeric character only. Similarly, users can be forced to enter only alphabetic data by using the *picture* attribute with the character *A*. An *X* character can be used to allow any character to be entered. Further, if any other character is used to describe the field, it will appear in the same position at data entry. For example, the entry

```
p1 = mytable.myphone, picture = "(###)-###-####";
```

will allow only numeric characters to be entered for the indicated field. In addition, the characters *(*, *)*, and - will appear in the field at data entry time at the designated position, as shown below:

```
[(   )-   -    ]
```

The *format* attribute can be used to control the format of a decimal, float, smallfloat, or date type attribute. Users can be prevented from entering a new value to a specified field at record addition time by use of the attribute *noentry*. At data entry time, the field will be skipped. For example, if there is a field tag called *o4* which is used to describe an entry date, then today's date can be made the default and the user prevented from altering it by use of the *noentry* and *default* attributes, as shown below:

```
o4 = mytable.entrydate,default=today, noentry;
```

Similarly, the *noupdate* attribute can be used to prevent the user from updating a field.

The *right* attribute is used to right justify the data entered by the user. The *zerofill* attribute right justifies the field and fills it with leading zeros. If data entered in a field is very critical, then the user can be forced with use of the *verify* attribute to enter the data twice. If the entered data is not the same on both occasions, then the user has to repeat the process. A field can be displayed in reverse video mode with use of the *reverse* attribute. If a field is used to join two tables, then after a *query* operation is invoked, the join field is not cleared unless a *queryclear* attribute is specified.

6.3.4 Forms with Multiple Tables

In the last example, the form contained only one table. Multiple tables can be referenced in a single form. Different screen sections can also be used to interact with different tables. Here is a simple example of a form specification file which uses multiple screen sections:

```
database florist
screen
{

                        =======================
                           ORDER MAINTENANCE
                        =======================

Customer No  : [o1        ]    Order No. : [o2 ]

Order Amt.   : [o3        ]
Order Date   : [o4        ]
Description  : [o5                    ]
Delivery Chg.: [o6     ]
Paid         : [o7     ]

}
screen
{

                      ============================
                          CUSTOMER MAINTENANCE
                      ============================

Customer No. : [c1         ]

First Name   : [c2                  ]
Last  Name   : [c3                  ]
```

```
Address:
[c4                 ]
[c5                 ]
Town : [c6                 ]
State: [c7]
Zip  : [c8   ]

}
tables
        orders, customers
attributes
c1 = customers.c_no;
c2 = customers.c_fname;
c3 = customers.c_lname;
c4 = customers.c_addr1;
c5 = customers.c_addr2;
c6 = customers.c_town;
c7 = customers.c_state;
c8 = customers.c_zip;
o1 = orders.c_no;
o2 = orders.o_no;
o3 = orders.o_amt;
o4 = orders.o_date;
o5 = orders.o_desc;
o6 = orders.o_del_chg;
o7 = orders.o_paid;
end
```

The first screen section is used to interact with the customers table, and the second screen section is used to interact with the orders table. The two sections do not share any common field tags. When the form file is executed by use of the *sacego* utility, the customers form is displayed first. The user can select the desired option from the menu that appears in the top line. After completing the interactive session with the customers form, the user can display the orders form either by selecting the *Screen* option or by selecting the *Table* option. These options allow the user to toggle between the two screens/tables.

It is also possible to combine the two screen sections into a single screen section, as shown below:

```
database florist
screen
{
              =======================================
                  CUSTOMER AND ORDER MAINTENANCE
              =======================================

Customer No. : [c1         ]
First Name   : [c2                  ]
Last  Name   : [c3                  ]
Address:
[c4                     ]
[c5                     ]
Town : [c6                    ]       State : [c7]
Zip  : [c8    ]

------------------------------------------------------------------------

Customer No   : [o1         ]     Order No. : [o2 ]
Order Amt.    : [o3         ]  Order Date   : [o4          ]
Description   : [o5                           ]
Delivery Chg.: [o6      ]     Paid          : [o7      ]
}
tables
        orders, customers
attributes
c1 = customers.c_no;
c2 = customers.c_fname;
c3 = customers.c_lname;
c4 = customers.c_addr1;
c5 = customers.c_addr2;
c6 = customers.c_town;
c7 = customers.c_state;
c8 = customers.c_zip;
o1 = orders.c_no;
o2 = orders.o_no;
o3 = orders.o_amt;
o4 = orders.o_date;
o5 = orders.o_desc;
o6 = orders.o_del_chg;
o7 = orders.o_paid;
end
```

```
PERFORM [Query] Next  Previous  Add  Update  Remove  Table  Screen ...
Searches the active database table            ** 1: customers table**

                    =======================================
                          CUSTOMER AND ORDER MAINTENANCE
                    =======================================

Customer No. : [          ]
First Name   : [                   ]
Last  Name   : [                   ]
Address
[                 ]
[                 ]
Town : [                  ]       State : [  ]
Zip  : [       ]
------------------------------------------------------------------

Customer No   :                  Order No. :
Order Amt.    :               Order Date   :
Description   :
Delivery Chg.:                Paid         :
```

Figure 6.3 Initial Display of Form with Multiple Tables

When the form is displayed, only one of the two tables will be active. The field delimiters of the active table will be displayed to indicate the active fields of the selected table. The name of the active table will also be displayed. For example, when the customers table is active, the screen will look as shown is Figure 6.3. If the *Table* option is now selected, the orders table becomes the current table. The screen will appear as shown in Figure 6.4. The field delimiters appearing in the customers table are erased and now appear with the fields associated with the orders table. Also, the name of the active table is displayed.

The two columns *c1* and *o1* have the same information, namely *Customer No.* It is possible to have a single entry for both the fields in the *attributes* section by combining the lines

```
c1 = customers.c_no;
o1 = orders.c_no;
```

into a single line:

```
c1 = customers.c_no = orders.c_no;
```

```
PERFORM  Query  Next  Previous  Add  Update  Remove  [Table]  Screen ...
Selects the current table                         ** 2: orders table**

               ========================================
                    CUSTOMER AND ORDER MAINTENANCE
               ========================================


Customer No. :
First Name   :
Last  Name   :
Address


Town :                                State :
Zip  :
--------------------------------------------------------------------

Customer No   : [          ]     Order No. : [   ]
Order Amt.    : [          ]  Order Date   : [          ]
Description   : [                                  ]
Delivery Chg.: [        ]     Paid         : [        ]
```

Figure 6.4 After Table Option is Selected

and by renaming the field tag *o1* to *c1*. When the customers table is active the *Customer No.* field refers to the *c_no* column of the customers table; otherwise, it corresponds to the *c_no* field of the orders table. This mechanism to join two fields is particularly useful for implementing referential integrity. For example, if only orders for customers who have an entry in the customers table are to be accepted, then the following lines in the *attributes* section can be used to implement this check:

```
c1 = orders.c_no = *customers.c_no;
```

The asterisk indicates that the customers table is the master. This line in the attributes section is used to prevent entry of any value into *orders.c_no* that does not already exist in *customers.c_no*. If different attributes are to be associated with the common field tag, depending on the table which is active, then the two lists of additional attributes must be specified on different lines. For example,

```
c1 = orders.c_no,verify;
   = *customers.c_no;
```

will ask for verification of the *customer no.* field only when the orders table is active. But

```
c1 = orders.c_no = *customers.c_no, verify;
```

will ask for verification of the *customer no.* field when either of the two tables is active.

6.3.5 The Lookup Join

When a table is active and data is entered in a field, it is possible to treat this data as a key value in another table. If this key value is located in that "foreign" table, then an associated value from that table can be retrieved and displayed on the screen. The *lookup* join can be used to implement this feature in a form. The field tags for fields in which the data is retrieved and displayed as a result of a *lookup* join do not have a separate entry in the attributes section. For example, consider the following form specification file:

```
database florist
screen
{
                 =============================
                      ORDER MAINTENANCE
                 =============================
```

```
Customer No. : [c1          ]
        First Name    : [c2                  ]
        Last  Name    : [c3                  ]
Order No. : [o2 ]
Order Amt.    : [o3         ]  Order Date     : [o4          ]
Description   : [o5                               ]
Delivery Chg.: [o6      ]     Paid           : [o7     ]
}
tables
        orders, customers
attributes
c1 = orders.c_no,
        lookup c2 = customers.c_fname,
               c3 = customers.c_lname
        joining *customers.c_no;
o2 = orders.o_no;
o3 = orders.o_amt;
o4 = orders.o_date;
o5 = orders.o_desc;
o6 = orders.o_del_chg;
o7 = orders.o_paid;
end
```

During data entry, if a value is entered in the *Customer No.* field and if that value is found in the customers table, then the first and last name of that customer is displayed and the cursor moves to the amount field. If it is not found, an error message is displayed.

If a join is used in a form, it is advisable to have appropriate indexes on the join fields to improve the performance.

6.3.6 The Instructions Section

The process of running a form can be perceived as a series of user action and the system reaction. The user action can be a selection of an option, a data entry in a field, or entering in of the "ESC" key to execute a previously selected option. The system could react to these actions by moving the cursor to the next field, displaying an error message, or executing the user selected option such as adding a row or deleting one. The *instructions* section can be used to have additional control on the system reaction to user action.

In particular, the following user actions are recognized:

- Selection of an option such as *Add*, *Remove*, *Update*, or *Query*
- Data entry in a field
- An entering in of the "ESC" key to execute the selected option

The system can be made to respond to these user actions in the following ways:

- Move the cursor to a specified field
- Check for interfield consistency
- Compute a value based on data in one or more fields
- Display a computed value into a specified field
- Display an aggregate value into a specified field
- Abort the currently selected option
- Complete the currently selected option
- Execute a user-function written in the C language
- Display a message at the bottom of the form

The block which specifies the user action and defines the statements to be executed before or after that action is called a control block. The following control blocks are recognized:

- *before editadd of table-name*: The statements associated with this control block are executed immediately after the user selects the *add* option.
- *before editupdate of table-name*: The statements associated with this control block are executed immediately after the user selects the *update* option.
- *after editadd of table-name*: The statements associated with this control block are executed after the user enters the "ESC" key but before the row is added to the specified table.
- *after editupdate of table-name*: The statements associated with this control block are executed after the user enters the "ESC" key but before the row is updated into the specified table.
- *before editadd of field-name*: The statements associated with this control block are executed just before the cursor has moved to the specified field and while the user is in *add* mode.
- *before editupdate of field-name*: The statements associated with this control block are executed just before the cursor has moved to the specified field and while the user is in *update* mode.
- *after editadd of field-name*: The statements associated with this control block are executed just after the user has completed entering the data for the specified field while in the *add* mode.
- *after editupdate of field-name*: The statements associated with this control block are executed just after the user has completed entering the data for the specified field while in the *update* mode.

• *after add of table-name*: The statements associated with this control block are executed after the record is added to the database table.
• *after update of table-name*: The statements associated with this control block are executed after the record is updated into the database table.
• *after remove of table-name*: The statements associated with this control block are executed after the record is removed from the database table.
• *before remove of table-name*: The statements associated with this control block are executed after the user enters the "ESC" key but before the row is removed from the specified table.
• *after query of table-name*: The statements associated with this control block are executed after the user enters the "ESC" key while in query mode. The statements associated with this control block will not be executed when the user selects the *next* or *previous* options. The next control block can be used for this purpose.
• *after display of table-name*: The statements associated with this control block are executed after any operation that causes data to be displayed on the screen.

6.3.6.1 Statements Accepted in Control Blocks

The forms manager provides five different statements which can be used in the control blocks. The *let* statement can be used to display a value in a field. The displayed value can be a constant or a result of an expression. The statement

```
let x5 = x2 - x4
```

subtracts the values displayed in fields *x2* and *x4* and displays the result in field *x4*. The *nextfield* statement can be used to control the cursor movement. For example, execution of the statement

```
nextfield = x5
```

moves the cursor to the field labeled *x5*. The *comments* statement can be used to display a message at the bottom of the screen. The *bell* and *reverse* attributes can be used to ring the terminal bell and display the message in reverse video, respectively. The statement

```
comments bell reverse "This is not an acceptable value"
```

will ring the terminal bell and display the indicated message in reverse video mode. The *if... then... else* statement can be used to execute statements based on conditions which can be evaluated at run time. The *begin* and *end* constructs can be used to enclose multiple statements. The *else* part is optional. The statement

```
if (x4 > 100) then
  begin
    comments reverse "% Discount cannot be greater than 100!"
    let x4 = 100
  end
```

will display the indicated message and set the field *x4* to 100 only if the current value in the field is greater than 100. Finally, the *abort* statement can be used to exit the current option and return to the *perform* menu.

6.3.6.2 Examples Using Control Blocks

All the examples in this section will use the following form specification file:

```
database florist
screen
{
                 ============================
                     ORDER MAINTENANCE
                 ============================

Customer No. : [o1         ]
Order No.    : [o2 ]
Order Amt.   : [o3         ]  Delivery Chg.: [o4      ]
Tax          : [o5      ]     Total Amt.   : [o6      ]
Paid         : [o7      ]     Balance      : [o8      ]
Order Date   : [o9         ]
Description  : [o10                              ]

}
tables
        orders
```

```
attributes
o1 = orders.c_no;
o2 = orders.o_no;
o3 = orders.o_amt;
o4 = orders.o_del_chg;
o5 = displayonly type money;
o6 = displayonly type money;
o7 = orders.o_paid;
o8 = displayonly type money;
o9 = orders.o_date;
o10= orders.o_desc;
instructions
        after display of orders
                { charge a 6 % tax }
                let o5 = .06 * o3
                let o6 = o3 + o4 + o5
                let o8 = o6 - o7
        after editadd editupdate of orders
                let o5 = .06 * o3
                let o6 = o3 + o4 + o5
                let o8 = o6 - o7
end
```

When this form is compiled and displayed, it will appear as shown in Figure 6.5.

The field tags *o5*, *o6*, and *o8* do not represent any database columns. The values to be displayed in these fields are computed in the instructions section. The *after display of orders* control block is used to compute the values of the display fields when the *query*, *next*, or *previous* options of the *perform* menu are selected. The *after editadd editupdate* control block is used to compute and display the values for the same fields when the user has selected the *add* and *update* options, respectively, but the values are displayed only after the user enters the "ESC" key. If the values are to be displayed after the required information is entered by the user, then the lines

```
after editadd editupdate of orders
        let o5 = .06 * o3
        let o6 = o3 + o4 + o5
        let o8 = o6 - o7
```

must be changed to

```
after editadd editupdate of o_amt
        let o5 = .06 * o3
after editadd editupdate of o_del_chg
        let o6 = o3 + o4 + o5
after editadd editupdate of o_paid
        let o8 = o6 - o7
```

```
PERFORM [Query] Next  Previous  Add  Update  Remove  Table  Screen ...
Searches the active database table             ** 1: orders table**

                 ============================
                      ORDER MAINTENANCE
                 ============================

Customer No. : [           ]
Order No.    : [   ]
Order Amt.   : [           ]  Delivery Chg.: [        ]
Tax          : [        ]     Total Amt.   : [        ]
Paid         : [        ]     Balance      : [        ]
Order Date   : [           ]
Description  : [                              ]
```

Figure 6.5 Initial Display when Invoked

Let there be a restriction on the credit to be given on an order. If the amount paid is less than 50% of the total amount after the 6% tax and the delivery charges are added to the order, then the order is to be rejected. A message can be displayed in which the user is asked to reenter the amount paid. The cursor can be prevented from moving to the next field unless the user enters an amount which is at least equal to 50% of the total amount due. If the user has made a data entry error, she or he can rectify the same. Otherwise, the "DEL" key must be entered to abort the current order. Here is the rewritten *instructions* section:

```
instructions
  after display of orders
        { charge a 6 % tax }
        let o5 = .06 * o3
        let o6 = o3 + o4 + o5
        let o8 = o6 - o7
  after editadd editupdate of o_amt
        let o5 = .06 * o3
  after editadd editupdate of o_del_chg
        let o6 = o3 + o4 + o5
  after editadd editupdate of o_paid
        let o8 = o6 - o7
        if (o6/o7 > 2) then
          begin
           comments bell reverse "Only 50% credit allowed"
           nextfield = o7
          end
end
```

Another method is to abort the transaction completely without giving the user a second chance. This can be done by substituting the statement *abort* instead of the statement *nextfield = o7.*

6.3.6.3 Avoiding the ESC key

It is not always necessary to enter an "ESC" key to complete an operation. The *nextfield = exitnow* statement can be used to complete an operation without the ESC key being explicitly entered. For example, if the *add* and *update* operations are to be completed automatically after the user completes data entry for the *order description* field, then the *instructions* section can be rewritten as

```
after display of orders
  { charge a 6 % tax }
  let o5 = .06 * o3
  let o6 = o3 + o4 + o5
```

```
  let o8 = o6 - o7
after editadd editupdate of o_amt
  let o5 = .06 * o3
after editadd editupdate of o_del_chg
  let o6 = o3 + o4 + o5
after editadd editupdate of o_paid
  let o8 = o6 - o7
  if (o6/o7 > 2) then
    begin
     comments bell reverse "Only 50% credit allowed"
     nextfield = o7
    end
after editadd editupdate of o_desc
  nextfield = exitnow
end
```

6.3.6.4 Using Aggregate Functions

The *let* statement can be used to compute the aggregate value of a database field and to assign the result to another field. The aggregate functions available are *count*, *total*, *max*, *min*, and *average*. The aggregate function is computed over the current list of records. For example, after a query operation, the aggregate is computed over the selected set of records. The following file is an augmented version of the earlier form specification file in which summary information is displayed whenever a query is executed.

The aggregate functions are used with the *after display of orders* control block as opposed to the *after query of orders* control block so that the summary information will continue to be displayed even when the user is scrolling through individual records using the *next* and *previous* options. The summary information aggregates values over the specified fields of the retrieved rows. Additional control blocks are used to prevent the usage of this form for updates, additions, or removal of records.

```
database florist
screen
{
                            ============================
                                ORDER MAINTENANCE
                            ============================
```

```
Customer No. : [o1         ]
Order No.    : [o2 ]
Order Amt.   : [o3         ]  Delivery Chg.: [o4      ]
Tax          : [o5      ]     Total Amt.   : [o6      ]
Paid         : [o7      ]     Balance      : [o8      ]
Order Date   : [o9         ]
Description  : [o10                        ]


  =============== ONLY IN QUERY MODE ===============

          Total No. of orders: [o11       ]
          Last Order Date    : [o12       ]
         Total Order Amount : [o13       ]

}
tables
       orders
attributes
o1 = orders.c_no;
o2 = orders.o_no;
o3 = orders.o_amt;
o4 = orders.o_del_chg;
o7 = orders.o_paid;
o9 = orders.o_date;
o10= orders.o_desc;
o5 = displayonly type money;
o6 = displayonly type money;
o8 = displayonly type money;
o11= displayonly type char;
o12= displayonly type char;
o13= displayonly type char;
instructions
   before editadd editupdate of orders
    comments bell reverse "This form can be used only for a query"
    abort
   before remove of orders
    comments bell reverse "This form can be used only for a query"
    abort
   after display of orders
       { charge a 6 % tax }
       let o12 = max of o9
       let o13 = total of o3
```

```
            let o11 = count of o9
            let o5 = .06 * o3
            let o6 = o3 + o4 + o5
            let o8 = o6 - o7
    end
```

Note that if the type of the display field is different from that of the field on which the aggregate is computed, appropriate conversion is done before the result is displayed. No attempt is made here to clear the display fields. If the *o12* display field was declared as a type date field, then it would be initialized to *12/31/1899* after the query option is selected. (Why?)

6.3.6.5 Other Features of the Instruction Section

In addition to the features discussed in the previous section, the instructions section can also be used to:

- Change the characters used as delimiters to enclose fields
- Establish a composite join between two tables
- Provide a master/detail relationship between two tables

The characters used to enclose fields can be changed to <> by using the following *instructions* section:

```
instructions section
delimiters "<>"
end
```

A master/detail relationship between two tables should be established if they are joined by a one-to-many relationship. For example, several records from the orders table are associated with one record from the customers table. Therefore, the customers table is a master to the detail records in the orders table. If an order was associated with multiple customers, then a master/detail relationship between the two tables with the orders table as the master could also have been established. The master/detail relationship is extremely helpful for queries involving a join on the two tables. The following instructions section

```
instructions
        customers master of orders;
end
```

establishes a master/detail relationship between the customers table and the orders table, with the customers table as the master table. If a *query* operation is performed on the customers table for a specified customer table, then the orders for that customer can be retrieved simply by the user choosing the *detail* option.

Composite joins are used to establish a join between two tables on multiple columns. This is different than establishing multiple joins on individual columns. However, the individual columns must also be joined separately in the *attributes* section. Let "shipping" and "neworders" be two tables with the following definition:

```
shipping        neworders
========        =========
cust_no         cust_no
order_no        order_no
ship_date       order_amt
ship_cost       order_date
ship_type       order_desc
```

Then the two columns *cust_no* and *order_no* can be joined individually in the *attributes* section. If they are also joined by a composite join in the instructions section as shown below

```
instructions
  composites <shipping.cust_no, shipping.order_no>
           *<neworders.cust_no, neworders.order_no>
end
```

then only those records will be allowed to be added into the shipping table for which the combination of *cust_no* and *order_no* already exists in the neworders table. The combination is important. For example if a shipping record with *cust_no* = 12 and *order_no* = 4 is to be added, then there must be a record in the neworders table with *cust_no* = 12 and *orders_no* = 4. The presence of a record with *cust_no* = 12 and another record with *order_no* = 4 is not sufficient for the join condition to be satisfied.

6.3.6.6 The C Language Interface

Though the features provided by the screen forms management software is sufficient for most applications, occasionally it becomes necessary to use functions written in the C language to be interfaced with the forms manager. This feature gives the full power of the C language to the forms package. The structure of the C program is identical to that used earlier for interfacing with the report writer. The only difference lies in the utility to be used to create the customized *perform*. To create a customized version of *sacego*, the *cace* utility was used; to create a customized version of *sperform*, the *cperf* utility must be used.

The C-interfacing library provides five additional functions which can be used for interfacing with a form. They are tabulated in Table 6.2.

TABLE 6.2 Perform Library Functions

Function	Use	Arguments
pf_gettype	To retrieve the type and length of a display field	char *field_tag_name short *data_type short *length
pf_getval	To read a value from a display field	char *field_tag_name char *return_value short *data_type short *length
pf_putval	To put a value into a display field	char *val_to_be_put short *data_type char *field_tag_name
pf_nxfield	To move a cursor to a specified field	char *field_tag_name
pf_msg	To display a message at the bottom of the screen	char *message short reverse_flag short bell_flag

In addition to the control blocks discussed earlier, two new control blocks can be used to invoke user-defined C functions. They are *on beginning* and *on ending*. The C function in the *on beginning* control block is executed immediately after the user invokes the customized version of *sperform*. The C function in the *on ending* control block is executed just before the user exits the form. There can only be one C function invocation in these control blocks. No other statements are allowed.

It is very common in a data-processing environment to keep a log of all users who access a system. The next example shows how a log can be maintained for each user who attempts to access the form. When the form is invoked, a validation check is made to verify if the user is authorized to use the form. A list of authorized users is maintained in a file named formfile. Unauthorized users are not allowed to access the form. An entry is made in the log file to register the time when the form was invoked and when a session was terminated. The rewritten form specification file is

```
database florist
screen
{
              ============================
                  ORDER MAINTENANCE
              ============================

Customer No. : [o1         ]
Order No.    : [o2 ]
Order Amt.   : [o3         ]  Delivery Chg.: [o4      ]
Tax          : [o5      ]     Total Amt.   : [o6      ]
Paid         : [o7      ]     Balance      : [o8      ]
Order Date   : [o9         ]
Description  : [o10                          ]

}
tables
        orders
attributes
o1 = orders.c_no;
o2 = orders.o_no;
o3 = orders.o_amt;
o4 = orders.o_del_chg;
o5 = displayonly allowing input type money;
o6 = displayonly type money;
o7 = orders.o_paid;
o8 = displayonly type money;
o9 = orders.o_date;
o10= orders.o_desc;
instructions

{ Validate user and make an entry in the usage log}
        on beginning
                call val_user(0)
        on ending
```

```
        call val_user(1)

        after display of orders
                { charge a 6 % tax }
                let o5 = .06 * o3
                let o6 = o3 + o4 + o5
                let o8 = o6 - o7
        after editadd editupdate of o_amt
                let o5 = .06 * o3
        after editadd editupdate of o_del_chg
                let o6 = o3 + o4 + o5
        after editadd editupdate of o_paid
                let o8 = o6 - o7
                if (o6/o7 > 2) then
                  begin
                   comments bell reverse "Only 50% credit allowed"
                   nextfield = o7
                  end
end
```

The C file containing the invoked functions is

```
#include "ctools.h"
#include <stdio.h>

valueptr valid();

struct ufunc userfuncs[] =
{
   "val_user", valid,
   0, 0
};
valueptr valid(beg_or_end)
valueptr beg_or_end;
{
   char fuser[9], *cuserid(),user[9];
   int eof=2;
   long time(),now;
   char *ctime();
   FILE *fp,*flog;

   now = time((long *)0);
```

```
/* Open the log file */
flog=fopen("logfile","a");

/* Get the user login, could have used getlogin */
cuserid(user);

/* If invoked in the end control block */
if (beg_or_end->v_int == 1) {
   fprintf(flog, "Session terminated by %s on %s\n",
       user,ctime(&now));
   fclose(flog);
   intreturn(0);
}

/* Open the file with valid login names */
fp = fopen("formfile","r");

/* Check if user is in the formfile */
while (1)
{
   eof=fscanf(fp,"%s",fuser);

   /* If EOF then not found, return 1 */
   if (eof == EOF)
   {
      /* Display message with bell ring */
      /* and in reverse video mode */
      fprintf(flog, "Attempt made by %s to invoke this form on %s\n",
          user,ctime(&now));
      fclose(flog);
      fclose(fp);
      pf_msg("Not an authorized user",1,1);
      system("stty sane;echo");
      exit(1);
   }
   if (strcmp(fuser,user)==0)
      break;
}
fprintf(flog, "Session initiated by %s on %s\n",
    user,ctime(&now));
fclose(flog);
fclose(fp);
```

```
        intreturn(0);
    }
```

The *pf_msg* function as described in Table 6.3 is used to display a message at the bottom of the screen. The second and third arguments are used to display the message in reverse video mode and to ring the terminal bell. Before the form is exited, the terminal must be reset. The UNIX command *stty sane* is used for this purpose. The *echo* statement following this is used to generate a new line.

The function *val_user* is used in both the *begin* and the *end* control blocks. The argument to this function is used to detect from which control block it was invoked.

The log file can also be used to maintain a log of all updates and inserts. The following form specification file is a modified version of the previous order maintenance form in which deletion of order records is disabled in the *instructions* section. In addition, a new C function called *upd_log* is invoked with different arguments after a successful *add* or *update* operation. This C function enters an entry in the log file which indicates the record updated or added:

```
database florist
screen
{
              ============================
                  ORDER MAINTENANCE
              ============================

Customer No. : [o1        ]
Order No.    : [o2 ]
Order Amt.   : [o3        ]  Delivery Chg.: [o4      ]
Tax          : [o5     ]     Total Amt.   : [o6      ]
Paid         : [o7     ]     Balance      : [o8      ]
Order Date   : [o9        ]
Description  : [o10                        ]

}
tables
   orders
attributes
o1 = orders.c_no;
o2 = orders.o_no;
o3 = orders.o_amt;
```

```
o4 = orders.o_del_chg;
o5 = displayonly allowing input type money;
o6 = displayonly type money;
o7 = orders.o_paid;
o8 = displayonly type money;
o9 = orders.o_date;
o10= orders.o_desc;
instructions

{ Validate user and make an entry in the usage log}
   on beginning
      call val_user(0)
   on ending
      call val_user(1)

   after display of orders
      { charge a 6 % tax }
      let o5 = .06 * o3
      let o6 = o3 + o4 + o5
      let o8 = o6 - o7
   after editadd editupdate of o_amt
      let o5 = .06 * o3
   after editadd editupdate of o_del_chg
      let o6 = o3 + o4 + o5
   after editadd editupdate of o_paid
      let o8 = o6 - o7
      if (o6/o7 > 2) then
        begin
         comments bell reverse "Only 50% credit allowed"
              nextfield = o7
        end

   after add of orders
      call upd_log(1)
   after update of orders
      call upd_log(2)

   { prevent order deletions }
   before remove of orders
      comments bell reverse "Cannot remove orders using this form"
      abort
end
```

The modified C program file is

```
#include "ctools.h"
#include <stdio.h>

valueptr valid(),upd_log();

struct ufunc userfuncs[] =
{
   "val_user", valid,
   "upd_log", upd_log,
   0, 0
};
valueptr upd_log(type_upd)
valueptr type_upd;
{
FILE *flog;
char cust_no[11],user[9];
long ord_no;

   /* Open the log file */
   flog=fopen("logfile","a");

   /* Get the user login, could have used getlogin */
   cuserid(user);

   /* Get the customer and order no */
   pf_getval("o1",cust_no,CCHARTYPE,11);
   pf_getval("o2",&ord_no,CLONGTYPE,0);

   if (type_upd->v_int == 1)
      fprintf(flog,"Add operation, User: %s Cust: %s Order: %ld\n",
                              user, cust_no, ord_no);
   else
      fprintf(flog,"Upd operation, User: %s Cust: %s Order: %ld\n",
                              user, cust_no, ord_no);
   fclose(flog);
}
valueptr valid(beg_or_end)
valueptr beg_or_end;
{
   char fuser[9], *cuserid(),user[9];
   int eof=2;
```

```
long time(),now;
char *ctime();
FILE *fp,*flog;

now = time((long *)0);

/* Open the log file */
flog=fopen("logfile","a");

/* Get the user login, could have used getlogin */
cuserid(user);

/* If invoked in the end control block */
if (beg_or_end->v_int == 1) {
   fprintf(flog, "\nSession terminated by %s on %s\n",
       user,ctime(&now));
   fclose(flog);
   intreturn(0);
}

/* Open the file with valid login names */
fp = fopen("formfile","r");

/* Check if user is in the formfile */
while (1)
{
   eof=fscanf(fp,"%s",fuser);

   /* If EOF then not found, return 1 */
   if (eof == EOF)
   {
      /* Display message with bell ring */
      /* and in reverse video mode */
      fprintf(flog, "Attempt made by %s to invoke this form on %s\n",
          user,ctime(&now));
      fclose(flog);
      fclose(fp);
      pf_msg("Not an authorized user",1,1);
      system("stty sane;echo");
      exit(1);
   }
   if (strcmp(fuser,user)==0)
      break;
```

```
        }
        fprintf(flog, "Session initiated by %s on %s\n",
            user,ctime(&now));
        fclose(flog);
        fclose(fp);
        intreturn(0);
    }
```

Note that the entry for an *update* operation is made after the update is successful. The log will therefore have the customer number and the order number of the updated entry. If these fields are themselves updated, then the original record cannot be traced from the log file.

6.3.6.7 More about Perform

Once the form specification file is compiled, *sperform*, or a customized version of it, can be used to run the form. In addition to the features discussed earlier, *perform* offers features to do the following:

- Automatic checking of data type of the data entered: If the user enters data that does not conform with the data type of the field, an error message is displayed and the data is not accepted.
- Cursor positioning: The "return" key moves the cursor to the next field. If autonext is enabled, the cursor moves to the next field after the current field is full. The next field itself may be programmed in the *instructions* section. The down-arrow key can also be used instead of the "return" key. The backspace or the left-arrow key can be used to move the cursor backward. The right arrow key moves the cursor forward one character at a time without erasing the character.
- Field data editing: The data entered in the field can be edited by first positioning the cursor appropriately and then using the editing capabilities. The ctrl-x key deletes the character beneath the cursor. The ctrl-d key deletes all characters from the current cursor position to the end of the field. The ctrl-a key toggles between insert and overwrite mode. The ctrl-p key can be used in update mode to restore the old value before the user enters the new value. In add mode it can be used to add more than one row with the same value in one or more fields. The ctrl-c key can be used to clear the fields while in query mode. On-line help is available by entering the ctrl-w key.
- Running UNIX commands: Entering an exclamation (!) key displays it at the bottom of the screen. Any UNIX command, followed by a return key, can now be entered. After executing the command, the message:

```
Type carriage return to continue
```

will appear at the bottom of the screen. A return key entered at this point will return the user back to the form.

6.4 Invoking Informix Menu

So far almost all the compilation and execution of forms, reports, and queries was done with UNIX-level commands. Programmers find it convenient to use UNIX-level commands, but on the other hand this is not the most user-friendly mechanism. INFORMIX provides a menu interface which enables the user to access the various components of the INFORMIX database system. The interface can be invoked by using the *isql* command. In the last chapter, the *isql* command was used to run SQL queries. If the command is invoked without any arguments, then the INFORMIX main menu is displayed as shown in Figure 6.6.

```
INFORMIX-SQL:  Form  Report  Query-language  User-Menu  Database  Table  Exit
Run, Modify, Create, or Drop a form
-----------------------------------------------Press CTRL-W for Help---------
```

Figure 6.6 INFORMIX Main Menu

An option from the menu can be selected by moving the highlight to the desired option and then pressing a "return" or by entering the first letter of the option. The space bar can be used to move the highlight. The options in the main menu are explained below:

Form	This option can be used to create, compile, delete, run, or modify a form. It can also be used to generate a default form.
Report	This option can be used to create, compile, delete, run, or modify a report. It can also be used to generate a default report for a table.
Query-language	This option can be used to create, edit, and run SQL queries.
User-Menu	This option must be used to create user menus. Menus provide a user-friendly interface to a system. The next section discusses how this option can be used to create and modify user menus.
Database	This option can be used to create, select, or delete a database. Database deletion involves the elimination of the database with all associated tables. A database selection must be done so that the SQL processor knows the database to work on.
Table	This option can be used to create a new table, modify or delete an existing table, or to retrieve information about a table.
Exit	This option allows the user to return back to the UNIX environment.

Each option on the menu displays a sub-menu. The sub-menus are shown in Figure 6.7.

6.5 User-Menus

The earlier sections explained the use of INFORMIX commands to run queries and generate reports and forms. End users cannot be expected to run these UNIX-level commands. In fact, it is not advisable to provide the user an access to UNIX commands. A mechanism must be provided to the end user who need not be aware of the operating system on which the application is running. A menu interface provides this mechanism. From a user's perspective, a menu consists of the following components:

- A menu title: This is the heading of the menu which appears at the top.
- A selection number: This number, when selected by the user, executes the action associated with it.

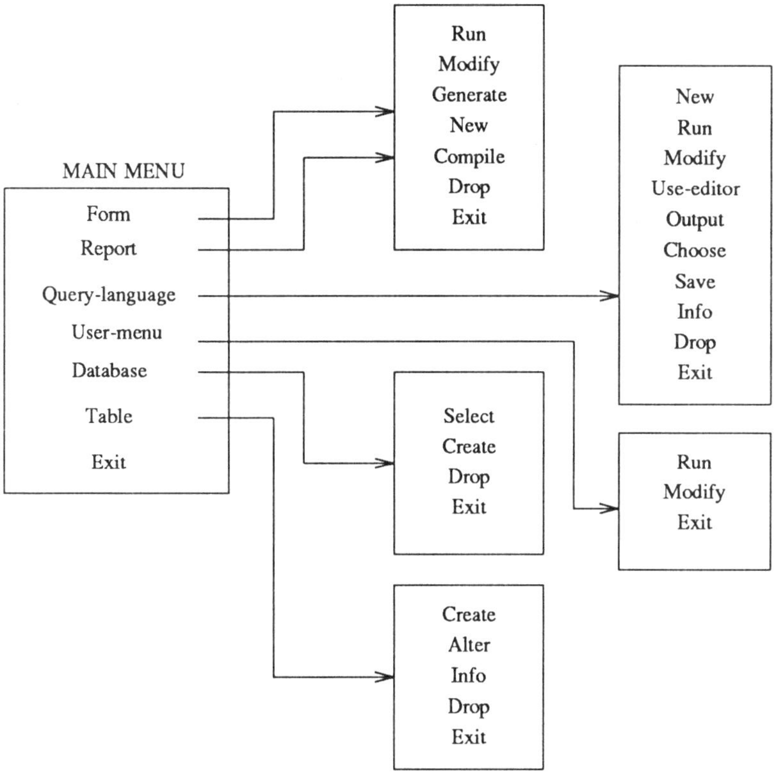

Figure 6.7 Informix Main Menu

- A selection text: This text describes the action which will be executed if the numeric option with which it is associated is selected.
- A menu prompt: A place on the screen where the user can enter the desired option.

The structure of a menu is shown in Figure 6.8. From a system designer's perspective, when a user selects a menu option, an action must be specified in terms of UNIX commands or INFORMIX utilities. The action can be classified into the following categories:

- Display a form: This action will execute *sperform* on a specified form which must be precompiled.

- Generate a report: This action will execute *sacego* on the specified report file which is assumed to have been precompiled using *saceprep*.
- Run a SQL query: This will run *isql* on the specified SQL script.
- Execute a UNIX command: This will execute the specified UNIX command. Of course, all the above actions can also be categorized under this action
- Display another menu: This will display the specified sub-menu.
- Exit the menu: When this is selected, the user is returned back to the calling program. If the current menu is a sub-menu, then the user is returned back to the parent menu. If the current menu is the main menu then the user is returned back to UNIX.

6.5.1 Designing a Menu Interface

This section discusses how menus can be used to design a front-end which isolates the user from the drudgery of running UNIX-level commands with all the options and syntax details. A menu must be associated with a database. The information about the structure of the menu, the selection text, the menu title, etc., is stored in two system tables: sysmenus and sysmenuitems. It is important to know the columns of these tables to understand the design procedure.

Table: sysmenus	**Table:** sysmenuitems
Fields:	**Fields:**
menuname	imenuname
title	itemnums
	mtext
	mtype
	progname
	nextmenu

The sysmenus table has two columns. The first column is used to store the name of a menu by which it can be identified. The second column is used to store the title of the menu. The second table, sysmenuitems, is used to store detail information about each menu. The first column identifies the parent menu with which this entry is associated. The column *itemnum* corresponds to the selection number of a menu. The column *mtext* stores the selection text associated with the *itemnum* option. The *mtype* column is used to store the type of action to be executed. The following types are recognized:

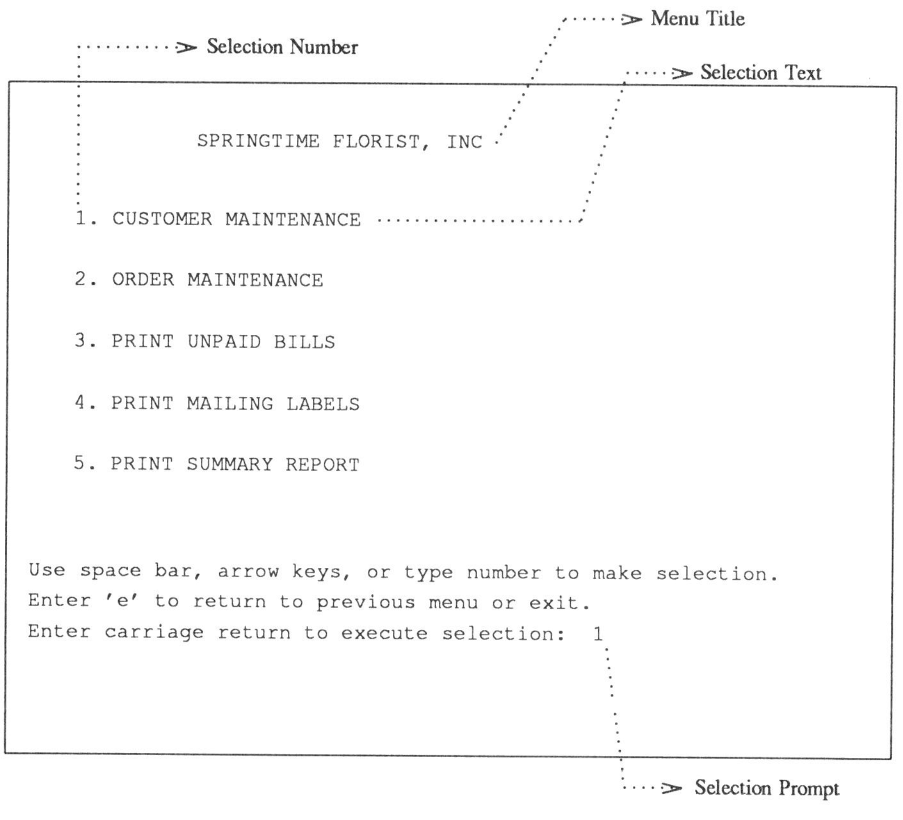

Figure 6.8 Structure of a Menu

M	Display another menu
P	Run a UNIX command
F	Display a user form
R	Generate a user-specified report
Q	Run an SQL query
S	Run a script menu (A script menu is one that includes more than one action for a single menu item)

The *nextmenu* column is not used. Clearly, the two columns, *menuname* in the sysmenus table and *imenuname* in the sysmenuitems table, can be looked at as join fields. Further, if a form is to be designed for interacting with these two tables, then there can be a master/detail relationship between the two tables sysmenus and sysmenuitems. In fact, that is exactly how the menu interface is designed. When the user invokes the *User-Menu* option of the INFORMIX menu, the screen shown in Figure 6.9 is displayed.

```
USER-MENU: [Run] Modify Exit
Run the user-menu for the current database
------------------- florist --------------------Press CTRL-W for Help---------
```

Figure 6.9 After Selecting the User-Menu Option

To create a new menu or to modify an existing one, the "modify" option must be used, after which the form shown in Figure 6.10 is displayed. The form interacts with the two menu maintenance tables sysmenus and sysmenuitems. A master/detail relationship is enforced on the two tables with sysmenus as the master of sysmenuitems. It is now a trivial task to enter information on the various components of the menu using this form. The first level menu must be named "main."

The lower part of the form corresponds to the table sysmenuitems. The *Detail* option of *perform* can be selected to make it the active table. The fields are self-explanatory. The field labeled "Selection type" is used to enter a value for the *mtype* columns. It is used to specify the type of action to be taken when the selection is invoked by the user. Values accepted by this field were discussed earlier. As an example, to enter the menu description for the menu shown in Figure 6.8, the user must make one entry to the sysmenus table and five entries to the sysmenuitems table. If an option is used to display another menu, then that menu must be described by the same procedure which is used to describe the *main* menu.

```
PERFORM: [Query] Next  Previous  Add  Update  Remove  Table  Screen  ...
Searches the active database table                ** 1: sysmenus table**
=========================MENU ENTRY FORM================================
Menu Name:  [          ]

Menu Title: [                                                          ]

------------------------SELECTION SECTION------------------------------

Selection Number:                      Selection Type:

Selection
Text:

Selection
Action:
```

Figure 6.10 Form for Entering Menu Data

6.5.2 Tying It Together

Menus with options to generate reports, display forms, or execute UNIX commands can be designed by the entering of the appropriate command name in the "Selection Action" field. If a customized version of *sperform* is to be used, then that command must be entered with the *-s* option to suppress copyright and other nonessential messages with a *P* for program as the action type rather than an *F* for form. Similarly, the *R* option for report should not be used if the report is to be generated from a customized *sacego*.

If the user is to be isolated from the UNIX environment, then an appropriate entry must be made in the user's .profile file to invoke *isql* automatically after login. The user can also be made to log off immediately after *isql* is used. The *isql* command has numerous options for the specification of different starting points. These are listed in Table 6.3.

In addition to these options, the first letters of the different sub-menus options can also be used. The most useful options are the *-s* and the *-u* options. The *-s* option, as explained earlier, is used to suppress redundant

TABLE 6.3 Important Isql Options

Option	Use
-s	To suppress copyright and other messages
-r	Display the *Report* option upon invocation
-q	Display the *Query-language* option upon invocation
-d	Display the *Database Menu* option upon invocation
-u	Display the *User-menu* option upon invocation

messages. The *-u* option can be used to display a specified menu as soon as the *isql* command is invoked. The following command, when invoked, suppresses all redundant messages and displays the *main* menu in the florist database:

```
isql -s florist -u main
```

This command is equivalent to

```
isql -s florist -ur
```

Here are some more examples:

```
isql -rc myrep
```

can be used to compile the report file myrep.ace and

```
isql -s -fr cust2
```

will suppress all copyright and other redundant messages and run the form cust2. Of course, *sacego* can also be used to do the same. The following line in the .profile file can be used to prevent non-UNIX users from getting to the UNIX environment after exiting from *isql*:

```
exec isql -s florist -u main
```

Of course, one can easily escape to the shell by using the *!* character or, better still, by running another shell. Well, don't tell the user about it!

6.6 Closing Thoughts

INFORMIX-SQL is a very powerful database management system. This chapter covered the salient features of the various components of the DBMS. For each command discussed here, there are numerous options. Though every attempt has been made to explain the important features, syntactic details are beyond the scope of this chapter. The INFORMIX reference manual is an excellent guide that designers must have at their sides. This chapter supplements the reference manual. It is by no means a substitute.

7 Embedded SQL

In Chapter 5 the SQL language was used to create a database and manipulate its contents. Though SQL is a very user-friendly language, it lacks several features. In particular, it cannot be used to write a query to implement any arbitrary retrieval. Also, there is no mechanism in SQL to have the information in the database interact with the outside world. For example, retrieving data from a table in a database based on information stored in a UNIX file outside the database is impossible. Of course, one can load the flat file into the database and then run a query against the loaded table, but there is no way to directly run a query against the database and a flat UNIX file.

The solution to this problem is to write a program, in a language such as C, which can interact with the UNIX file as well as the database files. The programmer will have to be aware of the internal structure of the database files. Even if that is known, the programming problem remains a nontrivial task. The ideal solution to this problem is to write SQL queries but, instead of redirecting the output to the screen or a file, make it available to the variables of a program written in a language such as C. This is possible by embedding SQL statements in the host language. In the UNIX environment the most popular host language for embedding SQL statements is C. However, one can embed SQL in other languages such as PL/1 and COBOL.

Programs written with SQL and the host language are called embedded SQL programs. The language itself is called embedded SQL. Programs written with embedded SQL can make use of the user-friendliness and power of SQL and the flexibility of the host language. This chapter discusses the embedded SQL package available from INFORMIX.

7.1 Implementation

Embedded SQL programs in the INFORMIX implementation consists of SQL statements embedded in C programs.

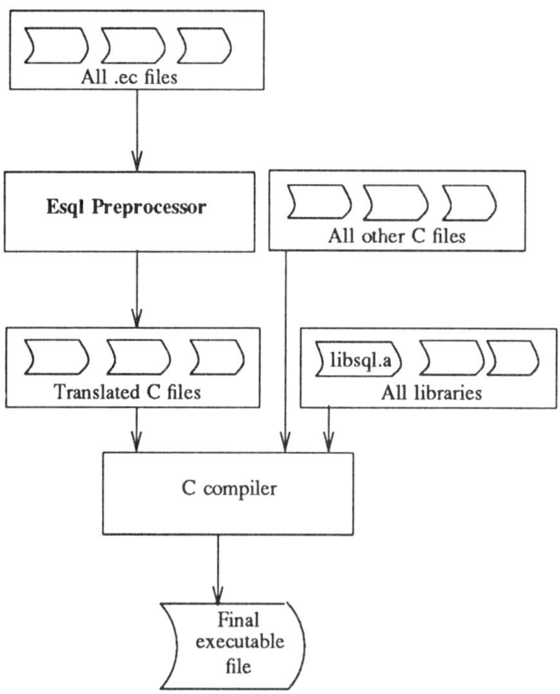

Figure 7.1 How Esql Works

All SQL statements must start with a dollar sign ($) and must be terminated by a semicolon. The *$* character must be the first non-white-space character on the line. In addition, C variables which are to be used to interface with SQL statements must also be identified with a declaration prefixed by the dollar sign. The *esql* program reads an embedded SQL program, identifies all statements starting with the *$*, and translates them into pure C code. Thus a program which had C and SQL statements is now made of pure C code only. The *esql* program then invokes the C compiler with the appropriate libraries and header files to generate the final executable code. The working of the *esql* program is shown in figure 7.1. All embedded SQL files must be suffixed by an *.ec*. The *esql* command can be used to invoke the embedded SQL processor, as shown below:

```
esql myprog.ec
```

A file suffixed *.c* is created and compiled with the required libraries to produce the final executable. In the above example, when *esql* is run on the file myprog.ec, a file called myprog.c is created and compiled with the required libraries to produce the final executable a.out. If the *-e* option is used, *esql* will stop after it generates the C program file. If other options are used, they are passed to the C compiler. For example, if a *-o* option is used with an argument, it will be used to name the final executable file.

7.2 Getting Started

Though the primary use of *esql* lies in its capability to be used as a Data Manipulation Language (DML) to manipulate the contents of a database, it can also be used as a Data Definition Language (DDL) to create and modify the database schema. All *esql* programs in this chapter will use the florist database used in Chapter 5. Here is an embedded SQL program to create a database and associated tables:

```
cat prog1.ec
main()
{

/* Create a database called florist */
$create database florist;

/* Make it the current database */
$database florist;
```

```
/* Create a table called customers */
$create table customers
(
c_no     char(10),
c_lname char(20),
c_fname char(20),
c_addr1 char(20),
c_addr2 char(20),
c_town   char(20),
c_state char(2),
c_zip    char(5)
);

/* Create another table called orders */
$create table orders
(
c_no     char(10),
o_no     integer,
o_amt    money,
o_date   date,
o_desc   char(30),
o_del_chg        money,
o_paid   money
);

}
esql progl.ec
a.out
```

Clearly, this program consists of a single *main* function with only SQL statements! All the SQL statements start with a *$* and are terminated by a semicolon. When the program is executed, the florist.dbs directory is created with the database and all the system and user files associated with it. The two user tables are empty. The database created with the *esql* program has the same structure as the database created with *isql*. All SQL statements can be run on this database by use of the *isql* command. For example, data from flat files can be loaded into the database by use of the *isql* command, as shown below:

```
cat ld.sql
load from "orders.d"
insert into orders;
load from "cust.d"
insert into customers
isql florist ld

11 row(s) loaded.

10 row(s) loaded.
```

Esql can also be used to load data into the database. This will be explained later. The contents of the cust.d file from which the customers table is loaded is

```
cat cust.d
2012428055|Doe|John|Apt. 2|782 Clifton Ave.|Shalantown|NJ|07104
8000011212|Smith|Mike|32 Palisade Ave.||Ringwood|NJ|07456
2011212451|McAlister|Todd|44 Park Ave.||Plainfield|NJ|07060
2013211234|Parab|Umesh|55 Slick St.||Midland Park|NJ|07432
2014561412|Dev|Kapil|55 Cricket Drive||Ocean|NJ|07712
2013211341|Botham|Ian|72 Fast Avenue||Nutley|NJ|07110
2014311211|Lillee|Dennis|92 Australia St.||Orange|NJ|07051
2018911211|Roberts|Maria|72 Cinconni Dr.||Lakewood|NJ|08701
2016667777|Marshal|Jennifer|11 Indies Lane||Paramus|NJ|07652
6091212121|Hadlee|Richard|112 Allround St.||Princeton|NJ|08540
```

and the contents of the orders.d file is:

```
cat orders.d
2012428055|1|45.70|12/12/1987|A dozen roses|5.00|15
2012428055|2|50|2/12/1988|Centerpiece|15.00|20
2013211234|1|872.00|1/24/1988|Wedding Arrang.|7.00|400.00
2013211234|2|70.00|1/24/1988|Birthday Arrang.|7.00|00.00
2013211341|1|25.00|2/12/1988|Basket Willis|6.00|55.00
2018911211|2|55.00|2/12/1988|Casket Spray|3.00|75.00
2016667777|4|75.00|3/27/1988|Birthday Arr.|4.00|85.00
6091212121|1|12.00|6/19/1988|Baby Girl Arr.|5.00|100.00
6091212121|2|50.00|2/2/1988|A dozen roses|2.00|10.00
6091212121|3|70.00|3/2/1988|Funeral Wreath|2.00|10.00
2123211411|1|100.00|3/12/1988|2 Dozen roses|5.00|90.00
```

Henceforth, it will be assumed in all examples in this chapter that the tables in the database are loaded with the two files shown here.

7.3 Retrieving Data

The SQL *select* statement can be embedded in C programs to retrieve data from the database. The retrieved data can then be processed by the C statements, thus giving the user the power of C and SQL in one program. The data is actually retrieved into the specified C variables. The user must make these variables known to the *esql* processor by prefixing the corresponding C declarations for these variables by a dollar sign as indicated earlier. The following program retrieves the first-name and last-name fields from the customers table where customer no. = 2012428055.

```
cat -n prog2.ec
$include  sqlca.h;
main()
{
/* C variables to accept SQL-retrieved data */
$char cc_fname[21], cc_lname[21];
/* Name of the database */
$database florist;
/* SQL statement which interacts with the C variables. */
$ select c_fname, c_lname into
   $cc_fname, $cc_lname
   from customers
   where c_no = "2012428055";
printf("First name            Last name\n");
printf("==========            =========\n\n");
printf("%s %s\n",cc_fname,cc_lname);
}
```

```
esql prog2.ec
a.out
First name          Last name
==========          =========

John                Doe
```

The italicized line numbers are, of course, not part of the program. The SQL *select* statement which does the actual retrieval is used in line 13. This statement is syntactically different from the *select* statement used by *isql*. Specifically, the *into* clause is provided here to specify a list of C variables in which the data is retrieved. The number of columns retrieved must therefore be equal to the number of C variables specified in the *into* list. Values for the retrieved columns of the selected row are assigned to the C variables *cc_fname* and *cc_lname*. Note that these variables were declared with the *$* to indicate that they would be used subsequently to interact with SQL statements. Also the size of the C character array must be greater than the size of the database column to accommodate the additional *NULL* character at the end of the retrieved string.

In the program just shown, we assumed that only one row will be retrieved after the query is executed. The set of variables declared to accept the retrieved data can handle only one row. When a *select* statement retrieves multiple rows, a different mechanism must be provided to handle them. The *cursor* object is used to provide this mechanism. A cursor is associated with a select statement. When the cursor is opened, the specified *select* statement is executed. Subsequently, the *fetch* operation can be performed on it repeatedly for the retrieval of one record at a time into the specified list of C variables. Here is a modified version of the previous program to handle multiple records:

```
cat -n prog3.ec
$include  sqlca.h;
main()
{
   /* C variables to accept SQL-retrieved data */
   $char cc_fname[21], cc_lname[21];
   /* Name of the database */
   $database florist;
   /* SQL statement which interacts with the C variables. */
   /* Associate cursor with the SQL statement          */
```

```
13    $declare cursor1 cursor for
14            select c_fname, c_lname into
15            $cc_fname, $cc_lname
16            from customers;
17
18    /* Initiate the execution */
19    $open cursor1;
20
21    printf("First name            Last name\n");
22    printf("==========            =========\n\n");
23    while(1)
24    {
25
26            /* Get the first record */
27            $fetch cursor1;
28
29            /* Was a record retrieved */
30            if (sqlca.sqlcode) break;
31            printf("%s %s\n",cc_fname,cc_lname);
32    }
33
34    /* Deactivate the cursor */
35    $close cursor1;
36
37  }
```

```
esql prog2.ec -o prog2
prog2
First name              Last name
==========              =========


John                    Doe
Mike                    Smith
Todd                    McAlister
Umesh                   Parab
Kapil                   Dev
Ian                     Botham
Dennis                  Lillee
Maria                   Roberts
Jennifer                Marshal
Richard                 Hadlee
```

The *select* statement retrieves multiple records and is identified by the "cursor1" cursor. When the cursor is opened (in line 19) by the use of an *open* statement, the *select* statement associated with it is analyzed and executed. The required rows are identified. A subsequent *fetch* operation (in line 27) on the cursor retrieves the desired columns of the first selected row into the list of C variables specified in the *into* clause of the *select* statement. This *fetch* operation can be repeated so that more records from the selected set can be retrieved. The *sqlca.sqlcode* variable is set to a nonzero value when no more records are available. Once the columns are retrieved in the C variables, the information can be processed further by use of additional C code.

The variables in which the data is to be retrieved can be specified in the *fetch* statement instead of the *select* statement. The *select* and the *fetch* statements in the previous program can be rewritten as:

```
$declare cursor1 cursor for
        select c_fname, c_lname
        from customers;
```

and

```
$fetch cursor1 into $cc_fname, $cc_lname;
```

7.3.1 Error Processing

After executing SQL statements within C programs, the user should check to see if the statement has been executed successfully. The elements of the *sqlca* structure can be examined to determine if any error occurred during the execution. This structure is declared in the header file sqlca.h as shown below:

```
struct sqlca_s
    {
    long sqlcode;
    char sqlerrm[72]; /* error message parameters */
    char sqlerrp[8];
    long sqlerrd[6];
        /* 0 - reserved         */
        /* 1 - serial value after insert or  ISAM error code */
        /* 2 - number of rows processed */
        /* 3 - estimated cost */
        /* 4 - offset into of an error */
        /* 5 - rowid after insert  */
```

```
        struct sqlcaw_s
         {
         char sqlwarn0; /* =W if any of sqlwarn[1-7] = W */
         char sqlwarn1; /* =W if any truncation occurred  */
         char sqlwarn2; /* =W if a null value returned */
         char sqlwarn3; /* =W if no. in sel. list != no. in into list*/
         char sqlwarn4; /* =W if no where clause on prepared update,
                         delete */
         char sqlwarn5; /* reserved */
         char sqlwarn6; /* reserved */
         char sqlwarn7; /* reserved */
         } sqlwarn;
        };

    extern struct sqlca_s sqlca;
```

All error codes are returned in *sqlca.sqlcode*. Its value must be examined after every SQL statement. For example, after a *fetch* operation, the value of the *sqlcode* element can be examined to detect end of input. A value of *SQLNOTFOUND* indicates that there is no further input to be processed. A negative value indicates that an error occurred during execution. This value can be printed; the manual documents the error message corresponding to this error number. If a C-ISAM error occurs, it can be detected by an examination of the contents of the variable *sqlca.sqlerrd[1]*. C-ISAM will be discussed in the next chapter.

In addition, the *sql_warn* structure can be used to detect other error conditions. The single character elements of this structure are set to 'W' to indicate a warning/error. The first element, *sqlwarn0* is set to 'W' to indicate that at least one warning condition occurred. This warning condition can then be identified by examination of the status of the other elements. For example, if truncation occurred in one or more elements, the variable *sqlwarn1* is set to 'W'. If a null value is encountered during aggregate function computation in an SQL statement, then the *sqlwarn2* element is set to 'W'. If the number of columns in a *select* statement does not match the number of C variables in the *into* clause, then the element *sqlcawarn3* is set to 'W'. If the *where* clause is missing in a prepared SQL *update* or *delete* statement, then all rows will be updated or deleted. This may be done inadvertently, and the *sqlwarn4* element is used to detect this situation. Prepared SQL statements are discussed later in this chapter.

The following program retrieves two records from the customers table and prints the name fields:

```
#include  <stdio.h>
$include sqlca;
main()
{
   /* C variables to accept SQL-retrieved data */
   $char cc_fname[21];
   $char cc_lname[21];
   int count_rec=0;

   /* Name of the database */
   $database florist;
   print_status("database open");

   /* SQL statement which interacts with the C variables. */
   /* Associate cursor with the SQL statement            */
   $declare cursor1 cursor for
       select c_fname
       into $cc_fname, $cc_lname
       from customers;

   /* Initiate the execution */
   $open cursor1;
   print_status("open cursor");
   printf("First name           Last name\n");
   printf("==========           =========\n\n");

   while(1)
   {
      /* Start reading records */
      $fetch cursor1;
      print_status("fetch cursor");
  /* After two records or EOF */
      if (sqlca.sqlcode || count_rec++ == 2 )
         break;
      printf("%s %s\n",cc_fname,cc_lname);
   }

   /* Deactivate the cursor */
   $close cursor1;
   print_status("close cursor");
}
```

```
print_status(statmt)
char *statmt;
{
 fprintf(stderr,"==============================================\n");
 fprintf(stderr,"Status of SQLCA structure after %s\n",statmt);
 fprintf(stderr,"sqlcode: %ld\n",sqlca.sqlcode);
 if (sqlca.sqlerrd[1] < 0)
  printf("C-ISAM errror: %ld\n",sqlca.sqlerrd[1]);
 fprintf(stderr,"Number of rows processed: %ld\n",sqlca.sqlerrd[2]);
 if (sqlca.sqlerrd[4] > 0)
  fprintf(stderr,"Error at character number: %ld\n",sqlca.sqlerrd[4]);
 if (sqlca.sqlwarn.sqlwarn0 == 'W')
 {
  if (sqlca.sqlwarn.sqlwarn1 == 'W')
   fprintf(stderr,"Truncation occurred in some variable(s)\n");
  if (sqlca.sqlwarn.sqlwarn2 == 'W')
   fprintf(stderr,"NULL value encountered in aggr. calculation\n");
  if (sqlca.sqlwarn.sqlwarn3 == 'W')
   fprintf(stderr,"No. of cols. in select list != no. of host vars.\n"
  if (sqlca.sqlwarn.sqlwarn4 == 'W')
   fprintf(stderr,"Missing where clause in a update/delete statement")
 }
 if (sqlca.sqlcode < 0)
 {
  fprintf(stderr,"Aborting...\n");
  exit(1);
 }
}
```

When compiled and executed, the program displays:

```
esql prog4.ec
a.out 2>err.log
First name            Last name
==========            =========

John
Mike
cat err.log
==============================================
Status of SQLCA structure after database open
sqlcode: 0
```

```
Number of rows processed: 0
================================================
Status of SQLCA structure after open cursor
sqlcode: 0
Number of rows processed: 0
================================================
Status of SQLCA structure after fetch cursor
sqlcode: 0
Number of rows processed: 10
No. of cols. in select list != no. of host vars.
================================================
Status of SQLCA structure after fetch cursor
sqlcode: 0
Number of rows processed: 10
No. of cols. in select list != no. of host vars.
================================================
Status of SQLCA structure after fetch cursor
sqlcode: 0
Number of rows processed: 10
No. of cols. in select list != no. of host vars.
================================================
Status of SQLCA structure after close cursor
sqlcode: 0
Number of rows processed: 0
```

The *print_status* function is used to print the status of the *sqlca* structure. No errors or warnings are detected after the execution of the *database* or *open* statements. However, the *fetch* statement detects a problem in the *select* statement. The number of columns and the number of C variables in the select statement do not match. This is detected and reported by the *print_status* function. Though this program invokes the *print_status* function after every SQL statement, that could slow the program. In practice, the *sqlca.sqlcode* variable should be checked after every SQL statement where a possibility of an error is high, and the contents of the *sqlca* structure should be printed only if an error condition is detected. Warning situations can be detected, where appropriate, by examining the contents of the *sqlwarn* structure.

In any event, if an error condition occurs, an attempt must be made to report its cause before the program is terminated. If the *select* statement in the previous program is changed from

```
select c_fname
```

to

```
select c_fname, c_llname
```

the program will not report any error at compilation time because the compiler, of course, does not check the database schema to detect an error column name. However, when executed, the program terminates abnormally but gracefully! This is shown below:

```
a.out 2>err
cat err
=====================================================
Status of SQLCA structure after: database open
sqlcode: 0
Number of rows processed: 0
=====================================================
Status of SQLCA structure after: open cursor
sqlcode: -217
Number of rows processed: 0
Error at character number: 28
Aborting...
```

The character position where the error occurs is approximate. To get the exact location of the error, examine the SQL statement assigned to the variable *_sqlcmdtxt[]* in the generated C program.

7.3.2 Null Values and String Truncation

If a C variable to accept character data is declared with a length shorter than the length of the database column, then it is possible for the data to be truncated when retrieved in the C variable. This truncation can be detected with the examination of the contents of the *sqlca* structure as was done earlier. However, with use of this mechanism, it is not possible to identify the column which was truncated. Another problem is encountered when a null value is retrieved. It must be possible to detect that a null value was retrieved and process it accordingly. These two problems can be handled by the use of an indicator variable.

An indicator variable is a short integer which is associated with a host variable (A C variable in which the database value is to be retrieved). After a *select* statement is executed, the value of the indicator variable must be checked to identify if a null value was retrieved. This variable can also be used to detect the truncation of string data. If a null value is retrieved, the indicator variable is set to a negative value. If a string is truncated, then the indicator variable is set to the length of the untruncated string as stored in the database.

Here is a program which retrieves two records from the customers table:

```
cat prog5.ec
#include  <stdio.h>
$include sqlca;
main()
{

   /* C variables to accept SQL-retrieved data */
   $char cc_addr1[21];
   $char cc_addr2[12];
   $char cc_no[21];
   $short addr1_ind, addr2_ind;
   int count_rec=0;

   /* Name of the database */
   $database florist;

   /* SQL statement which interacts with the C variables. */
   /* Associate cursor with the SQL statement            */
   $declare cursor1 cursor for
    select c_addr1,c_addr2, c_no
       into $cc_addr1:addr1_ind, $cc_addr2:addr2_ind, $cc_no
       from customers;

   /* Initiate the execution */
   $open cursor1;
   printf("Address line1       Address line2\n");
   printf("=============       =============\n\n");

   while(1)
   {
      /* Start reading records */
      $fetch cursor1;

      if (sqlca.sqlcode || count_rec++ == 2 )
         break;
      if (addr2_ind < 0)
       fprintf(stderr,
        "NULL value encountered in c_addr2,c_no: %s\n", cc_no);
      if (addr2_ind > 0)
       fprintf(stderr,
        "c_addr2 truncated by %d characters,c_no: %s\n",
```

```
41              addr2_ind-strlen(cc_addr2),cc_no );
42
43          printf("%s %s\n",cc_addr1,cc_addr2);
44      }
45
46      /* Deactivate the cursor */
47      $close cursor1;
48  }
```

The program is simplified by the elimination of all error processing statements. Note that the *cc_addr2* variable is declared to have a length shorter than the length of the corresponding column in the customers table. When compiled and executed, the error messages displayed are

```
esql prog5.ec
a.out 2>err.log
Address line1          Address line2
=============          =============

Apt. 2                 782 Clifton
32 Palisade Ave.
cat err.log
c_addr2 truncated by 9 characters,c_no: 2012428055
NULL value encountered in c_addr2,c_no: 8000011212
```

C statements from line 35 to line 41 handle null values and truncation of character strings.

7.3.3 Using a Scroll Cursor

In the earlier examples, a cursor was associated with a *select* statement and the name of this cursor was used to execute the *select* statement and retrieve the selected records. Though this mechanism suffices for most applications, it does not allow scrolling through the set of selected records. Once a new record is fetched, the previous record is lost unless the program has explicitly copied it in C variables. It cannot be fetched again without the *select* statement again being executed. Also, there is no explicit mechanism to access any random record from the selected set. For example, if the program wishes to access only the first and the last record from the selected set, it still has to *fetch* all the records.

A scroll cursor is provided to circumvent this problem. Conceptually, it provides a pointer into the set of selected records. The *fetch* statement is modified to retrieve a record pointed by this pointer. In the absence of this pointer, the *fetch* statement retrieves the next record.

The keyword *scroll* is used to declare a cursor to have this additional feature. For example, the *esql* statement

```
$declare scr_cursor scroll cursor for
  select c_no,  o_amt
     int cc_no, c_o_amt
       from orders;
```

makes *scr_cursor* a scroll cursor. It can now be used in a *fetch* statement to retrieve any record based on the specified position. In general, the *fetch* statement is modified as follows:

```
fetch [position] cursor_name
```

For example, to retrieve the last record from the selected set, the following *fetch* statement can be used:

```
$fetch last scr_cursor;
```

Unlike the *fetch* statements used in earlier examples, the purpose of this statement is not only to retrieve the next record, but to first position the cursor as desired and then to retrieve the record. If a position is not specified, the next record from the set is retrieved. If specified, the position can be one of the following:

Position	Description
First	Fetch the first row
Last	Fetch the last row
Current	Fetch the same row again
Prior	Fetch the previous row
Previous	Same as prior
Relative *n*	If *n* is positive, position the cursor *n* records forward and then retrieve the record it points to. If *n* is negative, position the cursor *n* records backward and then retrieve the record it points to

Next	Fetch the next record. If no position is specified, this is the default
Absolute *n*	Get the *n*th record in the selected set

Consider the following *select* statement:

```
$declare cursor1 scroll cursor for
        select c_no
         into $cc_no
         from customers
         order by c_no;
```

A scroll cursor is associated with it. The set of records retrieved will be sorted on the *c_no* field. A *fetch* operation on the selected records can be made to scroll through this set, as shown in Figure 7.2.

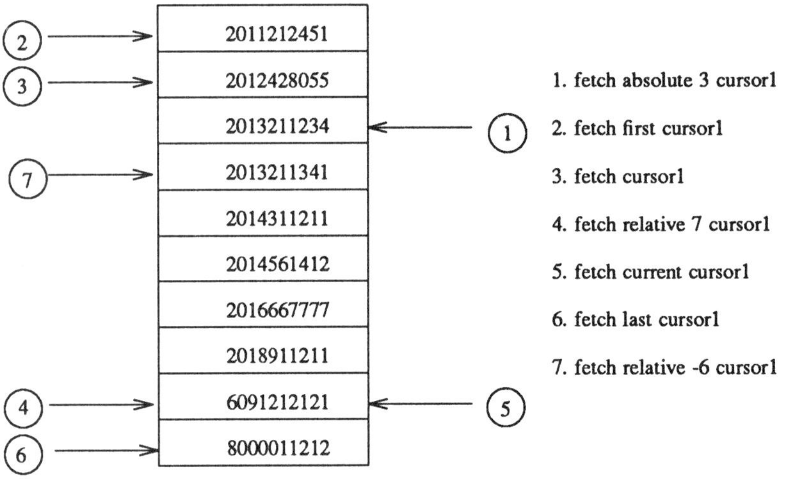

Figure 7.2 Scrolling in a Fetch Statement

The scroll feature is extremely useful, as it gives random access to any record in the selected set.

7.3.4 Retrieving Different Data Types

So far, the SQL statements in the *esql* programs were used only to retrieve character data. Of course, it is possible to retrieve other data types also. The host variables which accept the SQL columns must be declared appropriately. The programmer must be aware of the mapping between SQL data types and C data types. In addition, constants are defined in the SQL header file *sqltypes.h* to identify these data types. The mapping between the C and SQL data types and the corresponding constants defined in the header file is listed in Table 7.1.

Esql attempts to do appropriate conversion if the SQL data type does not match the C data type of the host variables. However, such conversion may result in roundoffs and truncation. The programmer must, therefore, declare the host variables correctly. *Esql* provides a powerful set of library functions to do conversion between the different data types. In particular, the functions which handle date and decimal data types are extremely useful. When a string is retrieved into a host variable which is declared as an array of characters, the trailing blanks are retained.

TABLE 7.1 RDSQL vs. C Data Types

SQL data type	C data type	RDSQL constant	C constant
char	char	SQLCHAR	CCHARTYPE CSTRINGTYPE CFIXCHARTYPE
smallint	short int	SQLSMINT	CSHORTTYPE
integer	long int	SQLINT	CLONGTYPE
serial	long int	SQLSERIAL	CLONGTYPE
smallfloat	float	SQLSMFLOAT	CFLOATTYPE
float	double	SQLFLOAT	CDOUBLETYPE
date	long int	SQLDATE	CLONGTYPE
money	struct decimal *or* dec_t	SQLMONEY	CDECIMALTYPE
decimal	struct decimal *or* dec_t	SQLDECIMAL	CDECIMALTYPE

Esql provides two other C data types for host variables. They are "string" and "fixchar". The "string" data type truncates trailing blanks from the retrieved data item; it inserts a null character in place of the first trailing blank. The "fixchar" data type does not terminate the string by a null character. Thus a host variable can be declared to have the same size as the corresponding database column. C functions, such as *strcpy*, which expect strings to be terminated by a null character will not function properly with "fixchar" data types. Figure 7.3 indicates how a "char" data type is moved into the host variable depending on the data type of the host variable. If there is a truncation of the data, then the *sqlca.sqlwarn.sqlwarn1* variable is set to 'W'. If there is an error in data conversion during the data transfer from the database to the host variable then the *sqlca.sqlcode* variable is set to a negative value which indicates an error.

The following program prints a report indicating the total amount due for each order. Note the use of the *dectodbl* function in lines 38 to 40 to convert a *dec_t* data type to a "double" data type and the *rdatestr* function in line 43 which converts a "long" data type to an array of characters which indicates the date that the long integer represents.

```
1  #include <stdio.h>
2  #include <decimal.h>
3  $include sqlca;
4  main()
5  {
6     $char cc_no[11], co_desc[31];
7     $long co_no;
8     $long co_date;
9     $dec_t co_amt,co_paid,co_del_chg;
10    char date_string[11];
11    double dbl_co_amt,dbl_co_paid,dbl_co_del_chg,tot_due,tot;
12    int i;
13
14    $database mydb;
15
16    $declare cursor1 cursor for
17        select c_no, o_no, o_del_chg,
18        o_amt, o_date, o_desc,
19        o_del_chg, o_paid
20        into
21        $cc_no, $co_no, $co_del_chg,
22        $co_amt, $co_date, $co_desc,
23        $co_paid
24        from orders
25        order by c_no,o_no;
26
27    $open cursor1;
28    printf("Customer No  Order No   Order Date  Tot. Amt");
29    printf("   Paid    Due\n");
30    printf("===========  ========   ==========  ========");
```

```
    printf("    ====    =====\n");
    while(1)
    {
            $fetch cursor1;
            if (sqlca.sqlcode) break;

            /* Convert dec_t to double */
            dectodbl(&co_amt,&dbl_co_amt);
            dectodbl(&co_del_chg,&dbl_co_del_chg);
            dectodbl(&co_paid,&dbl_co_paid);

            /* Convert long to date string */
            rdatestr(co_date,date_string);

            /* Calculate total amount and amount due */
            tot = dbl_co_amt + dbl_co_del_chg;
            tot_due = tot - dbl_co_paid;

            printf("%s  %4ld        %s   %6.2f  %6.2f  %6.2f\n",
             cc_no,co_no, date_string, tot, dbl_co_paid, tot_due);
    }
}
```

When compiled and executed, this program prints

```
Customer No  Order No   Order Date  Tot. Amt   Paid    Due
===========  ========   ==========  ========   ====   =====
2012428055      1       12/12/1987    50.70    5.00   45.70
2012428055      2       02/12/1988    65.00   15.00   50.00
2013211234      1       01/24/1988   879.00    7.00  872.00
2013211234      2       01/24/1988    77.00    7.00   70.00
2013211341      1       02/12/1988    31.00    6.00   25.00
2016667777      4       03/27/1988    79.00    4.00   75.00
2018911211      2       02/12/1988    58.00    3.00   55.00
2123211411      1       03/12/1988   105.00    5.00  100.00
6091212121      1       06/19/1988    17.00    5.00   12.00
6091212121      2       02/02/1988    52.00    2.00   50.00
6091212121      3       03/02/1988    72.00    2.00   70.00
```

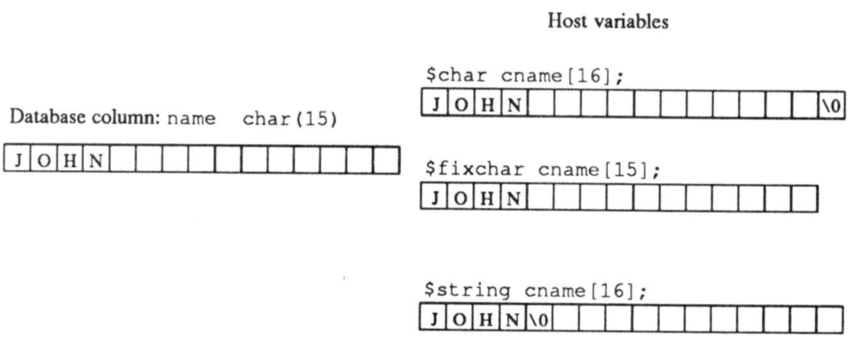

Figure 7.3 Transferring Character Strings into Host Variables

7.3.4.1 Other Functions for Data Type Conversion

There are several other functions available for data type conversion. The *rdatestr* function was used in the program to convert a long integer into a string data type. Similarly, the *rstrdate* function can be used to convert a date stored as a string into a long integer. The date string must have three numbers separated by a nonnumeric character, and the year must be a 4-digit number such as 1988. If the format of the string does not conform to this standard, then the *rdefmtdate* function must be used. It needs an additional argument to specify the format. Similarly, the *rfmtdate* function can be used to convert a date stored as a long integer to a string having a specified format. In addition to these conversion functions, several other functions are available for manipulation of date fields. For example, the *rtoday* function returns today's date as a long integer, and the *rdayofweek* function returns the day of the week, of any specified date, as an integer.

Functions are also available for conversion from decimal data type to other data types, and vice-versa. The *dectodbl* function was used earlier for conversion from decimal data type to double data type. Other functions include the *dectoasc* function which converts a decimal value to an ASCII string, the *deccvasc* function which converts an ASCII string to a decimal value, and the *dectoint* function which converts a decimal value to an integer. If an arithmetic operation is to be performed on a decimal data type, it can be done by first converting the value to an appropriate C data type and then performing the arithmetic operation or by use of some of the functions which are provided explicitly for arithmetic computation on decimal data types. The functions provided for this purpose include *decadd* for addition of values stored in decimal structures, *decmul* for multiplication, and "decdiv" for division. The previous program for computing the amount due on each order is rewritten below using some additional functions:

```
#include <stdio.h>
#include <decimal.h>
$include sqlca;
main()
{
   $char cc_no[11], co_desc[31];
   $long co_no;
   $long co_date;
   $dec_t co_amt,co_paid,co_del_chg,dec_tot;
   char date_string[14];
   double dbl_co_amt,dbl_co_paid,dbl_co_del_chg,tot_due,tot;
   int i;

   $database mydb;

   $declare cursor1 cursor for
      select c_no, o_no, o_del_chg,
      o_amt, o_date, o_desc,
      o_del_chg, o_paid
      into
      $cc_no, $co_no, $co_del_chg,
      $co_amt, $co date, $co desc,
      $co_paid
      from orders
      order by c_no,o_no;

   $open cursor1;
   printf("Customer No  Order No  Order Date  Tot. Amt");
   printf("   Paid    Due\n");
   printf("===========  ========  ===========  ========");
   printf("   ====    =====\n");
   while(1)
   {
         $fetch cursor1;
         if (sqlca.sqlcode) break;

         /* Convert dec_t to double */
         dectodbl(&co_paid,&dbl_co_paid);

```

```
40              /* Convert long to date string */
41              rfmtdate(co_date,"mmm. dd, yy",date_string);
42
43              /* Calculate total amount and amount due */
44              decadd(&co_amt,&co_del_chg,&dec_tot);;
45              dectodbl(&dec_tot,&tot);
46              tot_due = tot - dbl_co_paid;
47
48              printf("%s  %4ld       %s   %6.2f  %6.2f  %6.2f\n",
49               cc_no,co_no, date_string, tot, dbl_co_paid, tot_due);
50      }
51  }
```

When compiled and executed, the program generates the report shown earlier with one change: the date is printed in the format *mmm. dd, yy*. Here is the first detail line of the output report:

```
2012428055      1         Dec. 12, 87    50.70    5.00   45.70
```

The function *decadd* is invoked in line 44 to compute the total of the amount field and the delivery charge. The result is put in the decimal variable *dec_tot*. Also, in line 41, the *rfmtdate* function is used to retrieve the date string in the specified format: *mmm. dd, yy*.

7.4 Dynamic Select Statements

In all the *esql* programs examined in the previous section, the *select* statement was known at compile time. In practice this restriction is impractical. If the columns to be retrieved change, the program will have to be modified and recompiled. This is both inefficient and inelegant. Also, it should be possible to specify the values for the parameters in the *where* clause at run time. In the worst case, the entire query is known only at run time!

Consider a program which retrieves the name of a customer after prompting for the customer number. Clearly, the *esql* statements used so far will not suffice to write a program to do this. At compile time only the columns to be retrieved are known. The selection criterion is also specified at compile time but the values of the parameters in the *where* clause are known only at run time.

A new *esql* statement will be introduced at this point: the *prepare* statement analyzes a string having an SQL statement, checks for syntactic errors, and assigns an identifier to it. This identifier is associated with a cursor in a *declare* statement. This cursor can be used subsequently in an *open* statement to execute the query and in a *fetch* statement to retrieve a record from the selected set. Here is the required program:

```
1  #include <stdio.h>
2  $include sqlca;
3  main()
4  {
5     $char cc_no[11];
6     $string cc_lname[21],cc_fname[21];
7     $char query_string[300];
8     $char user_input[11];
9
10    $database florist;
11
12    /* Build the query */
13    strcpy(query_string,
14      "select c_no, c_lname, c_fname from customers ");
15    strcat(query_string," where c_no = ? ");
16    $prepare query1 from $query_string;
17    $declare mycursor cursor for query1;
18
19    printf("Input a 10 digit customer no: ");
20    scanf("%s", user_input);
21
22    $open mycursor using $user_input;
23
24    $fetch mycursor into $cc_no, $cc_lname, $cc_fname;
25    if (sqlca.sqlcode==SQLNOTFOUND)
26            fprintf(stderr,"Customer record not found\n");
27    else
28            printf("%s:%s:%s\n", cc_no, cc_lname, cc_fname);
29
30 }
```

A *?* character is used in place of all unknown parameters in the *where* clause of the query string. The *prepare* statement in line 16 checks for syntactic and semantic errors in the specified query string and assigns it an identifier. This identifier is subsequently used in line 17 to associate a cursor with the query. Note the use of the host variables in the *fetch* statement in line 24. The *into* clause cannot be used in a prepared *select* statement and therefore the *fetch* statement is used to specify the C variables in which the data is to be retrieved. The *open* statement in line 22 is also modified. This statement actually executes the prepared statement, and therefore all values used in the *where* clause must be known at this point. The *using* clause is used to specify the C variables whose values are substituted for the *?* in the *where* clause. When compiled and executed, the program runs as shown below:

```
a.out
Input a 10 digit customer no: 2012428055
2012428055:Doe:John
a.out
Input a 10 digit customer no: 2012331111
Customer record not found
```

If the columns to be retrieved are not known until execution time, then several additional statements are required to handle the problem. Figure 7.4 indicates the various steps required to process dynamic *select* statements in which information about columns to be retrieved is known only at execution time. Not knowing the columns to be retrieved poses the additional problem that memory must be allocated to host variables at run time. In fact, even the data types of the host variables are known only at execution time. *Esql* provides the *sqlda* structure and the *describe* statement to handle this problem. The *describe* statement examines the database schema stored in the system tables and the query string. It then describes the query into a *sqlda* structure which can be handled by the program, eliminating the need to parse the query string.

The *sqlda* structure provides information on the number of fields to be retrieved. In addition, for each field it provides information about its type and length. It also allocates a pointer for each field. Since the type and length of the data to be retrieved is now known, space can be *malloc*ed and the pointer for each field made to point to this space. When the *fetch* statement is executed, this *malloc*ed space is used as host variables into which to retrieve the data. The structure of the *sqlda* structure is:

```
struct sqlvar_struct
    {
    short sqltype;     /* variable type        */
    short sqllen;      /* length in bytes      */
    char *sqldata;     /* pointer to data      */
    short *sqlind;     /* pointer to indicator*/
    char  *sqlname;    /* variable name        */
    char  *sqlformat; /* reserved for future use */
    };
```

```
struct sqlda
    {
    short sqld;
    struct sqlvar_struct *sqlvar;
    };
```

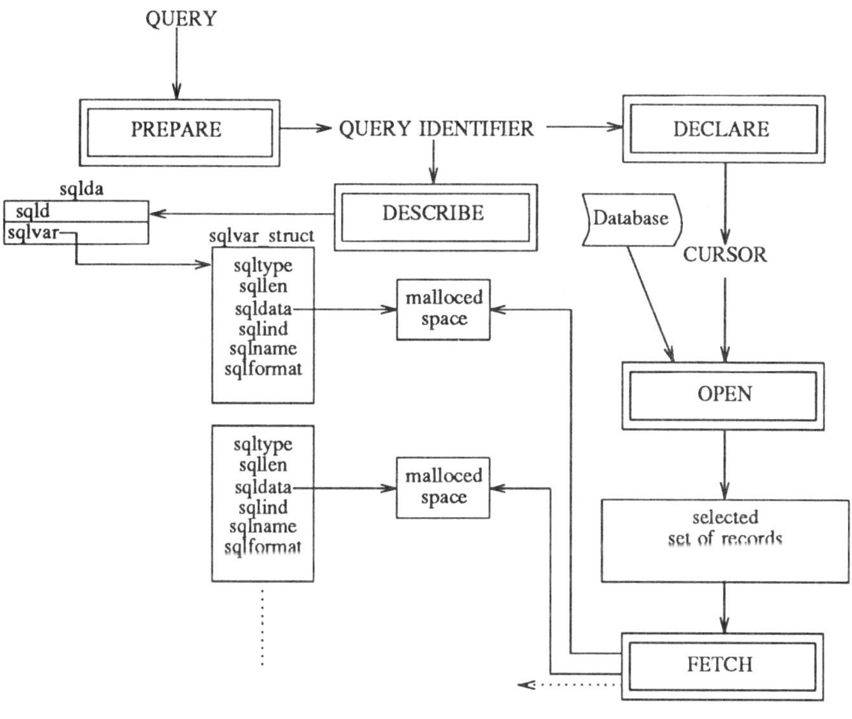

Figure 7.4 Managing Dynamic Select Statements

The *describe* statement populates some of the fields of the above structure. The field *sqld* is set to the number of columns to be retrieved. For each column the *sqlvar_struct* gives the length and type of each column in the database. The name of the column is stored in *sqlname*. Its type is indicated by the integer variable *sqltype*. The length of the field is given by the variable *sqllen* and *sqldata* should be made to point to space allocated to host the data. The pointer to the indicator variable can be used to detect null values and column truncation when the rows are fetched.

The following program illustrates how dynamic SQL statements can be processed by use of *esql* statements. The program prompts for the names of the columns to be retrieved, the names of the tables from which these columns are to be retrieved, and the selection criterion. The output is a series of records consisting of a tab-separated list of the required fields. To keep the program simple there is no error handling code in it.

```
$include sqlca;
$include sqlda;
$include sqltypes;
#define DAVAR sqlda_ptr->sqlvar
#include <stdio.h>
main()
{

   $char query_string[200];
   char list_of_cols[100],list_of_tabs[100],sel_cond[100];
   char achar, *malloc();
   int i;
   $struct sqlda *sqlda_ptr;

   /* select the database */
   $database florist;

   /* Input list of columns to be retrieved */
   printf("Please input a list of columns to be retrieved: ");
   scanf("%[^\n]%c",list_of_cols,&achar);

   /* Input tables involved in the selection */
   printf("Please input list of tables to be used: ");
   scanf("%[^\n]%c",list_of_tabs,&achar);

   /* Input the where condition */
   printf("Please input select condition, enter NO if none: ");
   scanf("%[^\n]%c",sel_cond,&achar);

   if (!strcmp(sel_cond,"NO"))
     sprintf(query_string,"select %s from %s",
                                list_of_cols, list_of_tabs);
   else
     sprintf(query_string,"select %s from %s where %s",
                                list_of_cols, list_of_tabs,sel_cond);
```

```
/* Assign  query identifier to the query string */
$prepare query_id from $query_string;

/* Describe cols. to be retrieved into the sqlda structure */
$describe query_id into sqlda_ptr;

/* For each column malloc enough space. */
/* Also assign the appropriate C type   */
for (i=0; i< sqlda_ptr->sqld; ++i)
{
  switch(DAVAR->sqltype)
  {
  case SQLCHAR:
    DAVAR->sqltype = CCHARTYPE;
    ++DAVAR->sqllen;
    DAVAR->sqldata = malloc(DAVAR->sqllen);
    break;
  case SQLMONEY:
    DAVAR->sqltype = CDECIMALTYPE;
    DAVAR->sqllen  = rtypmsize(DAVAR->sqltype);
    DAVAR->sqldata = malloc(DAVAR->sqllen);
    break;
  case SQLINT:
    DAVAR->sqltype = CLONGTYPE;
    DAVAR->sqllen  = rtypmsize(DAVAR->sqltype);
    DAVAR->sqldata = malloc(DAVAR->sqllen);
    break;
  case SQLDATE:
    DAVAR->sqltype = CSTRINGTYPE;
    DAVAR->sqllen  = rtypwidth(SQLDATE,DAVAR->sqllen)+1;
    DAVAR->sqldata = malloc(DAVAR->sqllen);
    break;
  default:
    fprintf(stderr,"Cannot handle column of this type\n");
    break;
  }
  ++DAVAR;
}

/* declare a cursor for the query_id */
$declare q_cursor cursor for query_id;
```

```
   /* Reset the sqlda_ptr->sqlvar (DAVAR) pointer */
   DAVAR -= sqlda_ptr->sqld;

   /* Identify the rows to be selected */
   $open q_cursor;

   while (1)
   {
     /* Retrieve each row */
     $fetch q_cursor using descriptor sqlda_ptr;
     if (sqlca.sqlcode) break;

     /* print each row */
     print_row(sqlda_ptr);
   }
 }
 print_row(ptr)
 struct sqlda *ptr;
 {
   int i;
   double dbl_val;
   struct sqlvar_struct *bkp_ptr;
   bkp_ptr = ptr->sqlvar;
   for (i=0; i< ptr->sqld; ++i)
   {
     switch(ptr->sqlvar->sqltype)
     {
     case CCHARTYPE:
     case CSTRINGTYPE:
       printf("%s\t",ptr->sqlvar->sqldata);
       break;
     case CDECIMALTYPE:
       dectodbl(ptr->sqlvar->sqldata,&dbl_val);
       printf("%.2f\t",dbl_val);
       break;
     case CLONGTYPE:
       printf("%ld\t",*(long *)ptr->sqlvar->sqldata);
       break;
     default:
       fprintf(stderr,"Unknown data type encountered\n");
       break;

     }
```

```
122        ++ptr->sqlvar;
123     }
124     printf("\n");
125     ptr->sqlvar = bkp_ptr;
126  }
```

When compiled and executed, the program retrieves the desired columns from the specified tables as shown below:

```
a.out
Please input a list of columns to be retrieved: c_no, o_no, o_date
Please input list of tables to be used: orders
Please input select condition, enter NO if none: NO
6091212121     3      03/02/1988
6091212121     2      02/02/1988
6091212121     1      06/19/1988
2016667777     4      03/27/1988
2018911211     2      02/12/1988
2013211341     1      02/12/1988
2013211234     2      01/24/1988
2013211234     1      01/24/1988
2012428055     2      02/12/1988
2012428055     1      12/12/1987
2123211411     1      03/12/1988
```

At execution time, the database is selected in the statement in line 16. Before line 38, the query string is completely defined. The *prepare* statement in line 38 associates a query identifier with the query string. The columns to be selected are known at this point. The *describe* statement in line no. 41 is used to get information on the columns to be retrieved. This information is provided in an *sqlda* structure pointed to by the variable *sqlda_ptr*.

The status of this pointer after the *describe* statement is executed is shown in Figure 7.5. It indicates the SQL data types and the length for the columns to be retrieved. The C statements from line 45 to line 74 change the elements of this structure to indicate the corresponding C data types for the columns to be retrieved. Note that the SQL data type for the field *o_date* returns a C long integer. However, the C data type specified for retrieval is CSTRINGTYPE. The number of bytes required to store this field in a "char" format is provided by the *rtypwidth* function in line 66. The additional 1 byte is provided to store the string terminating null character. These statements also specify the length of each C data field and the *malloc*ed space into which the data is to be retrieved.

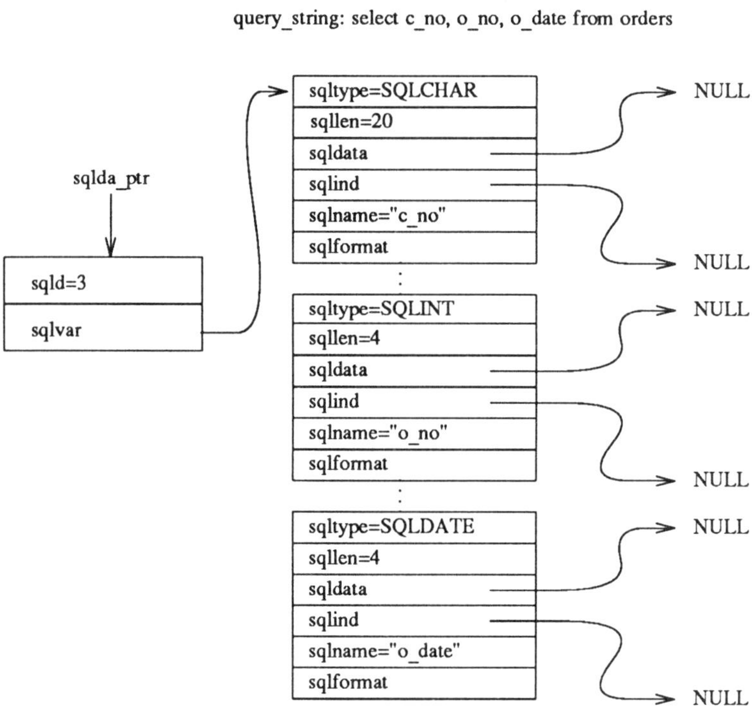

Figure 7.5 Sqlda Structure after Execution of *describe*

The *sqlda* structure after these statements are executed is shown in Figure 7.6. At line 80, the *sqlda_ptr->sqlvar* pointer is made to point back to the *sqlvar_struct* for the first field. This structure is used by the *fetch* statement to retrieve one record from the selected set. The retrieved record is printed in the *print_row* function.

As indicated earlier there is absolutely no error-processing involved in this program. Ideally, after every *esql* statement, the status of the *sqlca.sqlcode* variable must be examined and the contents of the *sqlca* structure dumped if an error is detected. Failure to detect an error code at an early stage may result in an abnormal termination at a later point which may be difficult to trace. The indicator variables must also be checked to detect null-valued fields and truncation of character strings. Of course, space must be allocated to the indicator variables for subsequent use by *fetch* statements.

This program cannot handle all data types; however, its modification to include other data types would be a trivial task. The two examples discussed here illustrate the use of *esql* statements to execute SQL *select* statements which are dynamically defined at execution time.

The next section discusses the use of *esql* statements to update, delete, or add information to the database.

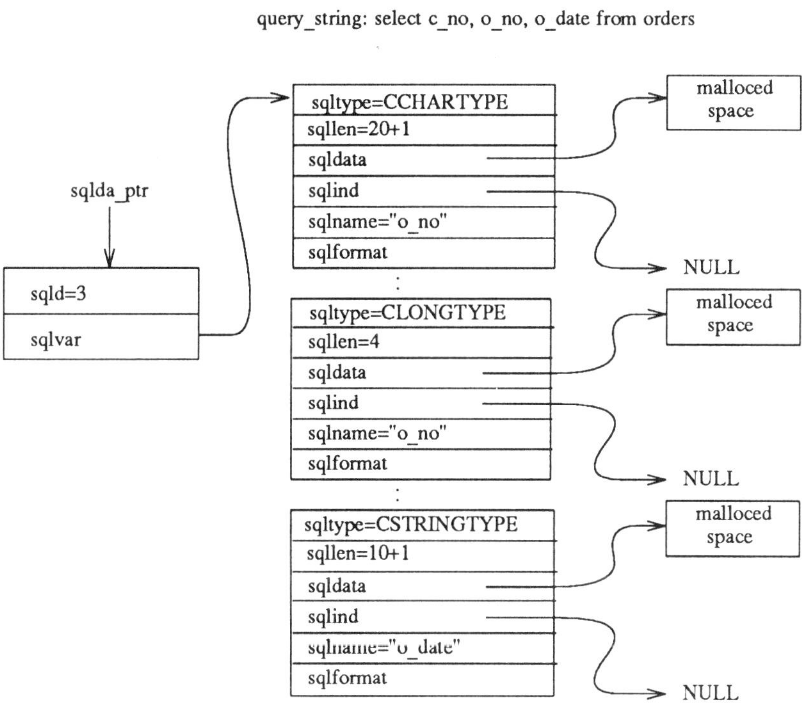

Figure 7.6 Sqlda Structure after Execution of Line No. 74

7.5 Updating Rows in a Table

Esql offers several different mechanisms for updating tables in a database. As in the case of the *select* statement, the *update* statement may not be completely known at compile time. If it is not known at compile time, then it must be prepared and then executed at run time.

If the *update* statement is known at compile time then the process is trivial. The *update* statement can then be executed like any other SQL statement. The following program updates the customer number in the customers file from 2012428055 to 2019061277.

```
#include <stdio.h>
$include sqlca;
main()
{

$database florist;

$update customers set c_no="2019061212"
   where c_no = "2012428055";
if (sqlca.sqlcode)
   fprintf(stderr,"Error in update, code:%d",sqlca.sqlcode);
else
    printf("Number of rows updated: %d\n", sqlca.sqlerrd[2]);
}
```

The syntax of the *esql update* statement is the same as that of the SQL *update* statement discussed in Chapter 5. The *sqlca* structure can be used to detect errors in the statement. The *sqlca.sqlcode* variable returns the status of the update. The number of rows updated is returned in the *sqlerrd[2]* element of the *sqlca* structure. Here is a sample run of the program:

```
a.out
Number of rows updated: 1
```

If the *update* statement is not known at compile time, then a mechanism similar to the one used to handle dynamic *select* statements can also be used here. The *update* statement is "built" in a string at execution time. During this process of defining the string, a *?* can be used in place of a value. This is particularly useful in a situation where the *update* statement is defined at compile time but the values to be used either in the *set* clause or the *where* selection clause are not known until execution time. The next *esql* program typifies such a situation. Its objective, once again, is to change the customer number in the customers file; however, the new number and the existing number to be updated are known only at execution time. Here is the program:

```
1  #include <stdio.h>
2  $include sqlca;
3  main()
4  {
5
6     $char upd_string[200],old_no[11],new_no[11];
7
8     $database florist;
9
10    /* build the update statement */
11    strcpy(upd_string,"update customers set c_no= ? where c_no = ?");
12
13    /* Process the update statement in the upd_string */
14    /* Assign it a statement identifier */
15    $prepare upd_id from $upd_string;
16
17    /* Get the old code and the new code */
18    printf("Input old customer code: ", old_no);
19    scanf("%s",old_no);
20    printf("Input new customer code: ", new_no);
21    scanf("%s",new_no);
22
23    /* execute the prepared statement */
24    $execute upd_id using $new_no, $old_no;
25
26    /* Display the returned status */
27    if (sqlca.sqlcode)
28      fprintf(stderr,"Error in update, code:%d",sqlca.sqlcode);
29    else
30      printf("Number of rows updated: %d\n", sqlca.sqlerrd[2]);
31 }
```

In line 11 the *update* statement is hard-wired in the program. It could have been defined at execution time. If the *where* clause were to be omitted, all the rows would be updated. If an update statement is defined at compile time, then steps must be taken to detect this situation. After a *describe* statement is executed, the *sqlca.sqlwarn.sqlwarn4* variable, which was discussed earlier, is set to 'W' if the prepared *update* statement does not have a *where* clause. Once detected, the program can take appropriate steps, if needed, before actually executing the statement. Here is a simple example where the user inputs the name of the table, the fields to be updated, the set of new values, and the selection condition, if any. If the selection condition is missing, then the program prompts for a confirmation before updating the database.

```
#include <stdio.h>
$include sqlca;
main()
{

   $char upd_string[200];
   char c_table[25], c_list[200],c_sel[200],resp[3];
   short proceed;
   $struct sqlda *sqlda_ptr;
   $database florist;

   /* Get information from user to form the update string */
   printf("Input table to be updated: ");
   gets(c_table);
   printf("Input a line of comma separated update list: ");
   gets(c_list);
   printf("Input a line of selection condition, NO otherwise: ");
   gets(c_sel);

   /* Form the update statement */
   if (strcmp(c_sel,"NO")!=0)
     sprintf(upd_string,
        "update %s set %s where %s", c_table, c_list, c_sel);
   else
     sprintf(upd_string,"update %s set %s ", c_table, c_list);
   /* Process the update statement in the upd_string */
   /* Assign it a statement identifier */
   $prepare upd_id from $upd_string;

   /* Check the update statement */
   if (sqlca.sqlcode)
   {
     fprintf(stderr,"Error in statement: %s\n", upd_string);
     exit(1);
   }

   /* Detect if the where clause is missing */
   $describe upd_id into sqlda_ptr;

   /* If the where clause is missing, then confirm execution */
   proceed = 1;
   if (sqlca.sqlwarn.sqlwarn4=='W')
   {
```

```
44        printf("Where clause missing, enter Y to proceed: ");
45        scanf("%s",resp);
46        if (strcmp("Y",resp)!=0)
47          proceed = 0;
48      }
49
50      /* execute the prepared statement */
51      if (proceed)
52        $execute upd_id;
53      else
54      {
55        fprintf(stderr,"Exiting program..\n");
56        exit(0);
57      }
58
59      /* Display the returned status */
60      if (sqlca.sqlcode)
61        fprintf(stderr,"Error in update, code:%d",sqlca.sqlcode);
62      else
63        printf("Number of rows updated: %d\n", sqlca.sqlerrd[2]);
64    }
```

The *describe* statement in line 38 is used in this program to detect the absence of the *where* clause.

7.5.1 Updating Selected Records

The SQL *select* statement can be used to select a set of records from a database, as was discussed earlier. At any time, only one record from the selected set is active. The *update* statement can be used to update this record by specifying the following *where* clause:

```
where current of cursor
```

If records selected from a table are to be updated, then the cursor associated with the *select* statement must be declared with the *for update* clause. The following program retrieves all the records from the orders file. It also opens a flat UNIX file with numbers of customers who should not have been charged a delivery fee. If there is an order record with a delivery charge for any of these customers, the delivery charge is zeroed; otherwise, the delivery charge is unchanged.

```
#include <stdio.h>
$include sqlca;
main()
{
   int eof,tot_upd=0;
   FILE *fp;
   char custno[70][11];
   short count=0,i,found;

   $char upd_string[200],cc_no[11];
   $struct sqlda *sqlda_ptr;

   /* Fill custno array with customer nos. */
   fp = fopen("custno.d","r");
   while (1)
   {
     eof = fscanf(fp,"%s",custno[count++]);
     if (eof==EOF) break;
   }

   $database florist;
   $declare cursor1 cursor for
       select c_no from orders for update;
   $open cursor1;

   sprintf(upd_string,
    "update orders set o_del_chg = 0 where current of cursor1");
   $prepare upd_id from $upd_string;
   while (1)
   {

     /* retrieve a record from the orders table */
     $fetch cursor1 into $cc_no;
     if (sqlca.sqlcode) break;
     found=0;

     /* Is the customer no. in the list */
     for (i=0;i<count;++i)
       if (strcmp(custno[i],cc_no)==0) {
         found=1;
         break;
       }

```

```
44      /* If found set delivery charge to zero */
45      if (found) {
46        $execute upd_id;
47        ++tot_upd;
48      }
49    }
50    printf("Total number of rows updated = %d\n", tot_upd);
51  }
```

The list of customer numbers from the custno.d external file is first loaded in the array *custno.* All records from the orders file are retrieved one at a time with use of the *fetch* statement in line 33. The customer number of the fetched record is compared with the numbers stored in the *custno* array. If a match is found, then the record is updated by use of the *execute* statement in line 46. It is also possible to open a cursor to update only a specified list of columns by providing this list along with the *for update* clause, as in

```
declare cursor1 cursor for select statement
        for update of list of columns.
```

Updating a selected record does not change the position of the cursor.

7.6 Deleting Rows in a Table

The process of deleting rows in *esql* is identical to the process discussed in the previous section for updating rows. The SQL *delete* statement can be used to delete existing records from a table. If the statement is known at compile time, then the process is simple. The following *esql* program deletes the record for customer no. 2012428055 from the orders table:

```
$include sqlca;
$include sqlda;
#include <decimal.h>
#include <stdio.h>
main()
{
  $database florist;
  $delete from orders where
   c_no = "2012428055";

```

```
    printf("No. of rows deleted: %d\n",sqlca.sqlerrd[2]);
}
```

After the successful execution of a *delete* statement, the *sqlca.sqlerrd[2]* variable is set to the number of records deleted. If the *delete* statement is not known at compile time, then it can be prepared at run time and subsequently executed. The next program prompts the user for the customer number and then deletes the record from the customer table:

```
$include sqlca;
$include sqlda;
#include <decimal.h>
#include <stdio.h>
main()
{

    $char cc_no[11], del_string[200];

    $database florist;
    printf("Program to delete customer records\n");
    printf("Please input customer no: ");
    gets(cc_no);

    sprintf(del_string,"delete from customers where c_no = ?");

    $prepare del_id from $del_string;
    $execute del_id using $cc_no;

    printf("No. of rows deleted: %d\n",sqlca.sqlerrd[2]);
}
```

In this program only the value inside the *where* clause is provided dynamically at run time. It is possible to provide the entire selection condition for record deletion at run time. If the *where* clause is missing, *describe* will set *sqlca.sqlwarn.sqlwarn4* to 'W'. This is particularly useful if the *where* clause is provided dynamically at run time. Before the prepared statement is executed, the program should check the value of this variable to prevent an inadvertent deletion of all the records in the table.

7.6.1 Deleting a Selected Record

If a record is to be deleted based on a selection condition which cannot be specified in the *where* clause, then the program must *select* the required set of records, *fetch* one record at a time, and then use C code to check if the fetched record satisfies the condition to be applied for deletion. If it does satisfy the condition, then it can be deleted with use of the *where current of cursor_name* clause with the *delete* statement. Consider a situation in which the customer number of customers whose records are to be deleted are in a flat file called custno.d. Clearly, the mechanism used thus far to delete records will not suffice. The previous program which uses the *where current of cursor_name* clause with an *update* statement can be modified slightly to delete the required records. In fact, only two lines have to be changed. Line 27 has to be changed to

```
"delete from orders where current of cursor1");
```

and line 50 has to be changed to

```
printf("Total number of rows deleted = %d\n", tot_upd);
```

7.7 Inserting New Records

New records can be added to the database with the *insert* statement. If the entire statement is known at compile time, then the SQL *insert* statement can be used without any change. The following program inserts a new record in the orders table:

```
$include sqlca;
#include <stdio.h>
main()
{

 $database florist;
 $insert into orders values(
     "2012428055",1, 12.50, "12/12/88",
     "12 Roses", 1.50, 10.00
     );
```

```
   if (sqlca.sqlcode)
    fprintf(stderr,"Error in insert, sqlca.sqlcode: %d\n",
            sqlca.sqlcode);
  }
```

It is possible to buffer the records to be inserted. This is advantageous when several inserts have to be made to a table. The number of I/O operations is reduced significantly. Of course, at some point the buffered rows have to be flushed. This can be done explicitly by the program or it can be done when the buffer is full. Rows which are still in the buffer are not available to other users unless the buffer is flushed. To force buffering of rows to be inserted, a cursor has to be associated with the *insert* statement. After the cursor is *open*ed, a *put* statement can be used to insert a new record. The record is put into the buffer and *sqlca.sqlcode* is assigned a value of zero. A nonzero value would indicate that an error condition has occurred. The variable *sqlca.sqlerrd[2]* is ordinarily assigned a value of zero unless the buffer is flushed, in which case it is assigned a number which indicates the number of rows which are flushed. All rows inserted in the buffer can be flushed by using the *flush* statement.

When the cursor is closed, rows remaining in the buffer are all flushed. If the program exits without an insert cursor being closed, the rows in the buffer are not flushed and the *insert* operation is lost. The following program reads records with colon-separated fields from a file called custnew.d. The fields are read into the host variables and inserted into the database using the *put* statement. The status of the *sqlca.sqlcode* and *sqlca.sqlerrd[2]* variables is printed at different stages of the program. The first five records are flushed explicitly; after that the program flushes them, if the buffer is full. Finally, when the cursor is closed, the buffers are flushed again.

```
#include <stdio.h>
$include sqlca;
main()
{

  $char cc_no[11], cc_fname[21], cc_lname[21],cc_addr1[21];
  $char cc_addr2[21], cc_town[21], cc_state[3],cc_zip[6];
  char achar;
  int eof,count;

  $database florist;

  $declare ins_curs cursor for
```

```
    insert into customers ( c_no, c_fname, c_lname,c_addr1,
      c_addr2,c_town,c_state,c_zip)
      values ( $cc_no, $cc_fname, $cc_lname,
               $cc_addr1,$cc_addr1,$cc_town,$cc_state,$cc_zip);

  $open ins_curs;
  for (count=0;count<5;++count)
  { /* Read a record */
eof=scanf("%[^:]%c%[^:]%c%[^:]%c%[^:]%c%[^:]%c%[^:]%c%[^:]%c%[^\n]%c",
     cc_no,&achar,cc_fname,&achar,cc_lname,&achar,cc_addr1,&achar,
     cc_addr2,&achar,cc_town,&achar,cc_state,&achar,cc_zip,&achar);
   if (eof==EOF) break;
   $put ins_curs;
   printf("Sqlca.sqlcode: %d, sqlca.sqlerrd[2]: %d\n",
        sqlca.sqlcode,sqlca.sqlerrd[2]);
  }

  $flush ins_curs;
  printf("After flush:\n");
  printf("Sqlca.sqlcode: %d, sqlca.sqlerrd[2]: %d\n",
      sqlca.sqlcode,sqlca.sqlerrd[2]);

  printf("In while loop:\n");
  while (1)
  { /* Read a record */
eof=scanf("%[^:]%c%[^:]%c%[^:]%c%[^:]%c%[^:]%c%[^:]%c%[^:]%c%[^\n]%c",
      cc_no,&achar,cc_fname,&achar,cc_lname,&achar,cc_addr1,&achar,
      cc_addr2,&achar,cc_town,&achar,cc_state,&achar,cc_zip,&achar);
    if (eof==EOF) break;
    $put ins_curs;
    printf("Sqlca.sqlcode: %d, sqlca.sqlerrd[2]: %d\n",
        sqlca.sqlcode,sqlca.sqlerrd[2]);
  }

  $close ins_curs;
  printf("After closing cursor\n");
  printf("Sqlca.sqlcode: %d, sqlca.sqlerrd[2]: %d\n",
     sqlca.sqlcode,sqlca.sqlerrd[2]);
}
```

When the program is executed, the output is:

```
a.out < ins.d
Sqlca.sqlcode: 0, sqlca.sqlerrd[2]: 0
Sqlca.sqlcode: 0, sqlca.sqlerrd[2]: 0
Sqlca.sqlcode: 0, sqlca.sqlerrd[2]: 0
Sqlca.sqlcode: 0, sqlca.sqlerrd[2]: 0
Sqlca.sqlcode: 0, sqlca.sqlerrd[2]: 0
After flush:
Sqlca.sqlcode: 0, sqlca.sqlerrd[2]: 5
In while loop:
Sqlca.sqlcode: 0, sqlca.sqlerrd[2]: 0
Sqlca.sqlcode: 0, sqlca.sqlerrd[2]: 0
Sqlca.sqlcode: 0, sqlca.sqlerrd[2]: 0
Sqlca.sqlcode: 0, sqlca.sqlerrd[2]: 0
Sqlca.sqlcode: 0, sqlca.sqlerrd[2]: 0
Sqlca.sqlcode: 0, sqlca.sqlerrd[2]: 0
Sqlca.sqlcode: 0, sqlca.sqlerrd[2]: 0
Sqlca.sqlcode: 0, sqlca.sqlerrd[2]: 8
Sqlca.sqlcode: 0, sqlca.sqlerrd[2]: 0
Sqlca.sqlcode: 0, sqlca.sqlerrd[2]: 0
Sqlca.sqlcode: 0, sqlca.sqlerrd[2]: 0
After closing cursor
Sqlca.sqlcode: 0, sqlca.sqlerrd[2]: 3
```

If the program was terminated without the *close* statement being executed, then the last three inserts would have been lost. An *sqlda* structure can also be used instead of the host variables. Also, if the host variables to be used in the *insert* statement are not known at compile time, then a question mark (?) can be used in their place and the *from* clause of the *put* statement can be used to specify the host variables.

7.8 Handling Other SQL Statements

Other SQL statements not discussed in this chapter can be embedded in C programs without any change. These include statements to handle locking mechanism, transaction management, and audit trail maintenance. A number of INFORMIX products use *esql* to process database access request with dynamic management statements. The database access is actually satisfied by a back-end process which is implemented in C-ISAM. This back-end process is forked by the *esql* program. C-ISAM will be discussed in the next chapter.

8 C-ISAM

One of the major advantages of database management tools over standard UNIX utilities is that they provide a faster access to data. When a query is executed, either directly or indirectly, by the use of forms and reports, data must be accessed in the fastest possible time. It is the responsibility of the query processor to determine the fastest possible access method. This involves the selection of the appropriate index. It is the responsibility of the designer to create the required indexes. The SQL command to create an index was discussed in Chapter 5. The index has a definite structure based on proprietary implementation algorithms. If this structure is known to the programmer, then it is possible, at least in theory, to write C programs to create this index.

To eliminate the need to have the programmer know the intricacies of the index structure, INFORMIX provides a C library interface for manipulating an index in C programs. This library is called C-ISAM. Several methods of implementing an index are known. ISAM is the most popular among UNIX-based DBMS vendors. The implementation varies depending on the data structure used to store the index and the algorithms used to manipulate this structure. Most ISAM implementations use the B-Tree and its various variations as the basic storage structure. If all implementations were similar, then it would be easy to port databases across different DBMS!

In this chapter, the basic concepts of an index are discussed along with some theoretical concepts. Familiarity with these concepts is not required for the user to use C-ISAM but it is necessary to understand how it works and how to use it efficiently. The rest of the chapter discusses the numerous functions available in the C-ISAM library.

8.1 Theoretical Concepts

What is an index? Open any book and a few pages are reserved for an index. Imagine a fat book with numerous chapters and sections. As the number of sections grows, so does the index. At some point the index grows so big that an index to the index is required. As new sections and chapters are added to the book, the index to the index requires another level of index. Very soon we have a treelike structure. ISAM is merely an implementation of this multilevel index with a few restrictions on its structure.

Consider the supplier file shown below:

```
cat supp.d
 Q0IBX Inc.            P1
 S1TTR Systems Inc.    P2
 S1TTR Systems Inc.    P3
 S3DP-Suppliers.       P1
 S4Max Enterprises     P5
 S4Max Enterprises     P6
 S6Leonard Wholesalers P1
 S6Leonard Wholesalers P2
 S7Rose Machines, Inc. P1
 S7Rose Machines, Inc. P2
 S7Rose Machines, Inc. P7
 S7Rose Machines, Inc. P8
 T8Leyland Inc.        P2
 T8Leyland Inc.        P3
 T9Tremley Industries  P5
 T9Tremley Industries  P6
U10Davidson Plastics.  P3
U10Davidson Plastics.  P9
U11Jacobs Industries   P9
```

This is a file with fixed-length records consisting of three fixed-length fields.

The first field is the supplier number and is 3 characters long. The second field is the supplier name and is 20 characters long. Finally, the third field, representing the part supplied by the supplier, is 2 characters long. A single-level index on the file on the supplier no field is shown below:

```
 Q0 1
 S1 2
 S3 4
 S4 5
 S6 7
 S7 9
 T8 13
 T9 15
U10 17
U11 19
```

The first field is the supplier number and the second field is the record number in the original data file. Another level of index can be added to this single-level index, as shown below:

```
S4 4
T8 7
>  8
```

The second level of index has two fields. The first field has the supplier number and the second field has an index into the first-level index. For example, the first entry in this index indicates that all suppliers with a supplier number less than or equal to *S4* will have an entry in the first four records in the first-level index. The last entry indicates that all suppliers with a supplier number greater than T8 have an entry starting from the eighth entry in the first-level index. The complete index structure is shown in Figure 8.1. The record numbers associated with the data file are shown to explain the index structure. They are not stored physically along with the records. Also the record number associated with the first level index is not stored physically with it. It is more convenient to store the index in smaller units called nodes. Each node has a fixed size, normally equal to a block size of the file system. Because of the fixed size restriction, all entries in a node may not always be populated.

If each node can have only four entries, then the index structure shown in Figure 8.1 can be restructured as shown in Figure 8.2. To retrieve a record with a given key value, the search starts at the root node. For example, to search for the key value *S7*, it is clear from the root node that the entry for

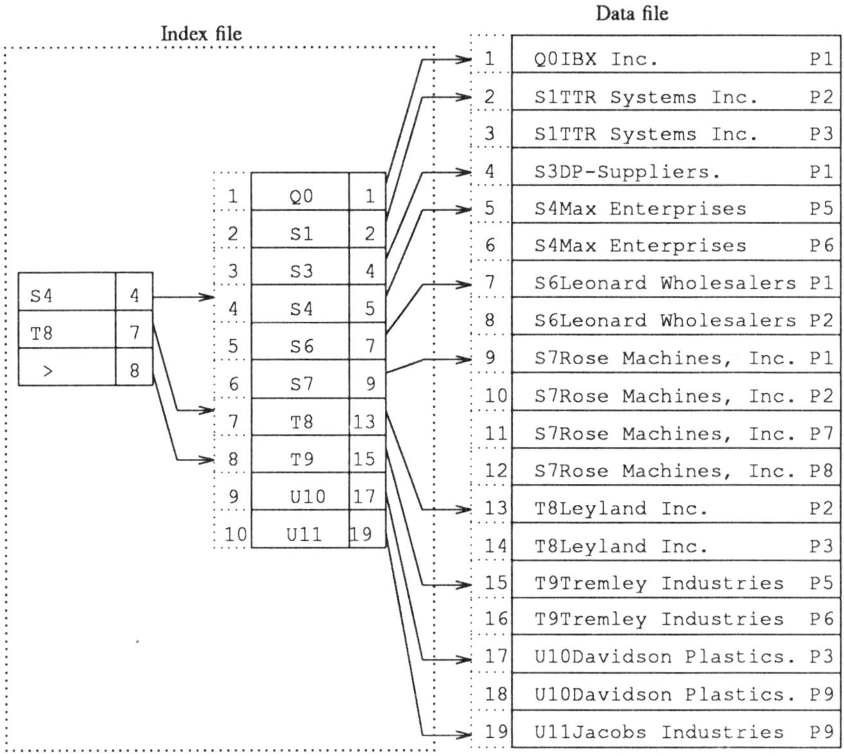

Figure 8.1 Simplified Structure of an Indexed File

S7, if it exists, must be in node *N1*. This eliminates the need to search nodes *N0* and *N2*.

If a new record is to be added, it can be appended or inserted in the data file. The key value, however, must be entered in the appropriate node. Adding an entry in the node is not always a trivial task. For example, an entry for key value *U12* can be added very easily as there is an unused entry in the *N2* node. However, if an entry for key value *S5* is to be added, then there is no room for it in the *N1* node. It must be split into two nodes, *N1* and *N4*. This change must be reflected in the parent node, which in this case is also the root node. There is an unused entry in the root node which eliminates the need to split it.

Addition of another record with supplier no. *S2* will split the node *N0* into

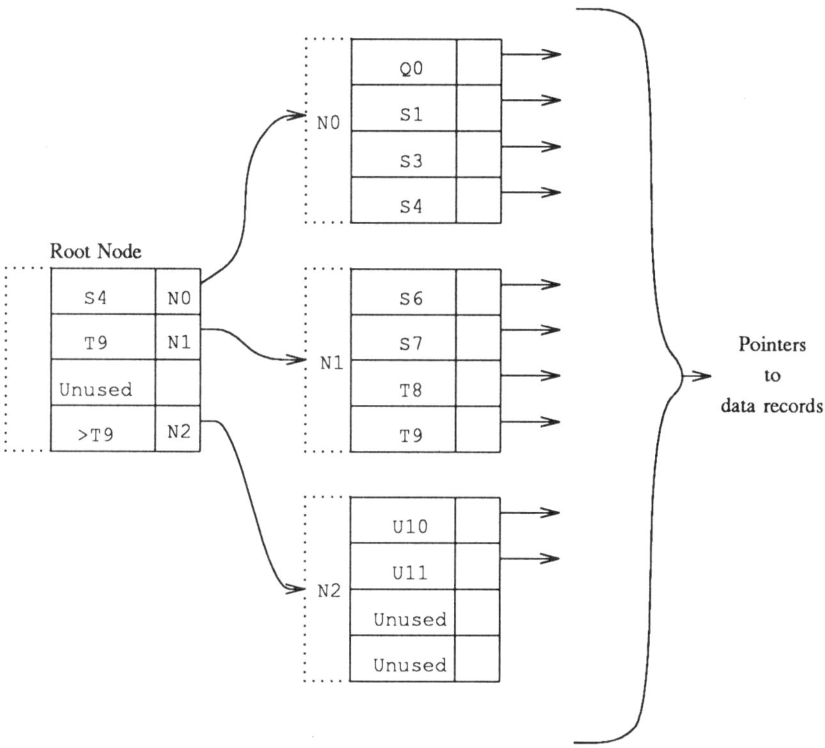

Figure 8.2 Index Stored in Multiple Nodes

two nodes *N0* and *N3*. This change must be reflected in the parent node. However, there is no more room in the root node and it must be split into two nodes. Also, a parent to these two nodes, a new root node, must be created. The new status of the index is shown in Figure 8.3.

Clearly, the index is stored in a treelike data structure. The distance between the root node and the end nodes is the height of the tree. To keep the tree balanced, the distance from any end nodes to the root node must always be the same. Each node size is equal to a block size of the file system or a multiple of it. As the number of key values increases, the height of the tree grows proportionately. As the height of the index tree increases, more nodes must be searched to locate the record requiring more disk access. One way to minimize the height of the tree is to pack as many keys as possible into a single node. This can be achieved by reducing the key size. One way is, of course, to select as the key a segment of the field as opposed to the whole key. If that is not acceptable for the application, then compression techniques must be used.

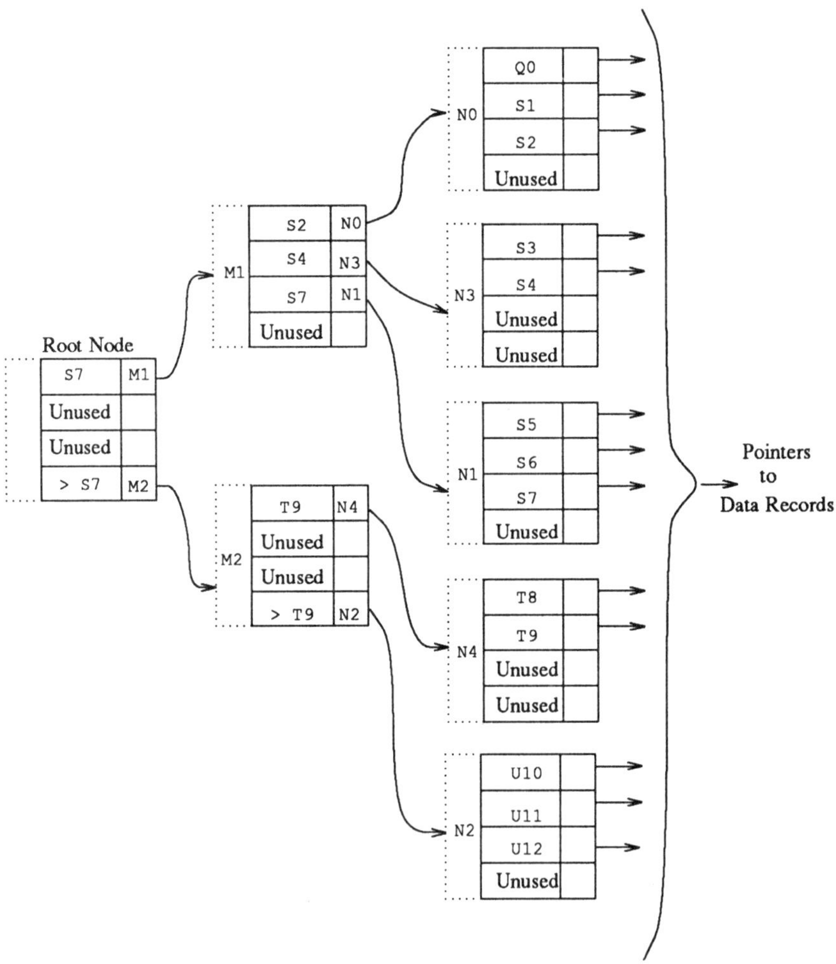

Figure 8.3 Status after Addition of *U12*, *S2*, and *S5*

Some ISAM packages compress key values automatically. C-ISAM requires that the user specify if the key has to be compressed. It accepts three types of compression. The first type involves removal of leading duplicate characters from the key. The second type involves removal of trailing blanks from the key. Finally, the third type involves removal of duplicate key entries from the index. Compression of key values must be applied only if the key values are long. Further, compression has its own overheads. The fact that a key was compressed must be recorded at the beginning of the key. The number of bytes used for recording this information should be smaller than the number of bytes compressed.

If records are deleted from the data file, then the corresponding entry from the index file is simply removed. When all entries in a node are deleted, then the node is marked "free." Subsequently, when a new node is needed, this node is reused. If a node marked "free" is not available, then a request is made to the UNIX file system for an additional block.

8.1.1 More on Index Structure

Some applications require that the data be accessed on different fields. For example, the index on the supplier no. field is useless to access the supplier file on the part no. field. A new index, often called the secondary index, can be created on an existing data file. Information about the index is stored in a node called the key description node. There are as many key description nodes as indexes. A key description node stores information about the key and its components. The flags indicating the compression type to be used on the keys are also stored here.

As nodes are freed they are not released to the operating system; rather, they are chained together to form a linked list of free nodes. When records are deleted from the data file they are simply marked "deleted" and filled with null characters, but they are not removed physically. The dictionary node keeps track of the free index nodes as well as the free records in the data file. In addition, it keeps track of the size of an index node, the number of indexes, the length of the data record, the record number of the last record in the data file, etc. The nodes in which the index itself is stored have key values, pointers to data records or other index nodes, and other miscellaneous information. This information includes the count of leading or trailing blanks for each key and the level of the index node.

All indexes on a table are stored in one physical file. As new indexes are added additional entries are made in the dictionary block and the key description block. Freed nodes are shared by all indexes of a table. Figure 8.4 shows how C-ISAM stores multiple indexes in a single file.

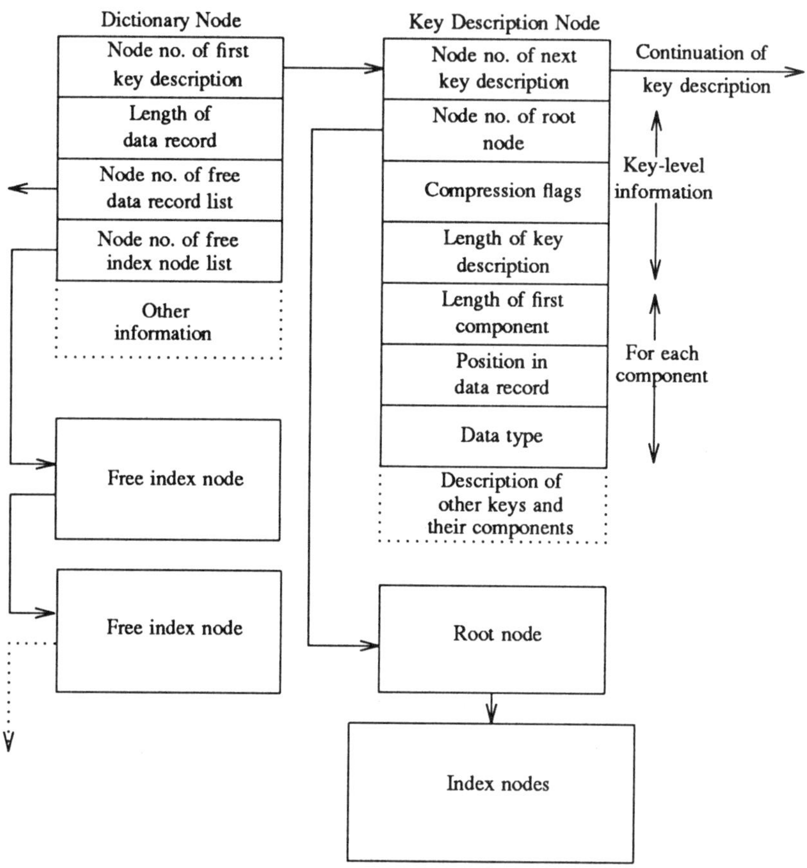

Figure 8.4 Structure of Nodes in a C-ISAM Index File

8.1.2 Structure of Data Records

The internal structure of a data file is much simpler than that of the index file. All records in the data file have a fixed size. This makes it easy to maintain. When a record is to be deleted, it is filled with null characters. The space is, of course, not returned back to the UNIX file system. When a new record is to be added, this space is reused.

Unlike any SQL implementation, C-ISAM does not maintain any names associated with fields of the record. A file is merely a collection of records.

Each record has a fixed number of bytes. It is the responsibility of the application program to map the byte positions into logically defined fields. The format of the data stored in the C-ISAM data file is machine-independent for most data types. This makes it easy to port C-ISAM programs and even C-ISAM data files to different machines.

8.2 From Concepts to Syntax

In the last section, basic principles of an ISAM structure were introduced. The later part of this section and Figure 8.4 showed how C-ISAM stores the indexes in a single file and maintains a separate data file. Given the structure of these two files, it is possible, at least in theory, to write a C program to access the data both sequentially as well as by using the index. C I/O functions can be used to read the data, and the *lseek* function can be used to position to any byte in the data file or index file. Such a program, however, would not only be extremely difficult to code but would, of course, require that the programmer understand every detail aspect of the structure of the index and the data file. In addition, maintaining the integrity of the index, keeping the tree balanced, and other such tasks are nontrivial for an average programmer. Further, some of the implementation details are proprietary and may not be known in the public domain.

So that these problems are avoided, INFORMIX provides a library of C functions to make life easy for the average programmer! This library of C functions along with all the header files, sample programs, and a utility called *bcheck* to check the integrity of the index together forms the C-ISAM package. The C functions provided by this library can be used like any other C function as long as the C-ISAM library is specified on the command line. For example, if the C program file which uses the C-ISAM functions is called myprog.c, then it can be compiled as:

```
cc myprog.c -lisam
```

All other *cc* options, including *-g*, *-p*, and -O, can also be specified as usual. The standard library directories are searched by the compiler to locate a file called libisam.a. If you are unable to locate the library or associated files, consult your local system administrator who may have renamed the library or moved it to a nonstandard directory.

8.3 Creating C-ISAM files

As explained in earlier sections, there are two physical files created by C-ISAM for each indexed file. One, suffixed *.idx*, stores the index, while the other suffixed *.dat* holds the data records. The function to create these files is *isbuild*. This function creates the index and the data files. The first argument to this function is the name of the index which serves as a common prefix to the *.dat* and the *.idx* files. Clearly, to create the index file it must have all the information indicated in Figure 8.4. To create the data file, it must have the length of each data record. Indeed, the second argument to the *isbuild* function is the length of the data record. The third argument is used to describe the index. The fourth argument is discussed later.

Information about the index involves specification about the index as well as a description of each of the component fields which constitute it. A key description structure is provided for this purpose and is shown below:

```
struct keypart
    {
    short kp_start;              /* starting byte of key part*/
    short kp_leng;               /* length in bytes*/
    short kp_type;               /* type of key part*/
    };

struct keydesc
    {
    short k_flags;               /* flags       */
    short k_nparts;              /* number of parts in key*/
    struct keypart
        k_part[NPARTS];                 /* each key part*/
                /* the following is for internal use only*/
    short k_len;                 /* length of whole key*/
    long k_rootnode;             /* pointer to rootnode*/
    };
```

These structures are defined in the isam.h header file along with all macro definitions. The *keydesc* structure is used to provide specifications about the index, while the array of *keyparts* structures having *nparts* components is used to describe detail information about each component of the index. The *k_flags* element can be set to any of the constants explained in Table 8.1. These constants are defined in the isam.h file. The *k_nparts* field is used to specify the number of components in the composite index.

Each component can then be described using a *keypart* structure. The

TABLE 8.1 Accepted Constants for *k_flags*

Constant	Use
ISNODUPS	To force uniqueness on the key; no two records with the same key value will be allowed in the file
ISDUPS	Allows records with the same key values
LCOMPRESS	Used to specify compression of leading duplicate characters in the key; used to squeeze more keys inside a single node
TCOMPRESS	Used to compress trailing duplicate characters
DCOMPRESS	Specifies compression of duplicates keys; used when duplicate keys are allowed
COMPRESS	Specifies all forms of compression

kp_start variable is used to specify the starting byte position of the component. Positions start from zero. The *kp_leng* variable specifies the length of the component, and the data type of the component is specified by the *kp_type* variable. Constants such as CHARTYPE and INTTYPE, defined in isam.h, are used to specify the data type. Table 8.3 lists the different data types supported by C-ISAM.

A structure of type *keydesc* must be declared in the program. Values describing the index and its components must be assigned to the different elements of this structure. The address of this structure forms the third argument to the *isbuild* function. The fourth and the final argument specifies the mode in which the files are to be opened after they are created. Two types of modes can be specified: one to specify the access mode (e.g., read only or write only) and the second one to specify the type of locking to be used. The access mode argument is similar to the second argument required for the C functions *open* and *fopen.* Locking mode specifies the type of locking mechanism to be used. Locking will be discussed in detail in a later section. At this point it suffices to say that if a file is to be opened for exclusive use, then the ISEXCLLOCK lock mode should be opened; otherwise, the ISMANULOCK mode is sufficient. Several constants can be used to specify the file opening mode. These are defined in the isam.h file and are listed in Table 8.2.

The following function creates a C-ISAM file called supfile. Actually two files are created: supfile.dat and supfile.idx:

```
isbuild("supfile",25,&mykey,ISINOUT+ISEXCLLOCK);
```

TABLE 8.2 Modes for Opening C-ISAM files

Mode	Description
ISINPUT	Open the file in input mode.
ISOUTPUT	Open the file in output mode.
ISINOUT	Open the file in input/output mode.
ISEXCLLOCK	Specifies an exclusive lock.
ISMANULOCK	Specifies a manual lock.
ISAUTOLOCK	Specifies automatic record locking.
ISTRANS	Enables rollback of transactions.

The length of each data record is 25 characters. The description of the index and its components is taken from the structure mykey. After the index and data files are created they are left open in exclusive mode for both input and output. Let us create an index on the first 3 bytes of the record. If these positions are used to store the supplier no. which is a character data type, then the structure mykey can be declared and initialized as shown below:

```
struct keydesc mykey;

mykey.k_flags = ISDUPS+TCOMPRESS;
mykey.k_nparts= 1;
mykey.k_part[0].kp_start=0;
mykey.k_part[0].kp_leng =3;
mykey.k_part[0].kp_type =CHARTYPE;
```

Here is the complete C program to create a C-ISAM file called supfile. **Though physically two different files are created, they will be collectively referred to as a single ISAM file in the rest of this chapter.**

```
#include <isam.h>
main()
{
        int fd;
        struct keydesc mykey;
```

```
        mykey.k_flags = ISDUPS+TCOMPRESS;
        mykey.k_nparts= 1;
        mykey.k_part[0].kp_start=0;
        mykey.k_part[0].kp_leng =3;
        mykey.k_part[0].kp_type =CHARTYPE;

        fd=isbuild("supfile",25,&mykey,ISINOUT+ISEXCLLOCK);
        isclose(fd);
}
```

If the ISAM file is built successfully, a nonnegative value is returned. Otherwise, a file descriptor is returned which can be used later in the program to manipulate the index file. The function *isclose* closes the opened ISAM file. It must be used to close all opened C-ISAM files before exiting from a program. Successful execution of the program shown above creates two files in the current directory: the supfile.dat file with no data in it, and the supfile.idx file with the dictionary and key description nodes.

8.3.1 Creating an ISAM file with No Index

The index specified at the file creation time is called the primary index. It is possible to create an ISAM file with no index! The index may be added at a later time, or it may not be required if record retrieval is to be based on the physical sequence number of the records in the data file. Here is a modification of the earlier program to create a C-ISAM file with no index on it:

```
#include <isam.h>
main()
{
        int fd;
        struct keydesc mykey;

        mykey.k_flags = ISNODUPS+TCOMPRESS;
        mykey.k_nparts= 0;
        fd=isbuild("newfile",25,&mykey,ISINOUT+ISEXCLLOCK);
        isclose(fd);
}
```

As expected, if the number of components in the key is specified as zero, then no index exists on the file.

8.3.2 Renaming and Deleting C-ISAM Files

The functions *isrename* can be used to rename the C-ISAM file. It needs two arguments. The first argument is used to specify the old name of the file, and the second argument is used to specify the new name. The names of the files are not hard-wired inside the C-ISAM files. Therefore the purpose of this function is merely to rename the two UNIX files suffixed *.idx* and *.dat*. To remove the C-ISAM file, the function *iserase* can be used. The *.idx* and the *.dat* files for the specified C-ISAM file are removed. The following program can be used to rename a C-ISAM file. It takes two arguments. The first argument is used to specify the old name of the C-ISAM file, and the second argument is used to specify the new name.

```
#include <stdio.h>
#include <isam.h>
main(argc,argv)
int argc;
char *argv[];
{
   int status;
   status = isrename(argv[1], argv[2]);
   if (status < 0)
      fprintf(stderr,"Cannot rename file, iserrno: %d\n", iserrno);
}
```

8.4 Adding Data to a C-ISAM file

Data can be added to a C-ISAM file by use of the *iswrite* function. The file must be first opened in write/output mode. A character array, representing the data record, must be declared and initialized appropriately. The *iswrite* function writes the contents of this array into the ISAM file. Consider the following layout of the supplier record:

Character Position	Data Content
1-3	Supplier no.
4-23	Supplier name
24-25	Part no. of part supplied

Let us assume for simplicity sake that all the fields are nonnumeric of C type *char*. Here is a program that reads records from the file sup.d and loads them into the C-ISAM file supfile that was created before:

```
#include <stdio.h>
#include <isam.h>
main()
{
        int fd;
        char *gets(), *eof;
        char myrec[26];

        /* Open the ISAM file(s) */
        fd = isopen("supfile",ISOUTPUT+ISMANULOCK);
        while(1)
        {
                /* read a record from the redirected flat file */
                eof=gets(myrec);
                if (eof == NULL) break;

                /* Write the record into the ISAM file */
                iswrite(fd,myrec);
        }
        isclose(fd);
}
```

In this program, the record in the flat file has the same format as the data record in the ISAM file. The internal record buffer can be built by collecting data from various sources. For example, the following program gets a list of part numbers from the partno.d file and prompts the user for the part name and the color of the part. It then stores the records in an ISAM file. The program starts by first creating an index file with a composite index on the part no. and part name fields. The format of the ISAM record is

Character Position	Data Content
1-2	Part no.
3-10	Color
11-20	Part name

Here is the program:

```
#include <stdio.h>
#include <isam.h>
main()
{
        char part_rec[21], *gets(), part_no[3];
        char part_name[11],part_color[9];
        int fd,eof;
        FILE *fp_nos;
        struct keydesc partkey;

        fp_nos = fopen("partnos.d","r");

        /* Set the index-level flags */
        partkey.k_flags = ISNODUPS;
        /* No. of components = 2 */
        partkey.k_nparts= 2;

        /* For the first component   */
        partkey.k_part[0].kp_start= 0;
        partkey.k_part[0].kp_leng = 2;
        partkey.k_part[0].kp_type = CHARTYPE;

        /* For the second component  */
        partkey.k_part[1].kp_start= 10;
        partkey.k_part[1].kp_leng = 10;
        partkey.k_part[1].kp_type = CHARTYPE;

        /* Create the ISAM file */
        fd = isbuild("partfile",20,&partkey,ISOUTPUT+ISMANULOCK);

        while(1)
        {
                /* read part no. from the flat file */
                eof=fscanf(fp_nos,"%s",part_no);
                if (eof == EOF) break;

                /* Prompt and get color and name of the part */
                printf("Input color for part no %s :", part_no);
                gets(part_color);
                printf("Input name for part no  %s :",part_no);
                gets(part_name);

                /* build the part record */
```

```
        stchar(part_no,part_rec,2);
                stchar(part_color,&part_rec[2],8);
                stchar(part_name,&part_rec[10],10);

                /* Write the record into the ISAM file */
                iswrite(fd,part_rec);
        }

        /* close the ISAM file */
        isclose(fd);
}
```

The function *stchar* is a C-ISAM function which is used to transfer a character string from a C variable to a C-ISAM record buffer. The first argument is the C variable representing a field, the second argument is a pointer into the data-record buffer, and the third argument specifies the number of characters to be transferred. Of course, the *sprintf* function with appropriate formats could have been used in place of the three *stchar* functions to transfer the data to the record buffer.

8.4.1 Using Different Data Types

C-ISAM supports numerous data types. It stores most of the data in machine-independent format. The programmer need not know the structure of the internal formats, as functions are provided specifically for transferring data from different C variable types to the record buffer, and vice versa.

The data types supported by C-ISAM, their C language equivalents, and the size of the field as stored in a C-ISAM file are shown in Table 8.3. Clearly, if a field is declared of type FLOATTYPE or DOUBLETYPE then the representation of the field in the ISAM file is dependent on the machine. If machine independence is required, then the DECIMALTYPE data type should be used in place of FLOATTYPE and DOUBLETYPE.

The decimal data type is used to store a number up to 32 significant digits with an optional decimal point and an exponent in the range of -128 to +126. The decimal point is never stored physically in the file. The numbers are stored in a packed format in the data file. Two digits are represented by a single byte. Another byte is used to store the sign and the exponent. For example, 4 bytes are sufficient to represent 6 significant digits: 1 byte for storing the sign and the exponent, and the remaining 3 bytes to store six packed digits. Similarly, a decimal field of size 8 can be used to store 14 significant digits. Though the internal structure used by C-ISAM to manipulate

TABLE 8.3 C-ISAM Data Types

C-ISAM Data Type	C Data Type	Size in File
CHARTYPE	char	as specified
INTTYPE	int	2
LONGTYPE	long	4
FLOATTYPE	float	sizeof(float) machine dependent
DOUBLETYPE	double	sizeof(double) machine dependent
DECIMALTYPE	struct decimal	as specified

decimal data types may not be known to the programmer, she or he should be able to determine the number of bytes required to store a decimal field in the C-ISAM file as explained above.

In addition to the functions available to convert decimal data type into other C data types, C-ISAM also provides numerous functions for arithmetic computation on decimal data types.

The internal structure of C-ISAM does not distinguish between DECIMALTYPE and CHARTYPE indexes.

The program that follows creates a C-ISAM file called part_inv which is used to store the inventory status of a part at a location. The different fields, their data type, and their positions in the record are

Character Position	Data Content	Data Type
1-2	Part no.	CHARTYPE
3-6	Quantity in stock	DECIMALTYPE
7-8	Location	INTTYPE

The program creates the C-ISAM file, reads data from a flat UNIX file, and then converts this data into C-ISAM format, after which the *iswrite* function is used to write the record into the C-ISAM file. Here is the complete program:

```
#include <stdio.h>
#include <isam.h>
#include <decimal.h>
main()
{
        char part_rec[9], part_no[3];
        float stk_qty;
        int location,fd,eof;
        dec_t  dec_stk;
```

```
        struct keydesc partkey;

        /* Set the index-level flags */
        partkey.k_flags = ISNODUPS;

        /* No. of components = 1 */
        partkey.k_nparts= 1;

        /* For the first component    */
        partkey.k_part[0].kp_start= 0;
        partkey.k_part[0].kp_leng = 2;
        partkey.k_part[0].kp_type = CHARTYPE;

        /* Create the ISAM file */
        fd = isbuild("part_inv",8,&partkey,ISOUTPUT+ISMANULOCK);

        while(1)
        {
                /* read a record from the redirected flat file */
                eof=scanf("%s%f%d", part_no, &stk_qty, &location);
                if (eof == EOF) break;

                /* convert stk_qty from float to decimal */
                deccvflt(stk_qty,&dec_stk);

                /* build the part record */
                stchar(part_no,part_rec,2);
                stdecimal(&dec_stk,&part_rec[2],4);
                stint(location,&part_rec[6]);

                /* Write the record into the ISAM file */
                iswrite(fd,part_rec);
        }

        /* close the isam file */
        isclose(fd);
}
```

The *deccvflt* function converts a C variable of type float to a decimal type. Other functions used to convert a C variable to a decimal type are listed in Table 8.4. The *stint* and *stdecimal* functions are similar to the *stchar* functions and are used to convert and transfer data from C variables to the record buffer. The *stint* function converts data from a C integer variable to a C-ISAM format, which takes 2 bytes. The *stdecimal* function does the same for a C variable of type dec_t or struct decimal. The number of bytes required to store the decimal type in the data record is the third argument to this function.

TABLE 8.4 Functions for Conversion to Decimal Type

Function	Use
Deccvasc	Convert from a character string to decimal
Deccvint	Convert from C integer to decimal
Deccvlong	Convert from C long to decimal
Deccvflt	Convert from C float to decimal
Deccvdbl	Convert from C double to decimal

8.5 Error Processing

All C-ISAM functions return a negative integer value if the function is not executed successfully. In addition, the global variable *iserrno* is set to indicate the type of error that occurred. Its value should be printed to debug the problem. If it is less than 100, then a UNIX error has occurred which can be printed by using the C library function *perror*. All C-ISAM error codes are well-documented in the reference manual.

The last program to create the C-ISAM file part_inv is rewritten below with additional code for error handling.

```
#include <stdio.h>
#include <isam.h>
#include <decimal.h>
main()
{
  char part_rec[9], part_no[3];
  float stk_qty;
  int location,fd,status;
  dec_t  dec_stk;

  struct keydesc partkey;
```

```
/* Set the index-level flags */
partkey.k_flags = ISNODUPS;

/* No. of components = 1 */
partkey.k_nparts= 1;

/* For the first component   */
partkey.k_part[0].kp_start= 0;
partkey.k_part[0].kp_leng = 2;
partkey.k_part[0].kp_type = CHARTYPE;

/* Create the ISAM file */
fd = isbuild("part_inv",8,&partkey,ISOUTPUT+ISMANULOCK);
if (fd < 0) {
  fprintf(stderr,"Cannot create ISAM file part_inv, iserrno: %d\n",iserr
  if (iserrno < 100)
      perror("UNIX error");
  exit(1);
}


while(1)
{
  /* read a record from the redirected flat file */
  status=scanf("%s%f%d", part_no, &stk_qty, &location);
  if (status == EOF) break;

  /* convert stk_qty from float to decimal */
  deccvflt(stk_qty,&dec_stk);

  /* build the part record */
  stchar(part_no,part_rec,2);
  stdecimal(&dec_stk,&part_rec[2],4);
  stint(location,&part_rec[6]);

  /* Write the record into the ISAM file */
  status=iswrite(fd,part_rec);
  if (status < 0) {
    fprintf(stderr,"Write error for part_inv, iserrno: %d\n",iserrno);
    if (iserrno < 100)
     perror("UNIX error");
    exit(1);
  }
```

```
    }

    /* close the ISAM file */
    status=isclose(fd);
    if (status < 0) {
      fprintf(stderr,"Cannot close ISAM file part_inv, iserrno: %d\n",iserrno)
      if (iserrno < 100)
          perror("UNIX error");
      exit(1);
    }
}
```

The programs in the remaining section of this chapter have very little or no error processing code to keep them short. In practice, error processing code must be incorporated where necessary. Debugging a program with no error processing code can be a programmer's nightmare!

8.6 Retrieving Data

Once an ISAM file is created and records added to it, several functions are available to retrieve these records. Retrieval of records can be based on the record's key value or on its position in the file. Sequential processing of a file is also possible by reading the first record and then reading the file sequentially until end of file is encountered.

8.6.1 Retrieval Based on a Key Value

To retrieve a record based on a key value, first the record buffer must be populated with only the key value. The *isread* function uses this key value, searches for a record which matches the specified key value, and then retrieves the rest of the record in the record buffer. A match criterion can be specified to indicate the retrieval mode. For example, it is possible to search for records which match the specified key value exactly by using the *ISEQUAL* mode. Other retrieval modes are shown in Table 8.5.

TABLE 8.5 Retrieval Modes

Mode	Description
ISEQUAL	Specifies retrieval of all records which match the key value exactly
ISGREAT	Retrieves all records with key value greater than the specified value
ISGTEQ	Retrieves all records with key values greater than or equal to the specified value
ISNEXT	Retrieves the next record from the selected set of records
ISPREV	Retrieves the record preceding the record just read from the selected set
ISCURR	Reread the last record read

The following program retrieves the supplier name of the specified supplier. The C-ISAM file used here was created in an earlier section:

```
#include <isam.h>
#include <stdio.h>
main(argc,argv)
int argc;
char *argv[];
{
        char sup_rec[21],sup_name[21];
        int fd,status;

        /* Open the C-ISAM file(s) */
        fd = isopen("supfile",ISINPUT+ISMANULOCK);

        /* argv[1] has the supplier no.    */
        /* Copy it into the sup_rec buffer */
        stchar(argv[1],sup_rec,3);

        /* Retrieve the record */
        status = isread(fd,sup_rec,ISEQUAL);

        /* Is it found */
        if (status < 0)
                fprintf(stderr,"Supplier no. %s not found\n",argv[1]);
        else
```

```
        {
                ldchar(&sup_rec[3],20,sup_name);
                printf("Supplier name: %s\n", sup_name);
        }
        isclose(fd);
}
```

When compiled and executed, the program displays the supplier name of the supplier no. which is specified on the command line. An error message is printed if the supplier cannot be located, as is shown below:

```
a.out U11
Supplier name: Jacobs Industries
a.out T11
Supplier no. T11 not found
```

The *isread* function retrieves the matched record from the ISAM file and stores it in the C buffer *sup_rec*. The *ldchar* function is used here to extract the supplier name from the *sup_rec* variable and move it to the C variable *sup_name*. The second argument specifies the number of characters to be moved.

8.6.2 Sequential Processing of Records

Some applications require processing of all records retrieved on a specific sorted order. The C-ISAM *isread* function can also be used to process records in ascending or descending order. To process in ascending key order, invoke the *isread* function with the ISFIRST search mode. Subsequent invocations of this function must be made with the ISNEXT search mode until the end of the file is encountered. To process the file in descending order of the index, invoke the *isread* function with the ISLAST search mode and subsequently with ISPREV mode until the beginning of the file is encountered.

The following program prints a single line for each supplier. The line consists of the supplier no. and the list of parts supplied by him.

```
#include <isam.h>
#include <stdio.h>
main()
{
        char sup_rec[26],prev_sup_no[4];
```

```
        int fd,status;
        struct keydesc mykey;

        /* Open the C-ISAM file(s) */
        fd = isopen("supfile",ISINPUT+ISMANULOCK);

        prev_sup_no[3] = NULL;

        /* Read the first record */
        status = isread(fd,sup_rec,ISFIRST);

        /* Copy the first sup_no to keep track of change */
        strncpy(prev_sup_no,sup_rec,3);
        printf("%.3s:%s",sup_rec,&sup_rec[23]);

        while(1)
        {
        /* Read subsequent records */
        status = isread(fd,sup_rec,ISNEXT);

        /* Check for end of file */
        if (status < 0)
                break;

        /* Check for new supplier */
        if (strncmp(sup_rec,prev_sup_no,3)!=0)
                {
                printf("\n");
                strncpy(prev_sup_no,sup_rec,3);
                printf("%.3s:%s",sup_rec,&sup_rec[23]);
                }
        else
                printf(":%s",&sup_rec[23]);

        }
        printf("\n");
}
```

When compiled and executed, the program runs as shown below:

```
cc -o prsup myprog.c  -lisam
prsup
 Q0:P1
 S1:P2:P3
 S3:P1
 S4:P5:P6
 S6:P1:P2
 S7:P1:P2:P7:P8
 T8:P2:P3
 T9:P5:P6
U10:P3:P9
U11:P9
```

8.6.3 Finding Records By Record Number

As discussed earlier, the .dat file has a simple structure consisting of a series of fixed-length records. When a record is deleted, a null character is padded at its end to signify that the space is reusable. C-ISAM provides functions to access the records based on their physical location in the file. The physical position of a record in the file is called its record number. The global variable *isrecnum* is set to the record number of the last record accessed. The current record, on the other hand, is the last record read. Other C-ISAM functions can also be used to make a record current. Several C-ISAM functions operate only on the current record.

The function *isstart* can be used for positioning within the data file by setting the value of the global variable isrecnum. The record pointed by this variable is made the current record. It can be read by invoking the *isread* function with the ISCURR retrieval mode. If retrieval is based on the physical location of the record in the data file, then the index is of no use. The fifth record in the supfile file can be read by using the following program:

```
#include <stdio.h>
#include <isam.h>
main()
{
        int fd;
        char sup_rec[26];
        struct keydesc mykey;

        mykey.k_nparts = 0;
```

```
        /* Open the file */
        fd = isopen("supfile",ISINPUT+ISMANULOCK);

        /* Identify the record */
        isrecnum = 5;
        isstart(fd,&mykey,0,sup_rec,ISEQUAL);
        /* Read it */
        isread(fd,sup_rec,ISCURR);
        printf("%s\n",sup_rec);

        /* Process the record here */
}
```

The *mykey.k_nparts* variable is set to zero to indicate that no index is used. It is passed as the second argument to *isstart.* The third and fourth arguments are irrelevant for this specific use of the *isstart* function. The fifth argument is used here to specify the positioning criterion with respect to *isrecnum.* If ISGREAT was used, it would have pointed to the sixth record. The *isstart* function does not actually read the record. It only makes it current. The *isread* function must be used, as stated earlier, to read it.

8.7 Deleting Records

Several functions are available for the deletion of existing records from a C-ISAM file. Deletion of a record based on the value of its key can be done by use of the *isdelete* function. Only one record can be deleted by use of this function. Therefore, the index to be used must have been created with the ISNODUPS option. C-ISAM inserts null characters in place of the record to be deleted and also places a null character at the end of the record. Subsequent additions of new records make use of this space.

To use the *isdelete* function, place the key value in the data record buffer at a position corresponding to the key definition when the index was created. The function can then be invoked with the file descriptor and the record buffer. It searches for the record with the given key value. If it is found, the record is deleted; otherwise, a negative value is returned which indicates an error condition. The following program can be used to delete a record from the C-ISAM file called partfile which was created and loaded earlier. The part number and part name of the record to be deleted have to be specified on the command line.

```
#include <isam.h>
#include <stdio.h>
main(argc,argv)
int argc;
char *argv[];
{
        char part_rec[21];
        int fd,status;

        /* Open the C-ISAM file(s) */
        fd = isopen("partfile",ISINOUT+ISEXCLLOCK);

        /* Copy argv[1], the part no., to the record buffer  */
        stchar(argv[1],part_rec,2);
        /* Copy argv[2], the part name. to the record buffer */
        stchar(argv[2],&part_rec[10],10);

        /* Only the key segment of the record is loaded */
        status = isdelete(fd,part_rec);
        if (status < 0)
          fprintf(stderr,"Record not deleted, iserrno: %d\n",iserrno);
        else
          fprintf(stderr,"Record deleted\n");

        isclose(fd);
}
```

To delete records from a file which has an index with duplicates, use the function *isdelcurr*. To use this function first make current a record to be deleted. As indicated earlier, one way to do so is to read it. The *isdelcurr* function takes the file descriptor as an argument and deletes the current record. The previous program to delete a record given the part number and part name can be rewritten with use of the *isdelcurr* function as shown below:

```
#include <isam.h>
#include <stdio.h>
main(argc,argv)
int argc;
char *argv[];
{
        char part_rec[21];
        int fd,status;
```

```
        /* Open the C-ISAM file(s) */
        fd = isopen("partfile",ISINOUT+ISEXCLLOCK);

        /* Copy argv[1], the part no., to the record buffer  */
        stchar(argv[1],part_rec,2);
        /* Copy argv[2], the part name. to the record buffer */
        stchar(argv[2],&part_rec[10],10);

        /* Read the record and make it current */
        status = isread(fd,part_rec,ISEQUAL);
        if (status < 0)
          fprintf(stderr,"Record not found, iserrno: %d\n",iserrno);
        else
          {
            isdelcurr(fd);
            fprintf(stderr,"Record deleted\n");
          }
        isclose(fd);
}
```

This program will delete a record even if the index on the file was created without a NODUPS option. If multiple records match the specified key, then the program should make these current, one at a time, by reading them using the *isread* function with the ISNEXT mode until no more matching records are found. As the records are being made current, they can be deleted, by use of the *isdelcurr* function.

A record can be deleted from a file by its location or record number from the beginning of the file being specified. The *isdelrec* function can be used for this purpose. It takes two arguments. The first argument is the file descriptor of the opened file, and the second argument is the record number of the record to be deleted specified as a long integer. Here is a small program which deletes a record from the file. The record number is specified as the first argument on the command line.

```
#include <isam.h>
#include <stdio.h>
main(argc,argv)
int argc;
char *argv[];
{
        int fd,status;
```

```
        long atol();

        /* Open the C-ISAM file(s) */
        fd = isopen("partfile",ISINOUT+ISEXCLLOCK);

        status = isdelrec(fd,atol(argv[1]));
        if (status < 0)
          fprintf(stderr,"Record not deleted, iserrno: %d\n",iserrno);
        else
          fprintf(stderr,"Record deleted\n");

        isclose(fd);
}
```

The record number is the physical location in the file. As records are deleted from the file, "holes" are created in it. If an attempt is made to delete one of these holes (an already deleted record) an error condition is returned.

When a record is deleted by use of any of the three functions discussed here, the global variable *isrecnum* is set to the location pointing to the deleted record.

8.8 Updating Records

The process of updating a record in a C-ISAM file is similar to the process of deleting discussed in the previous section. Three functions can be used to update existing records.

The *isrewrite* function updates a record by entering the new information in the record buffer. The key segment of the record buffer is used to locate the record. Once located, the remaining portion of the data in the buffer is used to update the record. Only one record can be updated in a function call. Therefore the *isrewrite* function can be used only if the index, which has been used, was created without an ISNODUPS option.

Here is a sample program to update a record from the file partfile. The first argument is the part number and the second argument is the part name. These two arguments are used to locate the record. Finally, the third argument is used to specify the new color of the part. This is the new information to be updated.

```
#include <isam.h>
#include <stdio.h>
main(argc,argv)
int argc;
char *argv[];
{
     char part_rec[21];
     int fd,status;

     /* Open the C-ISAM file(s) */
     fd = isopen("partfile",ISINOUT+ISEXCLLOCK);

     /* Copy argv[1], the part no., to the record buffer  */
     stchar(argv[1],part_rec,2);
     /* Copy argv[2], the part name, to the record buffer */
     stchar(argv[2],&part_rec[10],10);

     /* Copy the new color to the record buffer */
     stchar(argv[3],&part_rec[2],8);

     /* Locate the record and update it */
     status = isrewrite(fd,part_rec);
     if (status < 0)
       fprintf(stderr,"Record not updated, iserrno: %d\n",iserrno);
     else
          fprintf(stderr,"Record updated\n");
     isclose(fd);
}
```

As is clear from this example, the *isrewrite* function cannot be used to update the key which is used to locate the record.

Once a record is made current, it can be updated with use of the *isrewcurr* function. Unlike the *isrewrite* function, the *isrewcurr* function has no restriction on the type of index to be used. It can be used with an index created with the ISDUPS option. The next sample program updates the supplier name in the file supfile. The records to be updated are stored in a flat file called new.d. Records in this file have two fields. The first field is the supplier number and the second field is the new supplier name. The program reads a record from this file and tries to locate all records with the same supplier number in the C-ISAM file. The supplier name in all the matching records is then updated. The program is listed below:

```
#include <stdio.h>
#include <isam.h>
main()
{
   FILE *fp_new;
   char new_sup_no[4],new_sup_name[21],sup_rec[26],achar;
   int eof,fd;

   /* Open the two files */
   fp_new = fopen("new.d","r");
   fd     = isopen("supfile",ISINOUT+ISMANULOCK);

   while (1)
   {
      /* Read the two colon-separated fields from the flat file */
      eof = fscanf(fp_new,"%[^:]%c%[^\n]%c",
          new_sup_no, &achar, new_sup_name, &achar);

      /* Is it end of file */
      if (eof==EOF) break;

      /* Is the supplier no. valid? */
      stchar(new_sup_no,sup_rec,3);
      if (isread(fd,sup_rec,ISEQUAL)< 0)

        /* If not, print an error message */
        fprintf(stderr,"Record for %s not found\n",new_sup_no);

      else

       /* Update all records for this supplier */
        do
            if (strncmp(sup_rec,new_sup_no,3)==0)
            {
               stchar(new_sup_name,&sup_rec[3],20);
               isrewcurr(fd,sup_rec);
            }
           else
           break;
        while (isread(fd,sup_rec,ISNEXT) >= 0);
   }
}
```

isrewrec is another function available for the updating of a C-ISAM file. It is similar to the *isdelrec* function, as it is used to update a record which is identified by its record number. The following function invocation updates the third record in the file:

```
isrewrec(fd,3L,new_rec);
```

where *fd* is the file descriptor of the file that is opened for update, *3L* indicates that the third record is to be updated, and *new_rec* is the record buffer which has the new data to be updated. The *L* in *3L* is used to specify a long integer.

8.9 Using Multiple Indexes

Some applications require that the ISAM file be accessed on different combinations of fields. Also, different users may access the same file on different fields. When the ISAM file is first created, there may or may not be an index. If an index was defined at creation time then that index is called the primary index. All programs in the preceding sections used this index. The primary index is permanantly attached to the file. If a new application is to be developed, it may need to access the file on fields which are not defined in the current index. A new index must then be built to meet the new access requirement. This new index is called the secondary index. As new applications are built, newer access methods are required and more secondary indexes have to be added. As applications are changed, unwanted indexes, except the primary index, can be removed. Addition and deletion of indexes have no effect on the data file. Only the index file is changed. This section explains the C-ISAM functions available for the manipulation of multiple indexes.

Updates and addition of data records take more time as the number of indexes increases.

8.9.1 Adding a New Index

You can add a new index by first describing the index in a *keydesc* structure and then calling the *isaddindex* function. Of course, the file must be opened before the index can be added. The following program adds a new index on the part no. field to the supplier file. The primary index on this file was built earlier on the supplier no. field.

```
#include <stdio.h>
#include <isam.h>
main()
{
  int fd;
  struct keydesc newindex_key;

  newindex_key.k_flags = ISDUPS+COMPRESS;
  newindex_key.k_nparts= 1;
  newindex_key.k_part[0].kp_start=23;
  newindex_key.k_part[0].kp_leng =2;
  newindex_key.k_part[0].kp_type =CHARTYPE;

  fd=isopen("supfile",ISINOUT+ISEXCLLOCK);

  if (isaddindex(fd,&newindex_key) < 0)
    fprintf(stderr,"Error in index addition, iserrno: %d\n",iserrno);
  else
    fprintf(stderr,"Index added\n");
  isclose(fd);
}
```

It is an error to have multiple indexes on the same fields in the same sequence (iserrno=108). Also, an index with an ISNODUPS flag set cannot be built on a file if duplicate data already exists in the data file.

8.9.2 Deleting an Existing Index

An existing index can be deleted by use of the *isdelindex* function. The steps involved are identical to those for the addition of an exiting index. First a keydesc structure must be defined to describe the index. The *isdelindex* function can then be invoked on the opened file to delete the index. If an index exists which matches the given description, then it is deleted; otherwise, a negative value is returned and the global variable *iserrno* is set to indicate the error type. The following program deletes the secondary index created in the previous section on the file supfile.

```
#include <stdio.h>
#include <isam.h>
main()
{
```

```
    int fd;
    struct keydesc newindex_key;

    newindex_key.k_flags = ISDUPS+COMPRESS;
    newindex_key.k_nparts= 1;
    newindex_key.k_part[0].kp_start=23;
    newindex_key.k_part[0].kp_leng =2;
    newindex_key.k_part[0].kp_type =CHARTYPE;

    fd=isopen("supfile",ISINOUT+ISEXCLLOCK);

    if (isdelindex(fd,&newindex_key) < 0)
      fprintf(stderr,"Error in index deletion, iserrno: %d\n",iserrno);
    else
      fprintf(stderr,"Index deleted\n");
    isclose(fd);
}
```

The file on which an index is to be deleted must be opened for exclusive use by use of the ISEXCLLOCK lock mode. The primary index cannot be deleted.

8.9.3 Selecting an Index

It is the responsibility of the programmer to specify the index to be used. By default, the primary index is the one that is used for all access operations. If multiple indexes are present, then a new index can be used by invoking the *isstart* function. This function was used in an earlier example to access records based on their physical position in the data file.

The function *isstart* takes five arguments. The first argument is the file descriptor of the opened file. The second argument is the address of a structure of type keydesc describing the new index to be used. The third argument is the length of the key to be used. It is used to search for a record when only part of the index key value is known or is to be used. The fourth argument is the record buffer which can be used to pass the key value. Finally, the fifth argument is used to specify the mode for locating the starting record. These modes are shown in Table 8.5.

isstart does not read the record, it only sets the current index to be used and the starting position in it. The record can be read by use of the *isread* function with the ISCURR retrieval mode. The next program illustrates the use of the *isstart* function for retrieval of data from the supfile file. The user is prompted for the field to be used for searching the record and also its value. The index to be used for searching is selected by the *isstart* function, and the record is read by the *isread* function. Here is the program:

```
#include <stdio.h>
#include <isam.h>
main()
{
   char  value[4], sup_rec[26], which_field;
   int fd,status;
   struct keydesc sup_key, part_key;

   /* Open the ISAM file */
   fd=isopen("supfile",ISINOUT+ISEXCLLOCK);

   /* Build the key on supplier no. */
   sup_key.k_flags = ISDUPS+TCOMPRESS;
   sup_key.k_nparts= 1;
   sup_key.k_part[0].kp_start=0;
   sup_key.k_part[0].kp_leng =3;
   sup_key.k_part[0].kp_type =CHARTYPE;

   /* Build the key on part no. */
   part_key.k_flags = ISDUPS+COMPRESS;
   part_key.k_nparts= 1;
   part_key.k_part[0].kp_start=23;
   part_key.k_part[0].kp_leng =2;
   part_key.k_part[0].kp_type =CHARTYPE;

   while (1)
   {
      printf("Please enter P or S to specify field, Q to quit: ");
      which_field=getchar();

      gets(value); /* To ignore the newline character */
      if (which_field=='Q')
      {
         isclose(fd);
         exit(0);
      }

      /* Get the search value */
      printf("Please enter search value: ");
```

```
        gets(value);

        /* Select the appropriate index for searching */
        /* and move the key values */
        if (which_field == 'P')
        {
           stchar(value,&sup_rec[23],2);
           status=isstart(fd,&part_key,2,sup_rec,ISEQUAL);
        }
        else
        {
           stchar(value,sup_rec,3);
           status=isstart(fd,&sup_key,3,sup_rec,ISEQUAL);
        }

        /* If found, read and print the record */
        if (status >= 0)
        {
           isread(fd,sup_rec,ISCURR);
          printf("Record is %s\n", sup_rec);
        }
        else
           printf("Record not found\n");
    }
}
```

The program prints only the first matched record. It can be modified very easily to print all matched records by the invocation of *isread* with the ISNEXT retrieval mode until the key value changes.

8.10 Determining Index Structures

Before a new index is added, check and see if an existing index can be used. The *isaddindex* function will return an error code only if the index already exists on the same fields in the same sequence. The *isindexinfo* function can be used to retrieve information on the existing indexes on the file. It examines the dictionary node in the *.idx* file and uses a structure of type *dictinfo* to provide information about the indexes on the file and the records in it. This structure is defined in the isam.h file and is reproduced below:

```
struct dictinfo
    {
    short di_nkeys;     /* number of keys defined*/
    short di_recsize;   /* data record size    */
    short di_idxsize;   /* index record size   */
    long di_nrecords;   /* number of records in file*/
    };
```

Once the number of indexes is known, the same function can be used to retrieve information about each index. This information is retrieved in a structure of type *keydesc* which was used frequently in earlier programs to describe the index and its components.

The *isindexinfo* takes three arguments. The first argument is, as expected, the file descriptor of an opened C-ISAM file. For the retrieval of information in a structure of type *dictinfo*, the second argument should be the address of a structure of the same type and the third argument should be zero. For the retrieval of information on each index, the second argument should be the address of a structure of type *keydesc* and the third argument should be the number of the index on which information is desired. The index number of the primary index is 1. The following general purpose program can be used to print the information about the indexes on any C-ISAM file:

```
#include <stdio.h>
#include <isam.h>
main(argc,argv)
int argc;
char *argv[];
{
 struct keydesc key;
 struct dictinfo ind_info;
 int fd,i,k;


 /* Open the file */
 fd = isopen(argv[1],ISINPUT+ISMANULOCK);
 if (fd < 0)
 {
   fprintf(stderr,"ISAM open error, iserrno: %d\n", iserrno);
   exit(1);
 }

 /* Fetch information about ISAM file*/
```

```
isindexinfo(fd,&ind_info,0);

/* Print the information */
printf("No. of indexes on the file is : %d\n",ind_info.di_nkeys);
printf("Size of each record is        : %d\n",ind_info.di_recsize);
printf("No. of bytes in each node is : %d\n",ind_info.di_idxsize);
printf("No. of records in the file is: %d\n\n",ind_info.di_nrecords);

/* Print information about each index */
for (i=1;i<ind_info.di_nkeys + 1; ++i)
{
   /* Get the information about the component */
   isindexinfo(fd,&key,i);
   printf("\nInformation about index no. %d\n", i);
   printf("================================\n");

   /* Print flags set */
   flags(key.k_flags);

   /* Print information about each component of the index */
   printf("No. of components    : %d\n",key.k_nparts);
   for (k=0; k < key.k_nparts; ++k) {
      printf("Starting position is : %d\n", key.k_part[k].kp_start);
      printf("Length of key is     : %d\n", key.k_part[k].kp_leng);
      types(key.k_part[k].kp_type);
   }

 }
}
flags(flag)
short flag;
{
   printf("Flags set are         : ");
   if (flag & ISDUPS)
      printf("ISDUPS");
   else
      printf("ISNODUPS");
   if (flag & DCOMPRESS)
      printf(",DCOMPRESS");
   if (flag & TCOMPRESS)
      printf(",TCOMPRESS");
   if (flag & LCOMPRESS)
      printf(",LCOMPRESS");
```

```
    printf("\n");
}
types(type)
short type;
{
    printf("Type is                 : ");
    switch(type)
    {
    case CHARTYPE:
        printf("CHARTYPE or DECIMALTYPE\n");
        break;
    case LONGTYPE:
        printf("LONGTYPE\n");
        break;
    case INTTYPE:
        printf("INTTYPE\n");
        break;
    case FLOATTYPE:
        printf("FLOATTYPE\n");
        break;
    case DOUBLETYPE:
        printf("DOUBLETYPE\n");
        break;
    }
}
```

When compiled and executed, this program prints index information as shown below:

```
cc -o index_info index_info.c -lisam
index_info supfile
No. of indexes on the file is : 2
Size of each record is        : 25
No. of bytes in each node is : 1023
No. of records in the file is: 18


Information about index no. 1
==============================
Flags set are          : ISNODUPS,TCOMPRESS
No. of components      : 1
Starting position is : 0
```

```
Length of key is      : 3
Type is               : CHARTYPE or DECIMALTYPE

Information about index no. 2
===============================
Flags set are         : ISDUPS,DCOMPRESS,TCOMPRESS,LCOMPRESS
No. of components     : 1
Starting position is  : 23
Length of key is      : 2
Type is               : CHARTYPE or DECIMALTYPE
```

8.11 Clustering: Sorting the Data File

Some applications require that the data be processed sequentially on a specified index. The presence of an index on a field helps in the retrieval of the data records sequentially, but the records in the data file are not normally sorted on the index. If the records are unsorted in the data file for the index under consideration, then the file will be inefficient from the UNIX I/O point of view, as numerous blocks will have to be buffered for reading records in a sorted order. The solution, then, is to sort the data file on one of the existing indexes. The clustering mechanism is provided for this purpose.

The clustering process is not a simple sorting of the data file; all the existing indexes have to be rebuilt because the positions of the records in the data file change as a result of the sort. The function *iscluster* can be used to cluster a C-ISAM index file. The following program clusters the file supfile on the first three characters, which is the supplier no. field:

```
#include <isam.h>
#include <stdio.h>
main()
{
        int fd;
        struct keydesc key;

        /* Open the file in exclusive mode */
        fd = isopen("supfile",ISINOUT+ISEXCLLOCK);

        /* Specify the index on which to cluster */
        key.k_flags = ISDUPS+TCOMPRESS;
```

```
        key.k_nparts= 1;
        key.k_part[0].kp_start=0;
        key.k_part[0].kp_leng =3;
        key.k_part[0].kp_type =CHARTYPE;

        /* Start the clustering */
        fd = iscluster(fd,&key);

        /* If any processing is required, use the new fd */
        isclose(fd);
}
```

The clustering effect is not permanent. As records are added and deleted, the data file is no longer guaranteed to be sorted.

8.12 Locking Mechanism

If two processes try to update the same record, a control mechanism is required for the synchronization of their activities. The locking mechanism is used for this purpose. In the absence of this mechanism, the integrity of the system is lost.

Figure 8.5 illustrates how an update on a record can be lost in the absence of a locking mechanism. If a locking mechanism is provided, then one process can wait for the other to complete the update and release the record. Figure 8.6 shows how the update lost in Figure 8.5 can be retained by locking the record before it is updated and then releasing it after the update is completed.

Two levels of locking are generally available: file-level locking and record-level locking. These levels determine the granularity of the objects which can be locked. Some systems also provide a field level lock. It is conceivable to have even a byte-level locking. In addition to "granularity" of the objects which can be locked, another term associated with locking is "lock mode." There are two generally accepted lock modes: shared and exclusive. A process is expected to lock an object in exclusive mode if it intends to change it. Similarly, a process is expected to lock an object in shared mode if it is only going to read its contents. In exclusive mode the locked object is unavailable to all other processes for reading or writing. In shared mode, other processes can read the object but cannot modify it.

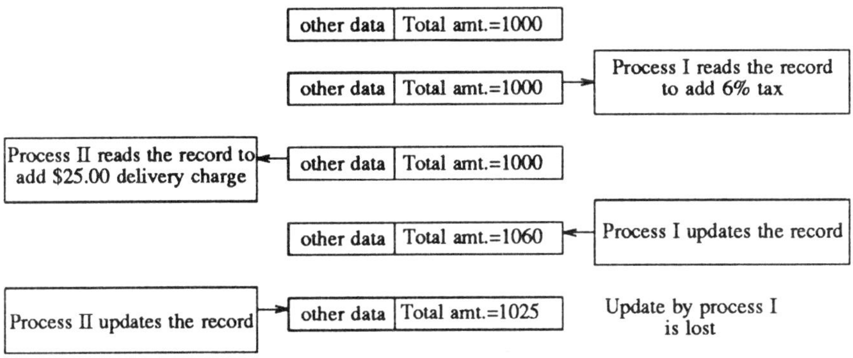

Figure 8.5 Update Lost in Concurrent Processing

8.12.1 Locking in C-ISAM

C-ISAM provides file-level and record-level locking. Locking can be achieved by explicitly invoking C-ISAM functions provided for this purpose or by specifying appropriate lock modes when opening the file with the *isopen* function. Within these two levels of locking there are two additional classifications: exclusive or manual mode. Similarly, a record can be locked in automatic or manual mode.

8.12.1.1 File-level Locking

The EXCLLOCK flag can be used with the *isopen* function call to lock the file for exclusive use of the program. No other programs/processes can access the locked file until it is closed by the invocation of an *isclose* function call. The next program illustrates the use of this locking mechanism:

```
#include <stdio.h>
#include <isam.h>
main()
{
   int fd;

   /* Open the file */
```

```
    fd = isopen("supfile",ISINOUT+ISEXCLLOCK);
    if (fd < 0)
        {
        fprintf(stderr,"ISAM open error, iserrno: %d\n", iserrno);
        exit(1);
        }
    /*******************************/
    /*  Do processing of data here */
    /*  The file is not available  */
    /*  for use by other programs. */
    /*******************************/

    /* Close the file before exiting */
    isclose(fd);
}
```

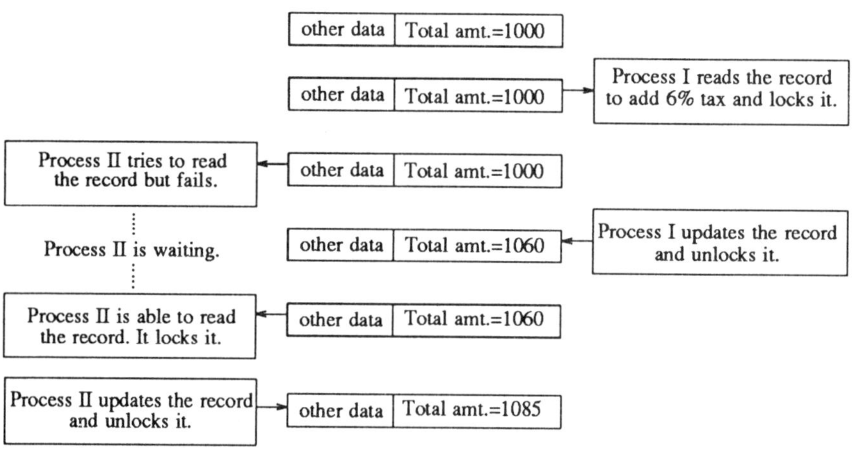

Figure 8.6 Use of Locks in Concurrent Processing

A file should not be locked for exclusive use unless absolutely necessary. For example, functions such as *iscluster*, *isaddindex*, and *isdelindex* require exclusive use of the file. Further, if a program needs to execute these critical functions, then the file should be opened in exclusive mode only during the execution of these functions. It should then be closed so that the exclusive lock is released and reopened again with a different lock mode. This increases the availability of the file.

When records are to be written to a file opened in exclusive mode, the *isflush* function can be used to force the writing of the records to the disk file. If the file is not opened in exclusive mode then this is not required because the records written are flushed immediately. The only argument to *isflush* is the file descriptor of the file into which records are to be written.

A less restrictive form of file locking can be implemented with use of manual locks. Manual file locking requires that the file be opened with the lock flag ISMANULOCK. When opened, the file is not locked in any way. If it needs to be locked at some point in the program, then the function *islock* should be invoked on the file. Once the file is locked in this way, other programs can still read it but cannot update it. This locked file can be subsequently unlocked by use of the function *isunlock*. The following program shows how *islock* and *isunlock* can be used to set and unset a manual lock:

```
#include <stdio.h>
#include <isam.h>
main()
{
   int fd;

   /* Open the file */
   fd = isopen("supfile",ISINOUT+ISMANULOCK);
   if (fd < 0)
       {
       fprintf(stderr,"ISAM open error, iserrno: %d\n", iserrno);
       exit(1);
       }

   /********************************/
   /*  Do processing of data which */
   /*  does not require the file to*/
   /*  be locked.                  */
   /********************************/

   /* Lock the file */

    islock(fd);

   /***********************************/
   /*  Do processing of data which    */
   /*  requires the file to be locked.*/
   /***********************************/
```

```
    /* Unlock the file here    */

    isunlock(fd);

    /* ...continue processing. */

    /* Close the file before exiting */
    isclose(fd);
}
```

8.12.1.2 Record-level Locking

Record-level locking provides the programmer with the ability to lock one or more records in a file. Compared to file-level locking, it increases the availability of the data in the file. Other records continue to remain unlocked and can be accessed regardless of the fact that some records in the same file are locked. Two forms of record-level locking are available: automatic and manual. The choice must be specified as an option when the file is opened with an *isopen* function call. Automatic record-level locking requires the use of a ISAUTOLOCK flag, and manual record-level locking requires the use of a ISMANULOCK flag.

If a file is opened with the automatic record-level locking flag set, then a record is locked when the *isread* function retrieves it. The locked record is subsequently unlocked when another C-ISAM function affecting the record is invoked. Only one record can be locked at a time with this mechanism.

If a file is opened with the manual record-level locking flag set, then the *isread* function must be invoked with the ISLOCK flag set to lock the retrieved record. Here is an example of an invocation of an *isread* function call with the *ISLOCK* flag set:

```
isread(fd,sup_rec,ISEQUAL+ISLOCK);
```

All the records, matching the key, are locked. To invoke the records, an *isrelease* function must be explicitly invoked, as in:

```
isrelease(fd);
```

Unlike automatic locks on records, manual locks can be applied to multiple records at the same time. There is, however, a limit which depends on the

UNIX version.

8.12.1.3 Handling Locked Records

When an attempt is made to retrieve a locked record, depending on the lock mode, the read may fail. The program must check if the read failed because of a lock or because of another reason. If an *isread* function call returns a negative value, then the value of the global variable *iserrno* must be checked. If it is equal to the defined constant EFLOCKED then the file has an exclusive lock. If it is equal to the defined constant ELOCKED then it indicates other forms of locks.

8.13 Transaction Management

Transaction management was discussed in Chapter 5 (where SQL statements were used to do transaction processing). A transaction is characterized by the atomicity of its operations. Either all or none at all of the operations associated with a transaction are completed. To implement this feature, a log file is used. All operations within a transaction are written to the log file. If an operation within the transaction needs to be undone, this log file is used. This log file can also be used to recover the status of a database if a backup copy was taken when the transaction file was created.

Transaction management also requires that the transactions be isolated. Isolation of a transaction means that the effect of the transaction must not be visible until the transaction is completed. Within a transaction, C-ISAM locks records to be modified and unlocks them when the transaction is completed.

C-ISAM offers several functions which can be used for transaction management. The function *isbegin* can be used to start a transaction. Once started, the transaction can be completed by use of the *iscommit* function. A set of operations already executed within a transaction can be undone by use of the *isrollback* function.

Here is a simple program to add a supplier and a part record. The supplier record is added first. If the part record cannot be added, then the write operation to add the supplier record is undone.

```
#include <stdio.h>
#include <isam.h>
main()
{
```

```
        int fd_sup, fd_part, status;
        char sup_rec[26], part_rec[21];

        /* Open the log file */
        status = islogopen("logfile.4");
        if (status < 0)
                {
                fprintf(stderr,"Cannot open log file, exiting...\n");
                exit(1);
                }

        /* Open the two C-ISAM files */
        fd_sup  = isopen("supfile",ISINOUT+ISMANULOCK+ISTRANS);
        fd_part = isopen("partfile",ISINOUT+ISMANULOCK+ISTRANS);

        /* Read the part and supplier records */
        gets(sup_rec);
        gets(part_rec);

        /* Start the transaction */
        isbegin();

        if (iswrite(fd_sup,sup_rec) < 0)
                isrollback();
        else
                if (iswrite(fd_part,part_rec) < 0)
                        isrollback();
        else
                iscommit();
        /* End of transaction */

        /* Close all files */
        isclose(fd_sup);
        isclose(fd_part);
        islogclose();
}
```

8.13.1 Miscellaneous C-ISAM Functions

C-ISAM provides a host of other functions. The *isrecover* function can be used to rollforward a corrupted C-ISAM file from a backup copy and a log file. If a C-ISAM file is corrupted then it can be restored to a previous consistent state by the use of a backup. Once the backup is complete, the log file can be used to roll forward the C-ISAM file by use of the *isrecover* function. The log file must be the one that was started immediately after the backup was created.

The *isaudit* function can be used to manage audit trail capabilities. Unlike the transaction log, audit trails can be set separately for each C-ISAM file.

8.14 Bcheck: An Index Maintenance Utility

As records are added and deleted from the data file, the entries in the different indexes also have to be adjusted. For every record in the data file, there must be an entry in all the indexes of the file. The index can be corrupted in the event of a system crash. The *bcheck* utility is used to check the integrity of the index and rebuild it if necessary. The name of the file is the only argument required. Several options are also available. They are:

-i	Check index file only
-l	List entries in B-trees
-n	Answer no to all questions
-y	Answer yes to all questions
-q	Suppress printing of unwanted messages
-s	Change the node size of an index

In the absence of a *-y* or a *-n* option, the program runs in interactive mode expecting a "yes" or "no" answer to different prompts. Here is a sample session:

```
bcheck -y supfile
Copyright and version number messages

C-ISAM Files: supfile

Checking dictionary and file sizes.
index file node size = 1024
current C-ISAM index node size = 1024
Checking data file records.
Checking indexes and key descriptions.
Index 1 = unique key(0,3,0)
        1 index node(s) used --1 index b-tree level(s) used
```

```
Checking data record and index node free lists.
3 index node(s) used, 0 free --10 data record(s) used, 29 free
```

If an index cannot be recovered by use of the *bcheck* utility, then it must be rebuilt by use of a backup copy and a transaction log or an audit trail.

8.15 Closing Thoughts

C-ISAM forms the backbone of most INFORMIX products. The architecture of these products consists of a front-end and a common back-end. The back-end is implemented with C-ISAM function calls. An interprocess communication facility is used to provide the necessary exchange of information between the two processes.

The common back-end design makes it easy to port data and index files across the different products. In fact, it is possible to write C programs with C-ISAM functions to manipulate the files created by *isql* or *i4gl*. Optimization in INFORMIX products can be done in both the front-end and in the back-end process. A good understanding of the internal structure of an index is necessary so that the fields and the options for creating an index can be selected. There is a general misconception that the more the indexes, the better the performance. In fact, the addition of a useless or redundant index not only takes extra space but also slows all updates to the database.

9 INFORMIX-TURBO

The wide acceptance of UNIX in the on-line transaction processing (OLTP) environment has encouraged DBMS vendors to develop systems which break performance bottlenecks imposed by the UNIX file system.

If the UNIX file system is used, the DBMS loses control on the lower-level data organization of the database, leaving it to the operating system file-handling routines. Several DBMS vendors have attempted to bypass the UNIX file system to improve the performance. INFORMIX-TURBO is one such implementation. Performance benchmarks conducted by independent vendors using INFORMIX-TURBO further corroborate that UNIX can indeed be an ideal platform for high-volume OLTP applications.

INFORMIX-TURBO has a much improved fault tolerance mechanism, raw I/O facility, self contained archiving capabilities, better control over memory management, and many fine tuning capabilities which have made it the fastest DBMS in the UNIX environment for OLTP applications. The objective of this chapter is to describe the basic features of the TURBO server and explain how it satisfies the need for a high performance and fault-tolerant OLTP application. Differences between the standard INFORMIX database server and the TURBO server and utilities to convert existing databases to be managed by the TURBO server are also discussed.

9.1 On-Line Transaction Processing

Traditionally, all database applications were categorized as OLTP systems. With the increased demand for high performance DBMS, the term OLTP is used for systems which are characterized by the following features:

- High throughput: A fast response time is a prime requirement for OLTP applications. OLTP applications often strive to operate totally in real time.
- High availability: This requires that the system has a high uptime and has a built-in fault tolerance mechanism. This feature enables it to be up and running with minimum operator intervention after a system failure.
- High concurrency: This feature of OLTP applications enables multiple users to share the same data with minimum time, space, and resource overheads.
- Support for large databases: This factor makes the implementation of other OLTP features difficult. Support for large databases requires efficient access methods.
- Support for security: Most OLTP applications require that the contents of the database be well-secured. Security aspect must be provided by the DBMS to ease the development of OLTP applications.
- Other features: Other features which characterize an OLTP application include ease of operation, support for multiprocessor utilization, and capability to handle growth of the database and number of users without performance degradation.

DBMS which support the development of OLTP applications must be able to cater to all these requirements. The segment of the DBMS software that handles these requirements is called the database server. It is normally an independent process.

9.2 Database Servers

The task of the database server is to satisfy the requirements of user processes by completing the requested database manipulation operations.

There are numerous methods of implementing a database server. One possible implementation is to have a centralized database server. Such an implementation would have a better control over the database integrity because all requests to the database must go through the same process. However, these requests will have to be queued to be serviced, resulting in a slow response time. Sharing of critical resources can be better handled because only one process is involved in controlling them. Such servers are called multi-threaded servers.

Another implementation would be to have a server for each application process. The major disadvantage in this type of an implementation is the overhead associated with each process. All INFORMIX applications which use INFORMIX-SQL, INFORMIX-4GL, or INFORMIX-ESQL use this implementation. The application process spawns another process, which is the database server. The application process is called the front-end, and the database server is called the back-end. INFORMIX-TURBO is an implementation of the back-end process. The non-TURBO back-end is implemented with the C-ISAM package. It is referred to in INFORMIX literature as the standard back-end, or as INFORMIX-SE (Standard Engine).

The back-end process communicates with the front-end process with pipes. The interprocess communication protocol between the front-end and the back-end process is the same for both types of back-ends. The front-end and the back-end process pairs cannot run independently. With certain requirements, such as locking of rows, the activities of a process-pair must be communicated to other process-pairs. Another interprocess communication protocol is therefore required for the back-end processes to communicate. Figure 9.1 illustrates the two different types of database server implementations.

9.2.1 Selecting the Back-End

INFORMIX application programs can be made to select the appropriate back-end with the setting of the environment variable SQLEXEC. To select the TURBO back-end, the user must set the SQLEXEC variable to *sqlturbo*. The variable can be set to *sqlexec* if the standard server is to be selected. Of course, INFORMIXDIR must be set to the directory in which INFORMIX is installed. If the Bourne shell is in use and the TURBO back-end is to be used, the environment variables can be set as shown here:

```
INFORMIXDIR=/usr/informix
export INFORMIXDIR
SQLEXEC=$INFORMIXDIR/lib/sqlturbo
export SQLEXEC
```

The selection of the back-end process does not allow the user to interact with any type of a database. A database that is created with a TURBO back-end cannot be used with a standard back-end, and vice-versa. The internal structures of the databases created by the two back-ends are significantly different. Utilities are available for converting databases from the standard back-end to the TURBO back-end.

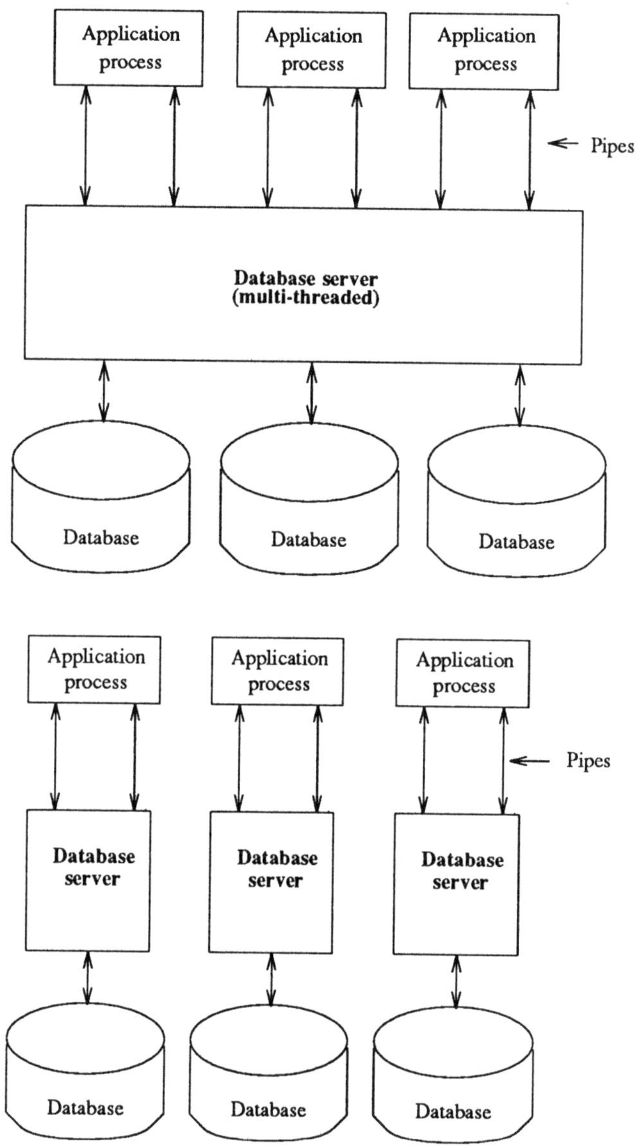

Figure 9.1 Database Server Implementations

9.3 Internal Database Structure

The internal structure of a database created with the standard back-end was explained in Chapter 6. For each database, a directory suffixed *.dbs* is created. There are two different distinct files for each table in the database. These files are suffixed *.dat* and *.idx*. The *.dat* file is used to store data and the *.idx* file is used to store the different indexes on the table. The contents of these files is manipulated by the *sqlexec* back-end. The allocation of blocks to these files is controlled by the UNIX file-system software. INFORMIX has no control over the physical location of these blocks or over the buffers which are allocated to these blocks during I/O operations.

The processing of rows can be expedited by the storage of the rows in physically contiguous blocks. If raw I/O is used, then the TURBO server can control the location of rows on the device. It is not necessary to have raw I/O to use the TURBO back-end, but using it definitely boosts the performance. To understand the organization of the raw device as used by INFORMIX-TURBO, it is important to know some of the terms explained in the following paragraph.

The highest unit of physical space is a chunk. A chunk can be either a complete raw device, a part of a raw device, or a file managed by UNIX. Allocation of a chunk reserves it for future use. A dbspace is a collection of chunks. More chunks can be added to a dbspace as space requirement arises. A single installation can have multiple dbspaces. When TURBO is initialized, the root dbspace is created. The name for the root dbspace can also be specified at this time. A database can span multiple dbspaces. A single dbspace can house multiple databases. A partition is allocated to each table. Unlike the ".dat" file, a partition also holds the index on the table. A partition is a collection of extents. The term "partition" should not be confused with the partitions used with UNIX disk devices. Future releases of TURBO plan to use the term "tblspace" for a partition.

When a table is created, a single extent is first allocated to it. If this extent is filled up, then more extents are assigned to this partition. An extent is made up of pages. A page is the basic unit of disk space and disk I/O. The page size is fixed for a machine and cannot be changed. The size of all other units has to be tuned for optimum performance. Partitions/tblspaces and dbspaces are logical entities. Chunks, extents, and pages are physical entities. The relationship between the different disk space units is illustrated in Figure 9.2.

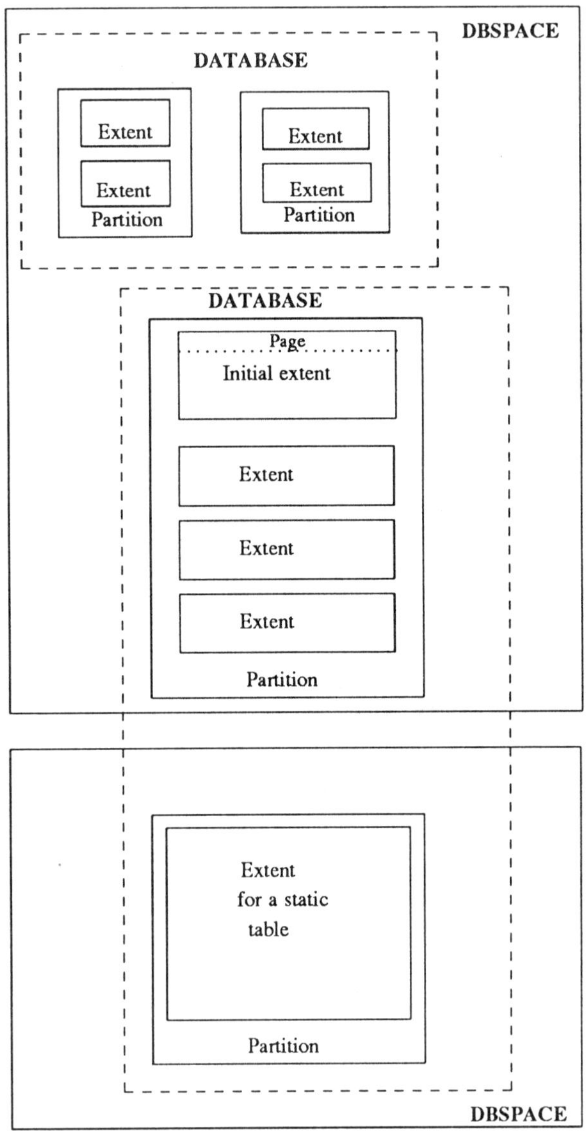

Figure 9.2 Relationship Between TURBO Disk Space Units

9.4 Creating Databases and Tables

The SQL *create table* and the *create database* statements are modified when used with the TURBO back-end. When a database is created, the name of the dbspace in which the database should reside can be specified. Strictly speaking, the name of the dbspace is used to specify the location of the system catalogs for the database. User tables can subsequently be created in a different dbspace. If the dbspace is not specified, then the system catalog for the database is placed in the root dbspace. Remember that there is no concept of a directory when raw device space is used. The following SQL command can be used to create a database in the "demospace" dbspace:

```
isql - -
> create database demodb in demospace;
Database created.
```

A table can also be created by use of the SQL *create table* statement. In addition to the column specifications, three other parameters can be specified at table creation time. They are listed below:

- Name of the dbspace: This specifies the dbspace in which the table will reside. A table does not have to reside in the same dbspace in which the database was created. If the name of a dbspace is not specified at table creation time, then the table is created in the dbspace in which the database was created.
- The initial extent size: When a table is created, an initial extent is assigned to it. The size of the initial extent can be specified in the SQL *create* statement. It must be an even multiple of page size. If it is not specified, the default size used is 16 Kbytes.
- The additional extent size: When the initial extent is completely used, a new extent must be assigned to the partition which holds the table. The size of this additional extent and all subsequent extents to be allocated to the table/partition can also be specified with the SQL *create* statement. It must be an even multiple of page size. If it is not specified, the default size used is 16 Kbytes.

Performance degradation occurs if more than eight extents are assigned to a table. To avoid this problem, the user must be able to predict the table size and growth factor and choose extent sizes accordingly.

Once the extent sizes are known, the SQL *create table* statement can be executed as shown below:

```
create table customers
(
c_no    char(10),
c_lname char(20),
c_fname char(20),
c_addr1 char(20),
c_addr2 char(20),
c_town  char(20),
c_state char(2),
c_zip   char(5)
) in rootdbs
  extent size 3500
  next extent 250;
```

In this example, the customers table is created in the dbspace named *rootdbs*. The initial extent size is 3500 Kbytes and the size of all subsequent extents will be 250 Kbytes.

9.4.1 Calculating Extent Sizes

To calculate the extent size, the following information is required:

- The page size
- The definition of the table to be created
- The description of all the indexes to be created
- The total number of rows currently available to be loaded in the table
- The expected growth of the table in a certain time period

Based on this information, the maximum number of data rows per page and the maximum number of index entries per page can be calculated. The following explanation uses, as an example, the customers table with two indexes. One index is on the *c_no* field and the other on *c_lname*.

Given the definition of the table, the total number of bytes required to store a single row can easily be calculated. The total number of bytes for each record in the customers table is 117. This is simply the sum of the number of bytes required to store each field. Rows cannot break across page boundaries. Therefore, some space is lost in each page. The number of rows which can be stored in a single page can be calculated by dividing the page size by the row size and truncating the result. Let the page size be 1024 bytes. For the customers table, the maximum number of rows which can be stored in a single page is 1024/117 = 8 rows.

The next step is to calculate the maximum number of index entries which can be stored in each page. The storage of index entries requires that in addition to the end nodes, the B+ tree itself be stored. If an overhead factor of 15% is associated with each entry, then the effective size of an index entry is (10 + 4)*1.15 + (20 + 4)*1.15 = 43 bytes. The number of index entries per page is 1024/43 = 23.

The final step is to calculate the number of pages in the initial extent and the subsequent extents. Let the number of rows to be loaded initially in the database be 10000. If 8 rows can be stored per page, then the total number of pages required to store data rows is 10000/8 = 1250. Similarly, the number of pages required to store index entries is 10000/23 = 435.

If the page size is 1 Kbyte then the size of the initial extent to store data rows and index entries is 1250 + 435 = 1685 Kbytes. If the table is expected to be static, then this is all we need to calculate.

For a dynamic table, we need to modify the size of the initial extent and calculate the size of the incremental extents. Let the table be expected to grow by 5000 rows by the end of the year. Further, let us assume that the table will be reorganized annually. Given these assumptions, the size of the subsequent extents can be calculated as follows. First, the 5000 rows must be spread over 8 extents. Each extent must therefore be able to handle 5000/8 = 625 rows. The total number of pages required to handle these rows is 625/8 = 79 pages and the total number of pages required to handle the index entries is 625/23 = 28 pages. The total number of pages required per additional extent is 79 + 28 = 107 pages. Given that the page size is 1 Kbyte, the size of each additional extent can be specified to be 107 Kbytes and the size of the initial extent is the number of Kbytes required to store the initial data plus space for one-eighth of the expected growth which is 107 + 1685 = 1792 Kbytes. Figure 9.3 illustrates how space is allocated to the customers table.

The above method gives only an approximate estimate of the extent sizes. It takes into consideration an approximate B+ tree overhead of 15%; it does not take into consideration the header and footer overheads within every page.

Though the performance deteriorates slightly after 8 extents have been allocated, TURBO can handle partitions with 200 extents.

9.4.2 Changes in System Catalogs

System catalogs consist of tables which INFORMIX uses to keep information about user tables and indexes. The internal organization of the databases and the tables is significantly different when the databases are created and managed by the TURBO back-end. Several changes were made to the systables, syscolumns, and sysindexes tables which store information on the tables, columns, and indexes, respectively. In particular, the systables table

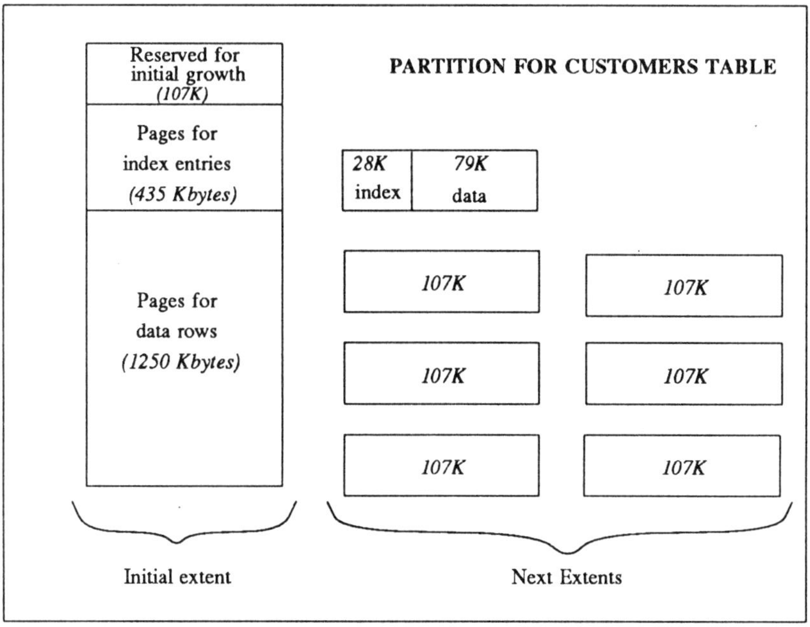

Figure 9.3 Estimated Extent Sizes for Customers Table

has the following five additional fields:

- Partnum: This is used to identify the partition which is used to store the table.
- Locklevel: This stores the lock mode for the table.
- Npused: This is used to keep track of the number of pages used by the table. (Not currently used)
- fextsize: This is used to store the size of the initial extent.
- nextsize: This is used to store the size of all subsequent extents.

Some of these fields are not currently used. This table is used when information about a user table and its extents is required.

9.5 Memory Management

Under the non-TURBO database server, each process has its own data space. This suffices for environments in which only one process is operating on the database or in which multiple processes are only querying the database. If several processes are accessing the database and even if only one of these processes is actively updating it, then it is difficult to ensure that the other processes are indeed reading the latest data. Some overhead is incurred to guarantee the validity of the row that is fetched by any process. The shared memory facility can be used to alleviate this problem.

9.5.1 Shared Memory

The shared-memory facility offered by most versions of UNIX allows multiple processes to share memory and consequently the data contained in it. The sharing is done by having participating processes access a common virtual memory space. The availability of hardware segment registers on most CPUs makes access to shared memory as fast as access to variables in the local address space. The use of shared memory enables all database servers to use the same data buffers. In addition, control information such as lock tables can also be shared among the processes. There is a system-dependent limit on the amount of memory that can be shared. In particular, the following four shared-memory parameters are relevant:

SHMMAX	Specifies the maximum size of a shared memory segment
SHMSEG	Specifies the maximum number of segments a process can attach
SHMMNI	Specifies the total number of segments for the system
SHMALL	Specifies the total number of shared memory pages for the system

The four parameters are not entirely independent of one another. The total shared memory that can be allocated is the product of the size of each segment and the maximum number of segments. This number must be approximately equal to the product of the shared-memory page size and the total number of shared-memory pages for the system. The larger the shared memory, the more data buffers that can be accommodated in it. The values of the above parameters can be changed only by the super-user. They are stored in a configuration file and are read when the kernel is regenerated.

The larger the shared memory, the more data buffers that can be allocated, resulting in improved TURBO performance. Enough memory must be left for other processes to execute. In a swapping environment, if not enough memory is available, then some portion of memory can be swapped. TURBO performance can degrade if the shared memory is swapped in and out frequently. Some versions of UNIX provide an option which prevents shared memory from being swapped out. If this option is exercised, then the performance of non-TURBO applications on the same system may be affected.

9.5.2 Controlling Access to Shared Memory

The ability to have different processes map the same memory in their user process space requires a mechanism to control access to it. TURBO uses latches to control access to shared memory.

Latches are also referred to as semaphores in INFORMIX literature. These latches/semaphores are distinctly different from UNIX semaphores. We will call them latches to avoid any confusion. A simplified structure of a latch appears as shown below:

Flag	Wait	User

A latch consists of three fields. *Flag* is a test and set field. The *wait* field indicates if another user is waiting for this latch. The *user* field indicates the owner of the latch currently held.

UNIX semaphores are used by TURBO to put processes to sleep and wake them up when waiting for system resources such as locks and buffers. A semaphore is a positive integer which can be used to control access to a shared resource. Most applications need several semaphores. System calls are available to create a set of semaphores. Additionally, a set of operations can be applied to a set of semaphores. The unique feature of these operations is that either all the operations are completed successfully or none at all. The set of operations can be viewed as a single indivisible atomic operation. Further, only one process can operate on a semaphore set. Multiple requests are queued and performed sequentially.

Three tunable parameters are used to control the number of semaphores for a system. The SEMMSL parameter is used to specify the maximum number of semaphores in a set. The SEMMNI parameter determines the maximum number of unique semaphore sets, and SEMMNS specifies the total number of semaphores for the entire system. Clearly, the SEMMNS parameter must be compatible with the product of SEMMNI and SEMMSL.

9.5.3 Changing Parameters

Changing the kernel parameters requires that the file from which these parameters are read during kernel generation be modified. For example, on the AT&T 6386 running UNIX System V Release 3.2, the system file /etc/conf/cf.d/mtune has to be modified. The shell script /etc/conf/bin/idbuild can be used for complete system reconfiguration. The new parameters become effective upon the next system boot.

Similar facilities are available for changing tunable parameters on other versions of the UNIX system.

9.5.4 Contents of TURBO Shared Memory

The shared memory used by INFORMIX TURBO contains a pool of data buffers and several control tables. The number of data buffers has a significant effect on the shared memory size. In addition, the following attributes also contribute to its size:

- Maximum number of users
- Maximum number of locks
- Maximum number of dbspaces
- Maximum number of chunks
- Maximum number of partitions
- Maximum number of buffers
- Maximum number of logical logs
- Size of physical log buffer

The numbers selected here affect the corresponding table size and the amount of shared memory that is available for data buffers.

9.6 Locking Mechanism

The importance of locking was explained in the previous chapter. Locking helps in maintaining the integrity of the database when multiple users are accessing the same data for retrieval and updates.

During updates, TURBO decides the level of isolation. When a row is read for an update, a shared lock is given to the updating process. Other processes can also be given a shared lock on the same row. The lock is promoted to an exclusive lock just before the update occurs. A row with an exclusive lock cannot be read or updated by any other process. A row with a shared lock can be read by any other process but not updated by it.

If a row were locked for exclusive use as soon as it was read for update, it would prevent other processes from accessing it until the update had been completed. This would minimize the availability of the record. The promotability of a lock increases the level of concurrency. Figure 9.4 illustrates the advantage of using promotable locks.

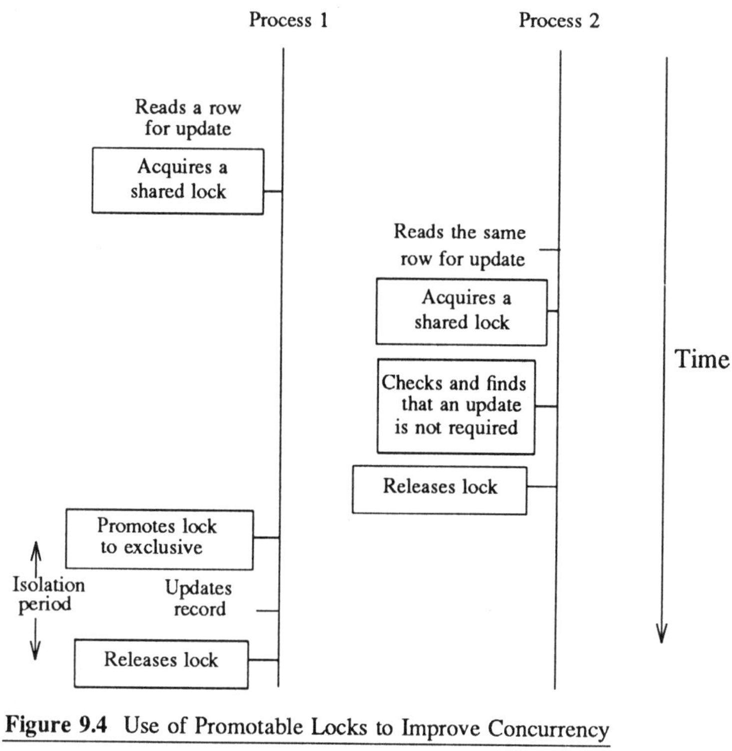

Figure 9.4 Use of Promotable Locks to Improve Concurrency

The promotability of locks makes it possible for process 1 and process 2 to simultaneously acquire a shared lock. If process 2 is going to relinquish the shared lock before process 3 promotes its lock, then there is no need to prevent two processes from acquiring a lock on the same record. The period of isolation is significantly reduced, increasing the level of concurrency.

9.6.1 Read-Only Locks

When multiple processes are accessing the database, a row read by one process may be deleted or updated by another process. TURBO provides different levels of guarantee to a process about the validity of a row that is being read.

9.6.1.1 Dirty Reads

Dirty reads provide no guarantee about the validity of a record. The rows that have been read with this level of validity may have been inserted by a transaction which may be rolled back at a later time. If the row itself exists, then it is possible that its updated contents may be rolled back after the row is read.

9.6.1.2 Committed Reads

Committed reads provide a guarantee that the row which is being read is not being modified by another process. It implements this level by trying to acquire a shared lock on the row. If the lock is acquired, then the test is successful and the lock is released immediately. After the read is completed, other processes can proceed to modify or even delete the row, because the shared lock is released.

9.6.1.3 Cursor Stability

This level of guarantee ensures that the record being read is not currently being modified and that it will not be modified until the reading process fetches another record. This guarantee is provided by the acquisition of a shared lock which is released only when the next record is fetched. It is possible for a process to select only a single row for reading without a cursor. This could result in the shared lock being held for a long time, as there are no more records to be fetched. To avoid this situation, in case of a single row selection without the use of a cursor, the shared lock is immediately released.

9.6.1.4 Repeatable Reads

This is the highest level of guarantee on the validity of the record being read. In the case of an explicit transaction, it guarantees that the record will not change during the course of the transaction. This level is implemented by the obtaining of a shared lock on the record being read. In addition, shared locks are also obtained for all records with the same key values as the current record. These locks guarantee that the selection of the record will not be affected by other processes.

9.6.1.5 Setting Read-Only Locks

Read-only locks can be set by use of the *set isolation* statement. This statement is an extension that is applicable only to TURBO back-ends. The statement

```
set isolation to dirty read
```

allows a record to be read even if it is currently undergoing an update. Other levels of read guarantees can be set by the following statements:

```
set isolation to committed read
set isolation to cursor stability
set isolation to repeatable read
```

The level of isolation can be changed dynamically. The default level of isolation is the committed read. If the database is not using logging, then only the dirty read level is applicable. Logging will be discussed later in this chapter.

If the front-end does not use explicit cursors for row retrieval, then the cursor stability and committed read levels have almost the same effect.

9.6.2 Locking Granularity

Locking granularity refers to the amount of data that is locked by a process. The level of concurrency is greatly enhanced with row-level locking. However, because of the finite number of locks available and the overhead associated with each lock, it becomes necessary to use locks at higher level.

TURBO provides four different levels of locking.

Row-level locking is the lowest level available. It provides the highest level of concurrency. A locked row is made inaccessible until the lock is released. The next higher level is *page level.* This level of locking is useful for sequential processing of rows. All the rows in the page are locked because the page itself is locked. This reduces the number of locks which are used, but at the same time it lowers the availability of multiple rows.

Table-level locks lock the entire table. If the number of rows to be processed in a transaction is large and if the rows are not physically in the same page, then table-level locking reduces the number of locks in use. It is also useful during a backup operation on a table. A table can be locked in either shared or exclusive mode. In shared mode, other processes have only read access to it. In exclusive mode, other processes have no access to the table for reading or for updating.

Finally, *database-level* locking provides a mechanism for locking the entire database. It can be used when changes are made to the entire database or when the whole database is being backed up. It should be used sparingly, as it makes the entire database unavailable for use.

9.6.2.1 Relevant Statements

To lock a database, the following statement can be used:

```
database dbname exclusive
```

where *dbname* is the name of the database to be locked. To lock a table, use the statement

```
lock table tablename in lockmode mode
```

where *tablename* is the name of the table and *lockmode* is the type of lock to be applied to the table. The two valid types are shared and exclusive, as explained earlier. Row-level locking can be set with either the *alter table* statement or the *create table* statement. To set row-level locking, use the following statements:

```
alter table tablename lock mode mode
   or
create table tablename
      rest of create statement
```

```
lock mode mode
```

where *tablename* is the name of the table to be locked and *mode* is the locking mode to be set on it. Applicable lock modes are "page", "row", and "page, row". TURBO can be made to choose between row-level and page-level locking by use of the *page, row* mode. This is not currently implemented. If you specify "page, row", it is set to page.

9.7 Fault Tolerance

The ability to restore a database from system crashes is an important feature for most OLTP applications. The ability to restore from a backup device is not enough for many applications. Cold start, as it is often referred to, loses transactions which may have been added to the database since the last backup. Besides, operator intervention is required for the restoration from a backup. The unavailability of the system during the restore process is another major disadvantage.

9.7.1 Types of Failures

Failures can be categorized in three classes:

- Secondary storage failure: Sometimes referred to as media failure, it is mostly caused by disk-head crashes. The entire contents of the disk may be lost.
- System failure: These can be categorized into two subclasses. In the first case, all information in memory at the time of the crash is available. Typical failure of this kind is caused by program errors such as a divide-by-zero condition which may force a *core dump* and abort the entire program. System failures may also be caused by a power outage, resulting in loss of information stored in main memory and subsequently the state of the database.
- Multiple failures: These are caused if the media on which a database as well as the media on which logs are written are both rendered inoperable. A cold start based on a backup copy is the only alternative to restoring it to a previous consistent state. If a backup was not taken, then it is the right time for the operator to find another job.

9.7.2 Theoretical Concepts

The basic mechanism for implementing transactions and recovery procedures is the use of logs. Under normal circumstances, for implementing transactions, a log contains information for undoing a transaction. In the event of a failure, a log will contain information for recovering to a stable and reliable database state. Consider the following transaction, written partially in pseudo-code, consisting of two updates:

```
begin work
update tab1 set col1 = 50
  where   col2 = 10
if cond1 then
  rollback work
update tab2 set col9 = 40
  where   col8 = 2
commit work
```

Here the *begin work* statement signals the start of a transaction. The transaction is committed when the *commit work* statement is encountered. All partially completed transactions are undone when the *rollback work* statement is executed. As transactions are partially completed, they are written to the log and the database. Information in a log file includes the following:

- An indicator indicating the start, commit, or abort point of a transaction
- Transaction identification information
- The type of operation in the transaction (insert, delete, or update)
- The preupdated image of the record
- The updated image of the record, if applicable

If a transaction were aborted, undoing the updates to the database in the absence of a log file would be difficult. Figure 9.5 shows the basic use of a log file.

All updates are added to the log. Transactions t1 to t4 are completed. Transaction t5 is currently proceeding. It may consist of multiple updates. Let t5 be the transaction described earlier for the updating of tables tab1 and tab2. Let the two updates be denoted by u1 and u2. If the transaction is to be rolled back after u1, then the required information is available in the log. If there is a disk crash, then the database can be restored from a backup. This will restore the status of the database just prior to transaction t1. The database can then be rolled forward by the redoing of all transactions up to and including transaction t4. Updates in transaction t5 are also done, but on finding that the

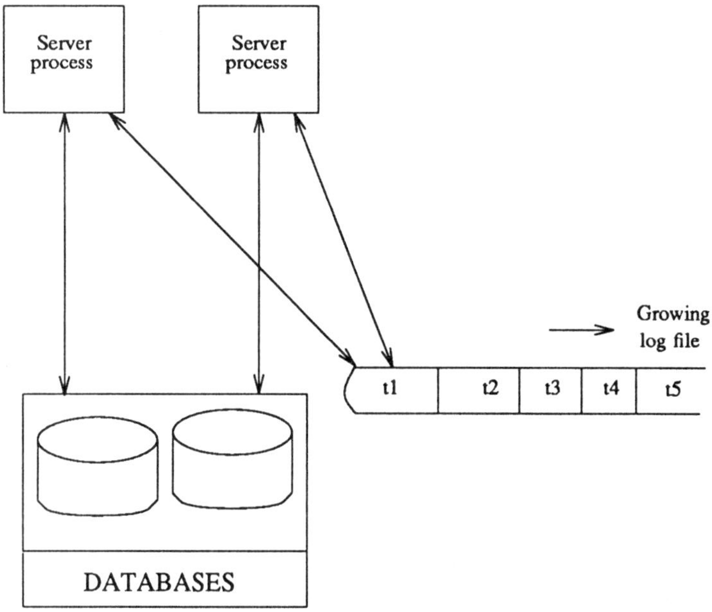

Figure 9.5 Basic Use of Log Files

transaction was not completed, these updates are undone. Information in the log is used to undo the incomplete transaction.

The log file is actually much more complicated; some DBMS servers use a separate log file for each database. TURBO uses a common log file for all the databases. Entries for a given transaction are not physically contiguous in the log file. Physical contiguity of transaction log entries would force transactions to be queued, resulting in performance degradation. The concurrent handling of multiple transactions is done only if the serializability property of transactions is maintained. In other words, the results of two transactions executing concurrently must be the same as if they were executed in a specific order.

The locking mechanism ensures that the results of partially completed transactions are not revealed to other transactions. Without this isolation property, the undoing of a transaction would require the undoing of all transactions which observed the partial results of a transaction. Each entry in the log file also indicates the database on which it is operating. The structure of a log file with concurrent execution of transactions on multiple databases appears as shown below:

Log File ⟶

Transaction T1 Update # 1	Transaction T2 Update # 1	Transaction T1 Update # 2	Transaction T1 Update # 3	Commit T1	

The sharing of one log file for several databases has one major potential problem. If the log file is corrupted, then none of the databases can be recovered completely. Further, to undo a transaction, multiple entries belonging to other databases have to be read to locate the required updates to be undone. This slows the rollback process within a transaction.

9.7.3 Effect of Buffered Writes

So far, the discussion on logging and recovery has assumed that transactions were written to the database and the log file as soon as the server requested them to be written. This simplifies the recovery process, as the dependence on the contents of main memory is minimal. Such writes, also referred to as unbuffered writes, are very inefficient. Most servers, including TURBO, use buffered writes. Buffered writes minimize I/O operations, as the data to be fetched or updated may still be in main memory; thus additional I/O operations are avoided. The disadvantage of buffered writes is that completed transactions may still be in main memory when a system crash occurs, resulting in loss of information in volatile storage.

Writes to the log file can also be buffered. Buffered logging improves performance by minimizing the number of I/O operations on the log file. However, some transactions are lost if the system crashes before they are written to disk. Additional buffers must be allocated for the log files in shared memory for buffered logging. Figure 9.6 shows how *write* operations perform an update on shared memory. The shared memory buffers are periodically written to the database and the log file.

9.7.4 Fast Recovery from System Crashes

If the system crashes while one or more database servers are actively updating the database, one simple method of recovery is to restore the database from a backup which was taken just before the log file was initialized. With use of the log files, all transactions in the log file can then be applied to roll forward

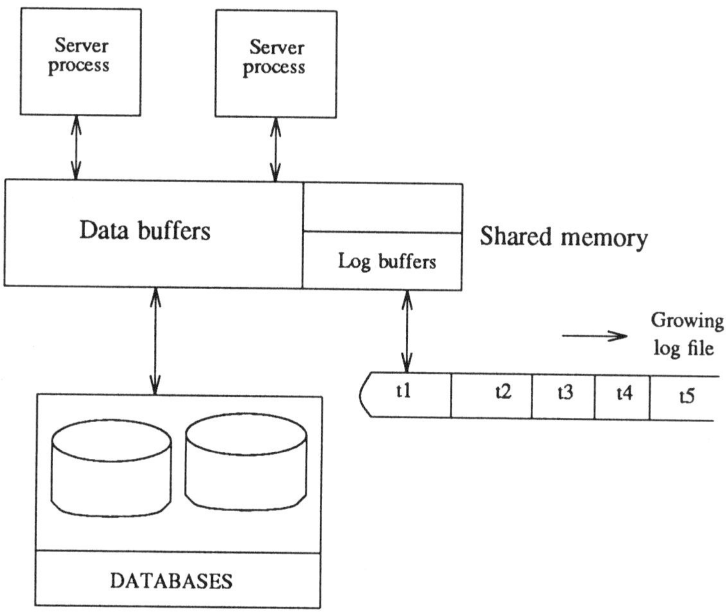

Figure 9.6 Logging with Buffered Writes

the database. After the roll forward is completed, all incomplete transactions are undone. If the information in the database itself was not lost, then this method is time consuming. The major disadvantage of this method is that the database is unavailable while it is being restored and also while completed transactions are applied to it after the restore.

To circumvent this problem and to provide a faster recovery mechanism, recovery procedures use a technique called checkpoints. A checkpoint is a point in time when all databases and log files are consistent. Consistency is achieved by the simple flushing of the data and log buffers to disk. When a checkpoint occurs, an entry is made in the log file. This entry indicates the transactions which were active at the time. When the system crashes, fast recovery is completed as follows:

- The last checkpoint record is located and read.
- The database status is restored back to the last checkpoint.
- The log is applied to the database, and all operations in it are redone.
- After the entire log is processed, incomplete transactions are undone. An incomplete transaction is one for which a commit record is not found.

This recovery process appears very trivial. However, there is one complication. How can the database be restored to the state that it had when the last checkpoint was written? This requires the use of another log! TURBO calls it the physical log, and the regular transaction log, the logical log. At the physical level, TURBO databases consist of many pages. When a page changes, its *before* image is written to the physical log. The *before* image refers to the status of the data page at the time of the last checkpoint. If it changes many times, then the *before* image need not be rewritten. In the event of a system crash, the status of the database at the time of the last checkpoint can be restored very easily by a simple copy of the pages in the physical log back to the database. Figure 9.7 illustrates the process of restoring the database to the last checkpoint.

In this figure, operations in the log file are labeled "T*ij*", where *i* is the transaction number and *j* refers to the sequence number of the update operation within the transaction. The subscript value of *b* is used to indicate the start of a transaction, and a value of *e* indicates the end of the transaction. For example, *T2b* indicates start of transaction number 2.

Pages in the database and the physical log are labeled "P*ij*", where *i* is the page number and *j* refers to the status of the page. If *j* is *b*, then the page is the before image. If *j* is *n*, then the page is the new updated image.

After the database is restored to the last checkpoint status, the recovery process is completed by a redoing of all operations in the logical file and an undoing of all incomplete transactions.

9.7.5 Physical Log and Checkpoints

Checkpoints, as discussed earlier, are times when the database and logical log buffers are flushed to disk. How frequently should checkpoints be written? If checkpoints are written too frequently, the advantage of having buffered I/O is lost. The frequency of checkpoints is also tied to physical log size. A checkpoint must occur before the physical log is filled up. If the physical log is made very large, then there are more pages to be processed in order for the database status to be restored to the last commit point, thus slowing the recovery process.

TURBO generates a checkpoint as soon as the log is 75% full. A checkpoint is also generated every 5 minutes if an update has occurred on a page which is not in the physical log. A checkpoint can also be forced by the Database Administrator.

Maintaining a physical log requires additional I/O operations whenever a new page has been updated. In an environment where frequent updates are made to the same physical segment of the database, the number of pages written to the physical log will be less, reducing the number of I/O operations. The capability of TURBO to allocate logically contiguous space to tables reduces the number of pages written into the physical log when records are updated sequentially.

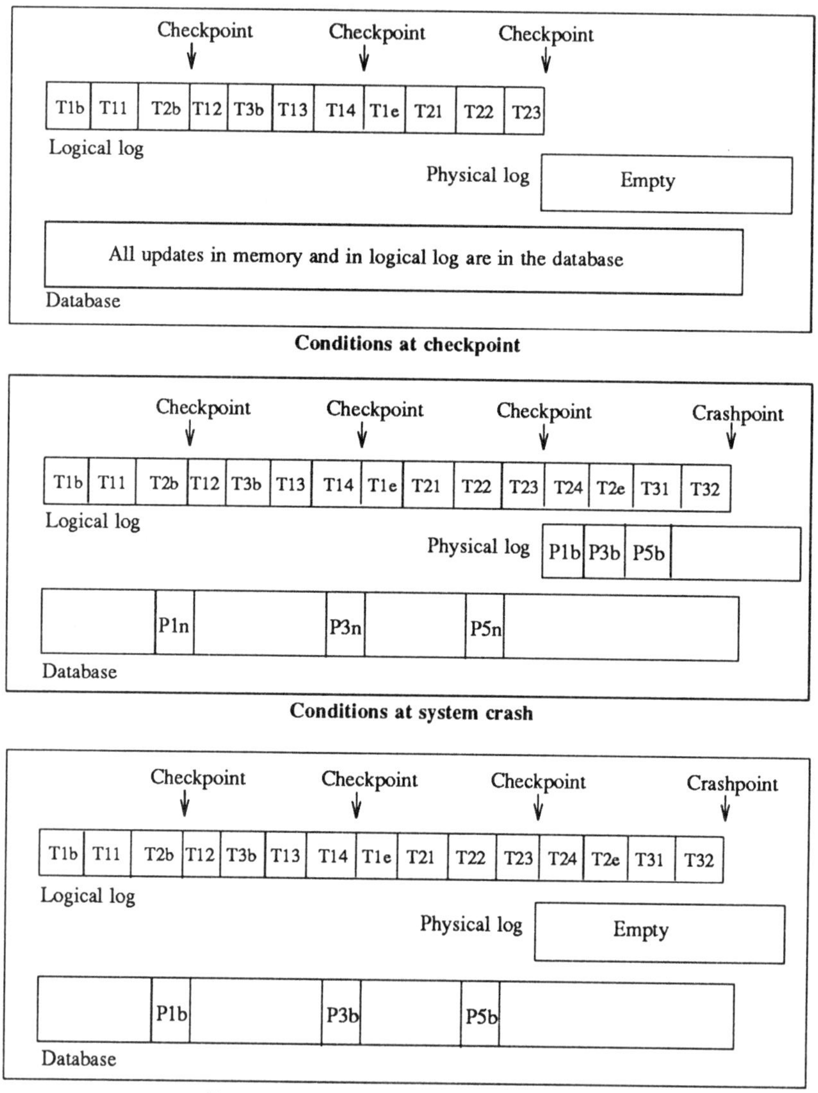

Figure 9.7 Restoring Databases to Last Checkpoint Status

9.7.6 Cutting Logs!

The logical log file as structured thus far has the history of all update events that occurred on all the databases. Clearly, for fast recovery only the latest segment of the log file containing active transactions is required. The remaining segment of the log file can be backed up to tape. This segment is useful when the disk on which the database itself is residing is corrupted.

TURBO allows logical logs to be split into multiple segments. The number of logical logs and their size can be specified to meet the needs of the application. If a log is filled up, it must be backed up to be reused. The TURBO feature to reuse a log after backing it eliminates the need to allocate large amounts of disk space to logical log files. The total amount of space available in all the logs determines the maximum length of a transaction. If the number of logs is small, then the backup frequency increases. If the log is large, then there are more transactions on it which may be lost if there is a crash on the disk where it is stored. Log files must not be stored on the same disk on which the database is stored. In the event of a media failure, recovery becomes almost impossible.

If a transaction starts in one logical log and continues into the last log, TURBO rolls back the transaction and kills the process that initiated the transaction. Long transactions should be avoided for other reasons also.

9.8 Backing Up Logical Logs

Logical logs must be backed up as they are filled. There are two different methods for backing up a log. In the first method, full logs are automatically backed up. This method requires continuous monitoring of the system. If all the logs are full and none are backed up, TURBO will stop and wait for a logical log to be backed up. In the second method, the logs are backed up as soon as they are filled. A tape drive is dedicated for this backup process.

9.9 From Theory to Practice

In the preceeding sections all the major features of TURBO and the theoretical foundations involved in its design were discussed. In the next few sections how TURBO can be initialized and how the different parameters can be changed with use of the user interface provided are discussed. It is assumed that TURBO is already installed on your system. The user interface to TURBO is provided via a program called *tbmonitor*. Almost all TURBO options can be set by use of this user-friendly program. When this command is entered, the main menu of TURBO is first displayed. This is shown in Figure 9.8.

```
INFORMIX-TURBO: [Status] Parameters Dbspaces Mode Checkpoint ...
Status menu to view INFORMIX-TURBO
-----------------Off-Line---------------Type CTRL-W for Help-----
```

Figure 9.8 Main Menu of *tbmonitor*.

9.9.1 Initialization

To configure TURBO initially, the *Parameters* option must be chosen. When this option is chosen, a new menu appears as shown in Figure 9.9. To set the basic parameters, select the *Initialize* option which displays the *DISK PARAMETERS* form as shown in Figure 9.10.

```
PARAMETERS: [Initialize] Shared-Memory Add-Log Drop-Log Physical-Log Exit
Initialize root dbspace and shared memory configuration
 -----------------Off-Line---------------Type CTRL-W for Help-----
```

Figure 9.9 PARAMETERS Menu of *tbmonitor*.

The items in the form are

- Page Size: This is the size of a page that is used by TURBO. It cannot be changed and is displayed only for reference.
- Sys. Log File: This is the file which maintains entries for TURBO activities. This file should be a regular UNIX file. A sample contents of this file is shown below.

```
Sat Mar 18 21:15:40 1989

21:15:40 1989

21:15:40 Turbo Initialized -- Complete Disk Initialized
21:15:43 Checkpoint completed
21:15:43 Quiescent Mode

Sun Mar 19 11:32:16 1989

11:32:16 Turbo Stopped

Sun Mar 19 11:32:46 1989

11:32:46 Turbo Initialized -- Shared Memory Initialized
11:32:46 Physical Recovery Started
11:32:46 Physical Recovery Complete: 0 Pages Restored
11:32:46 Logical Recovery Complete: 0 Committed, 0 Rolled Back
```

- Tape Device: This is the device name of the tape drive to be used for archiving dbspaces that belong to databases and also the associated logical log files.
- Tape Blk Size: This is the block size for the tape and should be chosen to be the maximum allowed to reduce the number of I/O operations.
- Total Tape Size: This is used to specify the tape capacity.
- Pathname: This is the raw device name which has been configured or partitioned for TURBO usage.
- Root Name: This is the name of the root dbspace. All logical logs, the physical log, and system information is stored here.
- Offset into device: This is zero for most cases unless a part of the device or partition is reserved for non-TURBO usage.
- Physical Log Size: This determines the size of the physical log. The effect of a small or big physical log was discussed earlier.
- Logical Log Size: This determines the size of the logical logs.

```
INITIALIZATION: Make desired changes and press ESC to record changes
Press DEL to abort changes.  Press F2 or CTRL-F for field-level help

                         DISK PARAMETERS

                                        Page Size: [     1] Kbytes

Sys. Log File [/sql/msg.log                                 ]
  Tape Device [                                             ]
Tape Blk Size [         16]  Kbytes    Total Tape Size [  4000] Kbytes

   Pathname [/dev/rhd0e                                     ]  Kbytes
  Root Name [rootdbs         ]                    Size [ 17000] Kbytes
                                  Offset into device [      0] Kbytes
                                   Physical Log Size [  1000] Kbytes
                                    Logical Log Size [  2000] Kbytes
                               Number of Logical Logs [     3]
```

Figure 9.10 Disk Parameters Specifications Form

- Number of Logical Logs: This determines the number of logical logs to be used. More logs can be added at a later time.

Once this form is filled, the "ESC" key can be entered to exit the form and to display the shared-memory parameters form as shown in Figure 9.11. The items in the form are:

- Page size: This is a display-only field and is shown here only for reference.
- Shared-memory size: This also is a display-only field. Its value changes as other parameters in this form are changed. The number of data buffers allocated in shared memory has a major impact on the size of the shared memory.
- Forced Residency: This is used to prevent shared memory from being swapped to disk. On most systems only root has this privilege.
- Maximum # of Logical Logs: This field is used to specify the maximum

number of logical logs.

- Maximum # of Users: This field is used to specify the maximum number of users on the system. A larger than expected number should be specified because it does not have a significant impact on the size of shared memory. It affects the size of some of the tables in shared memory.
- Maximum # of Chunks: This is used to specify the maximum number of chunks to be used. All these chunks need not be allocated initially. More can be added at a later time.
- Maximum # of Locks: This is impossible to predict accurately. It depends primarily on the types of transaction, the locking granularity used, and the number of processes running simultaneously. If row-level locking is used, then more locks are required. The total number of locks can be estimated as the product of the maximum number of processes expected to run simultaneously and the approximate number of locks required for each process.
- Maximum # of Open Partns: This figure depends on the number of processes running simultaneously and the average number of tables opened in each process.
- Maximum # of Buffers: This is probably the most important field in the form. The number of internal data buffers affects the number of I/O operations performed. A large size should not be chosen arbitrarily because it will increase the size of shared memory, reducing the space available to other processes.
- Maximum # of Dbspaces: This is the total number of dbspaces. All the dbspaces need not be allocated initially. More can be added in the future as explained later.
- Physical Log Buffer Size: This is the size of the physical log buffer. The larger it is, the more are the number of *before* image pages that it can store. The buffer is written to the physical log if it does not have space for a *before* image of a page which is to be updated. Unlike the data buffers, the pages in the physical log buffers are not constantly updated.

Once this form is filled, the "ESC" key can be entered to indicate the same. To confirm the settings, enter a "y" when the following prompt appears on the screen:

```
Do you want to keep these disk parameters? (y/n)
```

Once initialized, the disk and shared-memory parameters can be changed. They are stored in a file called tbconfig in the $INFORMIX/etc directory. This file is read by the *tbinit* process. This is the TURBO daemon. Another

```
SHARED MEMORY:  Make desired changes and press ESC to record changes
Press DEL to abort changes.  Press F2 or CTRL-F for field-level help

                         SHARED MEMORY PARAMETERS

Page Size: [    2] Kbytes          Shared memory size [     640] Kbytes
Forced Residency (Yes/No) [N]         Maximum # of Logical Logs [     4]

Maximum # of Users    [      20]      Maximum # of Chunks       [     8]
Maximum # of Locks    [    2000]      Maximum # of Open Partns  [   200]
Maximum # of Buffers  [     200]      Maximum # of Dbspaces     [     8]

                    Physical Log Buffer Size [    32] Kbytes
```

Figure 9.11 Form to Set Shared-Memory Parameters

file called tbconfig.std stores the default parameters. Here are the first five lines of this file:

```
head -5 /usr/informix/etc/tbconfig.std
USERS        20
LOCKS         2000
BUFFERS      200
BUFFSIZE      2048
PARTITIONS 200
```

9.10 TURBO Modes

TURBO operates in several modes. Some of the modes are temporary as TURBO makes a transition from one mode to another. TURBO modes can be changed at the command level by use of the *tbmode* utility or by use of the *Mode* option of the *tbmonitor* menu. This option displays the form shown in Figure 9.12.

```
MODE: [Startup]  On-line  Graceful-Shutdown  Immediate-Shutdown ...
Bring INFORMIX-TURBO to quiescent from off-line
--------------------Off-Line---------------Type CTRL-W for Help----
```

Figure 9.12 Changing TURBO Modes

Before TURBO is initialized, it is in *off-line* mode. In off-line mode, the TURBO daemon is not running and shared memory is not initialized. After TURBO is initialized, it is put in *quiescent* mode. In this mode, shared memory is initialized but database activities are not allowed. The TURBO administrator must bring the system on-line using the *On-line* option to let users use the TURBO back-end process for normal database activities.

If TURBO is in on-line mode, then bringing it in quiescent mode may be necessary, such as when backps of the entire TURBO system have to be taken. The transition from on-line mode to quiescent mode can be achieved by either letting all current users continue with their work or by killing all user TURBO processes and roll-backing incomplete transactions.

The *Graceful-Shutdown* option can be used to bring the system to quiescent mode by letting current users continue to work. If users are currently working on the system then TURBO provides an option to display the list of active users. This list is updated every 5 seconds. If all users exit from their TURBO processes, then the system would automatically go into quiescent mode.

If TURBO is to be brought down immediately without waiting for user processes to terminate normally, then the *Immediate-Shutdown* option can be selected. This option can be used when users leave their terminals with an "idle" INFORMIX process without any activity. An *isql* invocation which is not attached to any database is one such example.

If the TURBO system is to be backed up, then it is necessary to first bring it into quiescent mode. After bringing it into quiescent mode, when the backup starts, TURBO is put in *Backup* mode. The backup process executed by *tbmonitor* does not display the mode status. However, if *tbmonitor* is executed from a different terminal, then the mode status line will indicate *Backup* mode.

If dbspaces have to be restored, then TURBO must be brought off-line by selection of the *Turbo-Off* option. TURBO may be off-line for other reasons also. Once off-line, TURBO must be first brought into quiescent mode before it can be brought back on-line. When it goes from off-line mode to quiescent mode, it checks to see if the physical log has any entries. If it does, then it goes into fast recovery mode and restores the database to a consistent state, as explained earlier. After the recovery is complete, the TURBO system is put into quiescent mode. The *On-line* option can then be selected to bring TURBO back on-line and to make it available to all users. TURBO must be in quiescent mode to be brought on-line. Figure 9.13 illustrates the transition of TURBO to different modes.

9.10.1 The tbinit and tbmode Utilities

It is not always necessary to use *tbmonitor* to change TURBO modes. The *tbinit* and *tbmode* utilities can be used directly to change TURBO modes. *Tbinit* can be initiated from the command line to start TURBO in on-line or in quiescent mode. The *-s* option brings TURBO into quiescent mode.

Once started, *tbmode* can be used to change TURBO modes. The *-s* option initiates a graceful-shutdown, as explained earlier. The *-k* option initiates an immediate-shutdown and brings TURBO off-line. The *-u* option terminates all users and leaves TURBO in quiescent mode.

9.11 Archiving Logical Logs

As described earlier, logical logs are broken into smaller pieces so that they can be archived as they get filled. If buffered logging is set, then the buffer is not flushed until it is full. Unbuffered logging means the buffer gets flushed at a commit of a transaction. A logical log must be backed up before it can be reused. Each log is assigned a running serial number with which its logical sequence can be identified. This number is reset after an archive of the entire

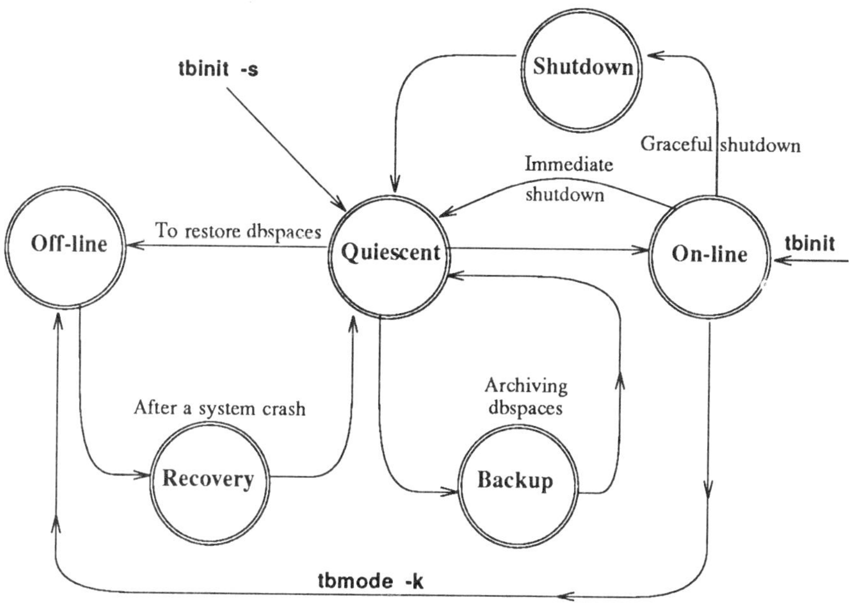

Figure 9.13 Transition of TURBO Modes

system is completed.

There are primarily two methods for backing up logical logs. One method involves backing up only logs which are used and filled by using *tbmonitor*. This could require continuous monitoring of the system. TURBO will stop if it cannot find a backed up logical log. Another method involves setting up a process to back up a log when it fills. This method has several advantages. First, the log is backed up as soon as it fills, reducing the system vulnerability in the event of a media failure on the disk used to store the logs. In addition, continuous backing of logs increases the logs' availability, thus preventing the situation of TURBO stopping because of the unavailability of logical logs. If continuous backup is required, then a terminal and a tape drive must be dedicated to the *tbmonitor* process. The continuous backup strategy still requires manual intervention when a new tape is to be mounted. This cannot be avoided because there is no way that the *tbmonitor* process can know that a new tape has been mounted.

9.11.1 Selecting the Log Backup Option

The desired logical log backup strategy can be selected by invocation of the *tbmonitor* utility. The *Logical-Logs* option can be used to display the menu shown in Figure 9.14.

```
LOGICAL LOGS: [Auto-Backup] Continuous-Backup Database Tape-Params Exit
Perform automatic backup of full logical logs
--------------------On-Line---------------Type CTRL-W for Help-----
```

Figure 9.14 Selecting Backup Strategy for Logical Logs

Once this menu is displayed, the required backup strategy can be selected.

9.11.2 The Tbtape Utility

This utility is invoked by *tbmonitor* to perform backup operations of logical logs. It can also be invoked directly as a UNIX command. When invoked with the *-a* option, it performs the automatic backup operation of logical logs. When invoked with the *-c* option, it performs continuous backup operation.

9.12 Backing Up the System

For the entire TURBO system to be backed up, it must first be brought into quiescent mode. The *Archive* option of the *tbmonitor* main menu must then be selected, followed by the *Backup* option of the *Archive* menu. Once this option is selected, TURBO starts an interactive session, prompting the administrator to mount a new tape every time a tape is filled up. After a tape is filled up, it displays the following message:

```
Please label this tape as number x in the archive sequence
Please mount next tape and press Return to continue ...
```

where *x* is the sequence number of the tape. It continues this interactive session until all the dbspaces are backed up. Finally, it displays the message:

```
Program over
Press Return to continue
```

The tapes must be labeled in the correct sequence. This sequence is used when the system has to be restored from a backup. In addition to the use of the *tbmonitor* menu interface, the *tbtape* command can also be used with the *-s* option to archive the entire TURBO system. The system must, of course, be in quiescent mode.

9.13 Restoring the System

The fast-recovery mechanism eliminates the need to do a database restore in the event of a system crash. However, a database restore is required if the database itself is corrupted due to an incorrect buggy program or due to a disk crash. Restores must be performed on the same device names and characteristics.

TURBO must be in off-line mode for restore to proceed. Once again *tbmonitor* can be used to restore the system. The *Archive* option must be selected first, followed by the *Restore* option. Before the database restore is initiated, any unbacked logical logs should also be backed up. TURBO displays the following prompt before the restore is started:

```
Would you like to backup logical logs?
```

A response of "y" backs up the logical logs. If these logs are already backed up, then there would not be any problem if the logs are backed up again. The roll forward process ignores duplicate logical logs. It uses the logical log sequence number to identify duplicate logs.

After the logical logs are backed, the first archived tape for the entire system must be mounted. TURBO initiates an interactive session, prompting for subsequent tapes to be mounted with the following message:

```
Please mount tape and press return to continue ...
```

This message is also displayed if the order of tapes is incorrect or if the tape drive is not ready.

After the system is restored to the old archived state, archived logical logs can be applied on it to roll forward the databases to a later date. The number of transactions lost would depend on the state of the data and logical log buffers at the time of the crash. Irrespective of the number of transactions lost, all databases would be restored to a consistent state, as explained earlier. The entire restore process is shown in Figure 9.15.

9.13.1 Tape Device Characteristics

All the archiving and restore tools provided by TURBO do not make use of standard UNIX tools such as *cpio* or *tar* because of the raw devices involved. TURBO uses its own technique. It reads tape parameters from the tbconfig file. In particular, the parameters TAPEDEV, TAPEBLK, and TAPESIZE provide information about the tape device name, the tape block size, and the total tape size, respectively.

Though the word *tape* is used throughout this chapter to refer to an archiving media, other devices besides tapes, such as floppies, can also be used.

9.14 Monitoring TURBO

Once the TURBO system is designed and implemented, its performance must be continuously monitored. Several TURBO parameters cannot be accurately computed. These parameters require fine tuning based on the system usage. TURBO provides options in the *tbmonitor* menu interface for the examination of performance parameters and the incorporation of changes to improve the performance. In addition, the *tbstat* utility can also be used to display the performance statistics available through *tbmonitor* and additional information. When the *Status* option of the main *tbmonitor* menu is selected, the menu shown in Figure 9.16 is displayed.

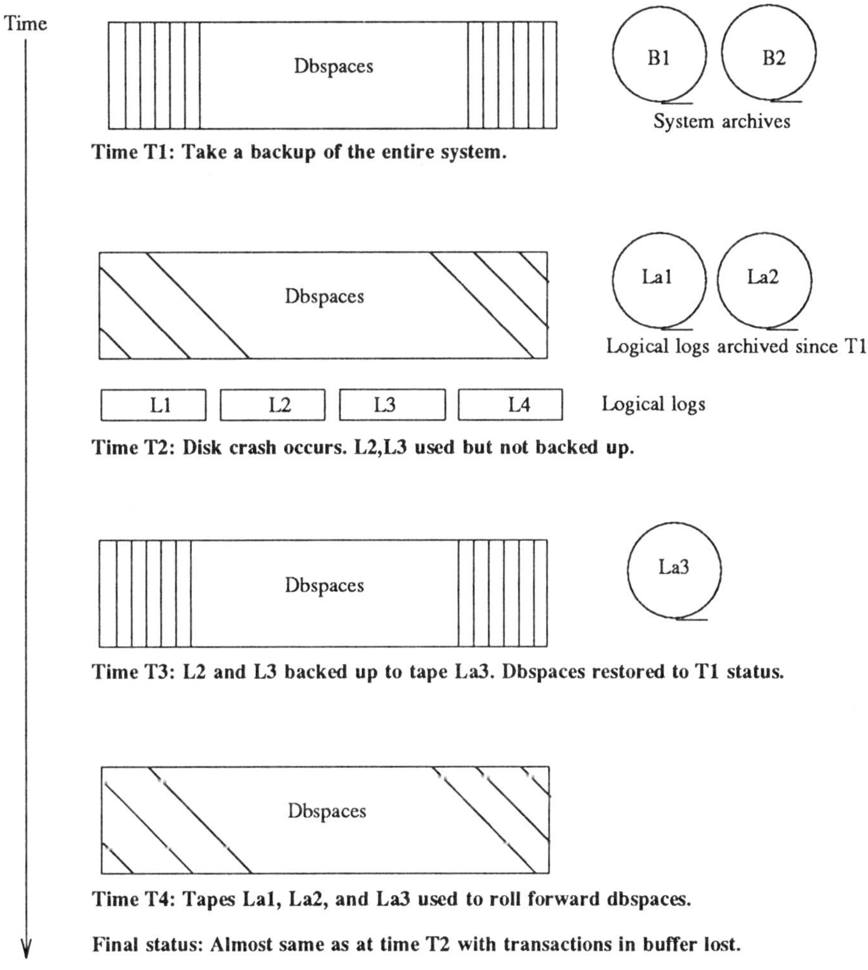

Figure 9.15 Restoring Dbspaces from Complete Archives and Logical Logs

9.14.1 The Profile Option

When the *Profile* option is selected, information on the following items is displayed:

- Boot Time: This refers to the time when the system was brought from off-line to quiescent mode after going through the recovery process.

```
STATUS: [Profile] Users Spaces Databases Logs Output Exit
Display system profile information.
  -----------------On-Line---------------Type CTRL-W for Help----
```

Figure 9.16 Status Menu of *tbmonitor*

- Current Time: This is the time for which the displayed information is valid.
- Disk Reads: The information associated with this label refers to the total number of actual reads on the physical disk.
- Buff. Reads: This information refers to the total number of reads from the buffers in the shared memory. This number and the total number of disk reads provide a measure of the use of buffering.
- % Cached: If d refers to the total number of disk reads and b indicates the total number of buffer reads, then % cached is calculated as $(b-d)/b*100$. Ideally, this number should be more than 90%. If the activities on the different databases are not localized, then this number will be low as more disk reads will be required.
- Disk Writes, Buffer Writes, and % Cached: These three items refer to the output operations on the system and provide a measure on the advantages of buffering for write operations.
- Over Part., Over Lock, and Over User: These three items refer to the number of attempts by user processes or users to exceed the limits set on maximum number of open partitions, maximum number of locks, and maximum number of users, respectively. These parameters are set when shared memory is initialized. If the display indicates that attempts were indeed made to exceed these limits, then the shared-memory parameters should be changed. Changing these parameters is an iterative process, because the display does not indicate the optimum values required for these parameters.
- Sys. Time: This is the total amount of system time consumed by all the *sqlturbo* processes. It is updated after a process terminates.

- User Time: This is the total amount of user time consumed by all the *sqlturbo* processes. It is updated after a process terminates.
- Checkpoints: This number refers to the number of checkpoint operations performed. A checkpoint, as explained earlier, flushes all buffers and ensures that what is on disk is consistent with the information in shared memory.
- Buffer Waits: A buffer in shared memory can only be updated by one process at a time. This count is incremented when a process waits for a buffer in shared memory to be free. This number is high if multiple processes are working on the same segment of a database at the same time.
- Lock Waits: When a process requests a row to be locked, it may already be locked. The process must then wait for the lock to be released. The number displayed is a count of all such waits.
- Lock Req.: This is a count of the total number of lock requests. This number must be compared with the total number of lock waits. If the number of lock waits is high with respect to the number of lock request, then the locking strategy must be changed. For example, consideration should be given to changing page-level locks on some tables to row-level locks. Such changes, however, may need the use of more locks.
- Deadlocks: This is a count of the number of situations in which granting a lock could have resulted in a deadlock. This is another indication of the locality of processing and the level of concurrency.
- Sem. Waits: Semaphores, as explained earlier, provide a mechanism to synchronize and manage the use of shared resources. The sharing of internal tables in shared memory is managed by the use of semaphores. Processes must check for the status of a semaphore to access these tables and must wait if the table is currently being updated. Such waits are of a short duration. The number associated with Sem. Waits is a count of these waits.
- Check Waits: The count displayed here refers to the number of times a checkpoint could not be completed immediately because of user processes locking some buffers.
- CALLS: The remaining items displayed refer to the different calls made by TURBO. They are further categorized as explained below:
  - Open: This count is incremented when a partition is opened.
  - Start: The count shown here is incremented when a change is made with respect to a position within an index.
  - Read: This count is incremented when a read operation is performed on a database. SQL statements such as *update* and *delete* also increment this count.
  - Write: This is a count of the number of write functions called.

- Rewrite: This is a count of the number of times an update occurs to the current row.
- Delete: This is a count of the number of times a row is deleted.
- Commit: This is a count of the number of times a transaction is committed.
- Rollback: This is a count of the number of times a transaction is rolled back.
- Total Calls: This is the sum of all the calls listed above. In addition, some other system calls are also included.

The statistics on calls provide invaluable information about the type of activities on the databases. For example, if there are very few deletes and updates, then fewer locks may be required and the shared memory parameters can be changed appropriately. These statistics can also be used to monitor activities during different time periods. This can be accomplished by resetting all profile counts to zero just before the start of the period to be monitored. The *tbstat* command with the *-z* option can be used for this purpose.

9.14.2 The Users Option

When the *Users* option is selected from the *Status* menu, information on all active TURBO processes is displayed. This information consists of the following items:

- PID: This is the process id. of the process.
- User: This is the login id. of the user who initiated the process.
- Locks Held: This is a count of the total number of locks held by the process.
- Disk Reads: This is a count of the total number of disk read calls.
- Disk Writes: This is a count of the total number of disk write calls.
- User Status: This is a composite display consisting of four components separated by a dash. Each component is indicated by a code. The first code indicates the wait status. The second code indicates the status of a transaction currently in progress. The third code indicates the type of I/O operation in progress. Finally, the fourth code indicates a D or an M if the process is either a daemon (*tbinit*) or a monitor (*tbmonitor*), respectively. These components can be represented by a dash if the codes are not applicable. Table 9.1 indicates the applicable codes.

TABLE 9.1 Codes used to display Process Status

Component no.	Code	Description
1	B	Waiting for buffer
1	C	Waiting for a checkpoint to complete
1	L	Waiting to lock a locked item
1	S	Waiting for a semaphore to be unlocked
2	T	Transaction in progress
2	R	Rolling back a transaction
2	B	Transaction started with BEGIN WORK
3	R	Read operation in progress
3	W	Write operation in progress
4	M	Process is *tbmonitor*
4	D	Process is a daemon

9.14.3 The Spaces Option

The *Spaces* option can be used to display information about the dbspaces in use. The following information is displayed:

- Id: This is a unique id. number assigned to the dbspace.
- Name: This refers to the name of the dbspace.
- Number of Chunks: This refers to the total number of chunks which make up the dbspace.
- When created: This displays the date when the dbspace was created.

A dbspace consists of one or more chunks which form a link list. The link list is maintained using a Chunk Id. To display information about the chunks associated with a dbspace, move the arrow key to the required dbspace and press the "F1" key. This displays the following information about each chunk.

- Chunk Id.: This is the chunk identification number. Its value is used to identify its position in the link list of chunks associated with a dbspace.
- Id. of Next Chunk: This id. is used to identify the next chunk in the dbspace following the current chunk. This number is set to zero for the last chunk.
- Pages in Chunk: This refers to the size of the chunk in pages.
- Pages Used: This refers to the number of pages used within the chunk.
- Full Pathname of Chunk: This is the device name or the name of a UNIX file where the chunk resides.

9.14.4 The Databases Option

The *Databases* option of the *Status* menu displays data on the databases managed by TURBO. This is categorized under the following headings:

- Database Name: This indicates the name of the database for which the following information is applicable.
- Owner: This is the login id. of the owner of the database.
- In Dbspace: This refers to the name of the dbspace in which the system catalogs of the database reside. Remember that the database itself can span multiple dbspaces.
- When Created: This indicated the time when the database was created.
- Log Status: This refers to the logging status of the database and is *B*, *U*, or *N* to indicate buffered logging, unbuffered logging, or no logging, respectively.

9.14.5 The Logs Option

If the `Logs` option is selected, then information on the physical and logical logs is displayed. The top portion shows information about the physical log. This information is displayed under the headings explained below.

- Buffer: This is the address of the physical log buffer.
- Buffsize: This is the size of the physical log buffer in pages.
- Bufused: This indicates the number of pages which are used in the physical log buffer.
- Numpages: This refers to the number of pages written to the physical log.
- Numwrites: This is the total number of writes to the physical log.
- Pages/IO: This is calculated from the previous two items as *Numpages/Numwrites*.
- Phybegin: This is the page number of the first page of the physical log file.
- Physize: This is the size of the physical log expressed in number of pages.
- Phypos: This is the page number in the physical log file which is currently in use.
- Phyused: This indicates the number of pages used in the physical log file. It is not the same as *Phypos* because the physical log file is circular. After the log is filled, it starts writing into it from the beginning. The difference between *Phypos* and *Phyused* is illustrated

in Figure 9.17.

- % Used: This indicates the percentage of pages used in the physical log. It is nothing but *(Phyused/Physize)*100.*

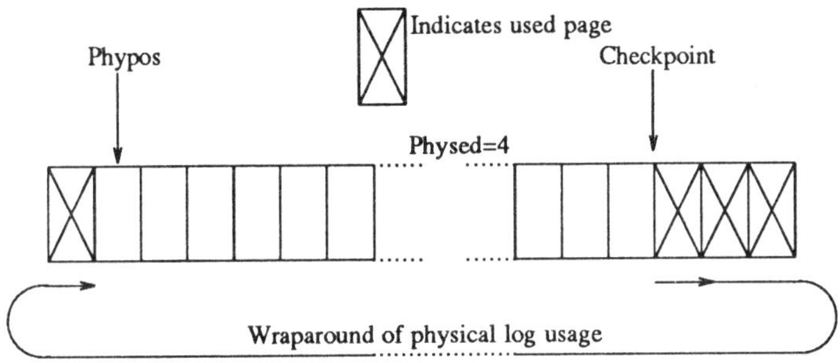

Figure 9.17 Difference between *Phypos* and *Phyused*

The lower portion of the screen displays information on logical logs under the headings described below:

- Number: This refers to the logical log number.
- Flags: These flags are used to display the status of each log. The codes used are explained in Table 9.2. Multiple codes can be indicated by being separated by dashes. Newly added logs are not used until after shutdown and archive.
- Uniqid: This refers to the unique logical sequence number assigned to each log as it is filled.
- Dbspace: This refers to the dbpspace in which the log is located.
- Pages: This is used to indicate the size of the logical log in pages.
- Used: This number indicates the number of pages used in the log.
- % Used: This number is calculated as *(Used/Pages)*100.*

In addition to the options discussed here, the *STATUS* menu has the *Output* option which is used to redirect the status information to another file. The selection of this option prompts for the name of the file to receive the output. All subsequent status information is appended to this file in addition to being displayed to the screen.

TABLE 9.2 Status Codes for Logical Logs

Code	Description
F	Indicates that the log is available for use.
B	Indicates that the log was backed up.
C	Indicates that the log is currently receiving transactions.
U	Indicates that the log is not yet released.
A	Indicates that the log was newly added.

9.14.6 The tbstat Utility

The *tbstat* utility is used by *tbmonitor* to display the statistics discussed above. Several options are available to provide additional statistics which are not available through *tbmonitor*. Some of these options are discussed in Table 9.3.

TABLE 9.3 Options to *tbstat*

Option	Description
-a	Prints all the information available through *tbstat*
-b	Prints information available through buffers
-c	Prints the contents of the tbconfig file
-d	Prints information about dbspaces and chunks
-t	Prints information about partitions
-u	Prints a list of users and their processes
-k	Prints information about logs
-z	Sets the profile counts displayed by *tbmonitor* to zero
-m	Prints the last 20 entries in the message log file

Here is an example of the use of the *tbstat* command:

```
tbstat -u
INFORMIX-TURBO -- On-Line -- Up 5 days 20:26:30 -- 180 Kbytes

Users
address  flags   pid  user     tty     wait  nlocks nreads nwrites
80400238 ------D 1896 informix console 0     0      9      1
80400288 ------D 0    informix console 0     0      9      1
```

```
80400238 ------D 4039  guest    console  0     0     0     0
 3 active, 12 total
```

The *address* fields in the display on users refers to the address of the user in the user table. The *wait* field identifies the lock on which the process is waiting. *Nlocks* provides a count of the locks used by the user process. Other fields were explained earlier.

9.15 Tuning TURBO

The main purpose of monitoring TURBO is to be able to choose the optimum values for parameters to improve performance. The *Parameters* option in the main menu can be selected to change these parameters. Once this option is selected, the menu shown in Figure 9.9 is displayed. The Shared Memory Parameters form shown in Figure 9.11 can be used to change the required parameters. This form is displayed when the *Shared-Memory* option is selected. After new values are entered, the new set of shared-memory parameters are recorded in the tbconfig file after the "ESC" key is pressed. The recording of the new set of values in the tbconfig file does not make the new set of values effective immediately. TURBO has to be brought to off-line mode and then to quiescent or on-line mode before the changes take effect.

9.15.1 Changing Logical Logs

Changing logical logs involves either adding new logical logs or dropping existing ones. The addition of new logs can be done by invoking the *Add-log* option of the *PARAMETERS* menu. When this option is selected, it displays the form shown in Figure 9.18. Only the dbspace name has to be entered; the logical log size is fixed when the disk parameters are set. It is displayed in this form only for reference. The *Drop-Log* option can be used to drop a logical log. A screen listing all the logical logs is displayed. The arrow keys can be used to select the log to be dropped. Pressing the "F1" key asks for a confirmation and only then is the log dropped.

A log cannot be dropped if it is not free. A free log is indicated by the *F* indicator in the *flags* field. There must be more than three logs in order for a log to be dropped.

```
Press ESC to add a logical log.
Press DEL to cancel the option and return to the Parameters menu.
Press F2 or CTRL-F for field level help.

                    ADDING A LOGICAL LOG

          Logical Log Size [          500] Kbytes

          Dbspace Name     [                    ]

Note: A system backup must be performed before the log can be used.
```

Figure 9.18 Form to Add New Logical Logs

9.15.2 Changing Physical Logs and Dbspaces

The *Physical-Log* option of the PARAMETERS menu can be selected to change the physical log size and the name of the dbspace in which it resides. It is advisable to make an archive copy of all dbspaces after the physical log parameters are changed.

The *Dbspaces* option of the main menu can be used to add and delete dbspaces. In addition, new chunks can be added to existing dbspaces with this menu.

9.16 Converting Old Databases

Databases created by using the regular back-end cannot, of course, be used with TURBO. These databases have to be converted to be handled by the

TURBO back-end. There are distinctly two phases involved in the conversion process. First, the schema of the existing database must be redefined in terms of SQL statements. This involves the specification of SQL statements to create the database, tables, and indexes. In addition, SQL statements to grant the existing permissions also have to be regenerated. Once the TURBO database, tables, and indexes are created, the data from the regular database must be unloaded to UNIX flat files and then reloaded into the TURBO database.

9.16.1 Using Existing Utilities

The *dbschema* utility described in Chapter 5 can be used to generate an SQL script which can recreate the old database. A set of SQL statements can be written to unload the data from existing tables to flat UNIX files and then upload the same data into the database created with TURBO. The environment variable *SQLEXEC* has to be set to *$INFORMIXDIR/lib/sqlexec* before *dbschema* is executed and then back to *$INFORMIXDIR/lib/sqlturbo* just before the database and associated tables and indexes are recreated using TURBO.

The process described above is simple for small databases using a few tables. However, in the absence of any utility to unload and load data from the old database to the new TURBO database, the process of writing SQL *unload* and *load* statements to do the same task can be extremely tedious. TURBO is equipped with two utilities to perform the database conversion tasks. They are *dbexport* and *dbimport*. These utilities are explained below.

9.16.2 Dbexport

This utility is used to generate a SQL script to recreate an existing database and to unload the data from the database into flat UNIX ASCII files. To illustrate the use of this utility, the sample florist database used in earlier chapters will be used here. The database schema is repeated here for reference:

```
create table customers
(
c_no    char(10),
c_lname char(20),
c_fname char(20),
c_addr1 char(20),
```

```
c_addr2 char(20),
c_town  char(20),
c_state char(2),
c_zip   char(5)
);
create table orders
(
c_no    char(10),
o_no    integer,
o_amt   money,
o_date  date,
o_desc  char(30),
o_del_chg       money,
o_paid  money
)
```

The customers table is loaded with 10 records and the orders table is loaded with 11 records. The *dbexport* utility can be executed on the florist database as shown below:

```
dbexport -q florist
```

This command creates a directory called florist.exp and a file called dbexport.out. The florist.exp directory has the SQL file to create the tables and indexes associated with the TURBO database. It also contains the unloaded ASCII data files. For the florist database the contents of the newly created directory are listed below:

```
ls florist.exp
custome100.unl
florist.sql
orders_101.unl
```

The dbexport.out file contains SQL statements, error messages, and warnings which were generated during the running of the program. The *-q* option is used to suppress the generation of the SQL commands to the screen. The generated SQL file is listed below:

```
cat florist.exp/florist.sql
{ DATABASE florist delimiter | }
grant dba to informix;

{ TABLE customers row size = 117 number of columns = 8 }
{ Unload file name = custome100.unl number of rows = 10 }
create table informix.customers (
   c_no char(10),
   c_lname  char(20),
   c_fname  char(20),
   c_addr1  char(20),
   c_addr2  char(20),
   c_town  char(20),
   c_state  char(2),
   c_zip  char(5));
revoke all on cutomers from public;
grant select on customers to public as informix;
grant update on customers to public as informix;
grant insert on customers to public as informix;
grant delete on customers to public as informix;
grant index on customers to public as informix;

{ TABLE orders row size = 75 number of columns = 7 }
{ unload file name = orders_101.unl number of rows = 11 }
create table informix.orders (
    c_no  char(10),
    o_no  integer,
    o_amt  money,
    o_date  date,
    o_desc  char(30),
    o_del_chg  money,
    o_paid  money);
revoke all on orders from public;
grant select on orders to public as informix;
grant update on orders to public as informix;
grant insert on orders to public as informix;
grant delete on orders to public as informix;
grant index on orders to public as informix;
```

The files suffixed *.unl* in the florist.exp directory are the flat ASCII data files.

9.16.2.1 Other Options to Dbexport

Dbexport comes equipped with many other options. Some of the important ones are discussed here. The *-o* option directs *dbexport* to create the ".exp" directory in the specified directory. For example,

```
dbexport -o /tmp florist
```

will create the florist.exp directory in /tmp instead of the current directory.

If the database to be converted is very large, then it may not be possible, due to disk space shortage, to unload ASCII data files of the entire database onto a disk. To circumvent this problem, the *-t* option can be used. This option takes as its argument the name of the tape device. In addition, the *-b* option can be used to specify the block size of the tape, and the *-s* option can be used to specify the size of the tape in Kbytes.

The *dbexport* utility locks the database in exclusive mode.

9.16.3 Creating a TURBO Database with Dbimport

Once the data from the standard database structure is loaded into flat files and the SQL script to create the database is ready, *dbimport* can be executed to complete the conversion process. The *SQLEXEC* environment variable must be reset to *$INFORMIXDIR/sqlturbo*. The *-i* option can be used to specify the input directory in which the SQL script and the ASCII files for creating and loading the database reside. The florist database can be recreated for the TURBO server with the following command:

```
dbimport -i /tmp florist
```

In addition, all the options discussed for *dbexport* also apply. The *-d* option can be used to specify the dbspace in which the newly created database is expected to reside. If this option is not specified, then the root dbspace is used.

By not changing the SQLEXEC environment variable, the *dbimport* and *dbexport* utilities can also be used to make copies of databases.

9.17 Closing Thoughts

TURBO provides the answer to critics who insist that UNIX is not a suitable platform for OLTP applications. It provides more than an answer to the basic requirements of OLTP applications. There are, however, some desirable features which may be available in future releases of TURBO. These are listed below:

- A single-server architecture. One multi-threaded server for multiple front-end processes can reduce the operating system overheads associated with multiple back-end processes.
- A mechanism to treat databases independently. Currently all databases share the same resources such as logs, locks, and internal shared-memory tables. Databases cannot be archived separately. All databases must share several characteristics such as buffered logging.
- Turbo requires monitoring. This cannot be viewed as a drawback. It is one of those unpleasant things in life that one has to live with.
- Several tools and fine-tuning steps require root privileges. The basic rule of isolating the task of the database administrator and the system administrator is violated.
- TURBO maintains statistics on multiple operations. Some of these figures are never used. Maintaining statistics consumes CPU time. It would be more efficient to provide options to the TURBO processes to suppress or activate the maintenance of statistics.
- Lack of a disk mirroring capability for databases and logs. Mirroring a log protects it against loss of any committed transactions. Mirroring a database guarantees continuous operation despite disk failures.
- TURBO does not have any feature to enforce referential integrity. All integrity rules must be enforced by application programs. Global integrity rules which can be enforced by the back-end can eliminate duplicate coding in application programs.

In spite of all these drawbacks TURBO is the most popular and the best database server in the UNIX environment. If you have a performance problem, give it a shot. You will not regret the decision.

Bibliography

Books

Becker, Richard A., and John Chambers, *S–An Interactive Environment for Data Analysis and Graphics,* Belmont, California: Wadsworth Advanced Program Books, 1984.

C-ISAM, Indexed Sequential Access Method, Informix Software, Inc., 1986.

Ceri, Stefano and Giuseppe Pelagatti, *Distributed Databases: Principles and Systems,* New York: McGraw-Hill, 1984.

Date, C. J., *An Introduction to Database Systems,* Vols. 1 and 2, Reading, Massachusetts: Addison-Wesley, 1983.

Date, C. J., *Relational Database, Selected Writings,* Reading, Massachusetts: Addison-Wesley, 1986.

Gonnet, G. H., *Handbook of Algorithms and Data Structures,* Reading, Massachusetts: Addison-Wesley, 1984.

Hawryszkiewycz, I. T., *Database Analysis and Design,* Sydney, Australia: Science Research Associates, Inc., 1984.

INFORMIX-ESQL/C, Embedded SQL for C, Informix Software, Inc., 1986.

INFORMIX-SQL, Reference Manual, Informix Software, Inc., 1986.

INFORMIX-SQL, User Guide, Informix Software, Inc., 1986.

INFORMIX-TURBO, Enhanced Database Server, Informix Software, Inc., 1987.

INFORMIX-TURBO, Programmer's Manual, Informix Software, Inc., 1986.

Jones, J. A., *Databases in Theory and Practice*, Pennsylvania: TAB Professional and Reference Books, 1987.

Kernighan, Brian and Dennis Ritchie, *The C Programming Language*, Englewood Cliffs, New Jersey: Prentice-Hall, 1978.

Kernighan, Brian and Rob Pike, *The UNIX Programming Environment*, Englewood Cliffs, New Jersey: Prentice-Hall, 1984.

Kochan, Stephen G., and Patrick Wood, *UNIX Shell Programming*, Hasbrouck Heights, New Jersey: Hayden, 1985.

McGilton, Henry and Rachel Morgan, *Introducing the UNIX System*, New York: McGraw-Hill, 1983.

Sobell, Mark, *Building Applications Using a 4GL*, Sunnyvale, California: Sobell Associates, 1986.

Tare, R. S., *UNIX Utilities*, New York: McGraw-Hill, 1987.

Thomas, Rebecca and Jean Yates, *A User Guide to the UNIX System,* Berkeley, California: Osborne/McGraw-Hill, 1985.

Ullman, J., D., *Principles of Database Systems*, Computer Science Press, 1983.

UNIX Programmer's Reference Manual–Check your local UNIX system documentation.

UNIX User's Reference Manual–Check your local UNIX system documentation.

Wiederhold, G., *Database Design*, New York: McGraw-Hill, 1983.

Articles

Aho, Alfred V., Brian W. Kernighan, and Peter J. Weinberger, *Awk–A Pattern Scanning and Text Processing Language*, Bell Laboratories, Murray Hill, New Jersey, 1978.

Astrahan, M. M. et al., System R: Relational approach to database management, *ACM Transactions on Database Systems*, Vol. 1, No. 2, June 1976.

Beech, David, The future of SQL, *Datamation*, Vol. 15, No. 4, Feb. 15, 1989.

Beech, David, New life for SQL, *Datamation*, Vol. 35, No. 3, Feb. 1, 1989.

Beeri, C., P. A. Bernstein, and N. Goodman, A sophisticate's introduction to database normalization theory, Proceedings of the fourth VLDB conference, Berlin, Sept. 1978.

Bernstein, P. A., Synthesizing third normal form relations from functional dependencies, *ACM Transactions on Database Systems*, Vol. 1, No. 4, Dec. 1976.

Bernstein, P. A., and D. M. Chiu, Using semi-joins to solve relational queries, *Journal of the ACM*, 28:1, 1981.

Cardinal, David J., File server offers transparent access to design tools, *Computer Design*, June 1985.

Chamberlain, D. D., et al., Sequel 2: A unified approach to data definition, manipulation, and control, *IBM Journal of Research and Development*, 1976.

Chen, P. P., Entity-Relationships model - Towards a unified view of data, *ACM Transactions on Database Systems*, Vol. 1, No. 1, March 1976.

Codd, E. F., A relational model for large databases, *CACM*, Vol. 13, No. 6, June 1970.

Dougherty, Dale, Awk: A not so awkward tool, *UNIX/World*, Vol. 4, No. 5, May 1987.

Fosdick, Howard, Programming SQL with cursors, *Database Programming and Design*, Vol. 2, No. 6, June 1989.

Hatch, Mark J., Michael Katz, and Jim Rees, AT&T's RFS and SUN's NFS, *UNIX/World*, Vol. 2, No. 11, Dec. 1985.

Kedem, Z. and A. Silberschatz, Controlling concurrency using locking protocols, Proceedings of the twentieth IEEE symposium on foundations of computer science, San Juan, Puerto Rico, 1979.

Kernighan, Brian, *PIC–A Graphics Language for Typesetting User Manual*, Bell Laboratories, Murray Hill, New Jersey.

Kernighan, Brian, *A TROFF Tutorial*, Bell Laboratories, Murray Hill, New Jersey, 1978.

Kocharekar, Raju, Nulls in relational databases, *SIGMOD Record*, Vol. 18, No. 1, March 1989.

Lachman, Ron, Yes!, UNIX exists in the MIS/DP environment, *UNIX/WORLD*, Vol. 5, No. 8, Aug. 1988.

Lesk, M. E., *Tbl–A Program to Format Tables*, Bell Laboratories, Murray Hill, New Jersey, Jan. 1979.

McClatchy, Will, SQL on the distributed DBMS front, *Information Week*, Issue 217, April 1989.

McMahon, Lee E., *SED–A Non-interactive Text Editor*, Bell Laboratories, Murray Hill, New Jersey, Aug. 1978.

Ossanna, Joseph F., *NROFF/TROFF User's Manual*, Bell Laboratories, Murray Hill, New Jersey, 1977.

Papadimitriou, C. H., Serializability of concurrent updates, *Journal of the ACM*, 26:4, 1979.

Potier, D. and P. Leblanc, Analysis of locking policies in database management systems, *Communications of the ACM*, Vol. 23, No. 10, 1980.

Radoff, David, 4GLs unbundled, *UNIX/World*, Vol. 6, No. 6, June 1989.

Ries, D. R. and M. Stonebraker: Effects of locking granularity in a database management system, *ACM Transactions on Database Systems*, Vol. 2, No. 3, Sept. 1977.

Sager, Gary, and Bob Lyon, Distributed file system strategies, *UNIX Review*, Vol. 3, No. 5, May 1985.

Schmid, H. A., and J. R. Swenson, On the semantics of the relational data model, Proceedings of the ACM SIGMOD conference, May 1975.

Spector, Alfred Z., and Michael L. Kazar, Uniting files systems, *UNIX Review*, Vol. 7, No. 3, March 1989.

Tanaka, Y. and T. Tsuda, Decomposition and composition of a relational database, *ACM Transactions on Database Systems*, Vol. 2, No. 2, June 1977.

Vaughan, Elizabeth, Pattern matching with regular expressions, *UNIX/World*, Vol. 4, No. 3, March 1987.

Verhofstad, J. S. M., Recovery techniques for database systems, *ACM Computing Surveys*, Vol. 10, No. 2, June 1978.

Vossen, Gottfried and Jim Yacabucci, An extension of the database language SQL to capture more relational concepts, *SIGMOD Record*, Vol. 17, No. 4, Dec. 1988.

Winston, Alan, Building the well-connected database, *UNIX/World*, Vol. 6, No. 6, May 1989.

Winston, Alan, A distributed database primer, *UNIX/World*, Vol. 5, No. 4, April 1988.

Winston, Alan, What's in the cards for 4GLs, *UNIX/World*, Vol. 5, No. 9, Sept. 1988.

Yannakakis, M., Serializability by locking, *Journal of the ACM*, Vol. 31, No. 2, 1984.

Index